The Supreme Court under Edward Douglass White, 1910–1921

CHIEF JUSTICESHIPS
OF THE UNITED STATES SUPREME COURT

Herbert A. Johnson, General Editor

The Chief Justiceship of Melville W. Fuller, 1888–1910
James W. Ely Jr.

The Supreme Court in the Early Republic:
The Chief Justiceships of John Jay and Oliver Ellsworth
William R. Casto

The Chief Justiceship of John Marshall, 1801–1835
Herbert A. Johnson

Division and Discord:
The Supreme Court under Stone and Vinson, 1941–1953
Melvin I. Urofsky

The Supreme Court under Edward Douglass White, 1910–1921
Walter F. Pratt Jr.

The Supreme Court under Edward Douglass White, 1910–1921

Walter F. Pratt Jr.

University of South Carolina Press

© 1999 University of South Carolina

Published in Columbia, South Carolina, by the
University of South Carolina Press

Manufactured in the United States of America

03 02 01 00 99   5 4 3 2 1

Library of Congress Cataloging-in-Publication Data

Pratt, Walter F., 1946–
   The Supreme Court under Chief Justice Edward Douglass White,
  1910–1921 / Walter F. Pratt, Jr.
     p. cm. — (Chief justiceships of the United States Supreme Court)
  Includes bibliographical references and index.
  ISBN 1-57003-309-9 (cloth)
  1. United States. Supreme Court—History—20th century. 2. White,
Edward Douglass, 1845–1921. I. Title. II. Series.
KF8742 .P73 1999
347.73'26'09—dc21   99-6156

Dedicated to Robert H. Birkby

CONTENTS

Illustrations	ix
Series Editor's Preface	xi
Preface	xvii
Acknowledgments	xix
Introduction	1
I The First Term	25
II The 1911–1912 Term	54
III The 1912–1913 Term	78
IV The 1913–1914 Term	97
V The 1914–1915 Term	112
VI The 1915–1916 Term	136
VII The 1916–1917 Term	156
VIII The 1917–1918 Term	186
IX The 1918–1919 Term	206
X The 1919–1920 Term	227
XI The Final Term	246
Conclusion	263
Appendix: Table of Cases	265
Selected Bibliography	279
Index	291

ILLUSTRATIONS

following page 96

Chief Justice Edward Douglass White

Chief Justice Edward Douglass White

Chief Justice White's Court, October 1911

Chief Justice White's Court, October 1920

Justice John Marshall Harlan

Justice Joseph McKenna

Justice Oliver Wendell Holmes

Justice William Rufus Day

Justice Horace Lurton

Chief Justice Charles Evans Hughes

Justice Willis Van Devanter

Justice Joseph Rucker Lamar

Justice Mahlon Pitney

Justice James Clark McReynolds

Justice John Clarke

Justice Louis Dembitz Brandeis

SERIES EDITOR'S PREFACE

The United States Supreme Court during the chief justiceship of Edward Douglass White was an institution beset by change. The years from 1910 to 1921 marked the emergence of the United States as a world power—albeit, a reluctant one. It is perhaps in the nature of courts and the legal profession that innovations occur much more slowly and deliberately than they do in less tradition-bound segments of our culture. Supreme Court opinions for this era provide ample evidence that the United States was moving rapidly from its traditional rural base to a distinctly urban environment. Growing integration of economic activity across state lines required adjustments in the inherited system of federalism. As a consequence the White Court had unique opportunities to establish constitutional and legal structures upon which an expansive nationalism might flourish. As might be expected, the justices moved slowly and deliberately in their task of striking a new federal balance. In doing so their decision-making was hindered by a need to confront an even more fundamental change.

It was the fate of the White Court to struggle with an upheaval in the way that words were defined and utilized. Since words are the building blocks of judicial opinions, this represented a substantial obstacle to "doing business as usual." At the outset the Court stressed traditional textual interpretation, drawing upon fixed definitions of words as the instruments for statutory construction. However, by 1912 the Court showed initial signs of moving toward acceptance of Justice Oliver Wendell Holmes's colorful statement in 1918, that words are the "skin of a living thought."[1] Hence, definitions might vary in the light of changed circumstances. Undoubtedly there is a close connection between substantive ideas and the words used to express those concepts. In addition, a new usage of words may also indicate that the decision-making process is itself in the process of change. What could account for such a pervasive alteration in the Court's approach to the definition of words?

---

1. See discussion on pages 195–98. The quotation is from *Towne v. Eisner*, 245 U.S. 418 (1918), discussed on page 196.

Immediately prior to the White era legal education was profoundly impacted by the introduction of the case method of law study. Beginning in 1870 and 1871 Christopher Columbus Langdell at Harvard Law School pioneered what he considered a "scientific" approach to law study. Close analysis of appellate court opinions forced students to become more precise in their use of language, and it also highlighted the degree to which words might carry connotations that rendered them ambiguous. Language thus acquired shades of meaning drawn from the circumstances in which it was used. Hence language might not be considered in a vacuum, and the "scientific" lawyer was alert to subtle changes in meaning that might have significance in the outcome of litigation before the courts. Not surprisingly, this new, and flexible, approach to textual analysis was part of the intellectual equipment of new justices who joined the Court during White's chief justiceship. By the 1913–1914 term of Court, the chief justice and Associate Justice Joseph McKenna made the transition from a strict deductive formalism to a studied inductive reasoning.[2] The rate of change in word usage seems to have accelerated markedly with the appointment of Justice Louis D. Brandeis in 1916. Pratt observes that "there were growing signs that the faith in words was weakening." However, the White Court remained very much in the grip of strict textual interpretation as it moved toward the era of World War I.

Undoubtedly, one of the dominating influences on Supreme Court adjudication was the deadening impact of a heavy caseload. For most of these years the justices were barely able to decide as many cases as they received each term. When one or more members were ill, or when vacancies occurred, the pending caseload began to rise. There were numerous relatively minor cases, bubbling up from the United States Circuit Courts of Appeal and other tribunals. Given the volume of pending business, the more important or more complex cases made substantial inroads upon the number of justices available to deal with the more mundane matters. Although Chief Justice White gamely took to himself the task of writing a large number of opinions, he was conspicuously unwilling, or unable, to fashion legislative proposals by which Congress might attempt to relieve the Court's backlog. As Pratt notes throughout this book, there was a sense of cultural lag that dogged the Court's work. At least part of that disconnectedness from current events and issues was due to the delay in deciding significant cases buried in the backlog. Welcoming newly appointed Justice John H. Clarke in 1916, White commented about the Court, "It is a great place, Judge, but we live in a cave."[3] In many ways it was a paper cave that proved impervious to the chief justice's persistent, but unimaginative, efforts to make light at the end of the paper

---

2. See the comment on page 100.
3. See page 149.

tunnel. Relief came with the statutory establishment of new certiorari rules first implemented in the 1916–1917 term. The 1916 statute substantially eliminated mandatory review of bankruptcy, trademark, and Federal Employer's Liability Act cases.[4]

Unlike the previous volumes published in this series, this one provides a chronological discussion of the Court's business within each term. Although this demands more diligence from readers wishing to trace topical developments, there is a countervailing advantage in encountering each decision in the way the justices did—in connection with other matters decided on the same day, or in proximity to each other. Viewed in this manner, the relationship between cases that otherwise might seem unrelated becomes clearer. Unquestionably there may be a conscious, or even subliminal, influence of one opinion upon the other when the matters are discussed in proximity. One example of this is the fact that the landmark opinion in *Missouri v. Holland* was issued on the same day that the Court's opinion was read in *South Covington & Cincinnati Street Railway Co v. Kentucky*. *Missouri* upheld treaty regulation of migratory waterfowl hunting, even though it was argued that such control would have violated the Constitution if it had been imposed by congressional statute. On the other hand, in permitting continued segregation of passengers by race, the Court in *South Covington* ignored the fact that the street railway crossed the Ohio-Kentucky state line and thus was technically a carrier in interstate commerce. Was the Court's strange oversight in *South Covington* a result of the justices' wish to mitigate the federalizing inroad blow of *Missouri*?[5] An interesting question, but one that would not be obvious in the absence of this volume's chronological format.

Within such a detailed and painstaking approach to the White Court, it is easy to lose the big trees within the forest. Procedurally the justices had to consider many cases that, in Pratt's phrase, were "insufferably insignificant."[6] However, the White Court made a definite contribution to the evolution of American constitutional law. Early on, the justices first applied the "rule of reason" to the adjudication of Sherman Act antitrust cases.[7] Subsequently the Court expanded the so-called federal police power by applying commerce clause regulation to food products, the "White Slave traffic," and alcoholic beverages.[8] On the other hand, they refused to allow regulation of

---

4. The improved review arrangement is discussed on pages 157–59.
5. See discussion on page 243–44.
6. See page 7.
7. *Standard Oil Company v. United States*, 221 U.S. 1 (1911), and *United States v. American Tobacco Company*, 221 U.S. 106 (1911), discussed on pages 37–44.
8. *Hipolite Egg Company v. United States*, 220 U.S. 45 (1911), dealing with adulterated food; *Hoke v. United States*, 227 U.S. 308 (1913) and *Caminetti v. United States*, 242 U.S. 470 (1917),

child labor under the aegis of the same commerce clause.⁹ It was left to Associate Justice Charles Evans Hughes to spell out the degree to which congressional power over interstate commerce led to a tacit authority to so regulate intrastate commerce that uniformity was not disturbed by state action.¹⁰

Chief Justice White and his colleagues also had to confront the complex issues of war powers and economic regulation that emerged from World War I. The wartime sedition case, *Schenck v. United States,* represents a significant stage in the development of the First Amendment, as does its sequel, *Abrams v. United States.*¹¹ In *Wilson v. New,* Chief Justice White approved Congress's mandate of an eight-hour day and a resulting increase in hourly wage. The chief justice affirmed the constitutionality of this statute by identifying the railroad industry as coming within the public interest, and thus within the scope of public regulation.¹² The *Selective Draft Law Cases* upheld federal authority to implement a draft as part of the federal government's exercise of its war powers. White, a former soldier in the Confederate States Army, wrote a strong defense of this exercise of national power.¹³ As Pratt notes, the First World War was instrumental in accelerating changes in American society and law that had already begun to take place.

Chief Justice White holds the historical distinction of being the first sitting associate justice to be appointed to the center chair in the Supreme Court chamber. For this reason, his chief justiceship provides food for thought concerning the wisdom of such a practice. Memorial tributes indicate that White was a friend to almost all of the justices on the Court; that might well have provided advantages in exercising leadership. At the same time, too long an association with the other associate justices may also have compromised White's ability to lead the Court aggressively into the twentieth century. Allegedly appointed by President Taft to keep the center seat warm for Taft, Chief Justice White proved to be a good place occupier, but less than dynamic either as the intellectual leader of the Court or as its administrative manager and political "point man." Taft required a bigger seat—both literally and figuratively—and his accession to the chief justiceship as White's successor showed him to be a much stronger leader and organizer than the amiable Louisianan had been. Next in the line of suc-

---

asserting federal commerce power to control interstate transportation of women for purposes of prostitution or other immoral activity; *National Prohibition Cases,* 253 U.S. 350 (1920).

9. *Hammer v. Dagenhart,* 247 U.S. 251 (1918).

10. *Minnesota Rate Cases,* 230 U.S. 352 (1913), and the *Shreveport Case,* 234 U.S. 342 (1914).

11. The *Schenck* case, 249 U.S. 47 (1919), is discussed on pages 215–17; *Abrams,* 250 U.S. 616 (1919), is discussed on pages 234–37.

12. 243 U.S. 332 (1917), discussed on pages 170–74.

13. 245 U.S. 366 (1918), discussed on pages 201–2.

cession after Taft was Charles Evans Hughes, who also served five years with White as his chief justice. Was Hughes's undoubtedly strong leadership after 1930 attributable to his fourteen-year absence from the deliberations of the Court, and his isolation from professional contact with its members during the Taft era?

We are indebted to Pratt for bringing the significance of the White Court to the forefront of our attention. There is a tendency to view the Supreme Court's work as being founded upon the decision of "great cases," and the White Court had a good share of those high-profile matters to decide. On the other hand, there was a heavy volume of lesser issues that had to be processed as the United States moved into being a world power and a combatant in the First World War. In small matters, as in the larger cases, the White Court moved slowly and hesitatingly into the new legal and constitutional world that would be twentieth-century America.

Herbert A. Johnson

PREFACE

The White Court found itself in the midst of a time when, in the phrasing of Thucydides, "Words had to change their ordinary meaning and to take that which was not given them."[1] American society in the second decade of the twentieth century found itself at the end of more than a generation of political turmoil, as first the Populists, then the Progressives fought for changes across the governmental landscape. As the critic Van Wyck Brooks wrote, contemporaneous with the White Court, "The most striking American spectacle today is a fumbling about after new issues which no one as yet has been able to throw into relief. We have seen one President advocating a 'New Nationalism,' another President advocating a 'New Freedom,' a well-known novelist talking about a 'New Patriotism'—phrases which illustrate just this vague fumbling, this acute consciousness of the inadequacy of the habitual issues, this total inability to divine and formulate new issues that really are issues."[2] Near the end of that decade Americans also found themselves confronting the byproducts of a war that challenged much they held dear. Although the White Court stood apart from the political maelstrom, it could not withdraw completely. Accordingly, throughout the decade the justices found themselves struggling to make sense out of the innovations in government. Try as they might, the justices found that they could not deal with those transformations without changing the meaning of words with which they had become familiar. As good lawyers, they struggled to confine change within existing categories. That they succeeded for so long is a compliment to their abilities. That they ultimately failed is a measure of the extent of change during the early part of the century.

My theme, therefore, is words. After all, appellate courts deal almost exclusively with words—printed words. They are separated from the witnesses of trial courts; and, except for the intervention of attorneys, the appel-

---

1. Thucydides, *The Peloponnesian War*, 3:82. James Boyd White has reminded us of the import of that statement in his *When Words Lose Their Meaning: Constitutions and Reconstitutions of Language, Character, and Community* (Chicago: University of Chicago Press, 1984).
2. Van Wyck Brooks, *America's Coming-of-Age* (New York: B. W. Huebsch, 1915), 167.

late judges deal only with nonspoken words. For the most part, the White Court dealt with familiar words, the rubrics of nineteenth-century American constitutional law. Gradually, however, those words came to have different meanings. There was no sharp discontinuity; but the meanings changed nonetheless. Accordingly, I have rejected the usual method of writing a history of this sort. I have chosen not to group cases from the entire period under common headings. Instead, I have chosen to write of the Court by term, allowing the cases for each term to illustrate the changes as they occurred. To me, it would be misleading to organize under a topic such as "Commerce Clause," for it is precisely such a heading that suffered a loss of meaning. To use the heading would be to deny what I believe to be true about the White Court; to use the heading would be to suggest an orderliness that I do not believe is present.

The Court itself *does* change, especially with the appointment of Brandeis in 1916. That appointment coincides almost precisely with the failing of White's health and the entry of the United States into the First World War. As a result, the one justice who is best suited to deal with the new meanings joins the Court at the very time the momentum of change is reaching a peak. It is, therefore, almost correct to say that there were two White Courts, not one. In the first, from 1910 to 1915, the justices dealt with few cases that caused them genuine discomfort, though there were any number of cases that pressed words to their limits, and even a few that pressed beyond those limits. In the second, from 1916 to 1921, the justices saw more and more new issues. Their fumbling attempts to deal with those issues showed how new they were and set the stage for other developments in subsequent decades.

Having said that this book is largely about words that lose their meaning, there are two other points that merit advance notice. First, the White Court is almost unique in that the appointment of a new chief justice did not mark a break with the past. By elevating White to the position of chief justice, President Taft assured continuity. It is therefore unlikely that there will be marked changes led by White. Second, the period itself is too short for any break with the past to be defined. At most there could be endings and beginnings. What those points mean for this volume is this, at least: I cannot argue that the White Court crafted a distinctive identity for itself. Instead, it, like the nation around it, struggled to come to grips with what it meant, and would mean, to live in the twentieth century. In that struggle, like the fulcrum of a seesaw, the Court saw arguments move sometimes this way, sometimes that. And, not unlike the fulcrum, the Court did not always have the power to affect those arguments. Instead, the Court had to wait for arguments to come to it. As a result, for the White Court we will see little initiative, though we will see creative recognition of the changes occurring around it.

ACKNOWLEDGMENTS

This book is dedicated to one of three teachers who have had the most significant impact on my professional life. To name three is not to minimize the importance of others. There are, indeed, others whose commitment and professionalism continue to motivate—Jim Ely, Kermit Hall, Bill Nelson, John Orth, and Russell Osgood. Having acknowledged the others, however, three stand out for their influence at critical junctures. The first was an eighth-grade teacher of American History—Mr. Moore (no eighth-grade teachers had first names). His energy still electrifies after these many years. The third was a teacher of contracts—Arthur Leff. His quick wit showed that controlled humor could be a teaching tool of enormous power. The second, to whom the book is dedicated is Robert Birkby. His unwavering inquiry in response to being greeted by "Good morning" was "What's so good about it?" The gleam in his eye, though, suggested that there really was something very good about the day, if only we students would make the effort to find it.

While writing this book I have had the good fortune to encounter others who have both helped me and taught me. The staff of the Notre Dame Law Library has been unfailingly helpful. Were it not for the fact that such assistance is their ordinary way of work, I would add the word *astonishingly*. But, for Dwight King, Carmela and Ken Kinslow, Patti Ogden, Lucy Payne, and, more recently, Mary Cowsert and Warren Rees, helping seems as effortless as breathing. They have enriched my understanding of the concept of professionalism. Several student research assistants have toiled magnificently in their efforts to uncover both the ordinary and the extraordinary—Lillian Cheng, Michelle Colman, Annejanette Heckman, Ed Leader, and Jim Neumeister. No single volume could ever contain all they found. Bob Rodes, at Notre Dame, and Herb Johnson, the general editor for this series, each gave the manuscript a careful and sympathetic reading. The finished product has benefited from their suggestions. I am even more confident that I have personally benefited from their example of how to be a true colleague. Others at Notre Dame have helped by being willing to listen to offhand questions and by offering encouragement throughout the life of the project.

Dean David T. Link of the Notre Dame Law School has supported the work with summer research grants and with flexibility in teaching schedules. My family has been unswerving in their support. I thank them all.

The Supreme Court under Edward Douglass White, 1910–1921

INTRODUCTION

When Edward Douglass White took his seat under the clock on December 19, 1910, the United States was on the eve of one of the most tumultuous decades in its history.[1] Only months before, Halley's comet had flashed across the sky, portending the end of the world to some. More earthly, though equally portentous, was the coalition of members from both parties who won restrictions on the powers of the Speaker of the House of Representatives in March, thereby eliminating a significant barrier to Progressive legislation.[2] The vote in the House foreshadowed a nationwide vote against conservatism in the fall, when progressive governors would be elected from New Jersey (Woodrow Wilson) to California (Hiram Johnson). The Democrats gained control of the House of Representatives for the first time in the twentieth century; and, along with reform-minded Republicans ("insurgents"), the Democrats would also control the Senate. In the words of historian George Mowry, with its nationwide success in the 1910 elections, the Progressive movement "separated an old and a new America."[3]

Many of those events were but prologue to the presidential election of 1912, with Theodore Roosevelt capturing the spirit of the moment, if not

---

1. The phrase "under the clock" was widely used to refer to the center seat on the Supreme Court's bench, the seat occupied by the chief justice. See, for example, Charles Henry Butler, *A Century at the Bar of the Supreme Court of the United States* (New York: G. P. Putnam's Sons, 1942), 76, 173. There are several surveys of the period that include the White Court; among them are Loren P. Beth, *The Development of the American Constitution, 1877–1917* (New York: Harper & Row, 1971); Alexander M. Bickel and Benno C. Schmidt Jr., *History of the Supreme Court of the United States: The Judiciary and Responsible Government, 1910–21* (New York: Macmillan, 1984); John W. Johnson, *American Legal Culture, 1908–1940* (Westport, Conn.: Greenwood Press, 1981); John E. Semonche, *Charting the Future: The Supreme Court Responds to a Changing Society, 1890–1920* (Westport, Conn.: Greenwood Press, 1978).
2. Henry F. Pringle, *The Life and Times of William Howard Taft* (New York: Farrar & Rinehart, 1939), 1:402–17.
3. George E. Mowry, *Theodore Roosevelt and the Progressive Movement* (New York: Hill and Wang, 1946; American Century Series ed., 1960), 10.

of the decade. Speaking to supporters in June 1912, on the eve of the Republican Convention, he said: "[W]e stand at Armageddon and we battle for the Lord."[4] Mark Sullivan would later recall Roosevelt's speech in terms that echoed Mowry's image, writing that the speech "made a very old word newly familiar to an America that was beginning to lose acquaintance with its Bible."[5] Likewise, the commentator Walter Weyl had written in 1912: "We are in a period of clamor, of bewilderment, of an almost tremulous unrest. We are hastily revising all our social conceptions. We are hastily testing all our political ideals. We are profoundly disenchanted with the fruits of a century of independence."[6] The presidential election of 1912 itself served to define the tumult of the decade, with Roosevelt and Wilson almost leaving the incumbent William Howard Taft on the sidelines as they debated the future of national governmental activities. Wilson's victory, combined with that of Democrats in both houses of Congress, returned the party to power for the first time since the Civil War, with the brief exception of two years under President Grover Cleveland.[7] Wilson's victory also brought southerners into control of the executive and legislative branches for the first time since the Civil War. More of an omen were the nine hundred thousand votes for the Socialist candidate, Eugene V. Debs—the party's highest total to date.

By the time of White's death, in May 1921, the Progressive Era (and the Democratic Party) was in eclipse, but not before seeing four amendments to the Constitution: in 1913, both the Sixteenth (income tax), and the Seventeenth (direct election of senators); in 1919, the Eighteenth (prohibition); and in 1920, the Nineteenth (women's right to vote).[8] No

---

4. *New York Times,* June 18, 1912. The quotation is also available in a book whose title comes from Roosevelt's remarks, Nell Irvin Painter, *Standing at Armageddon: The United States 1877–1919* (New York: W. W. Norton & Co., 1987), 268. Conversely, Loren Beth used the same image to describe four of Taft's five appointees to the Supreme Court. According to Beth, Chief Justice White, along with Justices Lamar, Lurton, Pitney, and Van Devanter, "saw themselves as soldiers at Armageddon fighting the progressive hosts exposed by the 1912 election." Beth, *Development of the American Constitution,* 66.

5. Mark Sullivan, *Our Times, 1900–1925,* vol. 4, *The War Begins, 1900–1914* (New York: Charles Scribner's Sons, 1946), 509.

6. Walter E. Weyl, *The New Democracy* (New York: Macmillan, 1912), 1, quoted in Neil A. Wynn, *From Progressivism to Prosperity: World War I and American Society* (New York: Holmes & Meier, 1986), 2. For other surveys of Progressivism, see Arthur S. Link and Richard L. McCormick, *Progressivism* (Arlington Heights, Ill.: Harlan Davidson, 1983); Lewis L. Gould, *Reform and Regulation: American Politics from Roosevelt to Wilson,* 2d ed. (New York: Knopf, 1986).

7. Between 1893 and 1895 the Democrats controlled both houses of Congress, as well as the presidency.

8. For the secretary of state's declaration that the amendments had been ratified, see the following: Sixteenth, February 25, 1913, 37 Stat. 1785; Seventeenth, May 31, 1913, 38 Stat. 2049; Eighteenth, January 29, 1919, 40 Stat. 1941; Nineteenth, August 25, 1920, 41 Stat. 1823.

other ten-year period had seen so many amendments, excluding the time of the Bill of Rights.⁹ The decade saw the culmination of an era in national legislation, with tariff reform (Underwood-Simmons Tariff, October 1913), the creation of the Federal Reserve system (Owens-Glass Act, December 1913), the Clayton Antitrust Act (October 1914), a child-labor bill (Keating-Owen Act, September 1916), and a workmen's compensation plan for federal workers (Kern-McGillicuddy Act, September 1916).¹⁰ Other events seemed genuinely more apocalyptic than assuring—the First World War, the Russian Revolution, a flu epidemic, labor unrest, and lynchings.

Outside the political arenas, other, contemporaneous events lent credibility to Virginia Woolf's enigmatic assertion that "on or about December 1910 human character changed."¹¹ Postimpressionism in art came to the United States with the Armory Show in New York in 1913; observations of a solar eclipse in 1919 confirmed the theory of relativity in science; and Freud's influence began to spread beyond psychology after his visit to the United States in 1909.¹² Between 1910 and 1921 the United States became, in a word, "modern."¹³ The United States changed from its agrarian (and rural) past to its industrial (and urban) future.¹⁴

Even the Supreme Court seemed poised for a new era in December 1910. To be sure, in August of that year Roosevelt had spoken for many when he criticized courts in his "New Nationalism" speech in Osawatomie,

---

9. The 1960s rivaled White's era, with three amendments: in 1961, the Twenty-third (electoral votes for the District of Columbia); in 1964, the Twenty-fourth (prohibition of poll tax as qualification for voting); and in 1967, the Twenty-fifth (provision for succession in case of president's illness). The Twenty-sixth Amendment (eighteen-year-olds voting) followed in 1971.

10. Underwood Tariff Act, Act of October 3, 1913, ch. 16, 38 Stat. 114; Federal Reserve Act, Act of December 23, 1913, ch. 6, 38 Stat. 251; Clayton Antitrust Act, Act of October 15, 1914, ch. 323, 38 Stat. 730; Keating-Owen Act, Act of September 1, 1916, ch. 432, 39 Stat. 675; Federal Employees' Compensation Act, Act of September 7, 1916, ch. 458, 39 Stat. 742.

11. Virginia Woolf, *Mr. Bennett and Mrs. Brown* (London: Hogarth Press, 1928), 4 (Woolf first read the essay to the Heretics in Cambridge, England, in May 1924). See also Peter Stansky, *On or About December 1910: Early Bloomsbury and Its Intimate World* (Cambridge, Mass.: Harvard University Press, 1996).

12. For a personal account of early exposure to Freud's work, see Abraham A. Brill, "The Introduction and Development of Freud's Work in the United States," *American Journal of Sociology* 45 (November 1939): 318–25. See also Frederick A. Hoffman, *Freudianism and the Literary Mind* (Baton Rouge: Louisiana State University Press, 1945).

13. Compare, Walter Nugent, *From Centennial to World War: American Society, 1876–1917* (New York: Macmillan, 1985), xi ("In those forty years [1870–1917] the United States underwent the several profound social processes collectively called modernization.")

14. John D. Buenker, "The Progressive Era: A Search for Synthesis," *Mid-America* 51 (1969): 175–93 (especially at 181 for observation that "[b]y 1920 the majority of Americans lived in

Kansas, urging the recall of federal judges.[15] He attacked the Supreme Court itself, predicting that the whole system of popular government would be overthrown if the Court continued with decisions such as *Lochner* and *E. C. Knight*.[16] He carried the criticism into the election of 1912 when he told the Progressive convention, "The American people, and not the courts are to determine their own fundamental policies."[17] The Progressive Party, formed as the National Progressive Republican League in January 1911, echoed that call. Even President Taft had criticized the Court, though privately and on grounds of inefficiency, not for particular results. In May 1909 he had written to his close friend and former colleague on the Court of Appeals for the Sixth Circuit, Judge Horace H. Lurton: "The condition of the Supreme Court is pitiable, and yet those old fools hold on with a tenacity that is most discouraging. Really, the Chief Justice [Fuller] is almost senile; Harlan does no work; Brewer is so deaf that he cannot hear and has got beyond the point of the commonest accuracy in writing his opinions; Brewer and Harlan sleep almost through all of the arguments. I don't know what can be done. It is most discouraging to the active men on the bench."[18]

In another letter, Taft chose to single out Justice William T. Moody, at fifty-six the youngest of the sitting justices, though crippled from arthritis: "It is an outrage that the four men on the bench who are over seventy should continue there and thus throw the work and responsibility on the other five. This is the occasion of Moody's illness. It is with difficulty that I can restrain myself from making such a statement in my annual message

---

urban areas for the first time in history.") Walter Nugent places the beginning of the "urban-metropolitan" America at 1915 or 1920, "the date depending on whether one stresses the statistics of agricultural stabilization, which favor the former, or the census revelations of 1920 of another sharp decline in aggregate population growth in the 1910–20 decade compared to the preceding several decades." *Structures of American Social History* (Bloomington: Indiana University Press, 1981), 121.

15. *New York Times,* August 30, September 1, 1910.
16. In *Lochner v. New York,* 198 U.S. 45 (1905), the Supreme Court declared unconstitutional a New York law limiting the hours of work of bakers. *United States v. E. C. Knight Co.,* 156 U.S. 1 (1895), was the Court's first interpretation of the 1890 Sherman Antitrust Act. The Court held that because manufacturing was not commerce, the act did not apply to the production of sugar within a single state.
17. *New York Times,* August 7, 1912.
18. Quoted in Pringle, *William Howard Taft,* 1:529–30. In light of that comment, Taft's own observation at the end of his judicial career is especially ironic. Taft wrote to his brother Horace on November 14, 1929: "I am older and slower and less acute and more confused. However, as long as things continue as they are, and I am able to answer in my place, I must stay on the court in order to prevent the Bolsheviki from getting control." Quoted in Ronald H. Romine, "The 'Politics' of Supreme Court Nominations from Theodore Roosevelt to Ronald Reagan: The Construction of a 'Politicization Index'" (Ph.D. diss., University of South Carolina, 1984), 34. (Romine says the letter is aimed at Brandeis.)

[to Congress]."[19] In response to Moody's disability, Congress passed a special act allowing him to retire immediately with full benefits.[20]

Within a year three of the septuagenarians would die—Rufus Peckham in October 1909, David Brewer in March 1910, and Chief Justice Melville Weston Fuller on July 4, 1910. (The fourth, John Marshall Harlan, followed in October 1911.) Justice Moody's retirement in November 1910 gave Taft a fourth appointment to make before Woolf's critical month of December. By breaking with tradition, and nominating a chief justice from within the Court, Taft gave himself five appointments within twelve months. No other president, except George Washington with his original appointments, has made as many appointments in so short a time.[21]

No one, however, was likely to associate Taft's appointments with Virginia Woolf's assertion. Indeed, almost as remarkable as the societal changes foreshadowed by the 1910–1912 biennium is the lassitude within the Supreme Court itself. Of the dozen men who served with White during his tenure as chief justice, four are likely to be included on a list of "great" justices—Brandeis, Harlan, Holmes, and Hughes.[22] Of those, only Holmes

---

19. Taft to Cabot Lodge, September 2, 1909, quoted in Pringle, *William Howard Taft*, 1:530. For a slightly more sympathetic portrayal of Taft's feelings toward Moody, see Archibald W. Butt, *Taft and Roosevelt: The Intimate Letters of Archie Butt Military Aide* (Garden City, N.Y.: Doubleday, Doran & Co., 1930), 2:437–39.

In 1913 Attorney General James C. McReynolds suggested a plan to allow the president to appoint an additional judge for each one who did not retire at seventy. The plan was limited to lower-court judges; but it became a basis for Franklin Roosevelt's "court-packing" plan some years later. By then, Justice McReynolds had himself become target of criticism on account of his age. See Department of Justice, *Annual Report of the Attorney General for 1913* (Washington, D.C.: GPO, 1913), 5. Also, one biographer of McReynolds reports that "McReynolds frequently objected to suggested candidates because of their age." Barbara Barlin Schimmel, "The Judicial Policy of Mr. Justice McReynolds" (Ph.D. diss., Yale University, 1964), 117.

20. Act of June 23, 1910, ch. 377, 36 Stat. 1861. The private act extended to Moody the provisions of an 1869 act that allowed *all* federal judges to retire at full pay at age seventy if they had served ten years. Act of April 10, 1869, ch. 22, §5, 16 Stat. 44, 45. Moody's act stipulated that he must retire within five months if he was to claim the benefits. On October 3 he notified President Taft that he would retire November 20, 1910, just three days short of the deadline (218 U.S. iv n. 5). For a survey of related provisions contemporaneous to the White Court, see William S. Carpenter, *Judicial Tenure in the United States* (New Haven, Conn.: Yale University Press, 1918).

21. Taft was well aware of the comparison with Washington. Pringle, *William Howard Taft*, 1:534. See also Elbert F. Baldwin, "The Supreme Court Justices," *Outlook* 97 (January 1911): 160; Edward Lowry, "The Men of the Supreme Court," *World's Work* 27 (April 1914): 630.

22. For a survey of ratings of justices, see Lee Epstein, Jeffrey A. Segal, Harold J. Spaeth, and Thomas G. Walker, *The Supreme Court Compendium: Data, Decisions, and Developments*, 2d ed. (Washington, D.C.: Congressional Quarterly, 1996), 369–70. On the reputations of Holmes and Brandeis, see G. Edward White, "The Canonization of Holmes and Brandeis: Epistemology and Judicial Reputations," *New York University Law Review* 70 (June 1995): 576–621.

served throughout White's time as chief justice. Harlan died within a year of White's appointment. Hughes spent but six of his more than seventeen years of judicial service under White; and Brandeis served with White for only five of what would be almost twenty-three years on the Court. In short, little of their "greatness" could be attributed to service between 1910 and 1921. Moreover, one would be hard-pressed to name a dozen "landmark" decisions from the White Court.[23] Even White's own reputation is based largely on decisions handed down before he became chief justice, or shortly thereafter—the *Insular Cases* and the "rule of reason" decisions in antitrust law.[24]

What is remarkable about the White Court is how it stood almost completely apart from the turmoil in the national and international arenas during the period. Part of the explanation lies in the fact that the Court, as an

---

23. One list includes these eleven cases among a list of "landmark decisions": *Standard Oil Co. v. United States,* 221 U.S. 1 (1911) (antitrust); *Pacific States Telephone & Telegraph Co. v. Oregon,* 223 U.S. 118 (1912) (republican form of government); *Houston, East & West Texas Ry. v. United States,* 234 U.S. 342 (1914) *(Shreveport Rate Cases)* (state regulation of interstate commerce); *Guinn and Beal v. United States,* 238 U.S. 347 (1915) (voting); *Truax v. Raich,* 239 U.S. 33 (1915) (aliens); *Wilson v. New,* 243 U.S. 332 (1917) (federal regulation of labor); *Buchanan v. Warley,* 245 U.S. 60 (1917) (race discrimination); *Selective Draft Law Cases,* 245 U.S. 366 (1918) (war powers); *Hammer v. Dagenhart,* 247 U.S. 251 (1918) (federal regulation of child labor); *Schenck v. United States,* 249 U.S. 47 (1919) (freedom of speech); *Missouri v. Holland,* 252 U.S. 416 (1920) (treaties and executive agreements). Epstein et al., *The Supreme Court Compendium,* 81–94. The second edition of the *Compendium* adds eight cases to that list, changing the heading to "Major Decisions of the Court." See Epstein et al., *The Supreme Court Compendium,* 2d ed., 105–7.

The *Oxford Companion to the Supreme Court of the United States* treats the following sixteen cases as worthy of a main entry: *Standard Oil Co. v. United States,* 221 U.S. 1 (1911); *Gompers v. Bucks Stove & Range Co.,* 221 U.S. 418 (1911); *Pacific States Telephone & Telegraph Co. v. Oregon,* 223 U.S. 118 (1912); *Weeks v. United States,* 232 U.S. 383 (1914); *Houston, East & West Texas Ry. v. United States,* 234 U.S. 342 (1914) *(Shreveport Rate Cases); Frank v. Mangum,* 237 U.S. 309 (1915); *Guinn and Beal v. United States,* 238 U.S. 347 (1915); *Clark Distilling Co. v. Western Maryland Railway Co.,* 242 U.S. 311 (1917); *Bunting v. Oregon,* 243 U.S. 426 (1917); *Buchanan v. Warley,* 245 U.S. 60 (1917); *Selective Draft Law Cases,* 245 U.S. 366 (1918); *Hammer v. Dagenhart,* 247 U.S. 251 (1918); *Schenck v. United States,* 249 U.S. 47 (1919); *Abrams v. United States,* 250 U.S. 616 (1919); *Missouri v. Holland,* 252 U.S. 416 (1920); *Duplex Printing Press Co. v. Deering,* 254 U.S. 443 (1921). Kermit L. Hall, ed., *Oxford Companion to the Supreme Court of the United States* (New York: Oxford University Press, 1992), passim.

24. The name *"Insular Cases"* refers to a group of decisions between 1901 and 1904 dealing with the application of the Constitution and Bill of Rights to overseas territories, especially those obtained by the United States after the Spanish-American War of 1898. For a discussion of these cases, see James E. Kerr, *The Insular Cases: The Role of the Judiciary in American Expansionism* (Port Washington, N.Y.: Kennikat Press, 1982). The "rule of reason" became the standard for applying the Sherman Antitrust Act after the Court's opinions in *Standard Oil Co. v. United States,* 221 U.S. 1 (1911), and *United States v. American Tobacco Co.,* 221 U.S. 106 (1911), both written by White.

institution, did not have command of its agenda. Not until 1925 would the Court have any significant control over its docket[25]—a fact suggesting both that White failed to use his position to promote change and that the Court had not been fully included in the Progressives' nationalization of American politics.[26] As a consequence, the White Court faced a high percentage of insufferably insignificant cases—ranging from disputes over land titles in the Philippines to quarrels about the language in wills from the District of Columbia. A court so burdened had neither the time nor the inclination to provide careful analysis of fundamental constitutional issues, or any other issues, for that matter. A second consequence of lacking control over its docket was the time lag between a case reaching the Court and the case being argued. Any judicial process tends to delay the resolution of critical issues, if for no other reason than that a court is a separate obstacle to overcome after the legislature and the executive. But during the White years that delay was exacerbated by the sheer number of cases. By the time the Court decided a case, the energy that had propelled the initial dispute was likely to have been diverted to other controversies. That was especially true in cases of public import, for which the Court's opinions frequently seemed anachronistic, a reminder of a political dispute already resolved. The opinions also ofttimes disclosed judges struggling to reconcile their views, formed during the "old" America, with the pressing demands of the "new" America.

Roosevelt attacked the courts for precisely that reason—they seemed so out of touch with the political processes. But the Court had its defenders, including the preeminent Court historian of the period, Charles Warren. Writing in 1913, Warren acknowledged the controversy: "During the past two years, there has been much agitation directed against the Supreme Court of the United States, frequent reference to 'judicial oligarchy,' 'usurpation' and the like, and demands for fundamental changes in the judicial system under the Constitution, not only of the States but of the United States." Even so, Warren explained, he wanted to disprove the allegation lest it gain credence by constant repetition.[27] According to Warren, the years 1887–1911 "constituted the period most productive of progressive and liberal—even radical—social and economic legislation in the United States." He explained that he had looked at 560 cases from the

---

25. Act of February 13, 1925, ch. 229, 43 Stat. 936.
26. On nationalization as being at the heart of the Progressive movement, see Morton Keller, *Regulating a New Society: Public Policy and Social Change in America, 1900–1933* (Cambridge, Mass.: Harvard University Press, 1994); Nugent, *From Centennial to World War*, 179.
27. Charles Warren, "The Progressiveness of the Supreme Court," *Columbia Law Review* 13 (1913): 294.

period, all decided under the due process or equal protection clauses. Of those cases, in only three had the Court declared a state law invalid: *Lochner,* plus *Connolly v. Union Sewer Pipe Co.* and *Allgeyer v. Louisiana.* Warren did, though, concede that the Court had struck down state laws thirty-four times under the rubric of *property* rights during the same period.[28] Moreover, as Louis Brandeis would later note, a single case might "do mischief way beyond the arithmetic ratio to totality of decisions."[29]

Even though the decisions were few in number, the critique of the Court was particularly sharp at the beginning of White's tenure as chief justice. As one scholar has commented, "In certain respects the 1909 term was the most dismal in the Court's history. Perhaps at no other time had the Court paid such a price for life tenure."[30] A contemporaneous observer predicted that the "historian of the future will probably say that at the time Mr. White was appointed Chief Justice, the Supreme Court, as well as the entire judiciary in America, was passing through the most distinct crisis in its history. The public had become suddenly distrustful of our courts and resented the absolute power of the judicial veto. Recall of judges as well as recall of judicial decisions was one of the flaming issues of the day. Indeed, antagonism to the power of judges was one of the basic creeds of a nascent political faith."[31] Writing in the *Outlook,* for which Roosevelt was a "contributing editor," Elbert Baldwin commented on the need for new justices: "The new members should help to expedite the seven hundred-odd cases on the docket, the largest number in the history of the Court since the passage of the Circuit Court of Appeals Act in 1891." With justices whose average age was sixty-four, Baldwin pointed to a second reason for needing new members of the Court: "the cases now mostly before the Court involve different principles and conditions from those which the Court had to decide when Justice Harlan, for instance, first came to Washington [in 1877]." Baldwin identified one group of cases as being especially important, those that would define what "the Sherman Anti-Trust Law is or is

---

28. Ibid., 294–95, 308. In *Connolly* the Court held that an Illinois statute was unconstitutional because its restrictions on trusts did not apply to agricultural products or to livestock (184 U.S. 540 [1902]). *Allgeyer* was the first case in which the Court struck down a state law for having infringed the "liberty of contract" protected by the due process clause of the Fourteenth Amendment (165 U.S. 578 [1897]).
29. Melvin I. Urofsky, "The Brandeis-Frankfurter Conversations," *The Supreme Court Review* (1985): 308.
30. Jeffrey B. Morris, "Chief Justice Edward Douglass White and President Taft's Court," *Supreme Court Historical Society Yearbook* (1982): 27. Morris's only citation to support that statement is Taft's letter to Lurton.
31. Samuel Spring, "Two Chief Justices: Edward Douglass White and William Howard Taft," *The American Review of Reviews* 64 (August 1921): 163–64.

not—that is to say, what is monopoly—for this law, in its operation, has caused much of the late litigation."[32]

In the face of such attention focused on the Court, Taft would seem to be the ideal president to provide the needed resuscitation. A former judge on the Court of Appeals for the Sixth Circuit, he cared more for the judicial office than any other—both for himself and for the country. In the words of his biographer, Taft's "absorption in the federal judiciary in general, and in the Supreme Court in particular, was complete."[33] Taft had twice declined Roosevelt's offer of appointment to the Supreme Court, preferring to wait for the chief justiceship to become available.[34] During the summer of 1910, while considering a replacement for Chief Justice Fuller, Taft is reported to have said to Justice Moody, "It does seem strange . . . that the one place in the government which I would have liked to fill myself I am forced to give to another."[35] According to former Attorney General George W. Wickersham, Taft made a similar comment when he signed White's commission as chief justice: "There is nothing I would have loved more than being chief justice of the United States . . . . I cannot help seeing the irony in the fact that I, who desired that office so much, should now be signing the commission of another man."[36] In light of Taft's professed concern for the Court, his appointments are perplexing at best. His failure to deal consistently with his own concern about the age of judges borders on the bewildering.[37] Taft did, however, remain true to one value of the "old" America—personal friendship. In the midst of an otherwise frustrating search for motive in each of Taft's appointments, the single factor common to all is that Taft knew, and liked, the man he appointed.

Never was personal friendship more important than with Taft's first appointment, that of Judge Horace Lurton, the very person to whom Taft

---

32. Baldwin, "The Supreme Court Justices," 160. Another contemporaneous commentator observed that "Taft's appointments greatly reduced the average age of the Court from what it had been for a number of years." Lowry, "The Men of the Supreme Court," 630.
33. Pringle, *William Howard Taft,* 1:529. See also Mark Sullivan, *Our Times: 1900–1925,* vol. 3, *Pre-War America* (New York: Charles Scribner's Sons, 1946), 7 (quoting Taft's wife).
34. Pringle, *William Howard Taft,* 1:102, 240–42, 264–65, 313–17, 378.
35. Butt, *Taft and Roosevelt,* 2:439.
36. Quoted in Pringle, *William Howard Taft,* 1:535.
37. For accounts of Taft's nominations, see Alexander M. Bickel, "Mr. Taft Rehabilitates the Court," *Yale Law Journal* 79 (November 1969): 1–45. (This article became the first chapter of Professor Bickel's contribution to the Holmes Devise History of the Supreme Court. Bickel and Schmidt, *History of the Supreme Court of the United States.*); Daniel S. McHargue, "President Taft's Appointments to the Supreme Court," *Journal of Politics* 12 (August 1950): 478–510. (This article is from McHargue's doctoral dissertation, "Appointments to the Supreme Court of the United States: The Factors That Have Affected Appointments, 1789–1932" [Ph.D. diss., University of California, Los Angeles, 1949].); Walter F. Murphy, "In His Own Image: Mr. Chief Justice Taft and Supreme Court Appointments," *The Supreme Court Review 1961:* 159–93.

had confided his concern about the Court's senescence. Born in Kentucky in 1844, Lurton grew up in Clarksville, Tennessee, a small town northwest of Nashville, near the border with Kentucky. In 1859 he went to Chicago to study at Douglas University, taking his parents with him. He never completed his degree, for with the outbreak of the Civil War, Lurton and his family returned southward. En route, Lurton joined the Fifth Tennessee Infantry Regiment, while his parents returned home to Clarksville. Lurton's experiences in the military have all the elements of legend. In the early months of the war Lurton earned promotion to sergeant-major, then suffered a lung infection that led to a medical discharge. He returned home to Clarksville but remained for only a few weeks before reenlisting to fight General Ulysses Grant's forces around Nashville. When Nashville fell, in February 1862, Lurton was among the thousands of Confederate soldiers taken prisoner. Lurton's captivity lasted only a few weeks, before he escaped to join the cavalry of General John Hunt Morgan. For more than a year Lurton and Morgan's cavalry harassed Union forces in the Ohio Valley. Then, in July 1863, Lurton was captured again. This time his imprisonment lasted some eighteen months, during which his lung infection recurred. His release came only a few months before the war ended. According to a romanticized account, President Lincoln personally ordered the release after listening to pleas from Lurton's mother. It seems more likely that Lurton himself secured his release by taking the oath of loyalty to the Union.[38] After his return from the war, Lurton studied law at Cumberland University, near Nashville, graduating in 1867. Once again he returned to Clarksville, where he became a civic leader as well as a respected attorney during the next two decades. In 1886 he won election to the Tennessee Supreme Court as a Democrat. Lurton earned high praise for his service on that court,[39] where he remained until 1893, when President Grover Cleveland appointed him to the United States Court of Appeals for the Sixth Circuit. While on the federal court, Lurton also taught law at Vanderbilt University, serving as dean of the law school from 1905 until his appointment to the Supreme Court.[40] Thus, by 1910 Lurton had almost a quarter of a century's experience on the state and federal courts. He was also approaching his sixty-sixth birthday.

---

38. See David M. Tucker, "Justice Horace Harmon Lurton: The Shaping of a National Progressive," *American Journal of Legal History* 13 (1969): 224 n. 3.

39. Samuel C. Williams, "Judge Horace H. Lurton," *Tennessee Law Review* 18 (1944): 242, 245 (the article contains the same text as Williams, *Phases of the History of the Supreme Court of Tennessee* (Johnson City, Tenn.: Watauga Press, 1944), 66, 69); *Green Bag* 5 (1893): 230, 232.

40. There is no full-length biography of Lurton. For information on his career, see John W. Green, "Judge Horace H. Lurton," in *Law and Lawyers: Sketches of the Federal Judges of Tennessee, Sketches of the Attorneys General of Tennessee, Legal Miscellany, Reminiscences by John W. Green* (Jackson, Tenn.: McCowat-Mercer Press, 1950): 79–84; Tucker, "Justice Horace Harmon Lurton," 223–32; Williams, "Judge Horace H. Lurton," 242–50.

If Taft doubted that Lurton's age posed a problem, his attorney general, George W. Wickersham, reminded him "that now, if ever the court needs young blood." Wickersham even recalled that one reason for Taft's having had "the support of the bar, and many of the conservative elements of the country, was that [he] would be conscientious in the selection of judges to build up that great court to the place that it formerly occupied." Taft's response was that of a person torn between duty to a friend and duty to his country: "I told George that the suggestions and the reasons tore my heart strings; that there was nothing that I had so much at heart in my whole administration as Lurton's appointment."[41] Taft had Wickersham consult with the justices of the Supreme Court, while Taft himself sought the advice of his cabinet. In the end, Taft's friendship for Lurton won out, as he explained to Lurton in a letter that was made public:

> It is just the simple truth to tell you that the chief pleasure of my administration, as I have contemplated it in the past, has been to commission you a Justice of the Supreme Court; and I never had any other purpose and was never shaken in it until there was presented to me the challenge whether I was not gratifying my personal desires at the expense of public interest in putting a Judge of your age upon the Bench under present conditions. For this reason, I took back my determination to appoint you, wiped it off the slate, and gave two or three days to the introspective process to know whether I was yielding to personal preference and affection at the expense of the public. I became convinced that I was not—that the circumstances justified the departure from the ordinary rule, and that I had the right to gratify my personal predilection by doing what I have done, because the motive in doing it included a desire to strengthen that Court as much as I could strengthen it.[42]

The Senate confirmed Lurton without opposition, enabling him to take his seat on January 3, 1910, the oldest man ever appointed to the Court up to that time.[43]

Just over two months after Lurton took his seat, Justice Brewer died, on March 28, 1910. Having chosen a southern Democrat, and a former Confederate, the Republican Taft turned northward and offered the position

---

41. Taft to Secretary of War John M. Dickinson, December 6, 1909, quoted in McHargue, "Appointments to the Supreme Court of the United States," 363.

42. Taft to Lurton (responding to Lurton's letter of thanks for the nomination), quoted in McHargue, "Appointments to the Supreme Court of the United States," 368. The letter was printed in "The Latest Addition to the Supreme Court," *Current Literature* 48 (March 1910): 271.

43. For a full account of the nomination of Lurton, see Pringle, *William Howard Taft*, 1:529–37; McHargue, "President Taft's Appointments to the Supreme Court," 482–87.

to the forty-eight-year-old Republican governor of New York, Charles Evans Hughes. Taft, and Roosevelt, had had mixed evaluations of Hughes; they respected his ability but disliked him personally.[44] By 1910, however, Taft's opinion changed. In 1908, Hughes had opened Taft's campaign for the presidency with a stirring speech in Youngstown, Ohio.[45] Later, after a personal visit with Hughes in Albany, New York, in March 1910 (a week before Brewer's death), Taft is reported to have said to his aide, "I don't know the man I admire more than Hughes. If ever I have the chance I shall offer to him the Chief Justiceship."[46] In light of Taft's longing for the chief justiceship himself, that statement is difficult to credit. Perhaps the personal ambivalence helps explain the careless letter Taft wrote to Hughes offering him the seat on the Court vacated by Brewer's death. Taft knew from their conversation that Hughes was anxious to leave politics; but he also recognized that the dynamic Hughes was a rising star in the Republican Party, one who loomed as a challenger to Taft's renomination in 1912.[47] Thus, Taft wrote, "I believe as strongly as possible that you are likely to be nominated and elected President some time in the future unless you go upon the Bench or make such associations at the Bar as to prevent."[48] Taft emphasized that Hughes would not have to leave the governor's office until the Court began its new term in the fall—a delay that would allow Hughes to deal with a special legislative session; and, somewhat optimistically, Taft suggested that the salary for an associate justice would soon be increased from $12,500 to $17,500.[49] Then, in a puzzling addition, he wrote: "The chief justiceship is soon likely to be vacant and I should never regard the practice of never promoting associate justices as one to be followed. Though, of course, this suggestion is only that by accepting the present position you do not bar yourself from the other, should it fall vacant in my term."[50] In a postscript, however, Taft took away what he had just

---

44. Pringle, *William Howard Taft*, 1:331, 533.
45. *New York Times*, September 6, 1908.
46. Butt, *Taft and Roosevelt*, 1:310.
47. Ibid., 1:223. Romine, "The 'Politics' of Supreme Court Nominations," 84, 194; Henry J. Abraham, *Justices and Presidents: A Political History of Appointments to the Supreme Court*, 3d ed. (New York: Oxford University Press, 1992), 168–69; Alpheus T. Mason, *William Howard Taft: Chief Justice* (New York: Simon and Schuster, 1965), 39–40; *Current Literature* 48 (June 1910): 594.
48. Taft to Hughes, April 22, 1910, quoted in Merlo J. Pusey, *Charles Evans Hughes* (New York: Macmillan, 1951), 1:271. Part of the same statement is quoted in Pringle, *William Howard Taft*, 1:532, with slightly different capitalization. The correspondence is also printed in *The Autobiographical Notes of Charles Evans Hughes*, eds. David J. Danelski and Joseph S. Tulchin (Cambridge, Mass.: Harvard University Press, 1973), 159–60.
49. The actual increase was only to $14,500. Act of August 23, 1912, ch. 350, 37 Stat. 360, 411.
50. Pringle, *William Howard Taft*, 1:532.

offered: "Don't misunderstand me as to the chief justiceship. I mean that if that office were now open, I should offer it to you and it is probable that if it were to become vacant during my term, I should promote you to it; but, of course, conditions change, so that it would not be right for me to say by way of promise what I would do in the future. Nor, on the other hand, would I have you think that your declination now would prevent my offering you the higher place, should conditions remain as they are."[51]

Two days later, Hughes wrote to accept the offer. He explained that he saw no opportunity for public service, other than the divided loyalties that would result from attempting to combine private practice of law with public service. That option not being attractive, Hughes viewed the Court as providing "a definite field of usefulness in the discharge of a function of national government of the gravest consequence to our people and to the future of our institutions."[52] He added a paragraph in response to Taft's comments about the chief justiceship: "Your expressions regarding the Chief Justiceship are understood and most warmly appreciated. You properly reserve entire freedom with respect to this and I accept the offer you now make without wishing you to feel committed in the slightest degree. Should the vacancy occur during your term I, in common with all our citizens, should desire you to act freely and without embarrassment in accordance with your best judgment at that time."[53]

The Senate confirmed Hughes unanimously in a five-minute executive session.[54] At forty-eight, Hughes would be the youngest of Taft's nominees; he was also the only one without prior judicial experience.[55] Hughes was a native of Glens Falls, New York, born there on April 11, 1862. An only child, he moved to New York City with his family before he was twelve. He excelled in school, becoming the youngest member of the 1881 graduating class at Brown University, where he ranked third. He then spent a year working to raise money before entering Columbia Law School, where he graduated in 1884. Within a few years he became a partner in a New York City law firm. Anxiety (from which he suffered all his life) forced him to leave private practice for teaching at Cornell Law School. After two years there, however, he returned to private practice in New York City in 1891. Hughes's adept handling of increasingly complex cases earned him appointment as counsel to New York state legislative committees investigating the gas and insurance

---

51. Pusey, *Charles Evans Hughes*, 1:271–72; also quoted in Pringle, *William Howard Taft*, 1:532, again with slight differences.
52. Pusey, *Charles Evans Hughes*, 1:272.
53. Ibid., 1:273.
54. Ibid.
55. McHargue, "Appointments to the Supreme Court of the United States," 374.

industries. His success in revealing abuses won him a national reputation that propelled him to election as governor of New York in 1906.[56] He was reelected in 1908 and served through the summer of 1910 before taking his seat on the Supreme Court in October.

Before Hughes could join the Court, however, Chief Justice Fuller died. Faced with a third nomination, Taft hesitated. Privately he repeated his irritation at judges who served beyond their abilities, commenting to his military aide Archie Butt, "If the justices would only retire when they have become burdens to the court itself, or when they recognize themselves that their faculties have become impaired, one could grieve sincerely when they pass away, and you would not feel like such a hypocrite as you do when going through the formality of sending telegrams of condolence and giving out interviews for propriety's sake."[57] A few days later, Taft visited the ailing Justice Moody. Taft resisted Moody's attempts to learn the name of the new chief justice, most likely because Taft had not decided on a nominee, for he waited more than five months after Fuller's death before naming White. The delay may not have had the significance attributed to it by some—Taft had previously announced that he would make no judicial appointments while Congress was in recess.[58] While Taft waited, Justice Moody announced his resignation, providing Taft yet another appointment.

The reasons for choosing White are difficult to discover.[59] Although Taft had intimated to Hughes that he would not rule out appointment of a sitting

---

56. For a contemporaneous account of the Court, along with comments about Hughes's decision to join the Court, see Edward G. Lowry, "Justice at Zero: The Frigid Austerities which Enrobe the Members of the United States Supreme Court," *Harper's Weekly Advertiser* (May 21, 1910): 8, 34.

57. Butt, *Taft and Roosevelt*, 2:433.

58. *New York Times*, July 5, 1910. See also "Rapid Changes in the Supreme Court," *American Review of Reviews* 42 (August 1910):136; *Current Literature* 49 (August 1910): 123 (no justice ever seated through recess appointment). On a related point, see Henry J. Abraham and Edward M. Goldberg, "A Note on the Appointment of Justices of the Supreme Court of the United States," *American Bar Association Journal* 46 (1960): 147–50, 219–22 (examines passage of time between date nomination sent to Senate and date final action by Senate—longer delay indicates greater significance for appointments).

59. There are only two full-length biographies of White. The most recent, Robert B. Highsaw, *Edward Douglass White, Defender of the Conservative Faith* (Baton Rouge: Louisiana State University Press, 1981), does not cite the earlier one, which was a published graduate thesis, Sister Marie Carolyn Klinkhamer, O.P., *Edward Douglas White, Chief Justice of the United States* (Washington, D.C.: Catholic University of America Press, 1943). On White in general, see Loren P. Beth, "Justice Harlan and the Chief Justiceship, 1910" *Supreme Court Historical Society Yearbook* (1983): 73–79; Newman Carter, *Court* "Edward D. White in Personal Retrospect," *Supreme Court Historical Society Yearbook* (1979): 5–7; Lewis C. Cassidy, "An Evaluation of Chief Justice White," *Mississippi Law Journal* 10 (February 1938): 136–53; Henry P. Dart, "Edward Douglas White," *Loyola Law Journal* 3 (November 1921): 1–13; Henry P. Dart, "Edward Douglas White," *Louisiana Historical Quarterly* 5 (April 1922): 145–51; Hugh J. Fegan, "Edward

justice, Taft is reported to have rejected out of hand a suggestion that he appoint Justice Harlan, the senior associate justice: "I'll do no such damned thing. I won't make the position of chief justice a blue ribbon for the final years of any member of the court. I want someone who will co-ordinate the activities of the court and who has a reasonable expectation of serving ten or twenty years on the bench."[60] That Taft might appoint from within the Court seemed to be known to the justices, and possibly even to the public; certainly Hughes's name was prominently mentioned as a candidate, especially in the New York press.[61] In response the justices let Taft know that they did not favor the appointment of Hughes, the junior member of the Court.[62] To explore the idea of appointing from within the Court, Taft again sent Attorney General Wickersham to poll the justices.[63] Wickersham reported a strong sentiment in favor of White, the most senior justice after Harlan. In the words of Justice Holmes, White was "the ablest man likely to be thought of." Although Holmes questioned White's administrative ability, he conceded that White would be "more politic" than Holmes himself and that White's "thinking

---

Douglass White, Jurist and Statesman," parts 1–3, *Georgetown Law Journal* 14 (November 1925): 1–21; (January 1926): 148–68; 15 (November 1926): 1–23; William H, Forman Jr., "Chief Justice Edward Douglass White," *American Bar Association Journal* 56 (1970): 260–62; Felix Frankfurter, "Chief Justices I Have Known," *Virginia Law Review* 39 (1953): 883–905, reprinted in *Supreme Court Historical Society Yearbook* (1980): 3–9; Virginia Van der Veer Hamilton, "In Defense of Order and Stability: The Constitutional Philosophy of Chief Justice Edward Douglass White," *Reviews in American History* 10 (1982): 105–8; W. O. Hart, "Edward Douglass White—A Tribute," *Loyola Law Journal* 7 (July 1926): 150–58; Richard Henry Jesse, "Chief Justice White," *American Law Review* 45 (May–June 1911): 321–26; Walter E. Joyce, "Edward Douglass White: The Louisiana Years, Early Life and on the Bench," *Tulane Law Review* 41 (June 1967): 751–68; Sister Marie Carolyn Klinkhamer, O.P. , "The Legal Philosophy of Edward Douglas White," *University of Detroit Law Journal* 35 (December 1957): 174–99; Sister Marie Carolyn Klinkhamer, "Chief Justice White and Administrative Law," *Fordham Law Review* 13 (November 1944): 194–231; Morris, "Chief Justice Edward Douglass White and President Taft's Court," 27–45; Spring, "Two Chief Justices: Edward Douglass White and William Howard Taft," 161–70; William Howard Taft et al., "Appreciation of Edward Douglass White," *Loyola Law Journal* 7 (April 1926): 61–94; Kenneth B. Umbreit, *Our Eleven Chief Justices: A History of the Supreme in Terms of Their Personalities* (New York: Harper & Brothers, 1938), 359–92.

60. Quoted in Pringle, *William Howard Taft*, 1:534. For a complete account of Harlan and the vacancy, see Beth, "Justice Harlan and the Chief Justiceship, 1910," 73–79.

61. Pusey, *Charles Evans Hughes*, 1:279; Beth, "Justice Harlan and the Chief Justiceship, 1910," 77 (quoting letter from Justice Lurton to Justice Harlan). For examples of speculation by the press, see the *New York Times,* April 21, 1910; April 26, 1910; July 5, 1910; September 4, 1910; November 26, 1910; November 29, 1910 (reporting that Hughes *will* be chief justice); December 12, 1910 (headline "White, not Hughes, for Chief Justice").

62. *New York Times,* December 18, 1910, magazine section, pt. 5; *American Review of Reviews* 43 (January 1911): 3; Frankfurter, "Chief Justices I Have Known," 891.

63. Pringle, *William Howard Taft*, 1:534–35.

[was] profound, especially in the legislative direction which we don't recognize as a judicial requirement but which is so, especially in our Court, nevertheless."[64] The *Green Bag*, in commenting on White's nomination, also hinted at a weakness in his executive ability, but praised his nomination nonetheless.[65] White himself was understandably pleased with the appointment—reportedly, his eyes filled with tears when he learned of his confirmation.[66]

Others, including Idaho's insurgent Senator William E. Borah, ranked White among the top ten justices who had sat on the Court, with Borah suggesting that he was "one of the great minds of the Supreme Court's history."[67] Some of the praise for White, especially that which ranked him along with Chief Justice John Marshall, seems today to be unlikely hyperbole.[68] Harold Laski certainly thought it an excess at the time.[69] It should not, however, be forgotten that Holmes had described White's thinking as "profound" and had intimated that White would indeed be able to lead the Court based on his intellectual power. Professor Edward Corwin turned the comparison ever so slightly, and in doing so probably reached the correct conclusion: "In its blended charm and force White's personality recalls the great Marshall himself."[70]

White was born in 1845 on his family's sugar plantation near Thibodaux, Louisiana, some thirty miles west of New Orleans. His early education came at the Jesuit College of the Immaculate Conception in New Orleans;

---

64. Holmes to Pollock, September 24, 1910, Howe, *Holmes-Pollock Letters: The Correspondence of Mr. Justice Holmes and Sir Frederick Pollock, 1874–1932*, ed. Mark DeWolfe Howe (Cambridge, Mass.: Harvard University Press, 1941), 1:170.
65. *Green Bag* 22 (1911): 102.
66. "The New Chief Justice," *Current Literature* 50 (January 1911): 16.
67. Charles W. Thompson, "The New Chief Justice of the United States," *New York Times*, December 18, 1910, magazine section, pt. 5, p. 2. One source suggested that Borah had been among the first to suggest White's appointment. See "The New Chief Justice," *Current Literature* 50 (January 1911): 17.
68. See, for example, Henry P. Dart, 149 Louisiana Reports xii (1922) (Dart was a lifelong friend of White's; he chaired the commission appointed by the Louisiana Bar Association to draft a resolution commemorating White; he read this resolution before the Supreme Court of Louisiana, October 3, 1921.) Dart himself recognized the eulogistic exaggeration in the comparisons; even so, he suggested that White would remain in the top rank of justices. Dart, "Edward Douglass White," *Loyola Law Journal*, 11. In 1938, and again in 1957, Justice Felix Frankfurter included White along with Marshall, Holmes, Brandeis, and Cardozo in what he termed a "roster of distinction." Felix Frankfurter, *Mr. Justice Holmes and the Supreme Court* (Cambridge, Mass.: Harvard University Press, 1938), 8–9; Felix Frankfurter, "The Supreme Court in the Mirror of Justices," *University of Pennsylvania Law Review* 105 (1957): 783.
69. Laski to Holmes, January 1, 1918, Howe, ed., *Holmes-Laski Letters* (Cambridge, Mass.: Harvard University Press, 1953), 1:123.
70. Edward S. Corwin, *The Twilight of the Supreme Court: A History of Our Constitutional Theory* (New Haven, Conn.: Yale University Press, 1934), 23.

in 1857, he went to Mount St. Mary's College, a preparatory school in Emmitsburg, Maryland. The next year he entered Georgetown College, another Jesuit institution. As was true for Justice Lurton, the outbreak of the Civil War cut short White's formal education. Soon after returning home from Georgetown, he enlisted as a private in the Confederate Army. He served fewer than two years before being taken prisoner at the fall of Port Hudson, on the Mississippi River below Natchez. He was paroled and sent home to Thibodaux. After the war ended, White read law in the New Orleans offices of a highly respected expert in civil law, Edward Bermudez, later chief justice of the state supreme court. In 1868 White was admitted to the Louisiana bar. He participated actively in the politics of the state under Reconstruction, siding with the Redeemers, who sought to end the control of state government by radical Republicans. The Compromise of 1877 saw the confirmation of White's political mentor, Francis T. Nicholls, as governor—a compromise furthered by Justice Harlan's service on the election commission. Shortly thereafter, in 1878, Nicholls rewarded White with nomination to the state supreme court. White served on the court from January 1879 until April 1880, when the state's constitution required that a new supreme court be appointed.[71] (White, only thirty-four, was not eligible for appointment since the new constitution required that justices be at least thirty-five.) White then returned to private practice in New Orleans.

In 1888 Nicholls again won election as governor; and again he rewarded White for his service in managing the campaign, this time with Nicholls's backing in the race for the United States Senate. White's short service in the Senate was marked by his support for measures that would benefit Louisiana, even when it required him to depart from his otherwise loyal backing of Democratic President Grover Cleveland. In particular, White opposed Cleveland's reform efforts to reduce tariffs, including that protecting Louisiana sugar. In part to silence White's opposition, but also in part to circumvent the opposition of New York's senators, Cleveland nominated White to the Supreme Court in February 1894 to replace Justice Samuel Blatchford, who had died in July 1893. In accord with custom, Cleveland initially nominated another New Yorker to succeed Blatchford. The Senate rejected that nominee and a second, choosing to support New York's senators in their quarrel with Cleveland over other matters. The president then turned to White, certain that he would be approved through an exercise of senatorial courtesy. Even though the Senate did just that, approving the nomination in only a few minutes, White refused to resign immediately. Instead, he chose to stay and fight (successfully) against tariff reform. White was finally sworn in as an associate justice on March 12, 1894.

---

71. Fegan, "Edward Douglass White, Jurist and Statesman," part 1, 8.

Sixteen years later, President Taft nominated White to be chief justice. By then, White had obviously earned the respect of his colleagues on the Court—witness their support for his nomination. He did so through ability and courtesy. He was an indefatigable walker, reported to be light on his feet in spite of his size—six feet tall and over two hundred pounds. In turn-of-the-century Washington, before automobiles came to dominate city streets, his walks made him known by sight to "[e]verybody in Washington."[72] Each day, on his walk home, often with another justice, he would stop to buy a single rose for his wife, whom he had married in 1894, after he joined the Court.[73] On other occasions, when visiting at the homes of justices, he would leave a rose for the wife and a cigar for the justice.[74] Justice Lamar's wife later described the Court as White's hobby: "He looked at every event from that angle."[75]

White's closest friend on the Court was Justice Holmes, with whom he often shared his walk home from the Court.[76] Holmes reciprocated the relationship, writing that White was "a great friend."[77] Each year, on the anniversary of one of Holmes's Civil War encounters, White would bring a red rose to be pinned on the elder justice's robes.[78] Justice McKenna was said to be White's next closest friend. McKenna and White, the only two Catholics on the Court, attended the same church in Washington, St. Matthew's; they also shared the walk home, McKenna to his apartment at 1150 Connecticut Avenue, and White to his residence at 1717 Rhode Island Avenue.[79]

Other than the respect shown by his judicial colleagues, reasons for White's nomination are not readily found. One theme that recurs in most discussions of the appointment is Taft's agreement with White's position

---

72. Rev. John Cavanaugh, C.S.C., "Recollections of Judge White," *The Annals of Our Lady of Lourdes* 38 (1921): 116; *New York Times*, May 18, 1921. See also Clarinda Pendleton Lamar, *The Life of Joseph Rucker Lamar, 1857–1916* (New York: G. P. Putnam's Sons, 1926), 172–73; George Shiras III, *Justice George Shiras Jr. of Pittsburgh* (Pittsburgh: University of Pittsburgh Press, 1953), 129–30.

73. The story about the single rose was an oft-remembered part of the lore surrounding White. See., for example, Thomas R. Marshall, *Recollections of Thomas R. Marshall* (Indianapolis: Bobbs-Merrill Co., 1925), 338; Shiras, *Justice George Shiras Jr. of Pittsburgh*, 129.

74. Lamar, *The Life of Joseph Rucker Lamar*, 180

75. Ibid.

76. Thompson, "The New Chief Justice of the United States," *New York Times*, 2; Lowry, "The Men of the Supreme Court," 631.

77. Holmes to Einstein, December 19, 1910, Jane Bishop Peabody, ed., *Holmes-Einstein Letters: Correspondence of Mr. Justice Holmes & Lewis Einstein, 1903–1935* (New York: St. Martin's Press, 1964), 57.

78. Dean Acheson, *Morning and Noon* (Boston: Houghton Mifflin, 1965), 59.

79. Butler, *A Century at the Bar*, 200.

in the *Insular Cases*.[80] Taft was governor in the Philippines at the time; he also worked on the brief for the United States. White's approach to applying the Constitution gave great flexibility to the administration and Congress, which doubtless appealed to Taft. Taft's political mentor, Roosevelt, liked White and opposed Hughes.[81] In addition, the appointment of White offered some hope for the impending presidential election. By the time he made the appointment, Taft knew of the disastrous results of the 1910 elections. He also had intimations of the looming split within his own party, as insurgent Republicans threatened to support another candidate.[82] The appointment of White, a Democrat, a southerner, and a Catholic, offered the prospect of attracting much-needed votes in 1912.[83]

Whatever else may be said about White's appointment, his age poses a conundrum. Taft had repeatedly said that he wanted to select younger men; he even explained his rejection of a distinguished public servant such as Rufus Choate in those terms: "He is sixty-five years old. What the country needs for Chief Justice is a man young enough to devote his strength and years to getting that court out of the slough of despond it has fallen into of late years."[84] Taft's appointment of White therefore went against his professed concerns. White, like Choate, was sixty-five, the oldest man ever appointed to the office of chief justice.[85] White's age combined with his political affiliation to weigh on Taft, with the result that on the morning of announcing White's nomination, Taft appeared to be "unusually concerned, and his customarily cheerful and calm manner was ruffled." Reflecting on the appointment, Taft said, "I suppose that an appointment which I have decided to make will bring on an avalanche of abuse from many leading Republicans." Then Taft continued, "I have decided to appoint White as

---

80. See, for example, Romine, "The 'Politics' of Supreme Court Nominations," 202; Umbreit, *Our Eleven Chief Justices,* 363–66 (White's nomination related to *Insular Cases* and the belief that he was a trustbuster).

81. Pringle, *William Howard Taft,* 1:535.

82. See Paolo E. Coletta, *The Presidency of William Howard Taft* (Lawrence: University Press of Kansas, 1973), 218–19.

83. See McHargue, "President Taft's Appointments to the Supreme Court," 493. Archie Butt's contemporaneous notes confirm Taft's desire to appeal to Catholic voters. Butt, *Taft and Roosevelt,* 2:443, 486. Taft's appointments of White and Lurton later brought southern support for Wilson to appoint Taft to the Court. *New York Times,* August 2, 1914.

84. Butt, *Taft and Roosevelt,* 2:442. Taft also explained his rejection of Elihu Root on similar grounds. See McHargue, "President Taft's Appointments to the Supreme Court," 492.

85. Beth, "Justice Harlan and the Chief Justiceship, 1910," 76. Of all the nominees for chief justice, only Charles Evans Hughes was older, being just two months shy of his sixty-eighth birthday when President Hoover nominated him in February 1930.

Chief Justice, and for three reasons I shall be greatly criticized. First, White is a prominent Democrat; second, he is a Catholic; and third, he was at one time a soldier in the Confederate Army. Still, I feel that I must appoint him, as I believe him to be the best qualified man in the country for that most important office."[86]

White was one of three Democrats appointed by Taft; the other two were Lurton and Lamar. According to one calculation, through 1932 there were some eighty justices, only seven of whom were appointed from a party different from that of the President making the appointment.[87] The unusual number of "off-party" appointments by Taft may well suggest nothing more than the fluidity of party labels at the time. Of course, it is also possible that Taft was trying to earn favor from Democrats in the hope of furthering his own chance of being appointed to the Court.[88]

In spite of White's age, many joined the justices in praising his appointment. The public is reported to have been in favor.[89] Writing in the *Outlook*, Elbert Baldwin attributed the Senate's speedy approval of the nomination of one of its former members (fifteen minutes in executive session) to its respect for "a man whose name, as a synonym of intellectual integrity and impartiality, may rank with the first dozen names of members of the Supreme Court since its creation." Baldwin also saw White as someone who had sufficient flexibility to deal with the contemporaneous intellectual turmoil in the law: "Justice White's decisions indicate the breadth, unpartisanship, humanness, and elasticity of a mind fitted to lead the deliberations of a continuous Constitutional Convention—for that to a certain degree is what the Supreme Court has become, despite its generally necessary affirmation of the principle of *stare decisis*—in its application and adaptation of the Constitution to the changes due to new conditions. Hence the elevation of such a man does not indicate that the leadership of the Supreme Court will be mechanical or 'fossilized.'"[90]

White's confirmation as chief justice gave Taft yet another appointment. He chose Joseph Rucker Lamar of Georgia. Baldwin's description of Lamar is suggestive of the lack of information about the new appointee: "Of all the

---

86. Charles E. Barker, *With President Taft in the White House* (Chicago: A. Kroch and Son, 1947), 38–39.
87. McHargue, "Appointments to the Supreme Court of the United States," 628.
88. Ibid., 629.
89. "The Progress of the World," *Review of Reviews* 43 (January 1911): 3. On reports of criticism of the nomination, see Francis McHale, *President and Chief Justice: The Life and Public Services of William Howard Taft* (Philadelphia: Dorrance & Co., 1931), 249; Murphy, "In His Own Image," 159, 171 (a cryptic reference to Senator Nelson of Minnesota having "never forgiven him [Taft] for appointing Edward Douglass White, a Democrat, to the chief justiceship."); *From the Diaries of Felix Frankfurter*, ed. Joseph Lash (New York: W. W. Norton & Co., 1975), 104 (Solicitor General Frederick W. Lehmann critical of the appointment of Democrats).
90. Baldwin, "The Supreme Court Justices," 157.

Judges, he seems the best worth looking at."[91] At least one author suggested that by the time Taft came to appoint Lamar he had run out of "first-rate" names. But that conclusion is difficult to accept in light of the repeated statements that Taft was so personally committed to the process.[92] Lamar did have the support of former justice Henry Billings Brown, who had previously recommended that Taft appoint Lamar to replace Justice Moody in the fall of 1910. Moreover, at the time of his nomination by Taft, Lamar was clearly a leader of the Georgia bar, as well as a highly respected historian of the state's law. Lamar had been born in 1857 in Ruckersville, Georgia, a small town east of Athens, on the border with South Carolina. He moved to Augusta when his father became pastor of the First Christian church there late in 1865. The church's parsonage was next door to that of the Presbyterian church, whose pastor was Woodrow Wilson's father. The future president and future justice became close friends, attending the same school until Wilson's father left for a church in South Carolina in 1870.[93] Lamar's father later took the family to Louisville, Kentucky, when he accepted a pastorate there. After graduating from his father's alma mater, Bethany College, in West Virginia, Lamar briefly studied law at Washington and Lee. He left to return to Augusta, where he read law in the office of a local attorney before being admitted to the Georgia bar in 1878. The following January he married the daughter of the president of Bethany College. They lived for brief periods in Louisville and at Bethany; then, in September 1880 they returned to Augusta, where Lamar became the partner of the lawyer in whose office he had read law. Before the end of that decade, Lamar served two terms in the state legislature while remaining active in a wide range of civic activities. In the 1890s he served with two others on a commission to revise Georgia's laws; he also became chairman of the board that examined applicants for membership in the state bar. Then, on New Year's Eve of 1902, Lamar learned that the governor had appointed him to the state's supreme court. Lamar easily won election to the court in 1904; but he resigned the next year, saying that he was opposed to the election of judges. He was also homesick for Augusta. Lamar's wife, Clarinda Pendleton Lamar, evocatively captured the spirit of the era when she described their new home

---

91. Ibid., 159.
92. The lack of suitable nominees is suggested in a book by John P. Frank, *Marble Palace: The Supreme Court in American Life* (New York: Knopf, 1958), 376; see also John P. Frank, "The Appointment of Supreme Court Justices: Prestige, Principles, and Politics," *Wisconsin Law Review* (1941): 172–210, 343–79, 461–512. Another survey of the process that led to Lamar's nomination reached the conclusion that the author could not "be sure what made Taft think of Lamar." McHargue, "Appointments to the Supreme Court of the United States," 400.
93. Lamar's wife reports that Lamar and Wilson did not meet again until 1913, at a reception for Wilson's inauguration. Although Lamar did not recognize his former friend, Wilson did remember, leading to a resumption of their friendship. Lamar, *The Life of Joseph Rucker Lamar*, 233–36.

in Augusta, where they lived until leaving for Washington: "But no city house is a home in the sense that a country house can be. No matter how fine it is, nor how saturated with memories it may become, it cannot take the place in one's affections, of living, growing things, of trees and flowers and birds."[94]

Lamar returned home and resumed his active practice of law. In 1908, President Taft came to Augusta with his family to recuperate from the presidential campaign. During that visit, the Lamars met the Tafts through their mutual friend and Augusta native, Archie Butt, the president's military aide. Taft visited Lamar again when he returned to Augusta in November 1909. As a result of those visits, it seems probable that Taft's nomination of Lamar was not unlike that of Lurton in being based on personal friendship.[95]

For his final appointment, to replace Moody, Taft turned westward. Once he looked in that direction, Taft could hardly have avoided Willis Van Devanter's name. For, in the words of a student of Van Devanter's life, "[t]here have been few occasions in American constitutional history where a purpose, so clearly stated, was worked for so diligently with such success."[96] For more than a decade Van Devanter had received the active support of Wyoming Republicans in his search for a seat on the Court. Although he had become a prominent Wyoming attorney by the time of his nomination in 1910, Van Devanter was born in Marion, Indiana, in 1859. After attending local public schools, he went to the forerunner of DePauw University. He had to withdraw from school briefly on account of his father's illness, but he resumed his education at Cincinnati Law School, from which he graduated in 1881, ranking second in his class. He then returned to Indiana, where he joined his father's law firm. When the senior Van Devanter retired in 1884, the other partner moved to Cheyenne, Wyoming. Van Devanter joined him soon thereafter. In 1888, Van Devanter won a seat in the territorial legislature, where he became a leader in the Republican Party. As Lamar would do in Georgia, Van Devanter served on a committee to codify the territorial laws, modeling them after the Ohio statutes he had studied at Cincinnati.

Based on his Republican activities, Van Devanter was appointed chief justice of the territorial supreme court in 1889. After Wyoming became a state in 1890, Van Devanter won election to the first state supreme court, though he

---

94. Ibid., 50–51.
95. For an account of Taft's visits to Augusta with the Lamars, see ibid., 161–65.
96. M. Paul Holsinger, "The Appointment of Supreme Court Justice Van Devanter: A Study of Political Preferment," *American Journal of Legal History* 12 (1968): 324. This article is based on the author's doctoral dissertation, which also provides further information about Van Devanter's career in Wyoming. M. Paul Holsinger, "Willis Van Devanter, the Early Years: 1859–1911" (Ph.D. diss., University of Denver, 1964). For another account of Van Devanter's early career, see Lewis Gould, "Willis Van Devanter in Wyoming Politics, 1884–1897" (Ph.D. diss., Yale University, 1966). And, for another account of Van Devanter's appointment, see Daniel A. Nelson, "The Supreme Court Appointment of Willis Van Devanter," *Annals of Wyoming* 53 (fall 1981): 2–11.

resigned after only four days to return to the practice of law and to active political life. His successes as leader of the state's Republican Party brought him an appointment as an assistant attorney general in the Department of the Interior in the McKinley administration. Van Devanter moved to Washington in 1897, where he succeeded in eliminating the backlog of cases in the department. Early in 1903, Roosevelt appointed him to a newly created seat on the Circuit Court of Appeals for the Eighth Circuit. Seven years later, Taft elevated Van Devanter to the Supreme Court, in spite of doubts about his production of opinions. Through his mentor, Wyoming Senator Francis E. Warren, Van Devanter attempted to explain his poor record by pointing to the illnesses that both he and his wife had suffered.[97] He seemed to sense, however, that Warren's prolonged campaign for his nomination might have begun to irritate Taft. As a result, Van Devanter sent Taft a telegram asking that his name be removed from consideration. Warren, however, did not retreat; he continued to importune Taft, both directly and indirectly. In the end, Taft capitulated, sending Van Devanter's name to the Senate along with those of White and Lamar on December 12, 1910.

Early the next month, the two most recent Taft nominees, now confirmed by the Senate, joined in the whirlwind of social activities that marked the new year. Since the first of January fell on a Sunday in 1911, official Washington observed New Year's Day on January second.[98] The newly invigorated Court undoubtedly participated fully in the seasonal parties. As Justice Hughes later recalled, "When at the beginning of 1911, Justices Van Devanter and Lamar came on the bench, we had a relatively young Court and the Justices went out a great deal. The older Justices too kept up the pace. Justice Holmes was a most popular guest and an inveterate dinner-goer." But the activities came with a price, with Hughes describing them as "very exacting." He added, "I was much in demand and invitations came long in advance; and when I tried to limit my engagements to a couple a week, and had made these, then others of such importance that I could not well refuse would come and I would find myself going three or four nights a week. One good feature of these parties was that we could get away early, shortly after ten as a rule; and I would then return to my library to read law until one or two o'clock in the morning."[99]

---

97. Taft accepted the explanation that Van Devanter himself had been ill, as had his wife. Even so, Van Devanter did not improve while on the Supreme Court. His annual average of opinions "was the lowest—14.15—of any Justice appointed between 1853 and 1943." Morris, "Chief Justice Edward Douglass White and President Taft's Court," 29. Complete comparative statistics are in Albert P. Blaustein and Roy M. Mersky, *The First One Hundred Justices* (Hamden, Conn.: Archon Books, 1978): 147–49. Although the low number of opinions suggests at least a failure to share the Court's workload, it may not be conclusive of the contribution made by a justice. For example, Blaustein and Mersky report that Van Devanter's close rival in opinions per term was Chief Justice Earl Warren, with 14.1.

98. For an account of the receptions, see Lamar, *The Life of Joseph Rucker Lamar,* 170–74.

99. Danelski and Tulchin, eds., *Autobiographical Notes of Charles Evans Hughes,* 165–66.

The next day, the justices again assembled, this time to make their way to a courtroom that everyone was coming to realize was inadequate. Plans were already being drawn for a new building north of the Capitol. For the moment, however, the justices had to do without private offices in the Capitol; "visiting attorneys who seek writs have to call upon the Judges at their private residences."[100] Messengers regularly traveled between the homes, carrying draft opinions and other Court business. Elbert Baldwin, again writing in the *Outlook*, provided a contemporaneous account, describing the Court's room in the basement of the Capitol as more "like a parlor," with poor lighting, poor heating, and poor ventilation (though he conceded that the ventilation was better than in other parts of the building).[101] The Court convened daily at noon, adjourned for lunch between 2:00 and 2:30, then sat until 4:30. The chief justice was paid $13,000 a year, though there was a proposal in Congress to raise the salary to $18,000.[102] Those salaries compared with an average banker's salary in 1910 of just over $7,700, a lawyer's of slightly more than $4,100, and a professor's of almost $2,900. In 1913, the average weekly wage of a clerk was $15, that of an accountant $30. The next year, Henry Ford would begin paying his workers the unheard-of salary of $5 a day (almost twice the average for industrial workers).[103] Throughout the tenure of White as chief justice, each justice had a clerical assistant (not yet formally known as a "law clerk").[104]

---

100. Baldwin, "The Supreme Court Justices," 156–60. See also Lowry, "Justice at Zero," 34.
101. Baldwin, "The Supreme Court Justices," 156.
102. Ibid., 160. In 1911 the salary of associate justices was raised to $14,500 and that of the chief justice to $15,000, where they remained until 1926. When measured against the consumer price index, the salaries were at their peak between 1911 and 1919, of any period between 1891 and 1953. U.S. Senate, *"Judicial and Congressional Salaries"—Reports of the Task Forces of the Commission on Judicial and Congressional Salaries pursuant to Public Law 220, 83d Congress,* 83d Cong., 2d sess., 1954, S. Doc. 97, pp. 63, 71.
103. Wynn, *From Progressivism to Prosperity,* 6; John Whiteclay Chambers II, *The Tyranny of Change: America in the Progressive Era, 1900–1917* (New York: St. Martin's Press, 1980), 54–55.
104. Chester A. Newland, "Personal Assistants to Supreme Court Justices: The Law Clerks," *Oregon Law Review* 40 (1961): 299–317. Newland notes that Congress first approved of assistants in the Sundry Civil Act of August 4, 1886 (ch. 902, 24 Stat. 222, 254.) with an annual salary of $1,600, which was increased to $2,000 by 1919. In 1919 Congress approved a second assistant, described as "law clerk," with a salary of $3,600. Act of July 19, 1919, ch. 24, 41 Stat. 163, 209. There was initial uncertainty about the status of the two, but in 1920 Congress made it clear that one would be paid $3,600 and the other $2,000—a law clerk and a stenographic clerk. Act of May 29, 1920, ch. 214, 41 Stat. 631, 686–87.

Justice McReynolds's first job after graduation from Virginia Law School was as secretary to Senator Howell Jackson, of Tennessee. One of McReynolds's first assignments from Jackson was to help draft the bill authorizing stenographers for the justices. Schimmel, "The Judicial Policy of Mr. Justice McReynolds," 61.

I

THE FIRST TERM

Edward Douglass White took the oath of office as chief justice on Monday, December 19, 1910, a day without oral argument or announcement of opinions. White then moved one chair to his left. Justice Harlan returned to the chief's right, the seat he had occupied for more than a decade, since Justice Stephen J. Field retired in December 1897. But before he resumed his accustomed seat, the ailing Harlan performed one last official duty as acting chief justice[1]—he administered the oath of office to Chief Justice White. Holmes described the scene in a letter to his young friend and American diplomat, Lewis Einstein: "White has taken the oath and is C.J.—Poor old Harlan, who is superseded, looks sad and aged. He has been presiding and now that excitement is off I shouldn't be surprised if he caved in. He is too old for work."[2] Harlan was undoubtedly disappointed,[3] both because he could not be chief justice and because he had had to administer the oath of office to a former Confederate. He did, however, allow himself one last conceit: As he is reported to have said to a friend, "On that day I wore my Grand Army and Loyal Legion buttons, so that they were plainly visible as I faced him; and I never more profoundly nor more solemnly pronounced the words of that oath than upon that occasion."[4]

When Van Devanter and Lamar took the oath of office on January 3, 1911, the Court had a full complement of members for the first time in more than nine months.[5] With that membership, the "White Court" began

---

1. One piece of Court mythology reported that White administered the oath to himself. Lowry, "The Men of the Supreme Court," 631.
2. Holmes to Einstein, December 19, 1910, Peabody, *Holmes-Einstein Letters,* 58.
3. Tinsley Yarbrough, *Judicial Enigma: The First Justice Harlan* (New York: Oxford University Press, 1995), 217–18.
4. Arthur Wallace Dunn, *From Harrison to Harding: A Personal Narrative, Covering a Third of a Century, 1888–1921* (New York: G. P. Putnam's Sons, 1922), 132–33.
5. For confirmation of this fact, as well as other valuable information about the Court, see generally, Hall, ed., *The Oxford Companion to the Supreme Court of the United States.* The information on gaps in the Court's membership is contained in a table at pages 983–87.

its work. In looking forward to the new year, Holmes had written, "We are to have two new men who have not put in an appearance yet, and with the New Year I suppose they will be re-arguing all their damned 'Great Cases.' I loathe great cases. They are not half as important as many small ones that involve interstitial developments of the law, but they make talk for the newspapers."[6] The two "new men" were, of course, Van Devanter and Lamar. White did all he could to ease their transition to the Court and to create a cohesive group. He earned accolades from Justice Hughes, who thought the addition of Van Devanter and Lamar, along with White's promotion, had changed the "atmosphere of the Court" so that it "became a reasonably happy family."[7] He specifically pointed to White's new attitude as contributing to the change:

> Chief Justice White assumed his new duties with manifest pleasure and with the most earnest desire to discharge them well. He was no longer distant or difficult. On the contrary, he was most considerate and gracious in his dealings with every member of the Court, plainly anxious to create an atmosphere of friendliness and to promote agreement in the disposition of cases.[8]

To deal with those cases, the White Court assembled on January 3, 1911. For the 1910–1911 term the Court had seen one of the sharpest rises in number of cases on its docket.[9] The more than eleven hundred cases represented both "great" ones and small ones. Within his first month as chief justice, White would preside over discussion about one of the centerpieces of Progressive reform legislation—the Food and Drug Act of 1906.[10] Before the second month was out, another key reform measure would be before the Court, the Employers' Liability Act of 1910[11] (the *second* Employers' Liability Act, the Court already having declared the first act unconsti-

---

6. Holmes to Einstein, December 19, 1910, Peabody, *Holmes-Einstein Letters*, 58. This letter echoed Holmes's dissent in *Northern Securities Co. v. United States,* 193 U.S. 197, 400–401 (1904) ("Great cases like hard cases make bad law. For great cases are called great, not by reason of their real importance in shaping the law of the future, but because of some accident of immediate overwhelming interest which appeals to the feelings and distorts the judgment.")
7. Hughes, *Autobiographical Notes,* 169.
8. Ibid.
9. Epstein et al., *The Supreme Court Compendium,* 2d ed., 72.
10. *Hipolite Egg Co. v. United States,* 220 U.S. 45 (1911). There was no oral argument in the case; briefs were submitted January 5, 1911.
11. The opinion would not be announced for almost a year, falling victim to Justice Van Devanter's "slow pen." *Second Employers' Liability Cases,* 223 U.S. 1 (1912).

tutional).¹² But the issues that were really "great" were those concerning trusts, about which the Court heard three oral arguments in White's first month. First came a relatively small case, but one that presented a key question concerning the ability of a patent holder to parlay the patent into control of retail prices.¹³ The issue would dog the Court for much of the next decade;¹⁴ but this first case paled in comparison with the other two, ones in which the United States government faced the tobacco trust and the oil trust, in the names of American Tobacco Company¹⁵ and the Standard Oil Company of New Jersey.¹⁶

Not surprisingly, the trust cases produced an outpouring of commentary from the press. The *Outlook* sent its special correspondent, Elbert Baldwin, to cover the argument in the tobacco case.¹⁷ Along with photographs of each of the justices, Baldwin offered a lively account of the Court's procedures. On each day that there was oral argument, the justices filed into the courtroom promptly at noon, only a few minutes after arriving at the Capitol. Chief Justice White, who led the procession across a public hallway and into the courtroom, was "the most impressive-looking of the company. . . . In physical appearance no man in public life, not even President Taft, better deserves the adjective 'ponderous.' . . . [but his] voice is like velvet." Possibly reflecting Roosevelt's own views, the article praised White at great length, suggesting that he might rank among the top dozen justices to have sat on the Court and concluding with the prediction that White's influence on the Court would "be exactly in line with John Marshall's."¹⁸

The image of Marshall was repeated in the description of his namesake Justice John Marshall Harlan, who was said to resemble closely the great chief justice. Little else was said about Harlan, other than to note his past career and to comment on his sense of humor, as exhibited during the argument in the tobacco case. Harlan had already served longer than all but five of his predecessors; within a year he would surpass all but two: Justice Stephen Field and Chief Justice Marshall himself. Harlan was born in 1833 in rural Boyle County, Kentucky, southwest of Lexington. He stud-

---

12. *Employers' Liability Cases,* 207 U.S. 463 (1908).
13. *Dr. Miles Medical Co. v. John D. Park & Sons Co.,* 220 U.S. 373 (1911).
14. See *Dr. Miles Medical Co. v. John D. Park & Sons Co.,* 220 U.S. 373 (1911); *Bauer & Cie v. O'Donnell,* 229 U.S. 1 (1913); *Boston Store of Chicago v. American Graphophone Co.,* 246 U.S. 8 (1918); *International News Service v. The Associated Press,* 248 U.S. 215 (1918); *United States v. Colgate & Co.,* 250 U.S. 300 (1919); *United States v. A. Schrader's Son, Inc.,* 252 U.S. 85 (1920).
15. *United States v. American Tobacco Co.,* 221 U.S. 106 (1911).
16. *Standard Oil Co. of New Jersey v. United States,* 221 U.S. 1 (1911).
17. Baldwin, "The Supreme Court Justices," 156–64.
18. Ibid., 157.

ied at both Centre College and Transylvania University. After being admitted to the bar in the decade before the Civil War, Harlan quickly distinguished himself both in the practice of law and in state politics. By the time the southern states began to secede, Harlan had sufficient influence to lead the state's legislature in refusing to join the breakaway. Even though he owned slaves (he freed them before the end of the war), he formed the Tenth Kentucky Volunteers, fighting on behalf of the Union until his father's death in 1863. Upon return to civilian life, he resumed an active role in state politics, first in Kentucky's Union Party, under whose banner he was elected attorney general for Kentucky. Harlan opposed the reelection of President Abraham Lincoln in 1864. But he moved toward the Republican Party in the years following the Civil War, gradually coming to accept the need for greater national activity in the face of efforts to prevent blacks from participating in the political life of the states. By 1868 he was fully in the Republican camp, campaigning for Ulysses Grant. Three years later, Harlan lost in his bid for governor, but he remained active in politics. In 1876, as head of the Kentucky delegation at the Republican Party's national convention, Harlan swung the state to Rutherford B. Hayes. He served on the commission sent to Louisiana to resolve the disputed election of 1876 when he met White during the discussions that led to the declaration that Francis Nicholls would become governor.[19] In return for Harlan's service, and as a sign of reconciliation with the South, President Hayes rewarded him with an appointment to the Supreme Court in the fall of 1877.[20] Before that, Harlan's only judicial service had been as a county judge in Kentucky, a part-time position he held for thirty-two months.[21] By 1911 Harlan had established a record distinguished for prescient (and sometimes truculent) dissents.[22]

Following Harlan into the courtroom was Justice Joseph McKenna, whose chin whiskers and Catholic religion attracted reporter Baldwin's attention. Felix Frankfurter would later remember McKenna as "that nice

---

19. Beth, *John Marshall Harlan*, 127.
20. Linda Carol Adams Przybyszewski, "The Republic According to John Marshal Harlan: Race, Republicanism, and Citizenship" (Ph.D. diss., Stanford University, 1989): x–xi.
21. David G. Farrelly, "Harlan's Formative Period: The Years Before the War," *Kentucky Law Journal* 46 (1958): 393.
22. The two most recent biographies of Harlan are Loren P. Beth, *John Marshall Harlan: The Last Whig Justice* (Lexington: University Press of Kentucky, 1992); Yarbrough, *Judicial Enigma: The First Justice Harlan*. Other worthwhile contributions include Loren Beth, "Justice Harlan and the Uses of Dissent," *American Political Science Review* 49 (1955): 1085–104; Jacob W. Landynski, "John Marshall Harlan and the Bill of Rights: A Centennial View," *Social Research* 49 (1982): 899–926; Przybyszewski, "The Republic According to John Marshall Harlan"; Sally Jo Vasicko, "Justice Harlan and the Equal Protection Clause," *Supreme Court Historical Society Yearbook* (1982): 46–56.

bird-like creature with a beard."[23] Born in Philadelphia in 1843, the first son of immigrant parents, McKenna had moved to California with his family in 1855. Ten years later he was admitted to the bar and elected as a Republican to be district attorney for Solano County. After serving a second, two-year term, he returned to private practice. In 1875 he successfully campaigned for a seat in the state legislature, where he became a close ally of Leland Stanford. In 1884 he won a seat in the United States House of Representatives after two unsuccessful attempts. He remained in the House until 1892, when President Benjamin Harrison appointed him to the Court of Appeals for the Ninth Circuit, raising cries of protest that the appointment was a political payoff to Stanford. While in the House, McKenna had formed another close political friendship, with Ohio's powerful Republican congressman, William McKinley. Not surprisingly, therefore, when McKinley was elected president in 1896 he looked for a cabinet position for McKenna, who could provide much-needed representation for the West. McKinley decided against nominating McKenna to be secretary of the interior, fearing that anti-Catholic factions would oppose McKenna's having control over schools on Indian reservations.[24] McKinley therefore appointed McKenna as attorney general, where he served only nine months before being appointed to the Supreme Court to replace another Californian, Justice Stephen J. Field. The nomination attracted little enthusiasm and modest opposition based on doubts about McKenna's abilities. Even so, the Senate unanimously confirmed the nomination.

After McKenna came the two remaining justices from before Taft's presidency—Oliver Wendell Holmes Jr. and William Rufus Day. Holmes earned reverential comments from Baldwin for his service in the Civil War and for his intelligence. In addition, Baldwin commented on what Holmes had revealed in his letter to Pollock—the close friendship between Holmes and White.[25] Approaching his seventieth birthday, Holmes had not yet been established as a giant standing astride the American judicial landscape. Having grown up among the elite of Boston society, he graduated from Harvard in June 1861. He promptly enlisted in the Union Army, with a commission as a lieutenant coming soon thereafter. Service in the war would prove to be a defining experience in his life. As he wrote half a century later, "You come down to truth in War. . . . [W]hen I saw the caissons

---

23. Frankfurter, "Chief Justices I Have Known," 891; reprinted in *Supreme Court Historical Society Yearbook*, 6.

24. Brother Matthew McDevitt, *Joseph McKenna: Associate Justice of the United States* (1946; reprint, New York: Da Capo Reprints, 1974), 90–91; Richard J. Purcell, "Justice Joseph McKenna," *Records of the American Catholic Historical Society of Philadelphia* 56 (September 1945): 194–99.

25. See also Lash, ed., *Diaries of Felix Frankfurter*, 314.

and the strings of horses, and heard the jingle of the sabres and the short command of the bugles I felt as if I touched the blue steel edge of actuality for half an hour."[26] On three different occasions during the war, Holmes suffered life-threatening wounds but returned to duty after each incident. He concluded his three-year service in July 1864 and returned to Boston, where he enrolled in Harvard Law School that fall. After graduation and admission to the bar, he practiced law in Boston for several years. He also edited the *American Law Review*, turning essays for that journal into his classic book, *The Common Law*, published in 1881. Following the appearance of that volume, Holmes was appointed to the Supreme Judicial Court of Massachusetts as well as to the law faculty at Harvard. Twenty years later, in 1902, President Roosevelt appointed Holmes to the "Massachusetts seat" on the Supreme Court after the death of Justice Horace Gray.[27]

Slight in stature, Justice William Rufus Day earned Baldwin's quip that he "seems all brain." Day was born in 1849 in Ravenna, Ohio, thirty miles southeast of Cleveland. From his hometown, a thriving county seat, Day went on to the University of Michigan, graduating in 1870. He then spent a year clerking for a local judge in Ravenna before returning for a single year of study at the university's law school. He was admitted to the Ohio bar in 1872, when he moved to Canton, Ohio, to begin practice. He rapidly won widespread respect for his excellence as a trial lawyer, with cases ranging from criminal to corporate. Along with his practice he became active in Ohio Republican politics, eventually developing a close friendship with William McKinley, whose home was also in Canton. The lasting strength of that friendship was evidenced by Day's giving each justice a carnation on McKinley's birthday every year.[28] The friendship led to Day's appointment as first assistant secretary of state under President McKinley, and also as secretary of

---

26. Holmes to Einstein, March 27, 1912, Peabody, *Holmes-Einstein Letters*, 67.
27. As would be expected, the literature on Holmes is extensive. The biographies range from Catherine Drinker Bowen's *Yankee from Olympus: Justice Holmes and His Family* (Boston: Little, Brown, 1944), to G. Edward White's *Justice Oliver Wendell Holmes: Law and the Inner Self* (New York: Oxford University Press, 1993). Other recent biographies include Gary J. Aichele, *Oliver Wendell Holmes, Jr.: Soldier, Scholar, Judge* (Boston: Twayne Publishers, 1989); Liva Baker, *The Justice from Beacon Hill: The Life and Times of Oliver Wendell Holmes* (New York: Harper Collins, 1991); and Sheldon M. Novick, *Honorable Justice: The Life of Oliver Wendell Holmes* (Boston: Little, Brown, 1989). See also Robert W. Gordon, ed., *The Legacy of Oliver Wendell Holmes, Jr.* (Palo Alto: Stanford University Press, 1992); Michael H. Hoffheimer, *Justice Holmes and Natural Law* (New York: Garland, 1992). The classic treatment of Holmes's life and career before joining the Court is the two-volume set by Mark DeWolfe Howe, *Justice Oliver Wendell Holmes: The Shaping Years, 1841–1870* (Cambridge, Mass.: Harvard University Press, Belknap Press, 1957), and *Justice Oliver Wendell Holmes: The Proving Years, 1870–1882* (Cambridge, Mass.: Harvard University Press, Belknap Press, 1963).
28. Pusey, *Charles Evans Hughes*, 1:283.

state. Day served for only four months in the latter position, resigning to head the American delegation to the peace conference at the end of the Spanish-American War in 1898. At the conclusion of the conference he returned to private life in Canton. Shortly thereafter, however, McKinley appointed him to the Court of Appeals for the Sixth Circuit, where he served with both William Howard Taft and Horace H. Lurton. Four years later, in 1903, President Roosevelt appointed him to the Supreme Court after Taft declined the nomination.[29]

Completing the procession of justices were Taft's four appointees—Lurton, Hughes, Van Devanter, and Lamar. Lurton's age merited no special mention (possibly because each of the five justices who preceded him into the courtroom was over sixty); but his style of questioning did, with Baldwin writing of Lurton that "he seems as pertinacious in asking questions of counsel from the bench as if he were a very young man, and his nasal Yankee voice has in it little of the soft Southern twang one might expect." Then, exercising a bit of journalistic license, Baldwin noted that Lurton and Harlan had been on opposite sides of a battle during the Civil War: "Colonel Harlan tried to train a cannon ball on [private] Lurton and company, but the Confederates won." Baldwin concluded his romantic vision with a keen insight into the continuity represented by the Court on the eve of the fiftieth anniversary of the outbreak of the Civil War: "The echoes of the Civil War are getting fainter, but the bringing together of two such men on the same bench revives a memory."[30]

Without an apocryphal story, Baldwin's evaluation of the three newest members of the Court was more abbreviated. Hughes's full beard and "virile manner and voice" attracted attention, as did his record as a progressive governor. Van Devanter received the singular compliment of being described as "a very human-looking document indeed." And, bringing up the rear was Lamar, who seemed "to be the best worth looking at" of all the justices.

So the justices must have filed into the courtroom on Thursday, January 5, the first day of oral argument under Chief Justice White.[31] Little was unusual about the docket for that day. To be sure, two of the four cases would attract considerable attention, *Hipolite Egg* and *Dr. Miles Medical*. The

---

29. The only biography of Day is Joseph E. McLean, *William Rufus Day: Supreme Court Justice from Ohio,* Johns Hopkins University Studies in Historical and Political Science, vol. 64 (Baltimore: Johns Hopkins Press, 1946). See also Vernon W. Roelofs, "William R. Day: A Study in Constitutional History" (Ph.D. diss., University of Michigan, 1942).

30. Baldwin, "The Supreme Court Justices," 158.

31. For a brief description of the operation of the Court by a former "secretary" to Justice Brewer, see J. F. Haig, "The Supreme Court of the United States," *Independent,* 69 (November 1910): 1038–39.

other two more closely resembled the usual fare for the White Court; eminently forgettable, they both involved minor procedural issues.[32] Yet, even they contained echoes of debates from an earlier time. Both cases involved charges that certain railroads had violated the 1906 Hepburn Act's ban on a railroad's shipping ore mined by a company owned by the railroad itself. (The act attempted to prevent what was termed "vertical integration," whereby a single railroad controlled all stages in the production of coal, from mining ore to selling to consumers.) Two years earlier, in one of the so-called "Commodities Cases," the Court had upheld the Hepburn Act but given it a restrictive construction by allowing railroads to control the *stock* of a mining company while prohibiting them from owning the *ore* itself.[33] Now that White was chief justice, all that remained of the dispute were procedural issues that did not reach the substance of the effort to control railroads.

From issues with little lasting significance, the Court turned to hear argument in two other cases. The first to be decided would be *Hipolite Egg*, through which the United States sought to seize fifty cans of preserved whole eggs, claiming that they were "adulterated" because one can had been found to contain a preservative, boric acid. The cans originated in St. Louis, where Hipolite had stored them for about five months before shipping them to Peoria, Illinois. There they were again stored, this time in a storeroom owned by the bakery that intended to use them in baked products.

The government pointed to section 10 of the Pure Food and Drug Act of 1906 to support its seizure of the eggs.[34] That section provided that if "any article of food that is adulterated and is being transported from one State . . . to another for sale, or, having been transported, remains unloaded, unsold, or in original unbroken packages" the article could be seized, so long as the government followed the process set out in the statute.[35] Hipolite challenged neither the procedures nor the assertion that the eggs were adulterated. Instead, it relied on an interpretation of the statute that involved two points: (1) that the statute did not cover goods used as raw materials, rather than for resale; and (2) that the cans were no longer in interstate commerce, having come to rest in the Peoria storerooms.

---

32. *United States v. Lehigh Valley Railroad Co.*, 220 U.S. 257 (1911); *United States v. Erie Railroad Co.*, 220 U.S. 275 (1911).
33. *United States v. Delaware & Hudson Co.*, 213 U.S. 366 (1909).
34. For explorations suggesting the variety of motives behind the act, see Peter Temin, *Taking Your Medicine: Drug Regulation in the United States* (Cambridge, Mass.: Harvard University Press, 1980); Donna J. Wood, *Strategic Uses of Public Policy: Business and Government in the Progressive Era* (Marshfield, Mass.: Pitman, 1986); Walter A. Trattner, "The Federal Food and Drugs Act: A Complete but Familiar Story," *Reviews in American History* 18 (1990): 390–94; Donna J. Wood, "Strategic Use of Public Policy: Business Support for the 1906 Food and Drug Act," *Business History Review* 59 (1985): 403–32.
35. Act of June 30, 1906, ch. 3915, 34 Stat. 768.

In an opinion whose mocking treatment of Hipolite's arguments belied the significance of the issue, Justice McKenna wrote sweepingly of the power to preserve the purity of food: "All articles, compound or single, not intended for consumption by the producer, are designed for sale, and, because they are, it is the concern of the law to have them pure."[36] McKenna seemed to be emboldened by Hipolite's concession that the eggs were adulterated. But the sweep of his language hid a serious question about the power of Congress to regulate goods that had come to rest inside a state. Thus, as McKenna wrote for the unanimous Court, "We are dealing, it must be remembered, with illicit articles." As a result, he could add, "There is here no conflict of national and state jurisdictions over property legally articles of trade. The question here is whether articles which are outlaws of commerce may be seized wherever found, and it certainly will not be contended that they are outside of the jurisdiction of the National Government when they are within the borders of a State."[37]

The final case on the first day of argument to the White Court implicated, without directly involving, both the Food and Drug Act of 1906 and the earlier Sherman Antitrust Act, two of the most significant attempts by reformers to enlist the federal government in regulation of the national economy. This final case, *Dr. Miles Medical Co. v. John D. Park & Sons Co.*,[38] originated in a suit filed by Miles seeking an injunction to prevent Park from encouraging Miles's wholesalers to sell below a price fixed by Miles. Miles had introduced the "Miles Plan" in 1903 in an attempt to protect its customers from competition. Under the plan, Miles contracted with druggists who would agree not to resell at a price other than that established by Miles. From the druggists' point of view, the plan offered maximum profits free from competition; from Miles's point of view, the plan gave greater control over its product and minimized the chance that a retailer would dilute the product, thereby harming public confidence. Miles spent more than one hundred thousand dollars putting the plan into operation, signing contracts with four hundred wholesalers and some twenty-five thousand retail druggists.[39]

The John D. Park & Sons Company, a Kentucky wholesaler, refused to participate in the Miles Plan, as it had refused to participate in similar plans for twenty years or more.[40] Instead, it acquired the drugs from a supplier will-

---

36. 220 U.S. at 54.
37. Ibid., 57–58.
38. 220 U.S. 373 (1911).
39. William C. Cray, *Miles 1884–1984: A Centennial History* (Englewood Cliffs, N.J.: Prentice Hall, 1984), 25.
40. See Herbert Hovenkamp, "The Sherman Act and the Classical Theory of Competition," *Iowa Law Review* 74 (July 1989): 1019–65.

ing to sell below the price fixed by Miles, and then resold. Miles sued, alleging that Park had interfered with its contractual relations. The lower federal courts ruled in favor of Park, denying the injunction. Although the vocabulary of the dispute suggested that it was a purely private matter, the argument took place in the long shadow of the Sherman Antitrust Act. Taken by itself, the Miles Plan resembled the vertical integration targeted by the Hepburn Act and by other aspects of antitrust policy—Miles, a producer of drugs, attempted to control the wholesale and retail market for the drugs. Park, represented by Alton B. Parker, the losing Democratic presidential nominee from 1904, pointed to that resemblance to support its contention that the plan was an illegal contract. As a result, Park argued, the plan could not be enforced by injunction.

The Supreme Court rejected Miles's arguments in an opinion by Justice Hughes. Responding to Miles's contention that there was no restraint of trade, Hughes wrote with much the same sweep that had characterized McKenna's opinion in *Hipolite:* "[T]he public interest is still the first consideration. To sustain the restraint, it must be found to be reasonable both with respect to the public and to the parties and that it is limited to what is fairly necessary, in the circumstances of the particular case, for the protection of the covenantee. Otherwise restraints of trade are void as against public policy."[41] Miles had attempted to evade that common-law principle by contending that its "medicines" were manufactured under secret processes that entitled it to patentlike protections for the products. The Court refused to allow the evasion, observing that Miles had done nothing to comply with the patent law. And, in what would become a long-running dispute among the justices, the Court ruled that the secrecy of the manufacturing process did not entitle the owner to control the entire chain of commerce involving the product.[42]

Writing alone, Justice Holmes entered an energetic dissent in keeping with his dislike of the antitrust law.[43] He concluded that Park had doubly interfered with Miles's contracts. First, it had interfered with the contracts with wholesalers by inducing one to sell at a lower price; second, it had interfered with the relationships with retailers. Holmes characterized the first relationship as one of agency, which allowed Miles, as principal, to control the actions of its agent, including the price at which it sold. The second relationship, sales at retail, differed only in form; it could just as easily have been set up as one of agency as well. Thus, Holmes concluded, Miles should have

---

41. 220 U.S. at 406.
42. The Court disdainfully rejected another claim based on the secrecy of the formula in *Jacobs v. Beecham,* 221 U.S. 263 (1911).
43. See, for example, Spencer W. Waller, "The Antitrust Philosophy of Oliver Wendell Holmes," *Southern Illinois University Law Journal* 18 (1994): 283–327; Danelski and Tulchin, eds., *Autobiographical Notes of Charles Evans Hughes,* 174.

the right to set those prices as well. Never a fan of antitrust laws, Holmes accused the majority of injecting its own antitrust policy into a new area, observing that "[o]n such matters we are in perilous country." His comments are worth reproducing at length, for they reveal much about his philosophy of competition, which he so often repeated during his career on the Court:

> I think that we greatly exaggerate the value and importance to the public of competition in the production or distribution of an article (here it is only distribution), as fixing a fair price. What really fixes that is the competition of conflicting desires. We, none of us, can have as much as we want of all the things that we want. Therefore, we have to choose. As soon as the price of something that we want goes above the point at which we are willing to give up other things to have that, we cease to buy it and buy something else. Of course, I am speaking of things that we can get along without. There may be necessaries that sooner or later must be dealt with like short rations in a shipwreck, but they are not Dr. Miles's medicines. With regard to things like the latter it seems to me that the point of most profitable returns marks the equilibrium of social desires and determines the fair price in the only sense in which I can find meaning in those words. The Dr. Miles Medical Company knows better than we do what will enable it to do the best business. We must assume its retail price to be reasonable, for it is so alleged and the case is here on demurrer; so I see nothing to warrant my assuming that the public will not be served best by the company being allowed to carry out its plan. I cannot believe that in the long run the public will profit by this court permitting knaves to cut reasonable prices for some ulterior purpose of their own and thus to impair, if not to destroy, the production and sale of articles which it is assumed to be desirable that the public should be able to get.[44]

Holmes sent a copy of his dissent to Sir Frederick Pollock, who responded: "It seems to me that the majority of your Honourable Court are being led into an archaic reaction by their anti-monopolistic zeal: and I cannot think that any sound doctrine of public policy requires you to favour the cheapening of Dr. Miles's medicines to the citizens of the United States."[45]

Of the other four cases argued during White's first full week as chief justice, only one produced an opinion of any significance—*Louisville & Nashville Railroad Co. v. Mottley*.[46] In 1871, Erasmus and Annie Mottley had accepted

---

44. 220 U.S. at 411–12.
45. Pollock to Holmes, May 3, 1911, Howe, *Holmes-Pollock Letters*, 1:178.
46. 219 U.S. 467 (1911). The other three cases involved minor questions about the interpretation of statutes.

passes allowing them lifetime free travel on the railroad in settlement of a suit for injuries suffered in a train collision. The railroad honored the passes for thirty-five years, until the passage of the Hepburn Act, which required railroads to post their tariffs and prohibited them from receiving "a greater or less or different compensation" from that posted. Given the statute's language, the Court easily concluded that the Mottleys had received a "different" rate. To make matters worse, their rate was not posted and available to all. On the matter of interpreting the statute, Harlan's opinion for the unanimous Court suggested greater willingness to look beyond the words of the statute than McKenna had shown in *Hipolite*. "Our duty is to ascertain the intention of Congress in passing the statute," Harlan explained. Then he continued, "That intention is to be gathered from the words of the act, interpreted according to their ordinary acceptation, and, when it becomes necessary to do so, in the light of the circumstances as they existed when the statute was passed." Even though he acknowledged that a decision in favor of the railroad would disadvantage the Mottleys, Harlan pressed on, "The court cannot mold a statute simply to meet its views of justice in a particular case."[47]

With that one minor difference between Harlan's opinion and McKenna's, the Court continued with an expansive concept of the power of Congress under the commerce clause, even when the exercise of that power invalidated a contract that had been valid at the time of its making—indeed, had been valid for more than three decades. As Harlan noted, it was "inconceivable" that individuals could, by contract, restrict the power of Congress to regulate interstate commerce.[48] To conclude otherwise, Harlan declared, "the result would be that individuals and corporations could, by contracts between themselves, in anticipation of legislation, render of no avail the exercise by Congress, to the full extent authorized by the Constitution, of its power to regulate commerce. No power of Congress can be thus restricted. The mischiefs that would result from a different interpretation of the Constitution will be readily perceived."[49]

---

47. 219 U.S. at 474. In another decision announced the same day, the Court held that a railroad could not use passes for transportation to pay for advertisements. Again writing for a unanimous Court, Harlan wrote, "The facts of the present case show how easily, under any other rule, the act can be evaded and the object of Congress entirely defeated. The legislative department intended that all who obtained transportation on interstate lines should be treated alike in the matter of rates and that all who availed themselves of the services of the railway company (with certain specified exceptions) should be on a plane of equality. Those ends cannot be met otherwise than by requiring transportation to be paid for in money which has a certain value known to all and not in commodities or services or otherwise than in money." *Chicago, Indianapolis and Louisville Railway Co. v. United States,* 219 U.S. 486, 496–97 (1911).
48. 219 U.S. at 482.
49. Ibid., 485–86.

All of these cases, from *Hipolite* to *Mottley*, came before the "great" cases of White's first fortnight of oral argument: *Standard Oil* and *American Tobacco*. Each of the two cases had been argued before—*Standard Oil* for three days in March 1910; *American Tobacco* for an equal time in January of the same year. Because not all nine justices could participate at those times, the Court ordered that each case be reargued. Now, with a full Court, the second *Standard Oil* argument took five days; the second *American Tobacco*, four days. Once again the cases recalled an earlier time, during the heights of Roosevelt's second administration when the initial suits had been centerpieces of his campaign against the trusts. For Chief Justice White, the cases also recalled his own unsuccessful effort more than a decade earlier to persuade the Court to adopt a "rule of reason" to determine which actions violated the antitrust law.[50] Then, he had been eighth in seniority on the Court, junior to all members except Justice Rufus Peckham, who had written both majority opinions. By 1911, White's position was stronger, his place as chief justice reinforced by being second in longevity only to Harlan.

The action against John D. Rockefeller, the Standard Oil Company, and more than seventy other corporations and individuals had begun in 1906. The United States alleged that Standard Oil had obtained control over 75 percent of the refining and marketing of petroleum in the United States. The complaint pointed to actions beginning in 1870 and continuing to 1906, all said to involve a conspiracy to restrain trade in petroleum and petroleum products. The special trial court ruled in favor of the United States on all but a few, minor points.

Twenty months after filing the suit against Standard Oil, the government filed another suit against James B. Duke's American Tobacco Company. Once again the suit involved more than seventy corporations and individuals, all of whom were said to have conspired together toward the control of more than 75 percent of the American market for cigarettes and other tobacco products.

These, then, were two of the "great" cases that Holmes so abhorred. Given the importance of the cases, it is not surprising that it took the Court some four months to produce its opinions, with *Standard Oil* being announced on May 15 and *American Tobacco* coming two weeks later. The two opinions fell amidst a group of almost fifty decisions handed down during that final fortnight of the term. None, however, attracted as much attention as the two antitrust cases. In each of those cases the Court sided with the

---

50. White had first articulated the rule of reason in two dissenting opinions: *United States v. Trans-Missouri Freight Association*, 166 U.S. 290 (1897); *United States v. Joint Traffic Association*, 171 U.S. 505 (1898). See Robert B. Dishman, "Mr. Justice White and the Rule of Reason," *Review of Politics* 13 (1951): 229–43.

government on the question of breaking up the monopoly; but the Court would not accept the government's reading of the Sherman Antitrust Act as barring *every* act that was in restraint of trade or an attempt to monopolize. Instead, the Court followed White's lead and adopted a rule that only "unreasonable" restraints were illegal.

The statutory language declared: "*Every* contract, combination in the form of trust or otherwise, or conspiracy, in restraint of trade or commerce, among the several States, or with foreign nations, is hereby declared to be illegal"; and "*Every* person who shall monopolize, or attempt to monopolize, or combine or conspire with any other person or persons, to monopolize any part of the trade or commerce among the several States, or with foreign nations, shall be deemed guilty of a misdemeanor."[51] In the face of that language, White's opinion is one of the few from this Court evincing more than a hint of modernity. The statute's language virtually thundered the absolute certainty of the nineteenth century; White's response was full of the soft contextualism that would come to epitomize the twentieth century. Eschewing an analysis of the text of the statute—possibly because the text had been so thoroughly parsed in prior decisions—he looked first at the legislative history. He conceded that "debates may not be used as a means for interpreting a statute"; but he quickly added that the "rule in the nature of things is not violated by resorting to debates as a means of ascertaining the environment at the time of the enactment of a particular law, that is, the history of the period when it was adopted."[52] In the history, White found little or no opposition to individual conduct, even when it tended to restrict trade. Instead, he located the origins of opposition to trusts in the animosity toward the royal prerogative in England. That opposition, he related, translated into animosity toward governmental favoritism in the United States. From that conclusion he drew the relativistic conclusion that there was a shifting opinion about what constituted an illegal act, "depending as it did upon the economic conceptions which obtained at the time when the legislation was adopted or judicial decision was rendered."[53] In light of that history, White could find no support for reading the act to prohibit "any act done by any of the enumerated methods anywhere in the whole field of human activity . . . if in restraint of trade."[54] He concluded that "it inevitably follows that the provision necessarily called for the exercise of judgement which required that some standard should be resorted to for the purpose of determining whether the prohibitions contained in the statute had or had

---

51. Act of July 2, 1890, ch. 647, 26 Stat. 209 (emphasis added). White quotes the sections in his opinion (221 U.S. at 49–50).
52. 221 U.S. at 50.
53. Ibid., 58.
54. Ibid., 60.

not in any given case been violated."⁵⁵ Since the legality of an act depended upon the circumstances and not upon the words of a statute, White pointed to "reason" as the only tool for evaluating an act in its context.

To reject reason, White suggested, would mean that every contract fell within the act's prohibitions. He spurned that interpretation as contrary to the basic principle of freedom of individuals to contract.⁵⁶ To support his conclusion, however, White had to distinguish the two precedents in which his dissents had first suggested the rule of reason, *United States v. Trans-Missouri Freight Association*⁵⁷ and *United States v. Joint Traffic Association*.⁵⁸ He acknowledged that certain language in those opinions could be read to support a rule that *all* restraints of trade were illegal. But, resorting to one of his favorite tactics for interpretation of both precedent and statutes, White announced that that reading was possible only if the language was read out of "context." When read in context, according to White, the language supported his "rule of reason."⁵⁹ To reach that conclusion, however, the chief justice had to engage in a bit of linguistic sleight of hand. He noted "that reason was resorted to for the purpose of deciding" the earlier cases; and from that he concluded that the *process* of reasoning supported a *substantive* rule of reason. He seemed not to consider that the process might properly have led to the conclusion that the statute provided an absolute bar on restraints of trade; instead, he concluded that the statute required an evaluation of each challenged act.

Justice Holmes considered White's rule to be his "greatest dialectical coup." As one of Brandeis's law clerks recalled, Holmes said of the opinion, "'The moment I saw that in the circulated draft, I knew he had us. How could you be against that without being for a rule of unreason? Of course,' [Holmes] added with a twinkle, 'the thought did occur to me that the rule might not prove to be self-elucidating.'"⁶⁰

Justice Harlan was livid, pounding the bench and shaking his fist at his colleagues as he announced his dissent. He agreed with the Court's conclusion that there had been a violation of the Sherman Act; but he rejected everything else in White's opinion. Justice Holmes later circumspectly referred to Harlan's "outbreak."⁶¹ Of the man who had been like a father to

---

55. Ibid.
56. Ibid., 63.
57. 166 U.S. 290 (1897).
58. 171 U.S. 505 (1898).
59. For other examples of this tactic, see *Weyerhaeuser v. Hoyt*, 219 U.S. 380, 394 (1911). The case involved interpretation of an 1864 grant of land to a railroad, as it affected the competing claims of a homesteader and a railroad. Justice Harlan also dissented in that case, siding with the homesteader. For another early example, see also *Southern Pacific Co. v. Interstate Commerce Commission*, 219 U.S. 433, 449 (1911) (context is opinion of ICC).
60. Acheson, *Morning and Noon*, 62.
61. Holmes to Pollock, March 21, 1912, Howe, *Holmes-Pollock Letters*, 1:190.

him, Justice Hughes recalled that Harlan had been "disturbed by the serenity of the Court [in the spring of 1911] and complained . . . that there were too few dissents."[62] As though he wanted to end the serenity and bring the term to a tumultuous end, Harlan delivered an oral dissent in the *Standard Oil* case with "a passionate outburst seldom if ever equaled in the annals of the Court."[63] As Hughes observed, Harlan "went far beyond his written opinion, launching out into a bitter invective, which I thought most unseemly. It was not a swan song but the roar of an angry lion."[64] The great advocate John W. Davis later remarked that "[t]hose who were present in the courtroom when these memorable decisions were handed down will not soon forget the almost savage vehemence with which Justice Harlan announced his disagreement."[65]

As had Holmes, Harlan recognized that the rule of reason would require much greater involvement by the courts in guiding antitrust policy. Harlan had joined the Court's opinions in both *Trans-Missouri Freight Association* and *Joint Traffic Association,* the two cases White distinguished in his majority opinion. As though he drew on the condemnations by Roosevelt and others in the political arena, Harlan now accused the Court of having "upset the long-settled interpretation of the act, [and of having] usurped the constitutional functions of the legislative branch of the Government."[66] Time and again, he returned to that theme, first accusing the Court of acting outside the Constitution: "It has, by mere interpretation, modified the act of Congress, and deprived it of practical value as a defensive measure against the evils to be remedied."[67] Then, as he neared the conclusion of his opinion, he reminded his audience of "the most important aspect of this case. That aspect concerns the usurpation by the judicial branch of the Government of the functions of the legislative department."[68] Reaching deep into his memory, Harlan linked the two great struggles of the nineteenth century:

> All who recall the condition of the country in 1890 will remember that there was everywhere, among the people generally, a deep feeling of unrest. The Nation had been rid of human slavery—fortunately, as all now feel—but the conviction was universal that the country was in real danger from another kind of slavery sought to be fastened on the American people, namely, the slavery that would result from aggregations of capital in the hands of a few individuals and corporations controlling, for

---

62. Danelski and Tulchin, eds., *Autobiographical Notes of Charles Evans Hughes,* 164, 170.
63. Ibid., 170.
64. Ibid.
65. John W. Davis, "Edward Douglass White," *American Bar Association Journal* 7 (1921): 381.
66. 221 U.S. at 83.
67. Ibid., 99.
68. Ibid., 103.

their own profit and advantage exclusively, the entire business of the country, including the production and sale of the necessaries of life.[69]

Harlan had a clear personal recollection of the first cases involving the Sherman Act, saying that "fifteen years ago, when the purpose of Congress in passing the Anti-trust Act was fresh in the minds of courts, lawyers, statesmen and the general public, this court expressly declined to indulge in judicial legislation, by inserting in the act the word 'unreasonable' or any other word of like import."[70] Only Harlan and White remained of the justices who had participated in those decisions; the other justices of that day had died or retired. As though he realized that he was soon to join them, Harlan drew on all his experience to pronounce this jeremiad:

> After many years of public service at the National Capital, and after a somewhat close observation of the conduct of public affairs, I am impelled to say that there is abroad, in our land, a most harmful tendency to bring about the amending of constitutions and legislative enactments by means alone of judicial construction. As a public policy has been declared by the legislative department in respect of interstate commerce, over which Congress has entire control, under the Constitution, all concerned must patiently submit to what has been lawfully done, until the People of the United States—the source of all National power—shall, in their own time, upon reflection and through the legislative department of the Government, require a change of that policy. . . . To overreach the action of Congress merely by judicial construction, that is, by indirection, is a blow at the integrity of our governmental system, and in the end will prove most dangerous to all. Mr. Justice Bradley wisely said, when on this Bench, that illegitimate and unconstitutional practices get their first footing by silent approaches and slight deviations from legal modes of legal procedure. . . . We shall do well to heed the warnings of that great jurist.[71]

Two weeks later, the Court returned to the Sherman Act with its decision in *United States v. American Tobacco Co.*[72] Organized in 1890, the same year that Congress passed the Sherman Act, the American Tobacco Company had grown to control some 95 percent of domestic cigarette produc-

---

69. Ibid., 83.
70. Ibid., 90.
71. Ibid., 105. The reference to Justice Bradley was to his opinion in *Boyd v. United States*, 116 U.S. 616, 635 (1886). Harlan's reference to Bradley's warning came two weeks after Justice McKenna used the same reference in his dissenting opinion in *Wilson v. United States*, 221 U.S. 361, 394 (1911).
72. 221 U.S. 106 (1911).

tion. The trial court agreed with the government that there had been a restraint of trade and enjoined the parties from voting the stock they owned in subsidiary corporations. White's opinion for the Court concluded that there had been a restraint of trade but reversed the trial court's judgment and remanded for hearings on how best to dissolve the combination. Before he reached that conclusion, however, the chief justice reviewed the holding in *Standard Oil*, asserting that there had been no departure from precedent, as though determined to taunt Harlan with White's victory: "In that case it was held, without departing from any previous decision of the court that as the statute had not defined the words restraint of trade, it became necessary to construe those words, a duty which could only be discharged by a resort to reason."[73] He went on to explain the basis for his "rule of reason":

> In other words, it was held, not that acts which the statute prohibited could be removed from the control of its prohibitions by a finding that they were reasonable, but that the duty to interpret which inevitably arose from the general character of the term restraint of trade should be given a meaning which would not destroy the individual right to contract and render difficult if not impossible any movement of trade in the channels of interstate commerce—the free movement of which it was the purpose of the statute to protect.[74]

Harlan responded with even sharper language, again calling attention to what he saw as a departure from precedent. To him, the assertion that the "rule of reason" did not represent a change in the law was as surprising "as would [be] a statement that black was white or white was black."[75]

The response to the opinions was immediate, with a cacophony that continues to the present day. The *New York Times* reported that "[r]epresentatives of 'big business' . . . did not hesitate to declare emphatically that the decision was all that the big corporations could ask."[76] In the words of a supporter of the decision, the editor of the *Wall Street Journal*, the Court had "read into the Sherman law an amendment that never could have passed the Congress of the United States."[77] Senator Robert La Follette's immediate reaction was that the Court had "amended the Sherman anti-trust law just as it was attempted over and over in the Senate . . . What they [the trusts] did

---

73. Ibid., 178–79.
74. Ibid., 179–80.
75. Ibid., 191.
76. *New York Times*, May 16, 1916.
77. Quoted in *Current Literature* 51 (July 1911): 1.

not get in the Senate they have now got from the court."[78] Later, speaking in New York City for the first time, La Follette repeated those thoughts, accusing the Court of adding to the Sherman Act "words that Congress had refused to write into it." As a result, he said, the Court had gone "outside of their functions."[79] Similarly critical was the early Marxist historian Gustavus Myers, who wrote that "[n]o power but the Supreme Court of the United States could or would have ignored the plain meaning of a statute of Congress, and construed that law to mean something far different than what it actually said."[80] William Jennings Bryan was even more scathing, saying that White had "waited fifteen years to throw his protecting arms around the trusts and tell them how to escape."[81] Criticism of the vagueness of the "rule" has continued to the present day, with one scholar writing tersely, "The notorious problem with the 'rule of reason' is its open-endedness, its incoherence, its unrealizability."[82]

By accepting the rule of reason, the Court effectively adopted Theodore Roosevelt's distinction between "good" trusts and "bad" ones while rejecting his call for greater intervention by the executive in enforcing the distinction.[83] That Solomon-like solution allowed the Court to temporize, retaining for itself the power, in Chief Justice John Marshall's famous phrase, "to say what the law is"[84] while allowing the executive to retain the initiative in deciding which organizations should be challenged. As Martin Sklar has argued, White's approach to antitrust law reflected his unwillingness to give up the notion of "freedom of contract"; instead, White opted for a system of regulating the national economy that combined market-based contract with external regulation by the government.[85] That freedom of contract was based in a nineteenth-century view

---

78. Ibid.
79. *New York Times,* January 23, 1912.
80. Gustavus Myers, *History of the Supreme Court of the United States* (Chicago: Charles H. Kerr & Co., 1925), 778–79. Myers's book was originally serialized in *The Call,* a socialist daily in New York City. *Current Literature* 51 (December 1911): 593.
81. *Current Literature* 51 (July 1911): 1.
82. Rudolph J. Peritz, "A Counter-History of Antitrust Law," *Duke Law Journal* 1990 (April): 265.
83. See Eleanor M. Fox and Lawrence A. Sullivan, "The Good and Bad Trust Dichotomy: A Short History of a Legal Idea," *Antitrust Bulletin* 35 (spring 1990): 57–82.
84. *Marbury v. Madison,* 1 Cranch (5 U.S.) 137, 177 (1803).
85. See Martin J. Sklar, "Sherman Antitrust Act Jurisprudence and Federal Policy-Making in the Formative Period, 1890–1914," *New York Law School Law Review* 35 (1990): 791–826. Professor Sklar first developed his argument in his doctoral dissertation, "The Corporate Reconstruction of American Society, 1896–1914: The Market and the Law" (Ph.D. diss., University of Rochester, 1982). He later published *The Corporate Reconstruction of Capitalism, 1890–1916: The Market, the Law, and Politics* (Cambridge: Cambridge University Press, 1988).

of contract being free from coercion, with both parties being of equal strength.[86]

The antitrust cases dominated the first months of White's tenure as chief justice—both in occupying almost half of the seventeen days in January 1911 allotted for oral argument and in attracting the attention of the public. Even so, they were but two of the even hundred opinions handed down in the winter and spring of 1911. At the end of that term, Holmes confided to Lewis Einstein, "As to the tobacco and oil cases; I was not satisfied but took the best I could get, and am very happy that they and some other troublesome matters are out of the way."[87]

Of all the cases decided during that first half-term, what is most striking is how they required the Court to look backward. In cases involving Indian tribes, counsel directed the Court's attention to treaties that were almost as old as Justice Harlan;[88] in cases involving railroads, the issues turned on construction of land grants from the Civil War[89] or on interpretation of statutes requiring that safety devices be installed on the railroad cars.[90] There were even two cases that required the Court to look to land claims dating from the eighteenth century.[91] To be sure, the Court occasionally focused on more recent political decisions. Even then, however, the Court found itself obligated to revive discussions from the last years of President Roosevelt's term and the first years of President Taft's—all at a time when the country was looking forward (at least politically) in eager anticipation of the 1912 presidential election. Thus, there was truth to the observation by the *Outlook*'s reporter Elbert Baldwin, that the Court revived memories by bringing the historical past as well as the personal past into the present. A personal remembrance had, after all, been at the heart of Harlan's dissents in the antitrust cases. White's majority opinions had hinted at rejecting that past in favor of a modern America; but White could not accept a complete break.

---

86. See Hovenkamp, "The Sherman Act and the Classical Theory of Competition." See also his "The Antitrust Movement and the Rise of Industrial Organization," *Texas Law Review* 68 (November 1989): 105–68.
87. Holmes to Einstein, June 24, 1911, Peabody, *Holmes-Einstein Letters,* 59–60.
88. In re Eastern Cherokees, 220 U.S. 83 (1911) (Treaty of Echola, May 23, 1836).
89. *Weyerhaeuser v. Hoyt,* 219 U.S. 380 (1911) (Act of July 2, 1864, ch. 217, 13 Stat. 365); *Northern Pacific Railway v. Trodick,* 221 U.S. 208 (1911) (same).
90. *Chicago, Burlington & Quincy Ry. v. United States,* 220 U.S. 559 (1911); *Delk v. St. Louis and San Francisco RR,* 220 U.S. 580 (1911); *Schlemmer v. Buffalo, Rochester & Pittsburg Ry.,* 220 U.S. 590 (1911). On the history of the Safety Appliance Acts, see Kurt Wetzel, "Railroad Management's Response to Operating Employee Accidents, 1890–1913," *Labor History* 21 (1980): 351–68; Steven W. Usselman, "Air Brakes for Freight Trains: Technological Innovation in the American Railroad Industry, 1869–1900," *Business History Review* 58 (1984): 30–50.
91. *Sena v. American Turquoise Co.,* 220 U.S. 497 (1911) (land grants from 1701 and 1728); *J. W. Perry Co. v. City of Norfolk,* 220 U.S. 472 (1911) (lease dated 1792).

He clung to the notion of freedom of contract, the central concept of nineteenth-century American law. But into that concept he injected a notion of context, a notion that gave to the courts a greater role. By so doing, the "rule of reason" in effect rejected the statist views of Theodore Roosevelt, who envisioned primacy for the administrative branch.[92] That White sided against Roosevelt personally seems unlikely. Instead, it seems more likely that he saw the rule of reason as restoring the antitrust law to the place originally intended by Congress, thereby protecting the notion of contract and allowing the voice of the people to speak, as he had done in the other celebrated decision of his early career, the *Insular Cases*. There, too, he had rejected an absolute rule (that the Constitution was effective wherever Congress acted) in favor of a more nuanced rule. White's opinion also preserved a role for the judiciary in the tiered structure of government. Rather than defer to the increasingly important executive,[93] the Court ensured that questions of antitrust policy would have to seek answers before the judiciary.

There were, however, cases that required more than a view of the past; they turned the Court's attention to glimpse the future. This requirement of dual vision came especially from cases involving administrative agencies. On the cusp of the administrative era, the Court was beginning to work out the relationship between courts and the newly empowered agencies. Here, too, White would come to play a significant role. One of his eulogists would later say that as Chief Justice Marshall had been to commerce, so the "definition of [the Interstate Commerce Commission's] powers and its workability as a practical agency [was] the work of Chief Justice White."[94] Holmes was even more direct in his praise of White's influence over administrative law, writing to Harold Laski that he thought "the credit is wholly his of making the relations between the Interstate Commerce Commission and our court clear and putting the whole important business on a sound and workable footing."[95] Even in these areas, however, the Court dealt with legislative compromises of the past. Thus, for example, *United States v. Grimaud* involved a challenge to regulations issued under the Forest Reserve Act of 1891.[96] Pierre Grimaud was indicted for grazing sheep without the permit required under regulations

---

92. Sklar, "Sherman Antitrust Act Jurisprudence and Federal Policy-Making in the Formative Period, 1890–1914."
93. See Peri Arnold, "The Intellectual Roots of the Progressive Era Presidency," *Miller Center Journal* 1 (spring 1994): 25–33.
94. Hiram M. Garwood, "Chief Justice Edward Douglass White," *Report of the Louisiana Bar Association for 1923* 24 (1923): 162.
95. November 26, 1920, Howe, *Holmes-Laski Letters*, 294.
96. 220 U.S. 506 (1911) (Act of March 3, 1891, ch. 561, 26 Stat. 1103). See also *Light v. United States*, 220 U.S. 523 (1911) (Holy Cross Forest Reserve, created by Act of March 3, 1891, ch. 561, 26 Stat. 1103).

issued by the secretary of agriculture. Grimaud challenged the authority of the secretary to issue regulations violation of which would be punishable as a crime. Crimes, he argued, could be defined only by direct legislative action.

Noting that the issue had produced disagreement among federal courts, Justice Lamar wrote for a unanimous Court upholding the regulations. Almost dismissing the regulations as matters of "administrative detail," he explained: "In the nature of things it was impracticable for Congress to provide general regulations for these various and varying details of management."[97] Without conceding that the secretary had unlimited power, the Court held that these regulations were acceptable under the authorization given by Congress.

One somewhat surprising example of deference to the new agencies came from the Court's looking to the agencies for help in interpreting statutes. The surprise is all the greater when one recalls that White's *Standard Oil* opinion had insisted that reason, or judgment, was required to apply the antitrust acts—traits usually associated with judicial rather than administrative offices. Responding to the apparent paradox, Justice McKenna wrote this about a statute he conceded was ambiguous: "[W]e must turn as a help to its meaning, indeed in such case, as determining its meaning, to the practice of the officers whose duty it was to construe and administer it. They may have been consulted as to its provisions, may have suggested them, indeed have written them. At any rate their practice, almost coincident with its enactment, and the rights which have been acquired under the practice, make it determinately persuasive."[98]

The strain between the old and the new appeared clearly in one other administrative law decision late in the term—*United States v. Johnson*.[99] *Johnson* was one of only two decisions this term with three dissenters; no other cases had more than two. *Johnson* alone had a written dissent. This case, like *Hipolite*, involved construction of a definition in the Food and Drug Act, section 8 of which defined "misbranded" as being any statement "which shall be false or misleading in any particular."[100] The United States had indicted O. A. Johnson for shipping drugs with labels containing a variety of claims,

---

97. 220 U.S. at 516.

98. *United States v. Hammers,* 221 U.S. 220, 228–29 (1911). The issue was whether a person who had made an entry onto public land could later assign the rights to the claim under the Desert Land Act of March 3, 1877, ch. 107, 19 Stat. 377, as amended by Act of March 3, 1891, ch. 561, §2, 26 Stat. 1095, 1096.

99. 221 U.S. 488 (1911). Only one other decision had a 6–3 vote, *West v. Kansas Natural Gas Co.,* 221 U.S. 229 (1911), but there was no written dissent.

100. The full statement is this: "That the term 'misbranded,' as used herein, shall apply to all drugs, or articles of food, or articles which enter into the composition of food, the package or label of which shall bear any statement, design, or device regarding such article, or the ingredients or substances contained therein which shall be false or misleading in any

including the statement that the drug cured cancer.[101] The trial court had dismissed the indictment, holding that the statute did not cover the labels used by Johnson. In agreeing with that conclusion, Justice Holmes wrote for the Court with his usual enigmatic grace: "What we have to decide is whether such misleading statements are aimed at and hit by the words of the act. It seems to us that the words used convey to an ear trained to the usages of English speech a different aim; and although the meaning of a sentence is to be felt rather than to be proved, generally and here the impression may be strengthened by argument, as we shall try to show."[102] The Court held that the prohibition did not reach all false statements, but only those "such as determine the identity of the article, possibly including its strength, quality and purity" as described in the preceding section of the act.[103] Drawing on the emerging acceptance of administrative agencies, Holmes pointed to the fact that the act directed questions about misbranding to the Department of Agriculture's Bureau of Chemistry, "which is most natural if the question concerns ingredients and kind, but hardly so as to medical effects."[104] In other words, false statements about a drug's curative abilities were not "misbranding," while false statements about chemical content would be.

Justice Hughes dissented for the first time in his judicial career. He expressed surprise at what he termed Holmes's "narrow construction" of the act.[105] Joined by Justices Harlan and Day, Hughes opened a crack onto the future, as he looked at "context" (legislative history) as well as administrative interpretation to support his conclusion. Oddly, he provided no citation for his references to changes in the original bill as it worked its way through Congress; presumably they resided in the memory of those in office.[106] He also noted, again without citation, that both the Department of Agriculture and the Department of Justice had used that interpretation in the earliest prosecutions.

One consequence of the Court's usual focus on the past was an attention to a rural, state-oriented America. The cases involving administrative agencies suggested the shape of the future of government—one in which

---

particular, and to any food or drug product which is falsely branded as to the State, Territory, or country in which it is manufactured or produced." 221 U.S. at 500–501.
101. Justice Hughes's dissent contains quotations from the labels, 221 U.S. at 499–500.
102. Ibid., 496.
103. Ibid., 497.
104. Ibid., 498. The next year, in what was known as the Sherley Amendment, Congress amended the statute to reject the outcome in *Johnson*. Act of August 23, 1912, ch. 352, 37 Stat. 416. The Court upheld the amendment in *Seven Cases of Eckman's Alternative v. United States*, 239 U.S. 510 (1916).
105. Danelski and Tulchin, eds., *Autobiographical Notes of Charles Evans Hughes*, 174.
106. See 221 U.S. at 503–4.

both legislative and judicial functions would be united in a single, administrative agency. But even these cases tended to involve a frontierlike America. One, for example, involved a claim to "desert" land near Los Angeles.[107] Occasionally, though, the Court caught a glimpse of the future, which was to be an urban, corporate America. One group of cases in particular examined the nature of corporate government. All involved criminal charges against corporations and consequent orders that officers or directors produce corporate books and records. The corporation, an artificial creature of law, was not alone in facing potential liability. The officers and directors, natural persons, faced the possibility of indictment for the same conduct, since they had controlled the acts of the corporation. Thus, the individuals of nineteenth-century, rural America found themselves entangled with the corporate forms of twentieth-century, urban America. The Court offered little solace.

One early case for the White Court was *Wilson v. United States*, which arose out of charges that Christopher C. Wilson had used the mails to further a conspiracy.[108] Wilson was president of the United Wireless Telegraph Company of Maine. When a grand jury asked to inspect corporate books in his possession, Wilson refused. The Court, speaking through Justice Hughes, rebuffed Wilson's claim of a privilege under the Fifth Amendment. That privilege, the Court held, applied only to private papers, not to papers that were public or to those that were required by law to be kept.[109] Wilson the natural person could have protected the papers, but Wilson entangled in the artificial corporation could find no protection. Justice McKenna alone dissented, revealing apprehension over the ease with which the Court had slipped into the twentieth century. He warned of the dangers of yielding to the "condition of modern civilization," as had been argued in a companion case that day.[110] One of those dangers was that words might lose their power to control action. As he asked rhetorically, "Is it possible that a written constitution is more flexible in its adaptations than an unwritten one?"[111] And he offered this warning: "The process of deterioration is simple. It may even be conceived to be

---

107. *United States v. Hammers*, 221 U.S. 220 (1911).
108. 221 U.S. 361 (1911).
109. Ibid., 380. At the end of the term, the Court applied *Wilson* to uphold a requirement by the ICC that railroads produce reports showing when employees had been required to work hours in excess of those permitted by statute. *Baltimore & Ohio Railroad v. Interstate Commerce Commission*, 221 U.S. 612 (1911). For discussion of the early rules as applied to the ICC, see R. Erik Lillquist, "Constitutional Rights at the Junction: The Emergence of the Privilege against Self-Incrimination and the Interstate Commerce Act," *Virginia Law Review* 81 (October 1995): 1989–2042.
110. 221 U.S. at 393. The companion case was *Dreier v. United States*, 221 U.S. 394 (1911) (the secretary of a corporation must produce books when ordered).
111. 221 U.S. at 393.

advancement, and that intelligent self-government can be trusted to adapt itself to occasion, not needing the fetters of a predetermined rule. It may come to be considered that a constitution is the cradle of infancy, that a nation grown up may boldly advance in confident security against the abuses of power and that passions will not sway more than reason."[112]

McKenna's apprehension of the future appeared in an opinion he wrote for the Court in the same term, *Fifth Avenue Coach Co. v. City of New York*.[113] This case involved a challenge to a ban on advertising on the exterior of "trucks, vans or wagons."[114] Before 1905 the coach company had placed advertisements only on the interior of its carriages. Beginning in that year, however, and continuing through 1907, the company replaced its "horse stages" with "automobile stages." The larger exterior surface on the new vehicles made advertising signs practicable. Accordingly, the company argued that it had a property right to earn income from selling space on the outside of its carriages. The state courts disagreed; and the Supreme Court affirmed the conclusion. For McKenna, the view of the urban environment was decidedly unattractive: "If [the coach company] be right, however the advertisements may be displayed is immaterial. There can be no limitation of rights by degrees of the grotesque. If such rights exist in plaintiff they exist in all wagon owners, and there might be such a fantastic panorama on the streets of New York that objection to it could not be said to have prompting only in an exaggerated aesthetic sense. That rights may not be pushed to such extremes does not help plaintiff. Its rights are not greater because others may not exercise theirs."[115] One would not have expected an issue such as advertising on the side of carriages to produce such an apocalyptic vision of the future. That it did is explicable in part by the growing tensions between urban and rural America.

By contrast, the decision in *Coyle v. Smith*[116] would not seem to require a pessimism about the future of the nation—after all, it involved what appeared to be no more than an amusing anecdote in the history of a new, predominantly rural, state. The 1906 enabling act that admitted Oklahoma to statehood provided that the capital would be in Guthrie, which had been the territorial capital.[117] The act further provided that the capital could not be

---

112. Ibid., 394.
113. 221 U.S. 467 (1911).
114. Ibid., 477. Various reports of the case are contained in the *New York Times*, September 5, 1907; June 6, 1908; January 6, 1909; May 30, 1911.
115. 221 U.S. at 483.
116. 221 U.S. 559 (1911).
117. That provision was the work of Henry Asp, a prominent Republican and chief attorney for the Santa Fe Railroad in Oklahoma. H. Wayne Morgan and Anne H. Morgan, *Oklahoma: A Bicentennial History* (New York: W. W. Norton & Co., 1977), 81.

changed before 1913, when the voters of the state would choose the location of the capital.[118] Impatient voters, led by Democrats who charged that Guthrie represented railroad interests, decided in June 1910 to test support for moving the capital. Almost 60 percent of the 161,000 votes cast favored moving the capital; of the 136,000 votes for another location, almost 70 percent favored Oklahoma City.[119] Five months later, the state legislature passed a law moving the capital to Oklahoma City. By a vote of 7–2, the Court upheld the state's action.[120] The Court, through Justice Lurton, reasoned that states were admitted to the union on the condition of equality with other states; Congress could not, therefore, impose conditions on the admission that it could not impose on the existing states.[121] That reasoning seems straightforward enough; but Lurton, the ex-Confederate, added "that the constitutional equality of the States is essential to the harmonious operation of the scheme upon which the Republic was organized. When that equality disappears we may remain a free people, but the Union will not be the Union of the Constitution."[122] That curious mix of states-rights equality with national sovereignty revealed how heavily memories of the Civil War still weighed in the minds of at least some of the justices. That *Coyle* was first argued on the fiftieth anniversary of President Lincoln's declaration that an insurrection existed only served to sharpen the recollection. With those memories, the nation continued to dangle perilously between old and new, between order and chaos.

The final "big" decision of the term captured yet one more force in the tensions of the Progressive Era—that between employer and employee. Fittingly, *Gompers v. Bucks Stove & Range Co.* arrayed two of the major antagonists against each other—the American Federation of Labor and the National Association of Manufacturers.[123] The case began when leaders of the American Federation of Labor and the publishers of its newspaper, the *American Federationist,* encouraged a boycott by putting the Bucks Stove Company on its "We Don't Patronize" list.[124] In response, the company (whose

---

118. Act of June 16, 1906, ch. 3335, 34 Stat. 267.
119. Edward E. Dale and Morris L. Wardell, *History of Oklahoma* (Englewood Cliffs, N.J.: Prentice-Hall, 1948), 324.
120. McKenna and Holmes dissented without an opinion.
121. For a discussion of this "equal footing" doctrine, see Luis R. Dávila-Colón, "Equal Citizenship, Self-Determination, and the U.S. Statehood Process: A Constitutional and Historical Analysis," *Case Western Reserve Journal of International Law* 13 (spring 1981): 337–40.
122. 221 U.S. at 580.
123. 221 U.S. 418 (1911). The Court's reporter of decisions omitted the apostrophe in "Buck's" throughout the United States Reports, though the lower courts used the apostrophe. See 33 App. D.C. 83, 516 (1909).
124. The history of the dispute is taken from the Court's opinion and from these sources: Samuel Gompers, *Seventy Years of Life and Labor: An Autobiography* (New York: E. P. Dutton & Co., 1925), 2:205–20; Harry W. Laidler, *Boycotts and the Labor Struggle: Economic and Legal*

president, James Van Cleve, was also the president of the National Association of Manufacturers) successfully sought an injunction prohibiting the publication of the statement in the AFL newspaper or anywhere else. The injunction came from a trial court in the District of Columbia, which reasoned that the AFL's actions amounted to coercion that others not deal with the company.[125] At Samuel Gompers's suggestion, the AFL decided to use the occasion as a test case to challenge what it saw as a growing abuse of injunctions by courts.[126] The officers of the AFL discussed the boycott at their national convention, which passed a resolution in favor of the boycott; and they distributed copies of the *American Federationist* containing a report of the convention's proceedings, including the resolution. For those actions, all three officers of the AFL were convicted of contempt of court and sentenced to prison. The Supreme Court granted certiorari to hear the case.

The Supreme Court unanimously reversed, remanding the case to the trial court for further proceedings. Writing for the Court, Justice Lamar began by disavowing any interest in discussing a violation of the First Amendment's protection of freedom of speech or of the press. All that was at issue, according to the Court, was the narrow question concerning the validity of an injunction against continuing a boycott.[127] The Court reasoned that the trial court had power to restrain the boycott, just as it would have the power to restrain any other injury to property. Thus, Bucks Stove became the individual harmed by the action of large, organized power:

> But the very fact that it is lawful to form these bodies, with multitudes of members, means that they have thereby acquired a vast power, in the presence of which the individual may be helpless. This power, when unlawfully used against one, cannot be met, except by his purchasing peace at the cost of submitting to terms which involve the sacrifice of rights protected by the Constitution; or by standing on such rights and appealing to the preventive powers of a court of equity. When such appeal is made it is the duty of government to protect the one against the many as well as the many against the one.
>
> In the case of an unlawful conspiracy, the agreement to act in concert when the signal is published, gives the words "Unfair," "We don't

---

Aspects (New York: John Lane Co., 1913), 134–50; Harold C. Livesay, *Samuel Gompers and Organized Labor in America* (Boston: Little, Brown, 1978) 144–47, 162; Gary Minda, "The Law and Metaphor of Boycott," *Buffalo Law Review* 41 (1993): 807–931; James G. Pope, "The Three-Systems Ladder of First Amendment Values: Two Rungs and a Black Hole," *Hastings Constitutional Law Quarterly* 11 (1984) 189–246.
125. 33 App. D.C. 83, 516 (1909).
126. Gompers, *Autobiography*, 2:206.
127. 221 U.S. at 436–37.

patronize," or similar expressions, a force not inhering in the words themselves, and therefore exceeding any possible right of speech which a single individual might have. Under such circumstances they become what have been called "verbal acts," and as much subject to injunction as the use of any other force whereby property is unlawfully damaged. When the facts in such case warrant it, a court having jurisdiction of the parties and subject-matter has power to grant an injunction.[128]

Even though the trial court had the power to enjoin the conduct, the Court held that the trial court had misused its power. The initial case was a civil dispute, between Bucks Stove and the AFL; thus, any contempt proceedings arising from that proceeding had also to be civil—especially since there never was an instance in which the government participated, as it would have had the case been a criminal one. The result was an inconsistency for which the trial court had to be reversed. Lamar reasoned that the sanction imposed here, imprisonment, was appropriate only in a criminal case; in a civil case, damages would be appropriately awarded to Bucks Stove; but here nothing had been awarded to Bucks Stove. Since the civil case had been settled, the civil side of the suit had dropped out; therefore, the case was remanded to the trial court with freedom to pursue the case as a matter of criminal contempt. In sum, the Court managed to follow a tortuous path to a conclusion that both reaffirmed the trial court's power and released the union officials from prison.

At the end of the term, Holmes reflected that it was "the most bothering term I have known or expect to know."[129] Holmes was almost certainly referring to the number of "big" cases involved, and possibly to the early friction between Harlan and White. Otherwise, there was little evidence of anything other than a smooth transition for White to the center seat. Likewise, the two new justices, Lamar and Van Devanter, had joined Taft's other appointees, Lurton and Hughes, at the far ends of the bench. No doubt, White's familiarity with the senior justices had eased his (and their) transition. For the newer justices, White's gracious welcome must also have contributed to the ease of transition. As Justice Lamar's wife recalled, "Nothing could have been kinder than the elder-brotherly attitude of the Chief Justice. He was interested in every detail that concerned the welfare or the happiness of each member of the Court. Was it the renting of a house, the engaging of a servant, or one of the more puzzling questions concerning the ethics of the position, he was both competent and willing to advise."[130]

---

128. Ibid., 439.
129. Holmes to Einstein, June 24, 1911, Peabody, *Holmes-Einstein Letters,* 60.
130. Lamar, *The Life of Joseph Rucker Lamar,* 179.

Hughes also remembered White's personal kindnesses, calling him a "very dear man—one of the dearest I have ever known." Toward the justices, White was "very warm-hearted and most solicitous that [they] should be as happy as possible."[131]

---

131. Lash, ed., *Diaries of Felix Frankfurter,* 313.

II

THE 1911–1912 TERM

The night before the Court reassembled for the 1911 term, Justice Harlan joined the Lamars for dinner at their home on New Hampshire Avenue, northeast of DuPont Circle. When Harlan began to leave, apparently to walk the seven blocks to his home, Mrs. Lamar prevailed on him to let her drive him in her electric car. She later recalled that he so filled the journey with questions about the car that both were surprised when they found themselves in front of his home.[1] Harlan attended the ceremonial opening of Court on Monday, October 9, as well as the session the next day. By late afternoon of this second day, however, he was ill and had to be taken home in a taxicab.[2] At the end of that week, Harlan died at his home. Four months would elapse before President Taft nominated Mahlon Pitney to replace Harlan. Also absent from the bench at the beginning of the term was Justice Day, who was at his home in Canton, Ohio, with his critically ill wife. He remained there until shortly after her death from cancer of the spine.[3] Justice Day returned to the bench on January 18, 1912.[4] Two more months passed before Pitney was confirmed, taking his seat on March 18. Thus, the Court was without a full bench for more than half of its term.

On February 19, President Taft announced the nomination of Mahlon Pitney to replace Justice Harlan. Taft had first offered the position to Secretary of State Philander Knox, who declined. Opposition from labor and from the fledgling NAACP caused Taft to reject his next two choices: Judge William Hook, of Kansas, and Secretary of Commerce and Labor Charles Nagel.[5] Taft then looked to New Jersey, according to some accounts in the

---

1. Lamar, *The Life of Joseph Rucker Lamar,* 181–82.
2. Beth, *John Marshall Harlan,* 189–90; Yarbrough, *Judicial Enigma,* 222.
3. McLean, *William Rufus Day,* 64; *New York Times,* January 6, 1912; January 9, 1912.
4. *New York Times,* January 19, 1912.
5. Robert D. Stenzel, "An Approach to Individuality, Liberty, and Equality: The Jurisprudence of Mr. Justice Pitney" (Ph.D. diss., New School for Social Research, 1975), 61. McHargue, "Appointments to the Supreme Court of the United States," 555.

hope of garnering support in the 1912 election.⁶ Those accounts are difficult to credit in light of Taft's vacillation between cabinet members and a federal judge from west of the Mississippi River. Admittedly, the nomination of Pitney came as Roosevelt moved ever closer to declaring openly that he was a candidate for the presidency. Only three days after Taft announced the nomination of Pitney, Roosevelt declared that his "hat was in the ring." The declaration came immediately before a speech in Columbus, Ohio, in which Roosevelt alienated many conservatives by repeating his support for the recall of judicial decisions.⁷ Much of the adverse reaction was to a proposal Roosevelt had *not* made—that *judges* be recalled. The actual proposal was that the people should have the power to recall judicial *decisions* in a limited class of state cases—those involving constitutional issues.⁸ Roosevelt would later use the term "judicial referendum" as more accurately describing his proposal.⁹ By using examples taken from decisions of the United States Supreme Court, however, Roosevelt almost invited the harshest of criticisms. Earlier in 1912, Senator Robert La Follette, also a candidate for the Republican presidential nomination, had drawn "deafening and long continued" applause for his announcement that he favored the recall of Supreme Court justices.[10] Roosevelt's challenge had grown steadily during the previous two years, beginning in the spring of 1910, shortly after the Senate confirmed Taft's nomination of Hughes. Thus, each of Taft's subsequent appointments, including that of White as chief justice, fell under Roosevelt's lengthening shadow. Moreover, each of the later appointments also came after the crushing defeat of Taft's conservative wing of the Republican Party in the 1910 elections. In the two years before the next elec-

---

6. Stenzel suggests this reasoning; but he also notes that Taft and Pitney exchanged letters in which Taft rejected the suggestion. Stenzel, "An Approach to Individuality, Liberty, and Equality," 60, 435. See also Alan R. Breed, "Mahlon Pitney: His Life and Career, Political and Judicial" (B.A. thesis, Princeton University, 1932), 39–40 (based in part on personal interviews with Justice Pitney's widow, brother, son, and other relatives, as well as Chief Justice Hughes and Justices Van Devanter and McReynolds).

7. The full text of the speech is printed in *The Works of Theodore Roosevelt*, vol. 17, *Social Justice and Popular Rule* (New York: Charles Scribner's Sons, 1926), 119–48. For discussion of the speech, and the reaction to it, see Mowry, *Theodore Roosevelt and the Progressive Movement*, 212–19. For a description of the debate about recall, especially among the legal community of the time, see Stephen Stagner, "The Recall of Judicial Decisions and the Due Process Debate," *American Journal of Legal History* 24 (1980): 257–72. Roosevelt responded to his critics in a speech on April 10, 1912, in Philadelphia, reprinted in *Works*, 190–203.

8. Pringle, *William Howard Taft*, 2:768–70; Sullivan, *Our Times*, vol. 4, *The War Begins, 1900–1914*, 536–39.

9. William G. Ross, *A Muted Fury: Populists, Progressives, and Labor Unions Confront the Courts, 1890–1937* (Princeton: Princeton University Press, 1994), 143 n. 53. Ross's book, especially pages 86–154, contains a detailed account of the efforts to make the courts more accountable to the public.

10. *New York Times,* January 23, 1912.

tion, Taft became increasingly disconsolate over the split within the Republican Party.[11] His attempts to build bridges proved futile, in politics generally as well as through his appointments to the Court. Indeed, at least one observer attributed Taft's loss in 1912 in part to his appointment of a Democrat, White, to the position of chief justice.[12]

Pitney was born on a farm near Morristown, New Jersey, on February 5, 1858. After attending local, private schools, he entered Princeton in the fall of 1875, as did Woodrow Wilson. The two were members of the same dining club throughout their four years at Princeton, though there is no evidence to suggest that they were close friends. Pitney did, however, attend a class reunion hosted by Wilson at the White House in November 1915.[13] Pitney returned home after graduation to work in his father's law office. Once admitted to the bar in 1882, the younger Pitney moved to Dover, New Jersey, to practice on his own. He rejoined his father seven years later, when the elder Pitney was appointed vice chancellor for New Jersey. The younger Pitney's success in practice led to his election to the United States House of Representatives in 1894 as a Republican. He was reelected in 1896, but he resigned shortly before his term ended to take the seat he had won in the New Jersey Senate in 1898. He had hoped to run for governor; but he could not win the support of the state Republican Party boss, William J. Sewall, who urged him to run for the state senate instead. Once more, Pitney's hard work placed him in line for the governorship; but, again, the political leaders thwarted his ambition. Before the 1901 election, the sitting governor appointed Pitney to the state supreme court. He served there until early 1908, when he was appointed chancellor, the highest judicial office in the state.[14] While in that office, Pitney continued to attract the attention of political leaders; within the state, many considered him a candidate for the United States Senate and for the governor's office.[15] Taft had included Pitney's name among those being considered for appointment to the Supreme Court in 1910.[16] But Taft apparently did not focus on Pitney until 1912, when Pitney attended a Lincoln's Birthday luncheon given in honor of the president, who was thought to be leaning toward appointing someone from New

---

11. Mowry, *Theodore Roosevelt and the Progressive Movement*, 183.
12. Joseph Benson Foraker, *Notes of a Busy Life*, 2d ed. (Cincinnati: Stewart & Kidd Co., 1916), 2:404.
13. Michal R. Belknap, "Mr. Justice Pitney and Progressivism," *Seton Hall Law Review* 16 (1986): 386.
14. The details of Pitney's career are taken from Breed, "Mahlon Pitney." On the structure of New Jersey courts, see generally William M. Clevenger, *The Courts of New Jersey: Their Origin, Composition and Jurisdiction* (Plainfield: New Jersey Law Journal Publishing Co., 1903).
15. Belknap, "Mr. Justice Pitney and Progressivism," 399–400.
16. Ibid., 400.

Jersey to the Supreme Court. Many had anticipated that the president would select Francis J. Swayze, then an associate justice of the state supreme court. Indeed, Pitney is said to have favorably mentioned his friend, Swayze, to the president. But, according to one report, Pitney and Taft spent most of the luncheon in a congenial discussion of golf, which they had once played together. After lunch, while traveling to New York City, Taft announced to those around him that he thought he would appoint Pitney to the Court.[17] Once he returned to Washington, Taft took time to study Pitney's opinions before publicly announcing the appointment.[18] Appropriately, Pitney learned of the news while playing golf in Atlantic City.[19] The foursome paused for a moment, then resumed their game, with Pitney recalling, "I had just made a peach of a drive, one of the best in my golfing career." The next day, he returned home and sent Taft a note saying he would consider the appointment. Two days later, he said he would accept if confirmed.[20]

Alone among Taft's nominations, Pitney's met with considerable opposition, especially from labor groups.[21] Even though Pitney had the support of Woodrow Wilson, by now governor of New Jersey, and other progressives,[22] the opposition forced the first significant delay in confirming an appointment since the contentious nominations by President Cleveland almost twenty years before, when White himself had joined the Court.[23] Although the opposition failed, the contest over the nomination reflected the continuation of the 1910 campaign debate about the role of the federal courts. This time, however, the debate focused on the Supreme Court, even if for only one brief moment. Once Pitney took the oath of office, on Monday, March 18, 1912,[24] he was transported into the cloistered time warp of the Court. The Court announced four, relatively insignificant, decisions that day before adjourning for two weeks.

---

17. Breed, "Mahlon Pitney," 22–23.
18. For accounts of the nomination of Pitney, see Romine, "The 'Politics' of Supreme Court Nominations," 504–7; McHargue, "Appointments to the Supreme Court of the United States," 403–7. The only significant published works on Pitney are Belknap, "Mr. Justice Pitney and Progressivism," and David M. Levitan, "Mahlon Pitney — Labor Judge," *Virginia Law Review* 40 (1954): 733–70. In addition to Breed's paper, one other unpublished work contains useful information: Stenzel, "An Approach to Individuality, Liberty, and Equality."
19. Breed, "Mahlon Pitney," 159.
20. Ibid., 29–30.
21. See the *New York Times* between February 19, 1912, and March 14, 1912.
22. On Pitney's relation to the Progressives, see Belknap, "Mr. Justice Pitney and Progressivism," 381–423.
23. Cleveland succeeded with his appointment of White only after two failed nominations, and eight months. See Umbreit, *Our Eleven Chief Justices,* 382. Cleveland's second nominee was delayed for five months, after which the Senate confirmed Justice Rufus Peckham.
24. For an account of the ceremony, see *New Jersey Law Journal* 35 (1912): 98.

Pitney's taking the oath of office marked the end of Taft's renewing the Court. In a little more than two years Taft had used six nominations to place five new men on the Court, the sixth nomination going to White himself. Three were Republicans, like Taft; three were Democrats. Three appointments came from the South (White, Lurton, Lamar), two from the East (Hughes, Pitney), and one from the West (Van Devanter). Taft had indeed reduced the average age of the justices to just over sixty years. But he had hardly made distinguished appointments. Only Hughes would claim a place in the pantheon of "great" members of the Court, and the bulk of his reputation would be made only after he replaced Taft as chief justice in 1930. Other than Lurton, who was a close friend, there is no evidence of a dominant reason behind any of the appointments. Instead, each seems to have been made from among the many names suggested. The one element that appears to unite the six is Taft's conservative eye on the election of 1912, with the defeats of 1910 firmly in his mind. As a result, he looked to states and groups that might offer him support. Possibly most telling is a remark attributed to Taft in the years after he left the presidency—he observed that he had appointed men who were the best lawyers in their states.[25] By that statement, as well as by the rough geographical balance he maintained in his appointments, Taft disclosed that he continued to view the Court as representing a nation of states rather than a single nation. Moreover, he had established cordial relations with both Lamar and Pitney, and apparently with Hughes as well, before nominating them. That personal contact suggests the America of the past, one where friendships mattered above most other relationships. Therefore, it is no surprise that Taft's Court continued to find itself slightly behind the changing political environment of the nation.

Harlan's death removed from the Court a significant dissenting voice, though not a prolific voice—for his career he averaged fewer than twenty-two opinions for the Court each term.[26] For the 1911 term that number would have placed him near the bottom of a table showing the justices' output. During the term the Court produced written opinions in 240 cases, representing almost 190 oral arguments. As had been true in recent terms, the Court continued its inability to keep pace with its docket.[27] Of course, part of the inability was the result of the Court being shorthanded. Justice Day would write only twelve opinions during the term, and Pitney only four after

---

25. Pringle, *William Howard Taft*, 1:536.
26. Blaustein and Mersky, *The First One Hundred Justices*, 148. For a contemporaneous account of Harlan's dissents, see Thomas J. Knight, "The Dissenting Opinions of Justice Harlan," *American Law Review* 51 (1917): 481–506.
27. *Annual Report of the Attorney General of the United States for the Year 1912* (Washington, D.C.: GPO, 1912), 58; Epstein et al., *The Supreme Court Compendium*, 2d ed., 72.

he joined the Court in March. Chief Justice White wrote the largest number (forty-four), followed closely by Holmes (forty-three), a pattern which continued throughout most of White's tenure as chief justice. McKenna was not far behind (thirty-six), while the other, junior justices wrote thirty or fewer: Van Devanter (thirty), Lamar (twenty-eight), Lurton (twenty-two), and Hughes (twenty). White's leadership in writing opinions for the Court followed the precedent of his immediate predecessors as chief justice—Morrison R. Waite and Melville W. Fuller—each of whom, on average, wrote more opinions than any other justice did. Indeed, White seemed to change his practice once he became chief justice—he averaged slightly more than thirty opinions per term as chief justice, an increase from his average of twenty-three while a justice.[28] Moreover, White dramatically reduced his separate opinions (both concurring and dissenting). At least for himself, White succeeded in his goal of reducing what he referred to as "this dissenting business."[29] In fact, as chief justice, White was second only to Chief Justice Marshall in having the lowest percentage of dissents.[30] White's leadership in writing opinions reinforced his now dual seniority. With Harlan's death, White was senior in length of service as well as in title. White's number of opinions is all the more impressive in light of his labored style of writing. In a generous understatement, an author writing after White's death said that he "did not possess a masterly instinct for the use of the written word."[31] Holmes prided himself in working rapidly, explaining to one correspondent, "Of one thing I can be certain, that whether my work is good or bad at least it is rapid, which I regard as an important element in decisions."[32] Brandeis later complained about Holmes's compulsion to finish a decision the same day it was given to him, adding that the desire for speed had become a "vice."[33] White, by contrast, toiled over his opinions, often going

---

28. Blaustein and Mersky, *The First One Hundred Justices*, 148.
29. Klinkhamer, *Edward Douglas White*, 61.
30. Thomas G. Walker, Lee Epstein, William J. Dixon, "On the Mysterious Demise of Consensual Norms in the United States Supreme Court," *Journal of Politics* 50 (1988): 383. See also Donald Carl Leavitt, "Attitudes and Ideology on the White Supreme Court, 1910–1920" (Ph.D. diss., Michigan State University, 1970), 377.
31. Spring, "Two Chief Justices: Edward Douglass White and William Howard Taft," 165. Spring also reported that "[m]any lawyers speak somewhat unkindly of his decisions because in form they tend to be involved and opaque." See also Chief Justice White," *Nation* 112 (June 1921): 781. ("His propensity for unwarranted antitheses and for artificial verbal logic make many of his opinions models of what judicial opinions ought not to be.")
32. Holmes to Einstein, April 10, 1915, Peabody, *Holmes-Einstein Letters*, 112. Writing to Sir Frederick Pollock, Holmes described himself as being "like the devil in a gale of wind." Holmes to Pollock, December 18, 1910, Howe, *Holmes-Pollock Letters*, 1:172.
33. Urofsky, "The Brandeis-Frankfurter Conversations," 311 (conversation of November 30, 1922).

to his study after guests left his home and working into the early hours of the morning.[34] After his own retirement, Justice Clarke recalled that "all Washington knew that the late Chief Justice White turned night into day when he was working on important cases."[35]

For the Court as a whole, the first three terms of White's service as chief justice saw an energetic burst of output. The number of opinions for the Court rose by more than a third when comparing the 1911 term with that of 1910. For the October 1913 term the number of opinions was higher than at any time since 1890, and it was almost 60 percent higher than the 1908 term, the last term in which the Court under Chief Justice Fuller had a full complement of justices.[36] In the midst of its burst of activity, the White Court also reduced the percentage of cases with dissenting opinions—to as low as 2 percent, from between 5 and 7 percent in the previous three terms.[37] No doubt, White's leadership affected those statistics.[38] The demonstrated respect of his senior colleagues, combined with his cultivation of the newer justices, made the Court a much more cohesive place. In short, White exhibited the kind of "social" leadership required for a community of judges from the "old" America.[39] As predicted by the *Green Bag* when White was appointed, he never developed the skills of a "task" leader. Hughes would later recall White's ineffective direction of conferences.[40] Louis Brandeis concurred, telling Felix Frankfurter that with Taft as chief justice "the judges go home less tired emotionally & less weary physically."[41] Hughes attributed his own success as chief justice "to the lessons I learned in watching White during the years when I was an associate Justice and seeing how it ought not to be done."[42] He explained: "[I]f I had any virtues as Chief Justice they were

---

34. For White, see for example, John H. Clarke, "Methods of Work of the United States Supreme Court Judges," *Ohio Law Reporter* 20 (1922): 401 (written by Clarke after he resigned from the Court); Cavanaugh, "Recollections of Judge White," 91. For Holmes, see for example, Francis Biddle, *A Casual Past* (Garden City, N.Y.: Doubleday, 1961), 263 (Biddle served as Holmes's "secretary" during the 1911–1912 term); Pusey, *Charles Evans Hughes,* 1:285.

35. Clarke, "Methods of Work of the United States Supreme Court Judges," 401.

36. Blaustein and Mersky, *The First One Hundred Justices,* 139; Epstein et al., *The Supreme Court Compendium,* 2d ed., 344.

37. Epstein et al., *The Supreme Court Compendium,* 2d ed., 197.

38. See Walker et al., "On the Mysterious Demise of Consensual Norms in the United States Supreme Court," 371.

39. See the description of "social" leadership and "task" leadership developed in David Danelski, "The Influence of the Chief Justice in the Decisional Process," in Walter F. Murphy and C. Herman Pritchett, eds., *Courts, Judges, and Politics: An Introduction to the Judicial Process,* 2d ed. (New York: Random House, 1974), 525–34.

40. Pusey, *Charles Evans Hughes,* 1:282–83.

41. Urofsky, "The Brandeis-Frankfurter Conversations," 322.

42. Lash, ed., *Diaries of Felix Frankfurter,* 313.

due to my determination to avoid White's faults. Very often he could not make up his mind and a favorite expression of his was, 'God help us,' as though he counted on God to decide a case. White was a very emotional man and at times he would deliver an extemporaneous oration of an hour's length. I would come home from Conference on Saturday with a strong feeling of frustration. White did not take hold the way that a Chief Justice should in guiding the discussion and taking a position in expounding the matters before the Court."[43] White did, however, make a minor change in the Court's procedures by placing some cases on a "summary" docket. For those cases, oral argument was limited to thirty minutes a side, instead of the usual two hours a side.[44] Just as important, however, was the fact that these terms saw few of Holmes's "great" cases.

The Court also engaged in creative interpretation of the occasional statute as a means of restricting its workload. One example of that tactic arose during this term from the fact that Congress was also the legislature for the District of Columbia. As a result, every law for the District was also a law of Congress. The Court was therefore confronted with an argument that a court's attempt to interpret an act authorizing the extension of the District's New York Avenue was a case "in which the construction of any law of the United States [was] drawn into question." Under federal statute, cases of that sort could be reviewed by a writ of error to the Supreme Court.[45] Almost in exasperation, the Court rejected the argument that this act was a "law of the United States." Appealing to strict construction, the Court reasoned that Congress could not have meant that cases such as this could be brought to the Court. Otherwise, "the appellate jurisdiction of this court has been largely and irrationally increased. We believe Congress meant no such result."[46]

Even in the face of an overwhelming number of cases on its docket, the Court could be expansive in its interpretation of jurisdictional statutes. One such case was *B. Altman & Co. v. United States*,[47] the central issue of which centered on interpreting the definition of "statuary" in the 1897 tariff act. As was typical for much of the Court's docket, the 1897 act had been superseded—

---

43. Ibid., 314.
44. Butler, *A Century at the Bar*, 87.
45. The language is from section 250 of the Judicial Code of March 3, 1911, ch. 231, 36 Stat. 1087, 1159.
46. *American Security and Trust Co. v. Commissioners of the District of Columbia*, 224 U.S. 491, 495 (1912). For another instance of the Court trying to protect itself from appeals, see *Norfolk & Suburban Turnpike Co. v. Virginia*, 225 U.S. 264 (1912). While admitting that its prior holdings were ambiguous, the Court announced that for the future it would not allow writs of error when the face of the record did not clearly show a decision on the merits.
47. 224 U.S. 583 (1912).

by the 1909 Payne-Aldrich Tariff. Even so, when the case reached the Court the key question was whether there was any right to review by the Court. In 1891, Congress had attempted to reduce the Court's workload by creating separate circuit courts of appeal and by making many decisions of those courts final.[48] Only the more important cases could be taken to the Supreme Court, including those in which "the validity or construction of any treaty made under its [the Constitution's] authority, is drawn in question."[49] In *Altman* there was no treaty, only a reciprocal agreement between the United States and France.[50] Nevertheless, the Court held that an appeal would lie. The Court conceded that "treaty" had a special meaning under the Constitution, as demonstrated by requirements for the Senate's advice and consent to agreements entered into by the president. But, invoking the "intention" of Congress, the Court asserted that such a special meaning was not appropriate for this section of the statute. Instead, according to the Court, "the purpose of Congress was manifestly" to allow disputes over matters of utmost importance to be reviewed by the Supreme Court.[51] And, without once referring to debates in Congress or any other source, the Court announced "that matters of such vital importance, arising out of opposing constructions of international compacts, sometimes involving the peace of nations, should be subject to direct and prompt review by the highest court of the Nation."[52] Therefore, in the best tradition of Humpty Dumpty, the Court announced that this agreement was a treaty.

Like so many cases on the Court's docket, *Altman*'s focus on the meaning of *treaty* in the 1891 act emphasized the Court's role as a kind of grammarian for debates that the nation and the states had hurried past. The major topics for this 1911 term were the role of the administrative state, at the national level, and the means of financing it, at both the national and the state levels. In addition, the Court continued to face more general issues of reform as well as continuing questions about competition within the economy.

As usual, questions about the administrative state focused primarily on the railroads. In particular, the issues turned on the relevance of state boundaries for punctuating regulations. Increasingly, those boundaries proved to be irrelevant, with the consequence that the word "state" came to have less definite meaning. One decision announced early in the term (though argued seven months earlier) illustrated the near futility of using state lines to delimit the power of the national government. The case, *Southern Railway Co. v.*

---

48. See Act of March 3, 1891, ch. 517, 26 Stat. 826.
49. 224 U.S. at 596.
50. Presidential Proclamation of May 30, 1898, 30 Stat. 1774.
51. 224 U.S. at 600, 601.
52. Ibid., 601.

United States,[53] involved application of legislation that was already a generation old, the Safety Appliance Acts of 1893 and 1903.[54] The United States sought civil penalties for the railroad's failure to have five cars equipped with automatic couplers. The use of automatic couplers reduced the chance for injury by eliminating the need for a crew member to step between rail cars to couple or decouple them manually. That three of the cars moved in *intrastate* commerce and two in *interstate* commerce, though momentarily joined in the same train, emphasized the impending collapse of the constitutional category of "commerce among the several States."[55] Congress had adhered to that category in the original act, requiring automatic couplers only on rail cars "*used* in moving interstate traffic." In 1903, however, Congress blurred the category by making the requirement apply not merely to *cars* that were so used, but to any *railroad* "*engaged* in interstate commerce." The amendment posed an intricate problem of statutory construction that drove the Court to a passing reference to debates on the floor of Congress and to the anomalous conclusion that part of the act was necessarily redundant.[56] Otherwise, the Court reasoned, the construction would run contrary to the intent of Congress. That left the Court with an interpretation that applied depending upon the nature of the railroad, not upon the use of the particular rail car. The effect of the interpretation would be to make the statute reach cars being used in intrastate commerce, but on rails of an interstate company. The Court accepted that consequence, noting that cars were often commingled on a single train, with both interstate and intrastate commerce. Justice Van Devanter offered this explanation in his opinion for the Court: "Besides, the several trains on the same railroad are not independent in point of movement and safety, but are interdependent, for whatever brings delay or disaster to one, or results in disabling one of its operatives, is calculated to impede the progress and imperil the safety of other trains. And so the absence of appropriate safety appliances from any part of any train is a menace not only to that train but to others."[57] Van Devanter concluded his opinion with an invocation of "practical considerations," repudiating adherence to the categories of interstate and intrastate that had for so long driven the Court's jurisprudence. Once the Court acknowledged that all rail cars were "interdependent" no matter where they served along the rail line, the potential for federal regulation seemed unlimited.

A similar conflation of interstate and intrastate occurred in *Northern Pacific Railway Co. v. Washington*.[58] The state had fined the railroad one thou-

---

53. 222 U.S. 20 (1911).
54. Act of March 2, 1893, ch. 196, 27 Stat. 531; Act of March 2, 1903, ch. 976, 32 Stat. 943.
55. U.S. Constitution, art. 1, sec. 8, cl. 3.
56. 222 U.S. at 26.
57. Ibid., 27.
58. 222 U.S. 370 (1912).

sand dollars for violating a state law limiting the number of hours a crew could be required to be on duty. The railroad contested the fine, arguing that the 1907 federal Hours of Service Law had superseded the state law.[59] The state responded by noting that the federal law did not become effective until March 4, 1908. Since the violations occurred in July 1907, the state argued that its law should apply. The train involved carried a mix of cargo sufficient to satisfy almost every possible permutation of intrastate and interstate commerce. Not surprisingly, therefore, Chief Justice White adopted a position similar to that of Van Devanter in *Southern Railway:* "In view of the unity and indivisibility of the service of the train crew and the paramount character of the authority of Congress to regulate commerce, the act of Congress was exclusively controlling."[60] For a unanimous Court, White also rejected the argument that state law could apply until the effective date of the federal law. To do so, he reasoned, would defeat the purpose of Congress in giving railroads time to adjust to the new law.[61]

The effect of these decisions was virtually to eliminate state lines from the vocabulary of discussions of the commerce clause. In their place were rail lines that, almost by necessity, involved interstate commerce. Furthermore, by almost equal necessity, parties began to look with increasing frequency to the national government for solutions. Illustrating that change of view, as well as the Court's acquiescence, was a series of decisions upholding the power of Congress to define the liabilities owed by railroads to shippers as well as to employees. For shippers, a significant problem arose when a shipment required more than one rail company to reach a destination. In those circumstances, if a shipment was damaged the shipper faced the almost impossible task of discovering which carrier was at fault. In response to that problem, Congress enacted the Carmack Amendment in 1906, which imposed liability on the initial carrier, the one with whom the shipper had dealt. By defining the obligations of contract, ordinarily a matter for state law, the statute left the carriers to resolve allocation of liability among themselves. The Court originally upheld the Carmack Amendment in *Atlantic Coast Line v. Riverside Mills*,[62] a case argued during the vacancy in the chief justiceship, though announced after White took the seat. Justice Lamar had appeared on behalf of the railroad. By reaffirming the constitutionality of that statute, the Court allowed Congress to compress a group of rail lines into a single

---

59. Act of March 4, 1907, ch. 2959, 34 Stat. 1415.
60. 222 U.S. at 375.
61. Ibid., 379–80 (citing the House Report on the bill for support).
62. 219 U.S. 186 (1911).

line.[63] In effect, the Court left Congress to determine the reach of interstate commerce.

With that reaffirmation of the relationship between carrier and shipper, the Court next considered Congress's attempt to define the relationship between carrier and employee. Here, again, Congress had acted to impose a greater liability on the railroads—this time by removing barriers to recovery by an injured party. The Court upheld that shift of liability in the much-delayed *Second Employers' Liability Cases*,[64] decided almost a year after argument. The historian Gustavus Myers drew on a slogan popular at the end of the previous century, suggesting that the Court had followed the election returns of 1910 and had an eye on the election of 1912.[65] The act at issue mirrored Progressive reforms in the states by redefining four key components of an employer's liability for injuries to employees.[66] First, it eliminated the fellow-servant rule, thereby imposing liability on a railroad for injuries caused by one of its employees to another employee. Next, the act imposed strict liability on an employer for violations of any statutory rule, thereby providing an additional incentive to comply with the statute. To further strengthen the support for the safety statute, the act provided that in cases other than those involving violation of statutory rules, an injured employee's fault would not bar recovery; instead, any monetary damages would be reduced in proportion to that employee's fault. Third, the statute eliminated the defense of "assumption of risk," again limited to instances involving breach of statutory duties—a defense based on the premise that an employee had willingly assumed any risk inherent in the employment. Fourth, the act allowed an action for wrongful death, thereby permitting those dependent upon a deceased employee to be compensated for part of their loss.[67]

In spite of approving such a radical restructuring of tort law, the Court was not willing to go beyond the clear language of the statute. Thus, later in the term, the justices refused to allow a widow to sue her late husband's

---

63. *Galveston, Harrisburg & San Antonio Railway Co. v. Wallace*, 223 U.S. 481 (1912). The Carmack Amendment was itself part of the Hepburn Act, Act of June 29, 1906, ch. 3591, 34 Stat. 584, 595, which amended the Interstate Commerce Act.

64. 223 U.S. 1 (1912).

65. Myers, *History of the Supreme Court of the United States,* 780. The phrase was made popular by humorist and political commentator Finley Peter Dunne, who wrote that the Court had followed the election returns of 1896 in reaching its decisions to allow the executive broad powers over territories acquired as a result of the Spanish-American War. Then-Justice White wrote the most important of those decisions, known as the *Insular Cases.*

66. Act of April 22, 1908, ch. 149, 35 Stat. 65, as amended by Act of April 5, 1910, ch. 143, 36 Stat. 291. The Court had declared the first act unconstitutional because it reached employees injured in intrastate commerce. *Employers' Liability Cases,* 207 U.S. 463 (1908).

67. 223 U.S. at 49–50.

employer. The Court pointed to language that made railroads liable to the injured employee and, in case of death, "to his or her personal representative, for the benefit of the surviving widow or husband and children of such employé; and, if none, then to such employé's parents."[68] The Court conceded that the purpose of any suit was to benefit the employee's survivors; but the language of the statute was clear in not allowing the survivors themselves to initiate the suit. Instead, only the "personal representative" of the employee could sue. In the face of such clear language, the Court said that it "must yield," even in a case in which it seemed to be a "useless circumlocution" to require that there be an administrator for the estate.[69]

Finally, the Court upheld the provision in the Liability Act that declared void all contracts that attempted to exempt the employer from liability under the statute.[70] The contract at issue dated from 1905, before either the original 1906 act or the expanded 1908 version. In the contract, the employee agreed that the railroad could deduct from his wages a fixed amount each month as contributions to a "Relief Fund" administered by the company. The fund would pay a benefit for any injury the employee suffered while employed by the railroad. Any employee who accepted payment from the fund waived any right to sue the company. In spite of that waiver, an employee sued the railroad and won a judgment for $7,500, even though he had accepted payments totaling $79 for the injury.

The Court brushed aside the suggestion that the statute did not apply to preexisting contracts. The Court pointed to language in the 1908 act that referred to any contract, "'the purpose or intent of which shall be to enable any common carrier to exempt itself from any liability created by this Act.'" Those words, Justice Hughes wrote for the Court, did not "refer simply to an actual intent of the parties to circumvent the statute"—there could be no intent in 1905 to evade a statute not yet passed. Instead, the "purpose and intent" was to be discovered in the "necessary operation and effect" of the contract.[71] Without reference to any proceedings in Congress, the Court simply asserted that no other conclusion would allow the act to "accomplish the object which it is plain that Congress had in view."[72]

Having concluded that Congress intended to void existing contracts, the Court then turned to the question of the power of Congress to do so. Once again the Court's rationale was largely consequential: "To subordinate the exercise of the Federal authority to the continuing operation of previous contracts, would be to place, to this extent, the regulation of interstate commerce

---

68. Act of April 22, 1908, ch. 149, 35 Stat. 65.
69. *American Railroad Company of Porto Rico v. Birch*, 224 U.S. 547, 557 (1912).
70. *Philadelphia, Baltimore & Washington Railroad Co. v. Schubert*, 224 U.S. 603 (1912).
71. Ibid., 613.
72. Ibid.

in the hands of private individuals and to withdraw from the control of Congress so much of the field as they might choose by prophetic discernment to bring within the range of their agreements.... It is of the essence of the delegated power of regulation that, within its sphere, Congress should be able to establish uniform rules, immediately obligatory, which as to future action should transcend all inconsistent provisions. Prior arrangements were necessarily subject to this paramount authority."[73] To support that conclusion, Justice Hughes looked no further than the previous term, when the Court had held that the Mottleys lost their entitlement to free passage once Congress amended the Interstate Commerce Act in 1906.

When the Court turned to innovations in financing the emerging administrative state, it found itself confronted with myriad provisions. Almost the only common element was that the states themselves had increasingly tried to annul the effect of state lines, reaching into other states to find property that could be the basis for taxation. The irony is obvious. At the very time the Court was struggling to maintain state boundaries, at least against the national government, the states were working to eradicate the lines for purposes of taxation. The result was that the states fueled arguments against the inviolability of state borders. The earliest example of this sort of case was *Southern Pacific Co. v. Kentucky*.[74] In spite of its name, the company was incorporated in Kentucky. The dispute arose when the commonwealth of Kentucky imposed a tax on the company's steamships that never entered Kentucky, but remained in New York City. In upholding the commonwealth's power to tax the steamships, the Court again avoided relying on sharply defined categories. Instead, writing for the Court, Justice Lurton explained that the "taxing power is one which may be interfered with upon grounds of unjustness only when there has been such flagrant abuse as may be remedied by some affirmative principle of constitutional law."[75]

---

73. Ibid., 613–14. Justice Lurton had used not dissimilar reasoning in upholding the Land Department's practice of granting a railroad priority to a claim of land based on the original filing, even against an intervening claimant. Any other interpretation, he reasoned, would invite private claimants to file claims based on the railroad's disclosure of its route, thereby defeating Congress's intention to encourage the development of railroads. *Stalker v. Oregon Short Line Railroad Co.*, 225 U.S. 142, 151–52 (1912).

74. 222 U.S. 63 (1911). The doctrines of these cases followed decisions announced the term before White became chief justice. See, for examples, *Western Union Telegraph Co. v. Kansas*, 216 U.S. 1 (1910); *Pullman Co. v. Kansas*, 216 U.S. 56 (1910); *Ludwig v. Western Union Telegraph Co.*, 216 U.S. 146 (1910). Similarly, the White Court struck down an Oklahoma statute that imposed a tax on income based on investments in land and bonds outside the state, based on precedent from the late Fuller Court. *Meyer v. Wells, Fargo & Co.*, 223 U.S. 298 (1912).

75. 222 U.S. at 76. There were, however, taxes the Court did declare unconstitutional. See, for example, *Atchison, Topeka & Santa Fe Railway Co. v. O'Connor*, 223 U.S. 280 (1912) (Colorado tax cannot be imposed on all of capital stock of railroad doing little business in the

The Court upheld another state tax in a case that afforded a different perspective on the expanding nature of commerce in the country. The 1 percent tax challenged in *Banker Brothers Co. v. Pennsylvania* was imposed on retail vendors.[76] Banker Brothers sold automobiles in Pittsburgh, ordering them from George N. Pierce Company of Buffalo, New York, only after a buyer had placed an order. Using the same analogy that Holmes had done in *Dr. Miles Medical,* Banker Brothers claimed to be a mere agent for Pierce. In that view, the cars were still in interstate commerce since they belonged to Pierce at all times until delivery to the buyer. The Court rejected the suggestion, noting that the contract for sale was made in Pennsylvania.

Justice Pitney also showed signs of impatience with the categories. He wrote for the unanimous Court in *United States Express Co. v. Minnesota,* a case involving a tax of 6 percent on gross receipts of express companies doing business within the state. The tax originated in a 1905 law providing that the tax on revenues was in lieu of all taxes on property.[77] Day conceded that there was difficulty in drawing a line between permissible and impermissible taxes. As he explained the problem, "The difficulty has been, and is, to distinguish between legitimate attempts to exert the taxing power of the State and those laws which, though in the guise of taxation, impose real burdens upon interstate commerce as such."[78] Seemingly impressed by the fact that the state had disclaimed any interest in taxing the *property* of the company, the Court accepted the tax on the almost intangible "income": "Upon the whole, we think the statute falls within that class where there has been an exercise in good faith of a legitimate taxing power, the measure of which taxation is in part the proceeds of interstate commerce, which could not, in itself, be taxed, and does not fall within that class of statutes uniformly condemned in this court, which show a manifest attempt to burden the conduct of interstate commerce, such power, of course, being beyond the authority of the State."[79]

All of these decisions resonated with themes from Chief Justice White's "rule of reason" in the antitrust cases. Just as the Sherman Act provided no absolute rule, so the Constitution gave no fixed categories. Instead, they were to be evaluated in accord with reason. Justice McKenna captured both the movement away from categories and the frustration from an absence of rules in an entirely different case, *Mutual Loan Co. v. Martell.*[80] The case arose out of an effort by Massachusetts to protect workers from creditors. The 1908 statute provided that all assignments of wages to secure loans of less

---

76. 222 U.S. 210 (1911).
77. 223 U.S. 335 (1912).
78. Ibid., 344.
79. Ibid., 348.
80. 222 U.S. 225 (1911).

than two hundred dollars would be ineffective unless accepted in writing by the employer and filed with a municipal clerk. George J. Martell, the employer, had never accepted the assignment, though it had been recorded. The loan company challenged the statute as being a denial of due process, because it lacked any connection with the subjects of the state's police power—traditionally the public's "health, safety, morals, or general welfare."[81] Writing for a unanimous Court, McKenna disavowed any categorical precision, belittling that most fundamental of rubrics, "police power." Instead, he conceded, the decision depended upon the particulars of the specific case: "In a sense, the police power is but another name for the power of government, and a contention that a particular exercise of it offends the due process clause of the Constitution is apt to be very intangible to a precise consideration and answer. Certain general principles, however, must be taken for granted. It is certainly the province of the State, by its legislature, to adopt such policy as to it seems best. . . . Legislation cannot be judged by theoretical standards. It must be tested by the concrete conditions which induced it [as was done in the state court]."[82]

Before McKenna announced his opinion in that case he was assigned to write the opinion in a similar case, *Southern Railway Co. v. Reid*.[83] Relying on state law, one D. L. Reid sued the railroad for refusing to accept her household goods for shipment. The railroad invoked federal law, contending that it had no obligation to accept the shipment in the absence of a published rate for the route she needed.[84] Once it established a rate, six days later, the railroad accepted the goods. Invoking a pointillist school of interstate commerce, McKenna wrote "that transportation of property between the States is interstate commerce, and may be of Federal rather than of state jurisdiction. We say may be of Federal jurisdiction, for interstate commerce in its practical conduct has many incidents having varying degrees of connection with it and effect upon it over which the State may have some power."[85] In light of the fear of secret rebates and discrimination in shipping, the Court concluded that Congress intended to occupy the entire field of setting rates for railroads.

Of all the decisions involving state taxation, however, possibly the most significant was one known not so much for the tax involved as for the method of enacting the tax. This decision, *Pacific States Telephone and Tele-*

---

81. Ibid., 227.
82. Ibid., 233.
83. 222 U.S. 424 (1912).
84. Section 2 of the Hepburn Act, Act of June 29, 1906, ch. 3591, 34 Stat. 584, 586, prohibited transportation before a rate had been set.
85. 222 U.S. at 434.

graph Co. v. Oregon,⁸⁶ grew out of the state of Oregon's initiative and referendum provisions. The initiative and referendum were two of the key reforms on the Progressive agenda. Supporters saw each as a means of providing a measure of direct democracy, circumventing the often corrupt legislative process. Oregon had amended its constitution in 1902 to establish both the initiative and the referendum, allowing voters to use general elections to enact legislation as well as to disapprove statutes enacted by the legislature itself. In 1906, voters had used the initiative to impose a 2-percent tax on the annual gross revenues of telephone and telegraph companies. The telephone company challenged the procedure as a violation of the provision in the United States Constitution that guaranteed all states a "republican form of government."⁸⁷ The company's argument was forthright and struck at the heart of Progressive reform: The initiative constituted direct democracy, not government through representatives, which was the essence of republican government. In spite of the importance of the substantive and procedural issues involved, the Court dismissed the case for want of jurisdiction, with White summarily explaining that the issue had "long since been determined by this court conformably to the practise of the Government from the beginning to be political in character, and therefore not cognizable by the judicial power, but solely committed by the Constitution to the judgment of Congress."⁸⁸ The holding that disputes over a "republican form of government" were not to be resolved by the courts was supported by longstanding precedent, dating back to an 1849 opinion by Chief Justice Roger Taney, *Luther v. Borden*.⁸⁹ White went beyond Taney, however, to predict that dire consequences would follow from the Court's entering into an inquiry about the form of government in a state. His description could only have come from a former Confederate with an image of the defeated South still in mind: To question a state's government would mean, he suggested, a declaration that there was no government at all, which in turn would require the Court to reconstruct a government, including admitting it to the Union, which would be contrary to the Constitution.⁹⁰

The *Pacific States Telephone* decision implied that the Court was willing to permit experiments with different procedures in state governments. The decision, announced on February 19, 1912, could not have come at a more

---

86. 223 U.S. 118 (1912). In a companion case, *Kiernan v. Portland*, 223 U.S. 151 (1912), the Court refused to consider a challenge to the use of the referendum to fund the construction of a bridge across the Willamette River.
87. The full provision is this: "The United States shall guarantee to every State in this Union a Republican Form of Government." U.S. Constitution, art. 1, sec. 4.
88. 223 U.S. at 133.
89. 7 How. (48 U.S.) 1 (1849).
90. 223 U.S. at 141–42.

opportune time to blunt the attacks on the courts. Almost three weeks earlier, Senator La Follette had seemed to collapse during a speech in Philadelphia. The apparent illness of La Follette prompted a rush by his supporters to endorse Roosevelt in the presidential campaign of 1912. A few days after the *Oregon* decision, Roosevelt squandered the advantage gained by calling for recall of judicial decisions. La Follette's illness had secured the reform cloak about Roosevelt's shoulders. But conservatives were all the more taken aback by the attack on the courts—an attack that seemed gratuitous in light of the Court's seeming support for the initiative and referendum. The support was only "seeming," however, because the disposition prevented the Court from dealing directly with the substantive issues involved.

Other cases before the Court reflected the congeries of interests that had comprised the Progressive movement in the states during the early part of the century, before it moved to the national level in the election of 1910 and the emerging campaign of 1912. An inevitable result of the Court's backlog of cases was that while the justices continued to deal with the movement at the state level, the political debate shifted to a different level, with resulting differences in issues. Even so, the Court did little this term to thwart reform. For example, the Court declined to give a limited interpretation to "practicing medicine" for purposes of a 1907 Texas regulatory statute.[91] The defendant was charged with violating the statute "by treating a named patient for hay fever by osteopathy, without having registered his authority," as required by the statute. Justice Holmes wrote with disdain for the defendant's claim that osteopathy was not medicine and therefore not subject to the act:

> In short, the statute says that if you want to do what it calls practising medicine you must have gone to a reputable school in that kind of practice. Whatever may be the osteopathic dislike of medicines, neither the school nor the plaintiff in error suffers a constitutional wrong if his place of tuition is called a medical school by the act for the purpose of showing that it satisfies the statutory requirements.
>
> An osteopath professes, the plaintiff in error professes, as we understand it, to help certain ailments by scientific manipulation affecting the nerve centres. It is intelligible, therefore that the State should require of him a scientific training. . . . An osteopath undertakes to be something more than a nurse or a masseur, and the difference rests precisely in a claim to greater science, which the State requires him to prove.[92]

---

91. *Collins v. Texas,* 223 U.S. 288 (1912).
92. Ibid., 296–97.

Similar results followed from states' attempts to regulate animal foodstuffs. For example, in 1907, Indiana enacted a statute that required the labeling of animal foods, including a list of their ingredients. The Court upheld the act, reasoning that the act was a clear exercise of the state's police power to protect the health of its citizens and that the act did not unduly interfere with interstate commerce. Furthermore, there was no conflict with the federal Pure Food and Drug Act, which covered only certain drugs, not animal foods.[93]

The statutory changes in common-law doctrines were nowhere more apparent than in the tort law, especially as applied between railroads and their employees. Under the common law, employees found barriers to their recovery for injuries suffered while on the job. Among them were the doctrines of the "fellow-servant rule," "contributory negligence," and of "assumption of the risk." The fellow-servant rule held, in general, that an employee could not recover for an injury caused by another employee—the reasoning being that the other employee, and not the employer, was responsible for the accident. Of course, few employees would have sufficient resources to make it worthwhile to sue them for damages. Related to the fellow-servant rule was the doctrine of assumption of risk, which held that an employee could not recover for injuries arising from risks about which he was aware—the theory being that those risks were part of the negotiations for salary and that the employee was being compensated for assuming the risks. Contributory negligence was a separate doctrine specifying that an employee could not recover for injuries to which the employee had contributed.

Once again the Court encountered changes to those common-law doctrines that occurred during the first phase of Progressivism. As the cases reached the Court, they did not always pose a direct challenge to the change in the rule of law. Rather, as was befitting a Court entitled "Court of the United States" and not merely the "Supreme Court," the issues were scattered across the legal terrain, as lawyers struggled to find a rubric under which their corporate clients could hope to succeed. For example, *Aluminum Company of America v. Ramsey* involved a challenge to a 1907 Arkansas law that abrogated the fellow-servant rule, but only for those employed by railroad corporations and companies engaged in coal mining.[94] The company did not challenge the substance of the rule; instead, it argued that the rule violated the equal protection clause of the Fourteenth Amendment,

---

93. *Savage v. Jones*, 225 U.S. 501 (1912). See also *Standard Stock Food Co. v. Wright*, 225 U.S. 540 (1912) (upholding Iowa law requiring label to disclose name of manufacturer and ingredients).
94. 222 U.S. 251 (1911).

because the statute did not apply to every employer. The unanimous Court, through Justice McKenna, rejected the argument with only a passing reference to well-established precedents.[95] Late in the term, Chief Justice White responded to a similar argument by a different company, saying that the questions "have been so plainly foreclosed by decisions of this court as to make further argument unnecessary."[96]

There was even an announcement by the Court that it, at least, was not to change the fellow-servant rule. Writing for the Court, Holmes acknowledged that the rule had been called "a bad exception to a bad rule"; but, he continued, "it is established, and it is not open to courts to do away with it upon their personal notions of what is expedient." Any remedy, he noted, was to be found in the legislature.[97]

There was, however, the occasional exception to the Court's willingness to accept new state laws. In this term, for example, the Court struck down an Arkansas law from 1907 that required railroads to pay for livestock killed on their lines. Under the law, if a railroad refused to pay within thirty days, the owner of the livestock was entitled to recover double damages in a lawsuit, plus attorney's fees.[98] The statute required no relationship between the amount demanded initially and the amount sought in a subsequent lawsuit; thus, railroads either had to pay the amount demanded or risk the outcome of a jury trial. The Court, through Justice Van Devanter, struck the statute down as being a violation of due process. In the eyes of the Court, the statute did not "merely provide a reasonable incentive for the prompt settlement, without suit, of just demands of a class admitting of special treatment by the legislature." Instead, it went further and attached "onerous penalties to the non-payment of extravagant demands, thereby making submission to them the preferable alternative. Thus, it takes property from one and gives it to another, not because of a breach by the former of a duty to the latter or to the public, but because of a lawful exercise of an undoubted right."[99]

The final days of the Court having a vacant position saw one more significant decision. *Henry v. A. B. Dick Co.* illustrated a continuing divide within the Court, but it does not fit into the categories discussed thus far.[100] This lone decision involved yet another dispute over the use of a patent to constrain retail sales. As successor to Thomas Edison, the A. B. Dick Company

---

95. Ibid., 255–56.
96. *Missouri Pacific Railway Co. v. Castle*, 224 U.S. 541, 544 (1912) (1907 Nebraska statute eliminated fellow-servant rule and established comparative negligence system under which award of damages would be reduced by proportion of fault borne by the employee).
97. *Beutler v. Grand Trunk Junction Railway Co.*, 224 U.S. 85, 88, 89 (1912).
98. *St. Louis, Iron Mountain & Southern Railway Co. v. Wynne*, 224 U.S. 354 (1912).
99. Ibid., 359–60.
100. 224 U.S. 1 (1912).

held a patent for its "rotary mimeograph" machine.[101] All sales were subject to a license that allowed the machine to be used "only with the stencil paper, ink and other supplies made by" the company.[102] The company sold a machine to a Christina B. Skou with the license affixed. She, in turn, bought a can of ink from Sidney Henry, even though the ink was not made by the company. The company sued Henry, claiming that he had contributed to an infringement of its patent. The suit properly began in federal court because the claim depended upon the extent of the company's rights under federal patent law, at least so a majority of the judges held. The Circuit Court of Appeals for the Second Circuit certified the question to the Supreme Court for an answer. In the absence of Justice Day, and the lack of a replacement for Justice Harlan, only seven justices participated in the decision, dividing four to three. Justice Lurton delivered the opinion of the Court, speaking for himself and Justices McKenna, Holmes, and Van Devanter. Chief Justice White dissented, joined by Justices Hughes and Lamar. Both Lurton and Van Devanter had written significant decisions on the issue while serving on circuit courts.[103]

Justice Lurton explained that the company sold its machines below cost, with the intention of making a profit from the sale of supplies.[104] The issue, then, was whether the holder of a patent could tie sales of its patented machine to sales of a related product, but not one covered by the patent. (The patent on the ink had expired.)[105] The issue resembled that in *Dr. Miles Medical*, in which the company had argued for protection of its secret (though not patented) process through controls on the market price for the goods. In turn, both cases touched on concerns raised in the antitrust cases of the 1911 term. Any attempt to control prices suggested a violation of the Sherman Act. Moreover, the American Tobacco Company had achieved its control of cigarette production, to a large degree, through control of patents on the machines needed to manufacture the cigarettes. Thus, even though *A. B. Dick* and *Dr. Miles Medical* were private actions not involving the

---

101. A. B. Dick himself originally owned a lumberyard in Chicago. In an effort to expand his business he experimented with ways to produce duplicate copies of a single form, which would allow him to learn the state of the market for his products. In the course of his experimentation, he discovered that Edison had filed two patents for a related device. Once he bought the patents from Edison in 1887, Dick closed his lumberyard to concentrate on the manufacture of the mimeograph. See Robert Conot, *A Streak of Luck* (New York: Seaview Books, 1979), 74, 84–85, 250; Francis Jehl, *Menlo Park: Reminiscences* (Dearborn, Mich.: Edison Institute, 1937), 1:94–99.
102. 224 U.S. at 11.
103. *Heaton-Peninsular Button-Fastener Co. v. Eureka Specialty Co.*, 77 F. 288 (6th Cir. 1896) (Lurton); *National Phonograph Co. v. Schlegel*, 128 F. 733 (8th Cir. 1904) (Van Devanter).
104. 224 U.S. at 26.
105. Ibid., 51 (dissenting opinion of Chief Justice White).

government, both held portents for antitrust law as well. In phrasing the issue, Lurton placed the company on the side of the public, and of morality, asking rhetorically: "Shall we deal with the statute creating and guaranteeing the exclusive right which is granted to the inventor with the narrow scrutiny proper when a statutory right is asserted to uphold a claim which is lacking in those moral elements which appeal to the normal man? Or shall we approach it as a monopoly granted to subserve a broad public policy, by which large ends are to be attained, and, therefore, to be construed so as to give effect to a wise and beneficial purpose?"[106] But Lurton did not stop there. He went on to emphasize that the owner of the patent had the right to decide whether to sell or not; and, having decided to sell, the owner created a market that would not otherwise have existed. "By selling it subject to the restrictions he took nothing from others and in no wise restricted their legitimate market."[107] Having identified the company with development of the market and with the moral sense of the nation, Lurton next wrapped the company's claim in the Constitution itself: "It must not be forgotten that we are dealing with a constitutional and statutory monopoly. An attack upon the rights under a patent because it secures a monopoly to make, to sell and to use, is an attack upon the whole patent system. We are not at liberty to say that the Constitution has unwisely provided for granting a monopolistic right to inventors, or that Congress has unwisely failed to impose limitations upon the inventor's exclusive right of use." Then he turned to the familiar trope that matters of policy were for Congress alone: "The field to which we are invited by such arguments is legislative, not judicial."[108]

White began his first written dissent as chief justice with an explanation: "My reluctance to dissent is overcome in this case: First, because the ruling now made has a much wider scope than the mere interest of the parties to this record, since, in my opinion, the effect of that ruling is to destroy, in a very large measure, the judicial authority of the States by unwarrantedly extending the Federal judicial power."[109] In White's opinion, the case involved a contract right, not a patent right. As a result, the matter should be resolved in state court, not in federal. Thus he rejected as inapplicable a line of English cases cited by Lurton, "in view of the distinction between state and national power which here prevails and the consequent necessity, if our institutions are to be preserved, of forbidding a use of the patent laws which serves to destroy the lawful authority of the States and their public policy."[110] Beyond the effect he saw on federalism, White envisioned an equally dire conse-

---

106. Ibid., 27.
107. Ibid., 32.
108. Ibid., 35.
109. Ibid., 49.
110. Ibid., 68.

quence for the economy: "[T]he effect of the ruling is to make the virtual legislative authority of the owner of a patented machine extend to every human being in society without reference to their privity to any contract existing between the patentee and the one to whom he has sold the patented machine."[111] The historian Gustavus Myers, who had excoriated White for his "rule of reason" decisions, was equally critical of Lurton's opinion. Emphasizing the one-vote margin, Myers wrote that because of *A. B. Dick*, "the power of the trusts was greatly enlarged and intrenched, and the prohibition of the Sherman Anti-Trust Act against restraint of trade was partially nullified."[112]

Although Justice Day had returned to the Court, the 4–3 vote emphasized the continuing vacancy on the bench, now in the middle of the 1911–1912 term. The Court decided three additional patent cases after Pitney took his seat, two of which involved a challenge to acquisition of a patent by the United States for military purposes. The two cases nicely illustrated the changing nature of the argument about governmental use of patents. In one, *United States v. Société Anonyme des Anciens Etablissements Cail,* the Court wrestled with the old, common-law doctrine of implying a contract under which the government promised to pay for the patent.[113] (Ordinarily, a person using a patented device without permission would be liable in tort. But the United States government, as a sovereign power, could not be sued in tort without its consent. Invoking the concept of an implied contract to pay for the device was the common law's method of avoiding the limitations of tort law.) The implication was clearly a fiction, but the Court would not accept what it said was the alternative—"the purpose to deliberately take property of another without the intention that he should be compensated—in other words, to do plainly a wrongful act."[114] The other case, *Crozier v. Fried. Krupp Aktiengesellschaft,*[115] involved the newer, statutory response to the problem. Enacted in 1910, the act treated the patent as having been taken through the exercise of eminent domain, with the Court of Claims authorized to set the amount of compensation due.[116]

The statutory replacement of common-law doctrine was typical of the Progressive responses to perceived problems. But, in the third of the patent cases, the Court demonstrated that there was still vitality to the common law. And, in doing so, it emphasized the pervasive influence of the railroad as a

---

111. Ibid., 54.
112. Myers, *History of the Supreme Court of the United States,* 782. (The book was originally published in 1912, contemporaneously with the decision in *A. B. Dick.*) The Clayton Act rejected the holding in *A. B. Dick.* Act of October 15, 1915, ch. 323, §3, 38 Stat. 730, 731.
113. 224 U.S. 309 (1912).
114. Ibid., 320.
115. 224 U.S. 290 (1912).
116. Act of June 25, 1910, ch. 423, 36 Stat 851.

metaphor. This third case involved George Westinghouse's patent, issued in 1887, for a device to prevent a converter from becoming overheated when used for a long time, thereby allowing a transformer to maintain voltage in electric wires. The lower courts found that the patent had been infringed, but awarded only a dollar in damages because Westinghouse could not prove that the other party had profited from the infringement. The patented device had been included as one of many components in another product, thereby making it impossible to trace any part of the profit to the patented item.

Writing for the unanimous Court, Justice Lurton announced a modification of the rule that required the defendant to bear the burden of separating the profits from each component. Lurton defended his conclusion as but an application of the doctrines from the railroad rate cases, in which categories blended into one: "The problem here, though different, was in many respects analogous to that presented in those cases in which it is necessary to separate the interstate from the intrastate earnings made by a railroad where the same track, rolling stock, depots and labor are employed at the same time in making gross receipts. These commingled expenses must be apportioned between the two classes of earnings in order to determine whether the intrastate rate is confiscatory."[117]

The Court announced its opinion in *Westinghouse* on Friday, June 7, 1912, the same day that the National Republican Committee met to begin resolving challenges to delegates chosen for the party's national convention. The Court adjourned for the summer the following Monday. A number of those delegates had been chosen in the nation's first-ever presidential primaries—yet another Progressive attempt to circumvent entrenched political powers. Roosevelt's victories in most of those primaries provided short-lived elation, for the committee resolved virtually every dispute in favor of Taft. Even Roosevelt's personal appearance in Chicago on the eve of the convention was not enough to sway the committee, in spite of his invocation of Armageddon. By the time Taft's nomination was secured, on June 22, it was clear to all that Roosevelt would break away from the Republican Party and run under his own banner. Before the summer ended, the Progressive Party had nominated Roosevelt to face Taft and the Democrat's nominee, New Jersey Governor Woodrow Wilson. With the Socialists also involved, the presidential election of 1912 would prove to be "the climactic battle of the progressive era."[118]

---

117. *Westinghouse Electric & Mfg. Co. v. Wagner Electric Mfg. Co.*, 225 U.S. 604, 617 (1912).

118. Link and McCormick, *Progressivism*, 41.

III

THE 1912–1913 TERM

The Court reassembled on October 14, 1912, only a month before the presidential election. What had been one of the most provocative campaigns in American history almost came to a tragic end that same day, when Roosevelt was shot while attending a rally in Milwaukee. Although wounded in the chest, Roosevelt delivered his speech as scheduled; but he then took two weeks off to recuperate. Early in November, Woodrow Wilson won the electoral vote by a landslide, though his popular vote was less than the combined totals for Roosevelt, who finished a distant second, and Taft. More indicative of the vigor of the debate, and of the divisions in American society, were the more than nine hundred thousand votes for the Socialist candidate and labor leader, Eugene V. Debs. That total represented the highest percentage ever won by a Socialist candidate, reflecting discontent that spread beyond the Socialist Party itself.[1] That displeasure found other voices, including a strike in a Lawrence, Massachusetts, textile factory, led by the Industrial Workers of the World (IWW), as well as on farms across the nation. In spite of the turmoil, the Court continued to be an institution apart, reflecting almost none of the political discord in its opinions during the term.

With all nine justices present for the entire term, the Court produced some 20 percent more opinions than in the previous term. Once again, more than 90 percent of those opinions earned the unanimous support of the justices.[2] Holmes (forty-four) and White (forty) once again wrote the largest numbers of opinions for the Court. Day (thirty-five), Lurton (thirty-three), McKenna (thirty-eight), and the rookie Pitney (thirty-one) would not be far behind. That left Lamar (twenty-eight), Van Devanter (twenty-four), and Hughes (sixteen) with the fewest opinions for the Court. Hughes's surprisingly low output would be explained at the end of the term, when he

---

1. For an account of the election, see Francis L. Broderick, *Progressivism at Risk: Electing a President in 1912* (New York: Greenwood Press, 1989).
2. Department of Justice, *Annual Report of the Attorney General of the United States for the Year 1913* (Washington, D.C.: GPO, 1913), 28 (all of the numbers include both original and appellate cases).

announced opinions for the Court in a series of cases, each challenging the authority of a state's railroad commission to set rates for intrastate traffic. The cases had been argued during the previous term, in April 1912, with the most significant ones being grouped under two titles, *The Minnesota Rate Cases*[3] and *The Missouri Rate Cases*.[4] At the time of oral argument Holmes had written of the "dreadful State rate cases," describing them as "involving fundamental questions and possibly endless figures for the wretches who have to write them."[5] In spite of those cases, Holmes found the new term to be "more satisfactory than . . . at the end of last term."[6] It would seem, therefore, that White and the new justices had settled well into their routine.

In addition to those significant pending cases, the Court's first fortnight of arguments contained almost another dozen cases involving some aspect of Congress's power to control interstate commerce. After this first wave of important cases, no doubt moved to the beginning of the term precisely because of their importance,[7] the Court settled back into its usual mix of modest cases among those that were utterly trivial. Early in the term, the Court's opinions revealed the continuing absence of national scope for a significant part of its docket. Two cases from the District of Columbia provide good illustration of that fact. One, *Taylor v. Columbian University*, required the Court to decide the meaning of a will leaving land to Columbian University (later George Washington University).[8] The other asked the Court to decide whether a bay window in a new house on Wyoming Avenue overhung an adjacent lot so much that it had to be removed.[9] Moving some distance geographically did not alter the nature of the disputes, as indicated by a dispute from the Philippines that turned on interpretations of a marriage in China in 1847.[10]

The first wave of important opinions did, however, serve to define the term. Once again, a significant number of cases raised constitutional issues that found their origins in Progressivism's first phase—attempts by cities and states to regulate businesses, as well as state and local efforts to tap new sources of revenue to support those attempts. Added to those opinions were an increasing number of cases from the first flexing of the Progressive muscle at the national level. Taken together, the decisions showed the Court's

---

3. 230 U.S. 352 (1913).
4. 230 U.S. 474 (1913).
5. Holmes to Einstein, April 25, 1912, Peabody, *Holmes-Einstein Letters*, 68.
6. Holmes to Einstein, October 28, 1912, Peabody, *Holmes-Einstein Letters*, 74.
7. See Danelski and Tulchin, eds., *Autobiographical Notes of Charles Evans Hughes*, 164–65.
8. 226 U.S. 126 (1912).
9. *Smoot v. Heyl*, 227 U.S. 518 (1913). See also *Camp v. Boyd*, 229 U.S. 530 (1913) (dispute over lot in D.C. begins with original sale in 1792).
10. *Sy Joc Lieng v. Gregorio Sy Quia*, 228 U.S. 335 (1913).

comfort with its vocabulary and the justices' continuing willingness to accept, if not support, new governmental activities.

The first week of the new term brought oral argument in only three cases. One involved a minor procedural point.[11] Each of the other two, however, stood at the head of a line of cases to be decided during the term. One line involved questions of statutory construction, with continuing focus on the difficult relationship between patent law and antitrust law. The other involved constitutional issues, providing occasion for the Court to repeat the mantra of the supremacy of the federal government over interstate commerce, and of the power given to administrative agencies.

Previewing the first line of cases, those involving statutory construction, was *Standard Sanitary Manufacturing Co. v. United States*.[12] Unlike cases such as *Dr. Miles Medical* and *A. B. Dick*, this case involved the government's use of the Sherman Antitrust Act to challenge a "license" granted by the holder of a patent. In 1899 James W. Arrott Jr. received a patent for a device to distribute enameling powder evenly over heated iron to produce a smoother surface for products such as bathtubs. Standard Sanitary had purchased the patent and licensed it to others on the condition that they agree to sell their products at a certain price and not sell any "seconds." The licensing arrangement proved to be remarkably successful, leading to the control of some 85 percent of the market by manufacturers licensed to use the Arrott patent. That control supported the Court's confidence in its understanding that the patent law did not reach so far into the economy as to permit a patent holder to monopolize the subsequent sale of its product. As Justice McKenna explained, "Rights conferred by patents are indeed very definite and extensive, but they do not give any more than other rights an universal license against positive prohibitions."[13] The positive prohibition in this case, of course, was the Sherman Act, which McKenna described as being "its own measure of right and wrong."[14]

Much more portentous of the patent and antitrust cases was *United States v. Winslow*, the first of what would become many attempts by the government to break up the United Shoe Machinery Company's control over machines used to assemble shoes.[15] The company began in 1899, with the combination of three groups of companies, each of which manufactured the machines

---

11. *Breese & Dickerson v. United States*, 226 U.S. 1 (1912).
12. 226 U.S. 20 (1912).
13. Ibid., 49.
14. Ibid., 49. For another example of expansive use of a patent, see *Virtue v. Creamery Package Manufacturing Co.*, 227 U.S. 8 (1913).
15. *United States v. Winslow*, 227 U.S. 202 (1913).

needed to assemble different parts of a shoe.[16] United Shoe eventually acquired some fifty other manufacturers of shoe machinery. As it grew, United Shoe stopped selling its machines; instead, it leased them, on the condition that they be used only with other machines from the company. Like the licensing agreements, these leases attempted to impose conditions on use of the machines. A lease of a lasting machine, for example, required that it be used only with a heeling machine manufactured by United Shoe. The United States charged individual organizers of the company as well as the company itself with violating the Sherman Act, both in the original merger of the companies in 1899 and in the later use of tying arrangements contained in the leases. The trial court, however, eviscerated the indictment by interpreting it to apply only to the original merger, thereby making irrelevant any evidence related to the later events. The trial court then ruled that the government's remaining evidence failed to show a violation of the Sherman Act. The Supreme Court affirmed.

The government brought the case to the Supreme Court for review under a 1907 statute that, unlike most other statutes of the time, expanded the Court's jurisdiction. But the Court had earlier declined to give the statute an expansive interpretation. As a consequence, the Court could not review the interpretation of the indictment. All the Court could do was review the charge that the formation of United Shoe had, by itself, violated the Sherman Act.[17] Even so, Holmes seized the opportunity to reiterate his theory of the benefits of competition in the marketplace: "On the face of it the combination was simply an effort after greater efficiency. The business of the several groups that combined, as it existed before the combination, is assumed to have been legal. The machines are patented, making them is a monopoly in any case, the exclusion of competitors from the use of them is of the very essence of the right conferred by the patents . . . and it may be assumed that the success of the several groups was due to their patents having been the best."[18] In Holmes's view, the corporations had not competed with each other prior to their combination—they had each made a different type of machinery. He could see no difference between a single corporation controlling 70 percent of the "three non-competing groups of patented machines collectively used for making a single product" and "three corporations making the same proportion of one group each." And, he concluded, "[t]he disintegration aimed at by the statute does not extend to

---

16. For a near-contemporaneous account of the company and the history of the case, see Eliot Jones, *The Trust Problem in the United States* (New York: Macmillan, 1921), esp. 161–83, 431–35.
17. See Criminal Appeals Act, Act of March 2, 1907, ch. 2564, 34 Stat. 1246.
18. 227 U.S. at 217.

reducing all manufacture to isolated units of the lowest degree. It is as lawful for one corporation to make every part of a steam engine and to put the machine together as it would be for one to make the boilers and another to make the wheels."[19]

Two months after the decision in *Winslow,* the Court heard argument in *Bauer & Cie v. O'Donnell.*[20] With no restrictive interpretation from the trial court, this case gave the Court its first unrestricted opportunity to consider the legality of a tying arrangement involving a patented article since *A. B. Dick* the term before. The Court had decided the earlier case in favor of the patent holder, though by a 4–3 vote. Now, however, the Court was at full strength, with Justice Day having returned from caring for his dying wife, and Justice Pitney having joined the Court only a week after the decision in *A. B. Dick.* Both of the additional justices joined the minority (White, Hughes, and Lamar) from the earlier case to provide a majority against the use of a patent to control subsequent sales.

Bauer was a German partnership that held the patent for a water-soluble albuminoid, which it sold under the name of Sanatogen. In the United States, Bauer sold only through the Bauer Chemical Company of New York. Printed on packages of Sanatogen designed for purchase by consumers was a "Notice to the Retailer," which stated that the package contained a patented product that was "licensed" "for sale and use at a price not less than one dollar." James O'Donnell, who operated a retail drug store around the corner from Ford's Theatre in Washington, D.C., refused to abide by that notice. When Bauer refused to sell directly to him, O'Donnell found a jobber who would do so. Bauer then turned to the courts to seek an order that O'Donnell stop violating the putative license.

On behalf of the Court, Justice Day wrote with assurance, pointing to the simplicity of the terms used in the patent law protecting "the exclusive right to make, use, and vend the invention or discovery."[21] He implicitly rejected the need to refer to any sources as guides for meaning:

> In framing the act and defining the extent of the rights and privileges secured to a patentee Congress did not use technical or occult phrases, but in simple terms gave an inventor the exclusive right to make, use and vend his invention for a definite term of years. The right to make can scarcely be made plainer by definition, and embraces the construction of the thing invented. The right to use is a comprehensive term and embraces within its

---

19. Ibid., 217–18.
20. 229 U.S. 1 (1913).
21. At the time of this decision, the language was codified in section 4884 of the Revised Statutes.

meaning the right to put into service any given invention. And Congress did not stop with the express grant of the rights to make and to use. Recognizing that many inventions would be valuable to the inventor because of sales of the patented machine or device to others, it granted also the exclusive right to vend the invention covered by the letters patent. To vend is also a term readily understood and of no doubtful import. Its use in the statute secured to the inventor the exclusive right to transfer the title for a consideration to others.[22]

Day then turned to the question of the power of a patent holder to control the retail price for the product. In doing so, he sought to narrow the issue. First, he noted that there was no right to control the retail price in the absence of some statutory protection, as decided by the *Dr. Miles Medical* case.[23] Next, although there was no precedent concerning a patent, decisions involving copyrights had held that the privilege of control ended with the sale by the copyright holder.[24] Since both the copyright and the patent statutes contained the term *vend*, Justice Day concluded that neither permitted control of the retail price. That left only the word *use*, contained in the patent law but not in the copyright law. Conceding that Congress would have had the power to enable a patent holder to control the retail price of an item, Day finally turned to the question of whether the act granted that power under the word *use*. He distinguished the *A. B. Dick* case as one involving the use of the leased product. By contrast, the price at which a product was sold was not a "use." Indeed, "it is a perversion of terms to call the transaction in any sense a license to use the invention. The jobber from whom the appellee purchased had previously bought, at a price which must be deemed to have been satisfactory, the packages of Sanatogen afterwards sold to the appellee. The patentee had no interest in the proceeds of the subsequent sales, no right to any royalty thereon or to participation in the profits thereof. The packages were sold with as full and complete title as any article could have when sold in the open market, excepting only the attempt to limit the sale or use when sold for not less than one dollar. . . . There was no transfer of a limited right to use this invention, and to call the sale a license to use is a mere play upon words."[25] The plurality from *A. B. Dick* (McKenna, Holmes, Lurton, Van Devanter) contented themselves with the simple notation that they dissented.

A similar confidence in meaning was evident through a number of other decisions involving statutory interpretation. The closest resemblance to

---

22. 229 U.S. at 10–11.
23. 220 U.S. 373 (1911).
24. *Bobbs-Merrill Co. v. Straus,* 210 U.S. 339 (1908).
25. 229 U.S. at 16.

Bauer came in *Smith v. Hitchcock*.[26] The case involved Ormond G. Smith's attempt to prevent the postmaster general from revoking second-class postal privileges previously enjoyed by publications such as *Tip Top Weekly* and *Work and Win*. The issue was whether the publications were "periodicals." During the summer of 1911, Justice Hughes had served on a commission that examined the rates charged for second-class postage.[27] The task lasted far longer than Hughes had expected, with the report not completed until February 1912. With that experience Hughes was presumably more familiar with the postal system than any other justice, though his committee discussed postal rates, while this case involved a different issue of statutory construction. But Hughes was hard at work on a series of complex rate cases.[28] So, White assigned Holmes the task of writing the opinion. Like Day, Holmes found little that was troublesome in the language of the statute. Holmes did, though, concede that there could be ambiguity, using expressions much like those he had used in *United States v. Johnson*, which had involved the meaning of *misbranded*:

> The noun periodical, according to the nice shade of meaning given to it by popular speech, conveys at least a suggestion if not a promise of matter on a variety of topics, and certainly implies that no single number is contemplated as forming a book by itself. But we can approach the question more profitably from the other end, and shall have gone as far as we need when we decide whether the numbers exhibited constitute so many books. The word book also, of course, has its ambiguities, and may have different meanings according to the connection in which it is used. . . . Without attempting a definition we may say that generally a printed publication is a book when its contents are complete in themselves, deal with a single subject, betray no need of continuation, and, perhaps, have an appreciable size.[29]

In that light, the items published by Smith were books, not entitled to the special mailing rates for periodicals.

One other decision concerning privileges revealed greater complexities in the statute granting those privileges. The case, *Lewis Publishing Co. v. Morgan*,[30] was argued two weeks after the decision in *Smith*. Lewis Publishing

---

26. 226 U.S. 53 (1912).
27. Danelski and Tulchin, eds., *Autobiographical Notes of Charles Evans Hughes*, 166.
28. Lash, ed., *Diaries of Felix Frankfurter*, 314.
29. 226 U.S. at 59.
30. 229 U.S. 288 (1913). For a similar dispute involving advertising, with an opinion decided the same term, see *Lewis Publishing Co. v. Wyman*, 228 U.S. 610 (1913) (publication that is almost entirely advertising is not entitled to second-class rates).

involved a challenge to two requirements in the statute: (1) that material for which the publication received payment be marked as "advertisement"; and (2) that publications file with the postmaster certain information about the publisher and stockholders.[31] Lewis Publishing argued that the requirements violated the First Amendment's guarantee of freedom of the press and the Fifth Amendment's guarantee of due process.

Although *Lewis Publishing* was argued in December 1912, Chief Justice White delayed six months before announcing his decision for a unanimous Court. Finally, during the last week of the term, he released the opinion amidst a group of almost sixty opinions. Referring to various government documents, White began his opinion with an expression of chauvinistic pride in the development of the postal system. Culminating with the 1912 statute involved here, that system had divided the mail into four classes, using first-class postage to subsidize second-class mail.[32] As was his style, White then posed the issue with such rhetorical contrasts that only a single answer was possible: "Was the provision [requiring labeling of advertisements and disclosure of ownership] intended simply to supplement the existing legislation relative to second class mail matter or was it enacted as an exertion of legislative power to regulate the press, to curtail its freedom, and under the assumption that there was a right to compel obedience to the command of legislation having that object in view, to deprive one who refused to obey of all right to use the mail service?"[33] In more direct language, the statute merely set rates. White supported that conclusion by reference to the language of the act itself. He reasoned that there could be no plan to interfere with the freedom of the press, pointing simply to the title of the act, which declared that it was a post office appropriation measure. Even more persuasive to White was the use of the word *enter,* a term already commonly used in the regulation of mail. White attached great importance to the use of that word, "since by practice and regulation prevailing during a long period of time, it had come to pass that the word 'enter' had exclusive relation to a duty to be performed in order to obtain the benefits of the second class classification. In the absence, therefore, of some express indication to the contrary, no other conclusion is possible, than that the word was used with reference to its received official and administrative significance."[34] As evidence of his common-law interpretation of the statutory language (he referred to the "common knowledge of mankind"), White

---

31. The requirements were contained in section 2 of the Post Office Appropriation Act of 1912, Act of August 24, 1912, ch. 389, 37 Stat. 539, 553.
32. 229 U.S. at 304.
33. Ibid., 308.
34. Ibid., 309.

rebuffed the publisher's attempt to rely on statements from debates in Congress and on administrative interpretations: "Without stopping however to review the subjects in detail we content ourselves with saying that we think neither the reference to expressions in debate, upon the concession for the sake of argument that they are competent to be looked at, nor an opinion of the Attorney General upon which reliance is placed, are adequate to control or modify the conclusion we have reached as to the meaning of the provision."[35] Having made that statement, however, White then proceeded to explain why the legislative history did not support the publisher's argument. Even with that concessionary detour, White relied primarily on his usual approach of using reason to decipher meaning. In the end, the requirements of the act were nothing more than extensions of existing rules. The labeling of advertisements was an extension of the requirement that advertising publications not be given second-class mailing privileges; the identification of stockholders and principal creditors was an extension of existing requirements that the names of owners and editors be disclosed. "We say this because of the intimate relation which exists between ownership and debt, since debt in its ultimate conception is a dismemberment of ownership and the power which it confers over an owner is by the common knowledge of mankind, often the equivalent of the control which would result from ownership itself."[36] White concluded by emphasizing the narrow scope of the Court's holding—it did not permit exclusion from the mails; neither did it involve regulation of the content of newspapers. Instead, it infringed only the right "of the publishers to continue to enjoy great privileges and advantages at the public expense."[37]

White's approach to statutory interpretation in *Lewis* was but a modification of one he had delivered a month before, in *United States v. Chavez*.[38] The case arose from Arnulfo Chavez's indictment for exporting two thousand Winchester cartridges from the United States to Mexico. The indictment was based on a joint resolution of Congress that made it illegal to export arms to a country after the president declared that the export would promote domestic violence. President Taft had made that declaration in an official proclamation the same day Congress passed the resolution.[39] The res-

---

35. Ibid., 311. The Court, through Justice Lamar, also rejected any reliance on congressional debates in *Omaha & Council Bluffs Street Railway Co. v. Interstate Commerce Commission*, 230 U.S. 324 (1913).
36. 229 U.S. at 315.
37. Ibid., 316.
38. 228 U.S. 525 (1913).
39. Joint Resolution of March 14, 1912, 37 Stat. 630; Presidential Proclamation of March 14, 1912, 37 Stat. 1733. The formulaic language of the joint resolution, followed by the president's proclamation, would be repeated just over twenty years later when President Franklin

olution and presidential declaration were attempts to curtail American involvement in the civil war in Mexico. Francisco I. Madero replaced Porfirio Díaz as president of Mexico in November 1911. Madero's complaint that arms from the United States were aiding insurgents prompted the congressional resolution. But the resolution did little to ease tensions between the two countries. A February 1913 coup removed Madero from office; the leaders killed him a few days later. Wilson's new administration, from March 1913, refused to recognize the new regime. Then, on April 9 local Mexican authorities arrested several American sailors who had gone ashore at Tampico. Later in the month, United States Marines occupied the Mexican city of Veracruz in response to reports that a boatload of German munitions was about to dock there. Both houses of Congress then voted to authorize the president to use armed force against Mexico. As the United States and Mexico moved toward what many feared would be open warfare, the Court heard oral argument in *Chavez* on April 11, 1913. When the decision followed four weeks later, nothing in the opinion hinted at the crisis between the two countries.

Chavez had been stopped in El Paso, Texas, before he could cross the border into Mexico. The trial court dismissed the indictment, reasoning that there could be no export without arrival in the foreign country. That commonsense ruling posed a problem for White's usual approach to statutory construction. Even so, he began with an assertion: "In common speech the shipment of goods from this to a foreign country without regard to their landing in such country is often spoken of as an export." For additional support, he pointed to two constitutional provisions with which he was familiar from the *Insular Cases*. One provision barred Congress from imposing duties "on articles exported from any State"; the other prohibited states from taxing exports.[40] But he conceded that it was also true that there was a consensus of opinion that "export" required both sending from and landing in. "But the question which we are called upon to solve, that is, the meaning of the words 'to export' as used in the joint resolution, may not be disposed of by any mere abstract consideration of the meaning of the words, but their signification must be determined with reference to the text of the resolution itself."[41] Relying solely on the text of the joint resolution, White pointed to the second section, which provided the sanctions for violating the prohibi-

---

Roosevelt imposed a similar prohibition on the export of arms to Bolivia and Paraguay. Joint Resolution of May 28, 1934, ch. 365, 48 Stat. 811; Presidential Proclamation of May 28, 1934, 48 Stat. 1744. The later proclamation would lead to the Court's decision in *United States v. Curtiss-Wright Export Corp.*, 299 U.S. 304 (1936), with its sweeping approval of broad executive power in foreign relations.
40. U.S. Constitution, art. 1, secs. 9, 10.
41. 228 U.S. at 530.

tion on export. That section used the term *any shipment*. With the joint resolution thus portrayed as equating export and shipment, there was no need to resort to legislative history. Instead, common, shared experience provided "the reasons which led to the prohibition against and punishment of shipment instead of export in the complete sense."[42]

White had used a similar argument concerning another statute, the act that created the government of Puerto Rico.[43] In *Porto Rico v. Rosaly Y Castillo*[44] the chief justice once again returned to subjects he had discussed in his *Insular Cases* opinions, which had so impressed Taft more than a decade earlier. Now, though, the issue concerned the meaning of the provision that there should be "a body politic under the name of The People of Porto Rico with governmental powers as hereinafter conferred and with power to sue and be sued as such." The specific question was whether the statement that the government could "be sued" was tantamount to an elimination of sovereign immunity. White emphasized that words had to be read in context, which meant that they might have one meaning in one place and a different meaning in another. "And this is made clear by bearing in mind that as usually applied the words to sue and be sued but express implications as to the existence of powers flowing from the matter to which they relate, while here if the words have the meaning insisted on they serve, if not to destroy, at least to seriously modify or greatly restrict the grant of powers conferred by the organic act."[45] Following that precipitous consequence, White suggested, would mean that the organic act had failed to create a government for Puerto Rico modeled on that of the United States. Instead, it would be "one in which the legislative power concerning claims of every kind against the government is subordinated to the judicial."[46] To avoid that consequence, White concluded that the words "to be sued" were redundant, because they simply confirmed what would be true from the grant of governmental power. In fact, the words were more than redundant, they were delusory, since the grant of governmental power carried with it a grant of immunity from suit without the consent of the government.[47]

Running parallel to this line of statutory construction cases was a series involving challenges to the constitutionality of statutes, both state and federal.

---

42. Ibid., 532.
43. Act of April 12, 1900, ch. 191, 31 Stat. 77. White reiterated his point that the same words might mean different things in different contexts in *McGowan v. Parish*, 228 U.S. 312 (1913).
44. 227 U.S. 270 (1913).
45. Ibid., 275. Later in the term White chided another court for interpreting an act "not by its true text, but by an imaginary context." *United States v. Anderson*, 228 U.S. 52, 59 (1913) (construction of the Indian Appropriation Act of July 4, 1884, ch. 180, 23 Stat. 76, and application of restrictions on cattle sales by Indians).
46. 227 U.S. at 276.
47. Ibid., 277.

The state statutes continued to represent the last wave of local, Progressive legislation; the federal statutes now began to reflect the first wave of national, Progressive legislation. For the state statutes there continued to be the usual challenges under the Fourteenth Amendment's rubrics of due process and equal protection. For the federal statutes the question was largely one of congressional power under the commerce clause.

Among the state statutes challenged this term was a mix of both regulatory and taxing questions. In all cases, however, the Court continued to show great deference to the state legislatures. In *Bradley v. City of Richmond* the Court upheld a municipal ordinance that imposed a license tax which varied according to the classification into which a business fell. One F. S. Bradley objected to categorizing "private bankers" according to the kind of property used to secure loans.[48] The Court readily held that the classification was not arbitrary and therefore did not violate the Fourteenth Amendment, even though the statute was conceded to be both a regulatory and a revenue measure. Likewise, in *Metropolis Theatre Co. v. City of Chicago* the Court upheld a 1909 Chicago license fee imposed on places of amusement, with the amount of the tax being based on the price of admission.[49] In writing for the unanimous Court, Justice McKenna accepted the use of "arbitrary" to describe the dividing line between the permissible and the impermissible. He went even further to concede the imprecision of the process:

> To be able to find fault with a law is not to demonstrate its invalidity. It may seem unjust and oppressive, yet be free from judicial interference. The problems of government are practical ones and may justify, if they do not require, rough accommodations—illogical, it may be, and unscientific. But even such criticism should not be hastily expressed. What is best is not always discernible; the wisdom of any choice may be disputed or condemned. Mere errors of government are not subject to our judicial review. It is only its palpably arbitrary exercises which can be declared void under the Fourteenth Amendment; and such judgment cannot be pronounced of the ordinance in controversy.[50]

---

48. 227 U.S. 477 (1913) (the distinction was between personal property and commercial property).
49. 228 U.S. 61 (1913).
50. Ibid., 69–70. See also *Rosenthal v. New York*, 226 U.S. 260, 271 (1912): "[T]he Federal Constitution does not require that all state laws shall be perfect, nor that the entire field of proper legislation shall be covered by a single enactment"; *Schmidinger v. City of Chicago*, 226 U.S. 578 (1913), upholding 1908 Chicago ordinance regulating sizes of bread loaves; *Hutchinson v. City of Valdosta*, 227 U.S. 303 (1913), upholding 1909 municipal ordinance requiring houses to install indoor plumbing if on a street where sewer mains are laid (Sarah M. Hutchinson argued the case *pro se*, one of the earliest instances of a woman arguing

McKenna used similar language in another Chicago case, one involving a 1907 city ordinance that required fencing or railings around elevator and hoist shafts in buildings under construction. Responding to the contention that the statute was underinclusive because it failed to deal with all dangerous situations and was therefore a denial of equal protection, McKenna wrote:

> The legislation cannot be judged by abstract or theoretical comparisons. It must be presumed that it was induced by actual experience . . . . If it be granted that the legislative judgment be disputable or crude, it is notwithstanding not subject to judicial review. We have said many times that the crudities or even the injustice of state laws are not redressed by the Fourteenth Amendment.
>
> The law may not be the best that can be drawn nor accurately adapted to all of the conditions to which it was addressed. . . . What the statute enjoins it enjoins not only of plaintiff in error but of all similarly situated. What it does not enjoin plaintiff in error cannot complain of.[51]

So, too, Justice Hughes wrote for the Court in upholding a Mississippi statute banning sale of all malt liquors, even if nonalcoholic.[52] As the Court had done in other cases, Hughes disclaimed any interest in evaluating the wisdom of the statute: "To hold otherwise would be to substitute judicial opinion of expediency for the will of the legislature, a notion foreign to our constitutional system."[53] He continued:

> It was competent for the legislature of Mississippi to recognize the difficulties besetting the administration of laws aimed at the prevention of traffic in intoxicants. . . . The statute establishes its own category. . . . The inquiry must be whether, considering the end in view, the statute passes the bounds of reason and assumes the character of a merely arbitrary fiat.
>
> That the opinion is extensively held that a general prohibition of the sale of malt liquors, whether intoxicating or not, is a necessary means to

---

before the Court); *Adams v. City of Milwaukee*, 228 U.S. 572 (1913) (McKenna), upholding 1908 city ordinance barring sales of milk from cows outside the city unless a certificate certifying that the cows are free from tuberculosis and contagious diseases; *Barrett v. Indiana*, 229 U.S. 26 (1913) (Day), upholding 1907 Indiana law regulating the width of entry into certain coal mines but not others; *Citizens' Telephone Co. of Grand Rapids v. Fuller*, 229 U.S. 322 (1913), upholding 1909 Michigan tax on telephone companies, excluding those with gross receipts less than five hundred dollars annually.

51. *Chicago Dock and Canal Co. v. Fraley*, 228 U.S. 680, 686–87 (1913).
52. *Purity Extract and Tonic Co. v. Lynch*, 226 U.S. 192 (1912).
53. Ibid., 202.

the suppression of trade in intoxicants, sufficiently appears from the legislation of other States and the decision of the courts in its construction.[54]

Just as the Fourteenth Amendment proved to be of little hindrance to state and local regulatory measures, so it also proved to be only a slight barrier to efforts by local governments to offer services, even when it meant competing with an existing commercial provider. Thus, when the city of Madera, California, began construction of a water plant, the current provider of water for the city sued to halt construction. Holmes's language for the Court was brusque in rejecting the franchise holder's argument:

> An appeal to the Fourteenth Amendment to protect property from a congenital defect must be vain. . . . It is impossible not to feel the force of the plaintiff's argument as a reason for interpreting the Constitution so as to avoid the result, if it might be, but it comes too late. There is no pretence that there is any express promise to private adventurers that they shall not encounter subsequent municipal competition. We do not find any language that even encourages that hope, and the principles established in this class of cases forbid us to resort to the fiction that a promise is implied.
>
> The constitutional possibility of such a ruinous competition is recognized in the cases, and is held not sufficient to justify the implication of a contract. . . . It is left to depend upon the sense of justice that the city may show.[55]

On occasion, to be sure, there was an exception. For example, in *City of Owensboro v. Cumberland Telephone & Telegraph Co.* the Court refused to uphold a 1909 ordinance requiring the company to remove its telephone poles from local streets, unless the company purchased a franchise from the city allowing it to maintain the poles under regulations to be passed.[56] Beyond the fact that the Court did not side with the local government, the exceptional nature of this case is indicated by the 5–4 division within the Court, one of only four such votes during the 1912–1913 term. The disagreement among the Court was over the meaning of the city's reserved power to "amend" or "repeal" franchises. Writing for the Court's majority,

---

54. Ibid., 204.
55. *Madera Water Works v. Madera,* 228 U.S. 454, 456–57 (1913). For similar cases, both involving Denver's decision late in 1907 to begin construction of municipal water works, see *City and County of Denver v. New York Trust Co.,* 229 U.S. 123 (1913); *Wheeler v. City and County of Denver,* 229 U.S. 342 (1913).
56. 230 U.S. 58 (1913). See also *Boise Artesian Hot and Cold Water Co., Ltd. v. Boise City,* 230 U.S. 84 (1913) (imposition of license fee is impairment of contract); *Old Colony Trust Co. v. City of Omaha,* 230 U.S. 100 (1913) (franchise is perpetual; Court rejects attempt to discover parties' intent, preferring a practical construction).

Justice Lurton reasoned that the power did not include the power to destroy, which he construed the ordinance to do. Justice Day disagreed, siding with the power of the municipality to control interests vital to the public.

Justice Lamar used the same image and echoed Chief Justice John Marshall in *McCulloch v. Maryland*[57]—that the power to regulate did not include the power to destroy—in striking down a 1901 municipal ordinance that repealed an 1868 charter authorizing a railroad to build double tracks through the city.[58] In Lamar's opinion, the case presented a stark conflict between the municipality's police power and the sanctity of contract guaranteed by the Constitution: "The power to regulate implies the existence and not the destruction of the thing to be controlled. And while the city retained the power to regulate the streets and the use of the franchise, it could neither destroy the public use nor impair the private contract, which, as it contemplated permanent and not temporary structures, granted a permanent and not a revocable franchise."[59] He even engaged in a bit of gloomy prediction, that the "destruction of great highways of commerce" would follow upon allowing the municipality to repeal the franchise.[60]

The one area in which states were most likely to find their laws struck down was that involving interstate commerce. In these cases the Court was extremely protective of the supremacy of national power. For example, the Hepburn Act of 1906 meant the invalidity of a state law requiring railroads to furnish cars within forty-eight hours of request.[61] And, insofar as there were difficult lines to be drawn to demarcate the power of states, the Court was not at all generous. Thus, to define the moment at which commerce became "interstate" or "foreign," and therefore no longer subject to state regulation, the Court chose the earliest possible moment—when the goods actually began their shipment.[62] As Justice McKenna explained, "the essential character of the commerce, not its mere accidents, should determine."[63] Once any other rule was applied, he wrote, "means will be afforded of evading the national control of foreign commerce from points in the interior of a State."[64]

---

57. 4 Wheat. (17 U.S.) 316 (1819).
58. *Grand Trunk Western Railway Co. v. City of South Bend*, 227 U.S. 544 (1913).
59. Ibid., 555.
60. Ibid., 556.
61. *Chicago, Rock Island & Pacific Railway Co. v. Hardwick Farmers Elevator Co.*, 226 U.S. 426 (1913). See also *Yazoo & Mississippi Valley Railroad Co. v. Greenwood Grocery Co.*, 227 U.S. 1 (1913) (penalty for delay in providing cars is unreasonable burden on interstate commerce); *St. Louis, Iron Mountain & Southern Railway Co. v. Edwards*, 227 U.S. 265 (1913) (1907 state statute invalid insofar as it imposes a penalty for delay in notifying consignee of arrival of freight).
62. *Texas & New Orleans Railroad Co. v. Sabine Tram Co.*, 227 U.S. 111, 123 (1913); *Railroad Commission of Louisiana v. Texas & Pacific Railway Co.*, 229 U.S. 336, 341 (1913).
63. 227 U.S. at 126.
64. Ibid.

All of these cases were, in a sense, but preamble to the two "big" cases of the term, *Hoke v. United States*[65] and *The Minnesota Rate Cases.*[66] *Hoke* was one of four decisions handed down on the same day, grouped under the title *White Slave Traffic Cases.*[67] Likewise, the *Minnesota Rate Cases* were a group of four cases, argued over four days in April 1912. Decided on the same day were the *Missouri Rate Cases,* a group of thirty-six cases joined for argument, first in October 1910, then reargued in April 1912.[68] Taken together, the cases defined the limits of federal and state power; moreover, they nicely illustrated the emerging Progressive legislative agenda, with *Hoke* showing the increasing nationalization of the agenda, and the *Rate Cases* the continuing vibrancy of the attempts at the state level.

Hoke involved a challenge to the 1910 Mann Act,[69] commonly known as the "White Slave Act." Effie Hoke was charged with inducing a woman to travel from New Orleans, Louisiana, to Beaumont, Texas, for the purpose of prostitution, in violation of the Mann Act.[70] Writing for a unanimous Court, Justice McKenna upheld the act against a wide-ranging attack. The key element of Hoke's challenge was that the act exceeded Congress's powers under the commerce clause because the statute went to matters of morality, which were issues reserved to the states.[71] As Hoke noted, there was no federal law against prostitution, that being a matter left to the police power of the states. Thus, the statute prohibited only an intention, not an intention to commit a crime.

---

65. 227 U.S. 308 (1913).
66. 230 U.S. 352 (1913).
67. *Athanasaw v. United States,* 227 U.S. 326 (1913); *Bennett v. United States,* 227 U.S. 333 (1913); *Harris v. United States,* 227 U.S. 340 (1913).
68. 230 U.S. 474 (1913). Justice Hughes wrote opinions in six other cases announced the same day, all depending upon the decision in the Minnesota cases. *Knott v. St. Louis Southwestern Railway Co.,* 230 U.S. 509 (1913); *Knott v. St. Louis, Kansas City & Colorado Railroad Co.,* 230 U.S. 512 (1913); *Chesapeake & Ohio Railway Co. v. Conley,* 230 U.S. 513 (1913); *Oregon Railroad & Navigation Co. v. Campbell,* 230 U.S. 525 (1913); *Southern Pacific Co. v. Campbell,* 230 U.S. 537 (1913); *Allen v. St. Louis, Iron Mountain & Southern Railway Co.,* 230 U.S. 553 (1913).
69. Act of June 25, 1910, ch. 395, 36 Stat. 825. On the Mann Act in general, see David J. Langum, *Crossing Over the Line: Legislating Morality and the Mann Act* (Chicago: University of Chicago Press, 1994).
70. Hoke, and her codefendant, Basile Economides, were charged with three counts of violating the Mann Act. Each count involved a different woman, one of whom was less than eighteen years old. The language of the indictment, and the sections of the Mann Act, are printed in the Court's opinion, 227 U.S. at 317–19.
71. Hoke also argued that the statute violated the privileges and immunities clause of the Constitution, which protected the right of interstate travel; and that there had been errors in the introduction of certain evidence. Neither of those arguments received significant attention from the Court.

McKenna began his opinion with a sweeping reaffirmation of the power of Congress under the commerce clause: "The power is direct; there is no word of limitation in it, and its broad and universal scope has been so often declared as to make repetition unnecessary. And, besides, it has had so much illustration by cases that it would seem as if there could be no instance of its exercise that does not find an admitted example in some one of them."[72] That power, he emphasized, included the power to reach commerce that included the movement of people, as well as property. He acknowledged that individuals had the right to move between states; but that right, which he termed one "exercised in morality," could not be extended to include an act of immorality. Articles, and by extension people, with intrinsic immorality, could be excluded from commerce, as evidenced by federal laws against obscene literature and lottery tickets.[73] McKenna acknowledged the difficulties of making rules for a federal system, but he emphatically reasserted the power of the national government, even when that power reached motives:

> Our dual form of government has its perplexities, State and Nation having different spheres of jurisdiction, as we have said, but it must be kept in mind that we are one people; and the powers reserved to the States and those conferred on the Nation are adapted to be exercised, whether independently or concurrently, to promote the general welfare, material and moral. This is the effect of the decisions, and surely if the facility of interstate transportation can be taken away from the demoralization of lotteries, the debasement of obscene literature, the contagion of diseased cattle or persons, the impurity of food and drugs, the like facility can be taken away from the systematic enticement to and the enslavement in prostitution and debauchery of women, and, more insistently, of girls.[74]

For final support he pointed to another of the key Progressive measures, the Pure Food and Drug law; and, in language that would later prove troublesome, McKenna wrote: "Let an article be debased by adulteration, let it be misrepresented by false branding, and Congress may exercise its prohibitive power. It may be that Congress could not prohibit the manufacture of the article in a State. It may be that Congress could not prohibit in all of its

---

72. 227 U.S. at 320.
73. Ibid., 321. The same day the Court announced its opinion in *Hoke*, it also upheld a conviction for mailing obscene material in interstate commerce. The letter was said to be too obscene to be placed in the record; but, the Court held that not to be a violation of the defendant's right under the Sixth Amendment to be notified of the charges against him. *Bartell v. United States*, 227 U.S. 427 (1913).
74. 227 U.S. at 322.

conditions its sale within a State. But Congress may prohibit its transportation between the States, and by that means defeat the motive and evils of its manufacture."[75]

At the end of the term, in opinions occupying over two hundred pages of the Court's official reports, Justice Hughes reaffirmed the power of Congress over interstate commerce while also affirming the power of states to control commerce within their boundaries. So long as Congress had not acted, Hughes reasoned, states retained the power to regulate rates charged on intrastate transportation, even when those rates affected interstate commerce, because of the geographical boundaries of the state. The focal point of the opinions was a series of actions by the state of Minnesota between 1905 and 1907, with the legislature first ordering a study of rail rates and the state's railroad commission following with new rates. The initial federal court held the rates to be unconstitutional because of their effect on interstate commerce, even though limited to intrastate commerce.

Hughes sorted through the mass of detail and argument (there were two amicus briefs, one written by thirteen attorneys on behalf of eight states, in addition to two briefs filed on each side) to focus on two issues: whether the state's action was a direct burden on interstate commerce, and whether the state's action conflicted with the Interstate Commerce Act.[76] He insisted that the two issues were separate—the first depending upon the Constitution in the absence of any action by Congress, the second depending only upon an act of Congress. For the first, his principle was as broad as McKenna's in *Hoke:* "There is no room in our scheme of government for the assertion of state power in hostility to the authorized exercise of Federal power."[77] But in the absence of action by Congress, there remained a wide range of activities subject to state power, activities which could not be said to be unregulated because they might be reached by Congress at a later time. Hughes emphasized that Congress had discretion to decide whether to act or not; until it did, the states had the power to govern. In words he repeated twice, he emphasized that the government was "a practical adjustment by which the National authority as conferred by the Constitution is maintained in its full scope without unnecessary loss of local efficiency."[78]

With those principles articulated, Hughes turned to a history of the regulation of rates charged by railroads. Hughes noted that the Court had

---

75. Ibid., 322. McKenna relied on *Hipolite Egg,* one of the first decisions of the White Court, to support that statement. The problem with the language would appear when the Court considered the Child Labor Law in *Hammer v. Dagenhart,* 247 U.S. 251 (1918).
76. The issue would return to the Court in the *Shreveport Rate Cases (Houston and Texas Railway Co. v. United States),* 234 U.S. 342 (1914).
77. 230 U.S. at 399.
78. Ibid., 402. See also ibid., 431.

approved the setting of railroad rates by the states, beginning with the Granger effort to reduce rates in the 1870s: "The extension of railroad facilities has been accompanied at every step by the assertion of this authority on the part of the States and its invariable recognition by this court."[79] He rejected the argument that a railroad could immunize itself from regulation by constructing its tracks across state lines. The only restriction on the state power was the paramount power of Congress—"a limitation may not be implied because of a dormant Federal power, that is, one which has not been exerted, but can only be found in the actual exercise of Federal control in such measure as to exclude this action by the State which otherwise would clearly be within its province."[80]

The question therefore became whether Congress had taken over the field through enactment of the Interstate Commerce Act. Hughes pointed to provisions in the original act, and in amendments stating that the act did not apply to intrastate transportation. With those provisions in mind, Hughes saw no need to refer to legislative histories or other sources to support his conclusion that the states retained the power to regulate intrastate rates: "Having regard to the terms of the Federal statute, the familiar range of state action at the time it was enacted, the continued exercise of state authority in the same manner and to the same extent after its enactment, and the decisions of this court recognizing and upholding this authority, we find no foundation for the proposition that the Act to Regulate Commerce contemplated interference therewith."[81] Establishing that principle did not end Hughes's burden; he still had to deal with the challenge to the rates as being set so low as to be confiscatory. His opinion continued for another forty pages, replete with tables and computations, all evidencing the months of study he had devoted to the cases. In the end, some rates were held to be confiscatory, others not. But the important point was that, at least for the moment, the Court had affirmed the power of states to regulate intrastate commerce.

For the greater part of the term, however, the Court continued to strengthen the ties unifying the nation's commercial activity—affirming congressional power and curtailing encroachments by the states. That nationalism received visual emphasis two weeks after the Court adjourned for the summer. At the end of that fortnight, veterans from both the North and the South began to assemble at Gettysburg to commemorate the fiftieth anniversary of the battle. With attendance estimated as high as fifty thousand, the *New York Times* termed the event a "genuine national reunion."[82]

---

79. Ibid., 416.
80. Ibid., 417.
81. Ibid., 420.
82. *New York Times*, July 4, 1913.

Chief Justice Edward Douglass White.
Photographer unknown.
From the Collection of the Supreme Court of the United States.

Chief Justice Edward Douglass White.
Photograph by George Harris and Martha Ewing.
From the Collection of the Supreme Court of the United States.

Chief Justice White's Court, October 1911. Photograph by Barnell M. Clinedinst. From the Collection of the Supreme Court of the United States.

Chief Justice White's Court, October 1920. Photograph by Barnell M. Clinedinst. From the Collection of the Supreme Court of the United States.

Justice John Marshall Harlan.
Portrait by Pierre Troubetzkoy.
From the Collection of the Supreme
Court of the United States.

Justice Joseph McKenna.
Photograph by George Harris and
Martha Ewing.
From the Collection of the Supreme
Court of the United States.

Justice Oliver Wendell Holmes.
Portrait by Charles Sydney Hopkinson.
From the Collection of the Supreme
Court of the United States.

Justice William Rufus Day.
Portrait by Rolf Stoll.
From the Collection of the
Supreme Court of the United
States.

Justice Horace Lurton.
Portrait by C. Gregory Stapko.
From the Collection of the Supreme
Court of the United States.

Chief Justice Charles Evans Hughes.
Portrait by George Burroughs Torrey.
From the Collection of the Supreme
Court of the United States.

Justice Willis Van Devanter.
Portrait by Thomas E. Stephens.
From the Collection of the Supreme
Court of the United States.

Justice Joseph Rucker Lamar.
Portrait by Julian Lamar.
From the Collection of the Supreme
Court of the United States.

Justice Mahlon Pitney.
Portrait by Adrian Lamb.
From the Collection of the Supreme
Court of the United States.

Justice James Clark McReynolds.
Portrait by Bjorn Egeli.
From the Collection of the Supreme
Court of the United States.

Justice John Clarke.
Portrait by Edith S. Wright.
From the Collection of the Supreme Court of the United States.

Justice Louis Dembitz Brandeis.
Photograph by George Harris and Martha Ewing.
From the Collection of the Supreme Court of the United States.

IV

THE 1913–1914 TERM

In many ways the 1913–1914 term marked a turning point for the Court's recognition of the changes that had been bustling around it. There was, to be sure, no cataclysmic break with the past, no single case which marked a divide between the old America and the modern. Even an event as catastrophic as the sinking of the *Titanic* could be translated into the sterile language of the law. Faced with multiple suits in American courts, the owners of the *Titanic* sought refuge in an American statute that set a lower limit on liability than did British law. With only Justice McKenna disagreeing, the Court held that the owners could claim the limited liability. In Justice Holmes's understated opinion for the Court there was no hint that the sinking of the largest passenger liner built to that time symbolized misplaced faith in technology and grandeur. Instead, there was only this terse statement: "The facts stated are as follows, with slight abbreviation. The Titanic, a British steamship, which had sailed from Southampton, England, on her maiden voyage for New York, collided on the high seas with an iceberg, on April 14 [1912], and sank the next morning, with the loss of many lives and total loss of vessel, cargo, personal effects, mails and everything connected with the ship except certain life boats."[1]

Possibly Holmes, and the Court, felt that the event was so recent that the facts remained in the shared memory of the community. If so, the old America was still present, though in a less obvious way than in an opinion such as *Grannis v. Ordean*.[2] Like so many other cases on the docket of the White Court, the issue was a small one—whether a defendant had been given proper notice of a lawsuit. There was no principle involved, only the factual question of whether the misspelling of the defendant's surname was of constitutional importance. In accord with state law, the plaintiffs had published notices in a local newspaper and mailed a notice to the defendant's last

---

1. *Ocean Steam Navigation Co., Ltd. v. Mellor*, 233 U.S. 718, 730 (1914). Privately, Holmes had written with no more emotion, "Naturally we all have been thinking about the Titanic." Holmes to Pollock, April 26, 1912, Howe, *Holmes-Pollock Letters,* 192.
2. 234 U.S. 385 (1914).

address. Unfortunately, all of the notices misspelled the defendant's name, using "Guilfuss" instead of "Geilfuss." Rejecting literalism, the Court unanimously held that the published notice was sufficient to alert those who knew the real Mr. Geilfuss to tell him of the suit. Even more revealing of the old America was the Court's quaint confidence that a letter addressed to "Albert B. Guilfuss, Milwaukee, Wisconsin," would be delivered by the post office. In 1895, Milwaukee was a rapidly growing town of more than two hundred thousand people; its population had almost doubled in the previous decade. Nevertheless, as Justice Pitney explained, "In view of the well-known skill of postal officials and employés in making proper delivery of letters defectively addressed, we think the presumption is clear and strong that the letters would reach" the correct destination.[3]

Even so, there were signs that the justices had begun to recognize the changes within the nation. Ironically, the voice of that recognition was the Court's second oldest member, Justice McKenna. Early in the term McKenna emphasized continuity with the past in upholding a Montana tax on all insurance companies doing business within the state, *New York Life Insurance Co. v. Deer Lodge County*.[4] The state levied the tax on the excess of premiums over losses and expenses, using only amounts from within the state. New York Life argued that the tax was a burden on interstate commerce, noting that its risk pool was national, not local. The Court rejected that argument, pointedly recalling how often it had held that insurance was not commerce. Of possibly more importance was the explicit recognition of the importance of continuity with the past. "For over forty-five years," McKenna wrote, the Court's precedents had "been the legal justification for such [state] legislation. To reverse the cases, therefore, would require us to promulgate a new rule of constitutional inhibition upon the States and which would compel a change of their policy and a readjustment of their laws. Such result necessarily urges against a change of decision."[5] Even so, the Court condescended to review the precedents, in light of the "earnestness of counsel,"[6] one of whom was Roscoe Pound, then a professor at Harvard Law School and the acknowledged founder of the new method of legal analysis known as "sociological jurisprudence." The result was a reaffirmation: "A policy of insurance, the cases declare, is a personal contract, a mere indemnity, for a consideration, against the happening of some contingent event, which may bring detriment to life or property." The Court saw no relevance to the fact

---

3. Ibid., 397–98.
4. 231 U.S. 495 (1913).
5. Ibid., 502.
6. Ibid. McKenna ended his opinion with a similar comment, writing that he had "gone beyond the citing of the authoritative cases only in deference to the able and earnest argument of counsel" (512).

that in the years since the Civil War, insurance had come to be sold in every state, as well as in foreign countries. The "character of the contracts," McKenna declared, did not "change by their numbers or the residence of the parties."[7] Neither was it important that the company had outgrown the boundaries of a single state and had to use the mail to conduct its business.

Later in the term, however, the Court would reveal fissures in this homage to the past. In *German Alliance Insurance Co. v. Lewis*,[8] the justices split 5–3 in upholding the constitutionality of a 1909 Kansas statute that required fire insurance companies to subject their rates to approval by the state's superintendent of insurance.[9] Although both *Deer Lodge* and *German Alliance* upheld Progressive-era state laws, the division within the Court in *German Alliance* emphasized the justices' awareness that this opinion broke with the past.

The difference is all the more suggestive given the sequence in which the cases were decided. *Deer Lodge* was argued November 11, 1913, and decided December 15 of the same year. *German Alliance* was argued December 10, 1913, the Wednesday before the announcement of the opinion in *Deer Lodge*. Thus, even though the decision came in April 1914, *German Alliance* would have been discussed in the Saturday conference immediately preceding the announcement of the result in *Deer Lodge*. Moreover, Justice McKenna wrote the Court's opinion in both cases. It is therefore puzzling that he wrote *German Alliance* without referring to *Deer Lodge*.

In *German Alliance* McKenna rejected the contention that insurance was nothing more than a private contract, with each policy being based on individual risks—a contention he had appeared to accept in *Deer Lodge*. Instead, he noted that it was "a matter of common knowledge" that insurance rates were based on general rules, of which a regulatory body could be as knowledgeable as could the parties.[10] Given that characteristic, the question for McKenna became whether the "business of insurance was so far affected with a public interest as to justify legislative regulation of its rates?"[11] Anticipating what would be heard from the dissenters, McKenna conceded that in "some degree the public interest is concerned in every transaction between men, the sum of the transactions constituting the activities of life. But there is something more special than this, something of more definite consequence, which makes the public interest that justifies regulatory legislation. We can best explain by examples."[12] In moving from his "matter of common knowledge" to "examples," McKenna straddled the nineteenth and twentieth centuries.

---

7. Ibid., 508–9.
8. 233 U.S. 389 (1914).
9. Justice Lurton did not participate, on account of illness.
10. 233 U.S. at 406.
11. Ibid.
12. Ibid.

But he was not quite prepared to make a complete break, for his examples were taken from decisions of the Court, not from the world in operation. In so doing, McKenna was following in the footsteps of Christopher Columbus Langdell, who as dean of the Harvard Law School had reshaped American legal education with his belief "that law is a science, and that all the available materials of that science are contained in printed books."[13] McKenna's "common knowledge" was akin to White's "context"—something known or knowable from the font of knowledge shared by all in a society. Both McKenna and White were moving away from a strict, deductive formalism; but neither was prepared to make a complete shift to studied, inductive reasoning. For the moment, both were content to rely on a body of knowledge that could reside in the common experience of judges.

So, when McKenna turned to his "examples" he looked first to *Munn v. Illinois*,[14] the classic statement of the power of government to regulate railroads as a business "affected with the public interest." He portrayed the conflict in *Munn* as one between, on the one hand, a "conservatism of the mind, which puts to question every new act of regulating legislation and regards the legislation [as] invalid or dangerous until it has become familiar," and, on the other hand, "government—state and National—[which] has pressed on in the general welfare." From that conflict had emerged a multitude of judicial decisions "where in instance after instance the exercise of regulation was resisted and yet sustained against attacks asserted to be justified by the Constitution of the United States. The dread of the moment having passed, no one is now heard to say that rights were restrained or their constitutional guaranties impaired."[15] After tracing a series of cases following *Munn*, he concluded: "The cases need no explanatory or fortifying comment. They demonstrate that a business, by circumstances and its nature, may rise from private to be of public concern and be subject, in consequence, to governmental regulation. . . . It would be a bold thing to say that the principle is fixed, inelastic, in the precedents of the past and cannot be applied though modern economic conditions may make necessary or beneficial its application."[16]

From those general principles he turned to specific examples of regulation of insurance, beginning as early as 1837. From then to McKenna's present, insurance had come to protect "a large part of the country's wealth."[17] He accepted as fact what he found in the familiar reports of judicial decisions

---

13. Quoted in Robert Stevens, *Law School: Legal Education in America from the 1850s to the 1980s* (Chapel Hill: University of North Carolina Press, 1983), 53. See also Paul D. Carrington, "Hail! Langdell!" *Law & Social Inquiry* 20 (summer 1995): 691–760.
14. 94 U.S. 113 (1876).
15. 233 U.S. at 409.
16. Ibid., 411.
17. Ibid., 413.

and enactments of state legislatures. He had no need to extend his search to the world of economists who wrote of what he termed the "substitution of certain for uncertain loss." Neither did he have to explore the "diffusion of positive loss over a large group of persons," though he knew that to be an effect of insurance. In short, McKenna was satisfied that material from his familiar world could show that insurance was now "a matter of public concern to regulate it." He did, though, appear to reject his own statement in *Deer Lodge* that the "character of contracts" did not "change by their numbers." For now he wrote with a hopeful "therefore": "Contracts of insurance, therefore, have greater public consequence than contracts between individuals to do or not to do a particular thing whose effect stops with the individuals."[18]

McKenna must have appreciated that he stood at a turning point between the past of individuals and the future of groups. But he refused to back away, emphasizing that "private" was the antithesis of "the public interest." Yet he could still describe "the ordinary businesses of the commercial world" as being "independent and individual, terminating in their effect with the instances." Insurance contracts were different, "interdependent."[19] The atomistic, nineteenth-century world of *Deer Lodge* met the organizational, modern world of the twentieth century.[20]

McKenna rejected as hyperbole suggestions that the Court's holding meant that government could regulate every aspect of human conduct, ultimately reaching the price of every item offered for sale. The possibility of regulating "price" represented the most apocalyptic of fears in the discussion among the justices. For price represented the most private of all elements of contract, the keystone in the arch of contract law. In previous terms the White Court had struggled with attempts by patent holders to control the resale price for their goods. The employers' liability cases had seen recitals of the respect shown to wages, the "price" presumptively negotiated between employer and employee to account for working conditions. To assuage fears, McKenna now offered reassurances of his sensitivity to making dramatic changes (though without referring to his apt language in *Deer Lodge*). He pointed to the history of insurance regulation, from which his examples had come. The novelty of regulation of price was no argument against its validity. After all, he noted, "[t]he power to regulate interstate commerce existed for a century before the Interstate Commerce Act was passed, and the Commission constituted by it was not given authority to fix rates until some years afterwards." Reflecting an almost Roosevelt-like view that big business required big

---

18. Ibid.
19. Ibid., 414.
20. For an essay on the distinction between "public" and "private," see Morton J. Horwitz, "The History of the Public/Private Distinction," *University of Pennsylvania Law Review* 130 (June 1982): 1423–28. The essay is part of a symposium devoted to the distinction.

government to control it, McKenna suggested that regulation "was exerted only when the size, number and influence of those agencies had so increased and developed as to seem to make it imperative."[21]

Justice Lamar, joined by Chief Justice White and Justice Van Devanter, could not accept McKenna's prophesy of the future. In fact, Lamar was so distressed that he responded with one of the only eight dissents he wrote during his five years on the Court.[22] The case, he began bluntly, "relates solely to the power of the State to fix the price of a strictly personal contract."[23] In that characterization, the regulation by Kansas represented a sharp break with the past. Fixing the price of a private exchange was equivalent to taking property in an eminent domain proceeding. He warned that "it must inevitably follow that the price to be paid for any service or the use of any property can be regulated by the General Assembly." He concluded with this further prediction of the loss of all that was important to nineteenth-century American law, if not to all nineteenth-century Americans: "[I]f this power be as extensive as is now, for the first time, decided, then the citizen holds his property and his individual right of contract and of labor under legislative favor rather than under constitutional guaranty."[24] Within the constraints of the judicial office, that statement was the equivalent, though from the opposite political spectrum, of Roosevelt's invocation of Armageddon some two years earlier. Turning to the merits of the dispute, Lamar began with the principle affirmed by McKenna in *Deer Lodge:* Insurance was not commerce; it was a private, personal contract, which, by definition, could not be "public." The Court's conclusion to the contrary was "not a mere entering wedge, but reaches the end from the beginning and announces a principle which points inevitably to the conclusion that the price of every article sold and the price of every service offered can be regulated by statute."[25]

Lamar responded to McKenna's history of insurance by conceding that there had been regulation; but Lamar found it telling that rates had never been controlled. In that history there was but one exception to the rule that rate-making statutes "related to a business which was public in its character

---

21. 233 U.S. at 415–16.
22. See Lamar, *The Life of Joseph Rucker Lamar,* 204. The complete list of cases in which he wrote dissents is this: *Quong Wing v. Kirkendall,* 223 U.S. 59 (1912); *Diaz v. United States,* 223 U.S. 442 (1912); *Pedersen v. Delaware, Lackawanna & Western Railroad Co.,* 229 U.S. 146 (1913); *German Alliance Ins. Co. v. Lewis,* 233 U.S. 389 (1914); *Wheeler v. Sohmer,* 233 U.S. 434 (1914); *United States v. Holte,* 236 U.S. 140 (1915); *Greenleaf Johnson Lumber Co. v. Garrison,* 237 U.S. 251 (1915); *United States v. Mosley,* 238 U.S. 383 (1915).
23. 233 U.S. at 419.
24. Ibid.
25. Ibid., 420.

and employed visible and tangible property which had been devoted to a public use."[26] By emphasizing the intangible character of insurance, Lamar focused on a second destructive characteristic of the case. The first had been the regulation of price, which both McKenna and Lamar discussed at length. But Lamar alone touched on the intangible nature of insurance. In doing so, he intimated an appreciation for the broader intellectual life of the early twentieth century, with its struggle to come to grips with elusive concepts such as relativity and the subconscious. But Lamar was not prepared to venture into conceptual speculation that might equate the intangible with the tangible. Instead, he focused on practical consequences. If insurance could be regulated merely because of its size, Lamar warned, then no part of the nation's economy would be exempt, pointing to farming and labor as examples. If that were to happen, then regulation would "destroy the right of private property and break down the barriers which the Constitution has thrown around the citizen to protect him in his right of property."[27]

The struggle to distinguish between public and private reverberated throughout the Progressive era. As the opinions in *German Alliance* had shown, the words *public* and *private* often were little more than the conclusions that followed an arduous train of reasoning. Lamar himself found it difficult to maintain the distinction. For example, in this same term he wrote the Court's opinion upholding the conviction of a railroad for hauling hay it owned but did not use, in violation of the Commodities Clause of the Hepburn Act.[28] This regulation was not, according to Lamar, a taking of "private" property, because the railroad was a "public" carrier. Beyond that question-begging assertion lay this explanation: "If such carrier hauls for the public and also for its own private purposes, there is an opportunity to discriminate in favor of itself against other shippers in the rate charged, the facility furnished or the quality of the service rendered."[29] Without mentioning it, Lamar had returned to Van Devanter's concept from *Southern Railway* that parts of a railroad were "interdependent." In that light, the Commodities Clause was nothing more than an effort by the federal government to prevent a conflict of interest from harming the public.

Although the justices had split in *German Alliance,* in general they still manifested a shared desire to maintain the states as established constitutional categories. But the boundaries of those categories continued to be permeable. Taxes, for example, had considerable leeway in reaching beyond

---

26. Ibid., 425.
27. Ibid., 430–31.
28. *Delaware, Lackawanna & Western Railroad Co. v. United States,* 231 U.S. 363 (1913). For the text of the clause, see 231 U.S. at 369. Act of June 29, 1906, ch. 3591, 34 Stat. 585.
29. 231 U.S. at 370.

state borders. A good example of that agreement comes from a decision announced only two weeks before *German Alliance*—*Browning v. City of Waycross*.[30] One E. A. Browning challenged an annual tax imposed by a municipal ordinance on lightning rod dealers, arguing that it interfered with interstate commerce. Browning portrayed himself as merely the agent for a St. Louis corporation, selling in Georgia for direct delivery from Missouri. Browning contended that there was but a single contract, for delivery *and* installation. The Court, through Chief Justice White, rejected that portrayal, just as it had done in *Banker Brothers,* when a car dealer claimed to be the agent for the manufacturer. Now the Court held that installation of lightning rods on houses was a local act, occurring after interstate commerce had ended. The parties could not, by contract, alter the intrastate character of the transaction. The tax, therefore, did not burden interstate commerce, even though all the materials came from other states. Then, as though to show that he was as capable as Lamar of apocalyptic vision, White added this gratuitous observation: "It is manifest that if the right here asserted were recognized or the power to accomplish by contract what is here claimed, were to be upheld, all lines of demarkation between National and state authority would become obliterated."[31]

The Court reached an apparently different conclusion when a question arose about a state's power to tax a corporation's capital stock regardless of where the owners of the stock held the certificates. In *Baltic Mining Co. v. Massachusetts,*[32] the Court reasoned that the tax was not on the property itself; rather, the tax was an excise tax that used the property as a measure. Likewise, in *Wheeler v. Sohmer* the Court upheld New York's power to tax promissory notes found in a safe deposit box in that state, even though the deceased owner was not a resident, and neither was the maker of the notes.[33] *Wheeler* was the most fractured opinion of the term, with only three justices supporting the judgment of the Court (an opinion written by Holmes, joined by Day and Hughes). McKenna, along with Pitney, concurred in the result but not the reasoning; and Lamar dissented, joined by White and Van Devanter. Holmes concluded that the state had the power to tax the notes on account of their situs in New York. McKenna did not accept that conclusion; instead, he reasoned that the state had the power to tax the transfer of property at death, even though it did not have the power to tax the property itself. The dissenters believed that the same principles applied to taxation of property as to taxation of inheritance; accordingly, New York should not have the power to tax these notes.

---

30. 233 U.S. 16 (1914).
31. Ibid., 23.
32. 231 U.S. 68 (1913).
33. 233 U.S. 434 (1914).

Other regulations were not so fortunate, finding themselves fenced by state lines. White himself reiterated the concerns in another insurance company case decided near the end of the term, *New York Life Insurance Co. v. Head*.[34] At issue in *Head* was a Missouri statute that required life insurance companies to retain a certain percentage of any cash value of a policy. Under the Missouri law, in the event of a default in payment the retained amount would be used to maintain the policy in force by paying the premiums as long as possible. The policy itself provided that New York law would apply; and New York did not require a company to retain any amount. White put aside any question of where the contract had been made, assuming that it was made in Missouri. The question then became whether Missouri could regulate *all* dealings under that contract. In explaining his conclusion that Missouri could not, White characterized the insurance contract as one "concerning a particular subject-matter not in its essence intrinsically and inherently local,"[35] which seems to reflect his agreement with Lamar in *German Alliance* that insurance was intangible. In White's terms, the issue was whether Missouri could prohibit a contract modification from being made in New York "simply because it modified a contract originally made in Missouri."[36] As was his style, White asserted that the statement of the issue provided the answer: "Such question, we think, admits of but one answer since it would be impossible to permit the statutes of Missouri to operate beyond the jurisdiction of that State and in the State of New York and there destroy freedom of contract without throwing down the constitutional barriers by which all the States are restricted within the orbits of their lawful authority and upon the preservation of which the Government under the Constitution depends."[37] The Court reached a similar conclusion in *Western Union Telegraph Co. v. Brown* when it held that a state could not impose its tort law in another jurisdiction to permit recovery when the other jurisdiction would not allow recovery.[38]

The Court did not, however, invalidate all state laws that might affect interstate commerce. It upheld a regulation of locomotive headlamps, saying that Congress could resolve any conflict that might arise from inconsistent state regulations.[39] The Court also allowed states to fix rates charged by passenger ferries operating on waters between two states, with emphasis on the fact that the states had regulated the rates for more than a century (with the implicit concurrent fact that Congress had *not* regulated the

---

34. 234 U.S. 149 (1914).
35. Ibid., 161.
36. Ibid.
37. Ibid.
38. 234 U.S. 542 (1914).
39. *Atlantic Coast Line Railroad Co. v. Georgia*, 234 U.S. 280 (1914).

rates).[40] The states were not, however, free to require a license of the same ferries. As Justice Hughes explained in the latter case, one otherwise qualified could not "be compelled to take out a local license for the mere privilege of carrying on interstate or foreign commerce."[41]

The Court found it equally frustrating to attempt to draw lines about the power of Congress, especially when the ICC attempted to reach within a state to regulate some aspect of commerce. Thus, in one of the most significant decisions of the White Court, *Houston, East & West Texas Railway Co. v. United States* (the *Shreveport Rate Cases*),[42] the Court upheld the ICC's requirement that rates within Texas not be less than rates charged for the same distance from the same point to Shreveport, Louisiana. That requirement arose out of a complaint filed with the ICC by the Railroad Commission of Louisiana. The state commission pointed out that Shreveport competed with two Texas cities, Houston and Dallas, for traffic out of eastern Texas. Within that area of competition, the state commission argued, the railroads favored the Texas cities by charging lower rates to and from them than for similar distances to Shreveport. The ICC found that the rates for westbound traffic out of Shreveport were unreasonably high. Accordingly, the ICC set maximum rates for that traffic—which the ICC clearly had the power to do, since the traffic was all interstate. Those rates, which the ICC declared to be reasonable, were still higher than the rates charged within Texas and approved by the Texas railroad commission. To combat that problem the ICC held that the intrastate rates amounted to unfair discrimination against Shreveport and ordered the railroads not to charge higher rates for Shreveport traffic than for intrastate traffic. In short, the ICC backed into ordering that intrastate rates be increased.

When the case reached the Supreme Court, argument focused on two issues: (1) whether Congress's constitutional power over interstate commerce could reach these intrastate rates; and (2) whether the statutory delegation of power to the ICC allowed the commission to regulate the intrastate rates. To resolve those issues, Chief Justice White assigned the opinion to Justice Hughes, who had written the opinions in the *Minnesota Rate Cases* and other highly technical cases. Hughes showed that he appreciated that the real controversy was one between the states of Texas and Louisiana. "Interstate trade," he wrote, "was not left to be destroyed or impeded by the rivalries of local governments."[43] And, reusing an image he had created in the *Minnesota Rate Cases*,

---

40. *Port Richmond & Bergen Point Ferry Co. v. Board of Chosen Freeholders of Hudson County*, 234 U.S. 317 (1914).
41. *City of Sault Ste. Marie v. International Transit Co.*, 234 U.S. 333, 341 (1914).
42. 234 U.S. 342 (1914).
43. Ibid., 350.

he explained that the purpose of Congress's plenary power over interstate commerce "was to make impossible the recurrence of the evils which had overwhelmed the Confederation and to provide the necessary basis of national unity."[44] Few could have missed the dual image thus invoked—the Confederation of 1781 and the Confederacy of 1861. From there, Hughes showed how the Court had reaffirmed Congress's power, building on the *Second Employers' Liability Cases,* the *Minnesota Rate Cases,* and *Southern Railway.* The result was a sweeping affirmation that Congress's power reached "all matters having such a close and substantial relation to interstate traffic that the control is essential or appropriate to the security of that traffic."[45] He knew full well what that statement meant: further erasure of state borders as barriers to congressional regulation. But, as though to reassure, he added, "[T]his is not to say that Congress possesses the authority to regulate the internal commerce of a state, as such." But Congress could "foster and protect interstate commerce."[46]

Once he defended the power of Congress, Hughes moved on to consider the power delegated to the ICC. With a brief quotation from a Senate report, he supported his statement that the purpose of the original 1887 interstate commerce act was to prevent discrimination in rates. Since the ICC had determined that there was discrimination, Hughes announced that the act was clearly intended to apply to situations such as this. With that conclusion, Hughes explained that the purpose of the act overrode a provision stating that the act would not apply to transportation "wholly within one State." In Hughes's words, "Wherever the interstate and intrastate transactions of carriers are so related that the government of the one involves the control of the other, it is Congress, and not the State, that is entitled to prescribe the final and dominant rule, for otherwise Congress would be denied the exercise of its constitutional authority and the State, and not the Nation, would be supreme within the national field."[47]

Yet, after the Hepburn Act of 1906 gave the ICC the power to regulate rates charged by pipelines, the Court held that the ICC could not reach a company that pumped oil from its own well, across a state line, to its own refinery. The statute used the now familiar language to define its reach—to anyone "engaged in the transportation of oil." But instead of using only the word *interstate,* the statute added that the transporter must be a "common carrier." The Court, through Justice Holmes, saw no reason to provide any further expla-

---

44. Ibid.
45. Ibid., 351.
46. Ibid., 353.
47. Ibid., 351–52. The full statutory provision is quoted in the opinion at 355–57. See also, Act of June 29, 1906, ch. 3591, 34 Stat. 584; Act of June 18, 1910, ch. 309, 36 Stat. 539, 545.

nation: "The circumstances in which the amendment was passed are known to every one."[48] In essence, the act was another skirmish in the battle against Rockefeller's Standard Oil Company, this time in its guise as controller of much of the transportation of oil in the country. The company required that anyone who wanted to send oil through its pipelines had to sell the oil to the company. Thus, the company would argue that it was not transporting oil for others, but only for itself. Based on his personal knowledge of legislative history, Holmes found no difficulty in holding that "common carrier" did not mean "common carrier in a technical sense."[49] Instead, the clause meant that those who transported oil were to be considered common carriers. The sale of oil to Standard Oil did not change the character. But not even Holmes was willing to allow the statute to apply to a company that pumped oil from its own well, across a state line, to its own refinery. Reflecting the same concerns that had animated the opinions in *German Alliance,* Justice Holmes wrote, "It would be a perversion of language, considering the sense in which it is used in the statute, to say that a man was engaged in the transportation of water whenever he pumped a pail of water from his well to his house."[50] Holmes seemed not to distinguish between the likely consumption of the water in the house and the probability that the oil would not be used at the refinery. Similarly, neither Holmes nor the Court seemed to recall the cases dealing with foreign commerce, in which the Court had held that foreign commerce began just as soon as the transportation began. Thus, one would have thought that pumping oil from a well would begin the interstate transportation of the oil, even if it did have to come to rest within a state while being refined before it could continue its journey. Neither did anyone recall the Court's holding that a railroad's fireman was engaged in interstate commerce when he was oiling an engine in preparation for taking it on an interstate journey.[51]

White concurred but noted that Holmes's exception made no sense. The company was plainly engaged in interstate transportation. But, because it used only its own oil, White explained, it was "engaged in a purely private business."[52] As such, the only way Congress could regulate its rates was to use eminent domain to take the company.

Justice McKenna dissented. He thought there was no showing that the pipeline companies had dedicated their property to the public. In his view,

---

48. *Pipe Line Cases,* 234 U.S. 548, 558 (1914).
49. Ibid., 560.
50. Ibid., 562.
51. *North Carolina Railroad Co. v. Zachary,* 232 U.S. 248 (1914). By contrast, a fireman was not engaged in interstate commerce while working on a switch engine within New Orleans, even though part of the task would involve handling cars that would be moved in interstate commerce. *Illinois Central Railroad Co. v. Behrens,* 233 U.S. 473 (1914).
52. 234 U.S. at 563.

voluntary dedication was essential to the holdings in prior cases, from *Munn* to *German Alliance*. The statute was therefore unconstitutional. That the companies had become dominant in the transportation of oil was of no consequence—it merely showed that they benefited from one of the essential characteristics of property, exclusive possession. To take that away, McKenna asserted, was to "take all that there is of property."[53] He resisted suggesting dire consequences from the decision, saying, "Alarms . . . are not arguments, and I grant that legislation must be practical."[54]

Holmes's interpretation, based solely on the language of the statute, continued to be the usual practice of the Court when dealing with statutory construction. But there were growing signs that the faith in words was weakening. For example, the Court was content to rely on common experience to support its conclusion that a mining company was engaged in business for purposes of the Corporation Tax Act of 1909.[55] The mining company had argued that it was not carrying on a business; rather, it was wasting its capital assets by mining the ore. It characterized the act as one designed to tax income; and, since the company had no income (only capital), it could not be taxed. The Court used a familiar image to explain its rejection of the argument, that the tax was not one on income, but an excise tax. In explaining that conclusion, Pitney returned to McKenna's disclaimer in *German Alliance*. The justices, Pitney explained, were "little aided by a discussion of theoretical distinctions between capital and income. Such refinements can hardly be deemed to have entered into the legislative purpose."[56] Without referring to any congressional materials, Pitney explained that the Court sought "the correct interpretation and construction of an act of legislation that was, at least, designed to furnish a practicable mode of raising revenue for the support of the Government."[57] Once again, though, the practicable was defined by the experienced.

Likewise, in *United States v. Antikamnia Chemical Co.* the Court held that the Food and Drug Act required labels to list derivatives of drugs as well as the drugs themselves, even though the words of the act expressed no such requirement.[58] Without having statutory language to support its conclusion, the Court relied on the purpose of the act: "to secure the purity of food and drugs and to inform purchasers of what they are buying."[59] Once again there

---

53. Ibid., 571.
54. Ibid., 575.
55. *Stratton's Independence, Ltd. v. Howbert*, 231 U.S. 399 (1913). The tax act was section 38 of the Tariff Act of August 5, 1909, ch. 6, 36 Stat. 11, 112. The Court had upheld the constitutionality of the act in *Flint v. Stone Tracy Co.*, 220 U.S. 107 (1911).
56. 231 U.S. at 414.
57. Ibid., 420.
58. 231 U.S. 654 (1914).
59. Ibid., 665.

was no citation of congressional materials, only the Court's assertion. That assertion, combined with a sense of helplessness in the face of "the ever increasing powers of the laboratory or the disguises of a technical nomenclature,"[60] impelled the Court to conclude that the purpose of the statute could not be met without including derivatives in the labeling requirement.

The Court did, however, begin to show small signs of a willingness to look outside its shared memory by examining certain congressional materials. For example, in another case involving the Food and Drug Act, the Court quoted a statement by one of the bill's sponsors in the Senate. The purpose of the quotation was to support the Court's reasoning that the government did not have to prove that an additive would cause injury, only that it "may" do so.[61] As Justice Day explained for the Court: "This is the plain meaning of the words and in our view needs no additional support by reference to reports and debates, although it may be said in passing that the meaning which we have given to the statute was well expressed by Mr. Heyburn, chairman of the committee having it in charge upon the floor of the Senate."[62] Likewise, Day also quoted the chair of the House Judiciary Committee to support a conclusion about a provision in an act dealing with fees charged by court clerks for filing records on appeal.[63] But debates on the floor were not acceptable. As Justice Pitney wrote, "the unreliability of such debates as a source from which to discover the meaning of the language employed in an act of Congress has been frequently pointed out . . . and we are not disposed to go beyond the reports of the committees."[64]

By the end of the term, the Court had handed down 293 opinions, the largest number in any term during White's tenure as chief justice. The Court achieved that record in spite of the fact that Justice Lurton was absent from December 3, 1913, to April 6, 1914, on account of illness. That he was not working at full strength at any time during the term is evident from the fact that he wrote only five opinions for the Court. Justice Lamar, who had celebrated his fifty-sixth birthday on the day the term began, was also ailing. He wrote only nineteen opinions for the Court during the term. Thus, the record output was achieved through the efforts of only seven justices, with White and Holmes again in the lead. In spite of that output, there was a continuing perception that elderly judges posed a problem, as evidenced by a proposal from Wilson's attorney general, James C. McReynolds, in his annual report dated

---

60. Ibid., 666.
61. *United States v. Lexington Mill & Elevator Co.*, 232 U.S. 399 (1914).
62. Ibid., 411.
63. *Rainey v. W. R. Grace & Co.*, 231 U.S. 703, 707 (1914).
64. *Lapina v. Williams*, 232 U.S. 78 (1914). The case dealt with the Immigration Act of 1907 and the meaning of *immigrants*. See also *Lewis v. Frick*, 233 U.S. 291 (1914). The Court also rejected use of list circulated by supporters of a bill to show which yachts would be taxed if the bill became law. *United States v. Goelet*, 232 U.S. 293, 298 (1914).

December 1, 1913. As was customary, the attorney general used the occasion to recommend new laws and other changes. Now, with the first opportunity for a Democratic administration in the twentieth century, McReynolds made this his first recommendation: "I suggest an act providing when any judge of a Federal court below the Supreme Court fails to avail himself of the privilege of retiring now granted by law, that the President be required, with the advice and consent of the Senate, to appoint another judge, who shall preside over the affairs of the court and have precedence over the older one. This will insure at all times the presence of a judge sufficiently active to discharge promptly and adequately the duties of the court."[65] Holmes, at seventy-two, and McKenna, who turned seventy two months before, were the only justices who would have triggered that provision, had it applied to the Supreme Court. With an average age now of sixty-two, the Court afforded less opportunity for criticism on account of the justices' ages. Even so, with Lurton seriously ill and Lamar showing signs of weakening, the Court continued to suffer from an inability of all nine justices to contribute equally. The effect on White was evident in his correspondence with the president of the University of Notre Dame, Rev. John W. Cavanaugh, C.S.C. Late in March the University notified White that he would receive the Laetare Medal. The *Catholic News* reported that the medal was "the most important distinction which a Catholic layman in this country can receive."[66] White wrote Cavanaugh to thank him, but declined the invitation to travel to Notre Dame to receive the award. White's letter was almost desperate in explaining his plight: "It is difficult for one unfamiliar with the situation in which I am placed to understand the circumstances by which I am environed and the absolute and imperative demands which are made upon my time during all the waking and a large part of the sleeping hours."[67] When the university repeated its invitation, White again declined, reporting that even the final argument for the term did not end the press of business, but only began "a week of the hardest kind of work."[68]

---

65. *Annual Report for 1913*, 5. McReynolds had explained the need for the act in these words: "Judges of United States courts, at the age of seventy, after having served 10 years, may retire upon full pay. In the past many judges have availed themselves of this privilege. Some, however, have remained upon the bench long beyond the time when they were capable of adequately discharging their duties, and in consequence the administration of justice has suffered. The power of Congress to correct this condition is limited by the provision of the Constitution that judges shall hold their offices during good behavior." McReynolds's successor, T. W. Gregory, repeated the recommendation, verbatim, in his report the next year. *Annual Report for 1914*, 10. Gregory repeated the recommendation in 1915. *Annual Report for 1915*, 9.
66. *Catholic News*, March 28, 1914 (clipping in collection UDIS, folder 129/01, University of Notre Dame Archives). See also *New York Times*, March 22, 1914.
67. White to Cavanaugh, May 12, 1914, Correspondence of Rev. John W. Cavanaugh, C.S.C., folder 3/21, University of Notre Dame Archives.
68. Ibid., June 4, 1917.

V

THE 1914–1915 TERM

When the Court assembled for the 1914–1915 term on October 12, James Clark McReynolds took the place of Justice Lurton, who had died during the summer. Of all the appointments to the Supreme Court during White's tenure, that of McReynolds is the most difficult to understand.[1] To be sure, his predecessor, Lurton, received his nomination solely on the basis of an especially close friendship with the president; but, at least of Lurton it could be said that he was an experienced judge who was courteous to all. Lurton, the former Confederate soldier, had even won the friendship of Justice Harlan, the former Union soldier, who was never able to forget his differences with Chief Justice White. Harlan and Lurton, however, were both members of the Beta Theta Pi fraternity (along with Lamar and Van Devanter).[2] In addition, Harlan and Lurton often joined Justice McKenna in playing golf.[3] Nothing of the kind could be said of Lurton's fellow Tennessean, McReynolds. Indeed, it seems probable that President Wilson nominated McReynolds to the Supreme Court to rid his cabinet of its most choleric member.[4]

---

1. McReynolds is generally rated as one of the "failures" among justices. See Blaustein and Mersky, *The First One Hundred Justices,* 48. On McReynolds in general, see Robert H. Birkby, "Teaching Congress How to Do Its Work: Mr. Justice McReynolds and Maritime Torts," *Congressional Studies* 8 (1981): 11–20; James E. Bond, *I Dissent: The Legacy of Chief Justice James Clark McReynolds* (Fairfax, Va.: George Mason University Press, 1992) ("Chief Justice" is a misprint); Doris Ariane Blaisdell, "The Constitutional Law of Mr. Justice McReynolds" (Ph.D. diss., University of Wisconsin, 1954); Stirling P. Gilbert, *James Clark McReynolds, 1862–1946: Justice of the Supreme Court of the United States of America* (1946), microform, Pamphlets in American History, Biography, B1517; Stephen Tyree Early, "James Clark McReynolds and the Judicial Process" (Ph.D. diss., University of Virginia, 1954); Robert V. Fletcher, "Mr. Justice McReynolds—An Appreciation," *Vanderbilt Law Review* 2 (1948): 35–46; Calvin P. Jones, "Kentucky's Irascible Conservative: Supreme Court Justice James Clark McReynolds," *Filson Club History Quarterly* 57 (January 1983): 20–30; Schimmel, "The Judicial Policy of Mr. Justice McReynolds."
2. *New York Times,* February 10, 1911.
3. Ibid., April 4, 1910.
4. Josephus Daniels, *The Wilson Era: Years of Peace—1910–1917* (Chapel Hill: University of North Carolina Press, 1944), 540; William Gibbs McAdoo, *Crowded Years: The Reminiscences of*

McReynolds was born in Elkton, Kentucky, on February 3, 1862. His father was a well-respected doctor; his mother a member of a prominent local family.[5] When McReynolds left home in 1879 to attend Vanderbilt University in Nashville, Tennessee, he had never been more than a hundred miles from home.[6] His remarkable success at Vanderbilt culminated with his graduating first in his class in 1882. Chosen by the members of his class to deliver the valedictory address, McReynolds presaged much of his judicial philosophy with this remark: "Competition is strong. . . . If success is to be ours, it must be had at the price of constant labor and exertion, and he who enters faint-hearted into the race need not expect to reach the goal."[7] McReynolds spent a fourth year at Vanderbilt, during which he served as editor in chief of the student newspaper and supplemented his B.S. degree with postgraduate work in natural history and geology. He then enrolled in the University of Virginia, where he attended a special summer session to enable him to earn his LL.B. degree in one year, graduating in 1884. Upon graduation, he returned to Nashville for a short time before leaving to become secretary to United States Senator Howell Jackson, of Tennessee. When Jackson was appointed federal circuit court judge in 1886, McReynolds moved back to Tennessee to practice law. He never achieved great success as a lawyer, though colleagues recalled that he was well respected as an adviser to other lawyers and to corporations.[8] At the end of the century, he returned to his alma mater as a professor of commercial law and insurance at Vanderbilt Law School, where Horace Lurton was also teaching.

McReynolds began his national service in 1903 when he joined the Justice Department as one of a number of new attorneys employed to enforce the Sherman Act. He served slightly more than three years, earning a reputation as a trustbuster, even a radical in his animosity toward trusts. He left to become a senior associate in the New York City firm Cravath, Henderson and De Gersdorff, but was soon called back to Washington as a special assistant to handle the *American Tobacco* case.[9] Although the government won the case, McReynolds refused to accept the compromise settlement negotiated by the attorney general, choosing instead to resign. He returned to private

---

William G. McAdoo (Boston: Houghton Mifflin, 1931), 183–84. For a survey of the literature on McReynolds's appointment, see McHargue, "Appointments to the Supreme Court of the United States," 410–15.

5. Schimmel, "The Judicial Policy of Mr. Justice McReynolds," 3.
6. Blaisdell, "The Constitutional Law of Mr. Justice McReynolds," 1.
7. Schimmel, "The Judicial Policy of Mr. Justice McReynolds," 30–31.
8. Blaisdell, "The Constitutional Law of Mr. Justice McReynolds," 20.
9. Robert T. Swaine, *The Cravath Firm and Its Predecessors: 1819–1948*, vol. 2, *The Cravath Firm Since 1906* (New York: Ad Press, 1948), 13. According to Swaine, McReynolds did not become a partner in the firm (x, xi, 13).

practice in New York City, this time as a sole practitioner. His support of Wilson in the 1912 election won him appointment as attorney general after Wilson decided he could not risk naming Louis Brandeis to such a prominent position.[10] In private letters Brandeis himself used words such as "excellent" and "first rate" to describe the prospect of McReynolds's service.[11] And, in a gracious letter to McReynolds, Brandeis wrote that Wilson had "made the wisest possible choice."[12] Shortly thereafter, Brandeis reported that he had had a useful and "cordial" meeting with McReynolds to discuss pending antitrust litigation.[13] In spite of the early praise, the appointment soon proved to be a mistake, with McReynolds becoming such a contentious member of the cabinet that he could not get along with any of his colleagues.[14] That divisiveness prompted Wilson to appoint McReynolds to the first available seat on the Supreme Court. In spite of the friction McReynolds created, he did have the support of one of Wilson's closest advisers, Colonel E. M. House.[15] Moreover, in 1914 he had the respect of many for his knowledge of antitrust laws.[16] Once on the Court, McReynolds joined Hughes as the only justices without prior judicial experience.[17]

To write merely that the Court "assembled" early in October is to be blind to international events. Justice Lamar had spent the first part of the summer in Niagara, Canada, as a member of the ABC Conference to mediate the festering dispute between the United States and the revolutionary government in Mexico, a dispute that had brought the United States to the brink of military intervention in the Mexican civil war. Lamar returned to the Court tired, possibly showing the early signs of the heart disease that would kill him within fifteen months.[18] The conference provided a brief respite before relations

---

10. Arthur S. Link, *Woodrow Wilson and the Progressive Era, 1910–1917* (New York: Harper & Brothers, 1954), 28, 30–31; Alpheus T. Mason, *Brandeis: A Free Man's Life* (New York: Viking Press, 1946), 385–94.
11. Brandeis to Moses Edwin Clapp, March 5, 1913; Brandeis to Gilson Gardner, March 5, 1913, in *Letters of Louis D. Brandeis*, vol. 3 (1913–1915), *Progressive and Zionist,* eds. Melvin I. Urofsky and David W. Levy (Albany: State University of New York Press, 1973), 39.
12. Brandeis to McReynolds, March 5, 1913, ibid., 41.
13. Strum, *Brandeis: Justice for the People,* 208.
14. McAdoo, *The Crowded Years,* 184; Daniels, *The Wilson Era: Years of Peace, 1910–1917,* 115, 540–41; *Literary Digest* 49 (September 1914): 405–6; *Green Bag* 26 (November 1914): 499; James Kerney, *The Political Education of Woodrow Wilson* (New York: Century Co., 1926), 296–97; *Lawyer and Banker* 9 (February 1916): 21.
15. Blaisdell, "The Constitutional Law of Mr. Justice McReynolds," 53–59.
16. See, for example, Burton J. Hendrick, "James C. McReynolds: Attorney-General and Believer in the Sherman Law," *World's Work* 27 (November 1913): 26.
17. The Senate confirmed McReynolds's nomination on August 29, 1914; he took the oath of office on September 5, 1914.
18. For an account of Lamar's service with former Solicitor General Frederick W. Lehmann, see Lamar, *The Life of Joseph Rucker Lamar,* 241–69.

between the two countries worsened. The United States would respond to raids by Pancho Villa in early 1916 by sending a force of almost seven thousand men, under General John J. Pershing, into Mexico to search for Villa. Relations between the two countries worsened in the first half of 1916, sometimes seeming to verge on outright war. Tension lessened in the summer only to worsen late in the year, until the United States's forces withdrew from Mexico in January 1917.[19] The initial relief felt when war with Mexico seemed averted after the ABC Conference was matched by pride when the Panama Canal opened on August 15, 1914. But both of those emotions were overshadowed by alarm at the outbreak of war in Europe on August 1. In the words of Arthur S. Link, "To say that the outbreak of the First World War in August, 1914, came as a shock to the American people would be to make an understatement of heroic proportions."[20] Although most Americans thought the war would not ensnare them, the United States continued involvement in Mexico and the spread of the war in Europe served as unsettling backdrops to the Court's term. Yet they were distant backdrops, with opinions giving nary a hint of the events.

Domestically, the news was equally foreboding. The United States economy was in the midst of its worst depression in two decades, a downturn that seemed to sap the reform movement of most of its energy. The congressional elections of 1914, with their resurgence of conservatives, appeared to confirm the lethargy. When the new Congress assembled in December 1915, Wilson produced a set of reform proposals rivaling his first year in office. But, for the moment, there was a lull in the domestic political life of the country, as the nation nervously watched events in Europe as well as those on its doorstep.

In that hiatus, the Court filled its 1914–1915 term. It would be too much to suggest that the turmoil in Europe and in Mexico had a direct effect on the Court's decisions during this term. In fact, it is important that the international tumult not conceal the truth that this was still a Court of nineteenth-century, rural America, where the post office could deliver a letter in a city of a quarter of a million when the envelope bore no more address than "C. Ferger, Indianapolis."[21] The envelope was part of a bankruptcy proceeding; the issue concerned the sufficiency of the address quoted to provide notice of the proceeding to Mr. Ferger. That the Court may have recognized conditions were changing is suggested by its remark that the issue was "one of those apparently simple questions which has been the occasion of an immense amount of controversy."[22] Echoing Justice Pitney from the term

---

19. See Link, *Woodrow Wilson and the Progressive Era, 1910–1917*, 107–44.
20. Ibid., 145.
21. *Kreitlein v. Ferger*, 238 U.S. 21 (1915).
22. Ibid., 28.

before, Justice Lamar wrote that "letters directed to persons by their initials are constantly, properly and promptly delivered in the greatest cities of the country even when the street number is not given."[23] That a change was in the wind, however, is indicated by Justice Day's disagreement with Lamar's conclusion. While acknowledging the ability of the post office to deliver mail, he insisted on the need to distinguish urban from rural addresses. "It seems to me," he wrote, "that the same rule in scheduling creditors cannot be applied to those who reside in large cities, where it may be essential in order that the creditor receive notice that street and number shall be given, as is applied to creditors residing in small communities where the postal authorities may be presumed to know the residence of the creditor by a more general form of address."[24]

Admittedly, the Court continued as it had, with an agenda set by others; and the agenda remained one defined by elections held two or more bienniums in the past. The cases on the Court's docket also continued to fall primarily under one or the other of familiar rubrics—interstate commerce and police power. The latter provided an amorphous guide to the powers inherent in state governments. The former represented the equally amorphous restriction imposed on those powers by the United States Constitution.

In some instances, however, the Court itself acknowledged that the rubrics were beginning to fade. The Court admitted as much in yet another of the cases involving the Federal Employers' Liability Act, which had proved to be so perplexing in prior terms. Here the rubric of interstate commerce served to constrain the reach of national power. If there was no interstate commerce, there could be no exercise of national power. As Justice Lamar explained, a dilemma arose "owing to the fact that, during the same day, railroad employés often and rapidly pass from one class of employment to another." As a result, he acknowledged, "the courts are constantly called upon to decide those close questions where it is difficult to define the line which divides the State from interstate business."[25] A macabre example of the difficulties came in *St. Louis, Iron Mountain & Southern Railway Co. v. Craft*.[26] The original suit sought damages for the deceased railway worker's father, his only heir, and for pain and suffering by the worker before he died. As the Court noted, the father's right to recover was recognized by the common law, so long as the father had been dependent upon the worker for financial benefits. Thus, other than restrictions on the defenses available to the employers, the act had not made major changes in the nature of the suits. The suit for the

---

23. Ibid., 33.
24. Ibid., 39. Justice McKenna joined the dissent.
25. *New York Central & Hudson River Railroad Co. v. Carr*, 238 U.S. 260 (1915).
26. 237 U.S. 648 (1915).

worker's personal injuries, however, harbored a significant change. Under the common law any personal right of action died with the deceased worker. As the Court well knew from its study of the act in the 1911 term, a 1910 amendment to the Federal Employers' Liability Act had changed that rule by providing that "any right of action given by this Act to a person suffering injury shall survive to his or her personal representative."[27] The issue the Court had to resolve, however, was whether the deceased worker had actually "suffered" injury between the time he was run over by a train car and the time he died. The Court noted that there was conflicting testimony as to whether the worker was conscious during the half hour before his death. Resolution of that conflict lay in the hands of the jury. "But," the Court added in further recognition of the difficulty of maintaining definitions, "to avoid any misapprehension it is well to observe that the case is close to the border line, for such pain and suffering as are substantially contemporaneous with death or mere incidents to it, as also the short periods of insensibility which sometimes intervene between fatal injuries and death, afford no basis for a separate estimation or award of damages under statutes like that which is controlling here."[28]

The Court also found itself pressed to redefine *commerce* as it concerned a federal tax on exports in *Thames and Mersey Marine Insurance Company, Ltd. v. United States.*[29] Again reflecting the lag in issues reaching the Court, at a time when most other eyes were on the First World War, the justices looked back to the Spanish-American War. This case involved the War Revenue Act of 1898, which had imposed a stamp tax on insurance policies covering exports against marine risks.[30] Thames & Mersey sought a refund of the tax paid, claiming that it amounted to a tax on exports, which the Constitution prohibited.[31] Although only a few months before, in *Deer Lodge,* the Court had declared that insurance was not commerce, it now concluded that a marine insurance policy was "an integral part of the exportation" of goods, adding the observation that "the business of the world is conducted upon this basis."[32] Then, joining the two wartime eras, Justice Hughes pointed for support to the War Risk Insurance Bureau, created by Congress in 1914 to provide government insur-

---

27. Ibid., 657. The amendment was an Act of April 5, 1910, ch. 143, 36 Stat. 291. Earlier in the 1914 term the Court had emphasized the importance of the amendment, saying that in the absence of the amendment, the employee's right to recover would not survive him, even when he lived for six hours after the accident. *Garrett v. Louisville & Nashville Railroad Co.,* 235 U.S. 308, 312 (1914).
28. 237 U.S. at 655. Later in the term the Court relied on *Craft* to dispose of a case in which the deceased worker had survived for less than two hours before dying. *Kansas City Southern Railway Co. v. Leslie,* 238 U.S. 599 (1915).
29. 237 U.S. 19 (1915).
30. Act of June 13, 1898, ch. 448, 30 Stat. 448.
31. U.S. Constitution, art. 1, sec. 9.
32. 237 U.S. at 26.

ance against the risks of war.[33] Seen in that light, the conclusion was inevitable: The tax on insurance was "as much a burden on exporting as if it were laid on the charter parties, the bills of lading, or the goods themselves. Such taxation does not deal with preliminaries, or with distinct or separable subjects; the tax falls upon the exporting process."[34]

The same commerce clause that allowed such an expansion of national powers also served to provide a boundary beyond which a state legislature might not go. Indeed, in one of the cases held over from the previous term, *Sioux Remedy Co. v. Cope*,[35] the Court struck down a South Dakota law that imposed restrictions on the right of foreign corporations to sue in state courts. As interpreted by the state's supreme court, the law required out-of-state corporations to submit to the jurisdiction of state courts before they could sue in those courts. That is, for a corporation to sue in state court, it first had to subject itself to *being sued* in state court. Most corporations preferred to litigate in federal courts, a process that both gave them a single body of law with which to deal and protected them from the more advanced stages of Progressive regulation. Thus, when sued (as a defendant) in state court, corporations would try to find a way to remove the dispute to federal court. On occasion, however, corporations had no choice but to sue (as a plaintiff) in state courts. The South Dakota law required that corporations chartered in other states had to give up the protection of federal courts if they wanted to sue in the state courts. The case arose from an effort by the Sioux Remedy Company to recover payment for merchandise it had shipped from Iowa to F. M. Cope in South Dakota. The state courts refused to allow the company to pursue the remedy, noting that it had failed to comply with the law. The Supreme Court held that the denial of access to the state courts was an interference with interstate commerce. Reflecting the expanding boundaries of the concept "interstate commerce," announced by Hughes in the *Shreveport Rate Cases* and his own opinion in *Southern Railway,* Justice Van Devanter explained for the unanimous Court that "the right to demand and enforce payment for goods sold in interstate commerce, if not a part of such commerce, is so directly connected with it and is so essential to its existence and continuance that the imposition of unreasonable conditions upon this right must necessarily operate as a restraint or burden upon interstate commerce."[36] The potential burden on interstate commerce was, in Van Devanter's mind, exacerbated by the potential for conflicting regulations from different states: "If one State can impose such a condition others can, and in that way corporations engaged in inter-

---

33. Act of September 2, 1914, ch. 293, 38 Stat. 711.
34. 237 U.S. at 27.
35. 235 U.S. 197 (1914).
36. Ibid., 202–3.

state commerce can be subjected to great embarrassment and serious hazards in the enforcement of contractual rights directly arising out of and connected with such commerce."[37]

Another instance of the breakdown of categories occurred with application of the states' police powers. Here the instance arose from attempts by states to regulate conditions under which employees worked. A decade before, the Court had provoked stinging criticism on account of its view that the employment of bakers was not sufficiently dangerous to merit legislative intervention.[38] Yet, in an almost contemporaneous decision, the Court had upheld a state's regulation of the hours worked in mines and smelters.[39] In truth, both cases reflected the Court's reliance on common experience to assess the need for special regulation of the employment. By the 1914–1915 term the Court faced an argument that the logic of the mining decisions allowed states to require mine owners to provide aboveground wash houses when a certain number of miners so requested.[40] In upholding the statute, the Court rejected the suggestion that its prior decisions were based on concerns about the safety of miners, concerns that ended once they returned aboveground. As Justice McKenna explained for the unanimous Court: "We are unable to concur in this reasoning or to limit the power of the legislature by the distinctions expressed. Having the power in the interest of the public health to regulate the conditions upon which coal mining may be conducted, it cannot be limited by moments of time and differences of situation."[41] Even so, McKenna acknowledged that the "conditions to which a miner passes or returns from are very different from those which an employé in work above ground passes to or returns from, and the conditions of actual service in the cases are very different"; and, he concluded that those differences could form the basis of a legitimate discrimination on the part of the legislature.[42] In short, what the Court did was once again attenuate the distinction that had formed the basis of its prior decision, stretching lines yet closer to their breaking points. In doing so, the Court seemed to signal approval for a wide range of Progressive-era state legislation that sought to regulate the conditions of employment.[43]

---

37. Ibid., 205. The Court used a similar rationale in striking down a local ordinance that prohibited street railways from carrying more than a third more passengers than it had seats. *South Covington & Cincinnati Street Railway Co. v. City of Covington*, 235 U.S. 537, 547–48 (1915).
38. *Lochner v. New York*, 198 U.S. 45 (1905).
39. *Holden v. Hardy,* 169 U.S. 366 (1898).
40. *Booth v. Indiana*, 237 U.S. 391 (1915).
41. Ibid., 396.
42. Ibid.
43. During the same term the Court also upheld several other restrictions on the freedom of contract between employers and employees. See., for example, *Rail & River Coal Co. v. Yaple*, 236 U.S. 338 (1915), Ohio statute required miners' pay be based on coal as it came from the mine, not after it was screened; *Miller v. Wilson*, 236 U.S. 373 (1915), California

In a separate case, Justice Day summarized the difficulties involved with defining these police powers. For the Court, he wrote that although "[t]he limitations upon the police power are hard to define, . . . its far-reaching scope has been recognized in many decisions of this court."[44] Then, he continued with a definition so capacious as to be practically useless: "The police power, in its broadest sense, includes all legislation and almost every function of civil government. It is not subject to definite limitations, but is coextensive with the necessities of the case and the safeguards of public interest."[45] The case which provoked that summary was one involving a 1911 Florida law prohibiting the shipment of fruit that was "immature or otherwise unfit for consumption." In upholding the statute, absent congressional legislation, the Court acknowledged that it was one in which the state looked outside its borders, for the state sought to protect both its own citizens and those of other states, not unlike Missouri had attempted with insurance in *New York Life Insurance Co. v. Head*.[46] Since the effect of the statute was to bar both intrastate and interstate shipment, the Court resorted to an old diversion, classifying the fruit as "not legitimate subjects of trade and commerce."[47] (The classification in effect stood *Hipolite* on its head. In *Hipolite,* Justice McKenna had supported the national government's reach into the states by saying that the product was "illicit." Now, in the Florida case, Justice Day supported a state government's reach into interstate commerce by saying that the product was "not legitimate.") Here, though, the prohibition was not limited to fruit that would cause physical harm to the consumer; the fruit need only be immature. Nevertheless, Justice Day justified the classification by reading the statute to mean that the fruit was both immature *and* unfit for consumption.[48] Day acknowledged that the rule extended beyond the borders of Florida, taking "judicial notice of the fact that the raising of citrus fruits is one of the great industries of the State of Florida." With that in mind, he concluded that the "protection of the State's reputation in foreign markets, with the consequent beneficial effect upon a great home industry, may have been within the legislative intent, and it certainly could not be said that this legislation has no reasonable relation to the accomplishment of that purpose."[49]

---

statute prohibited employment of women for more than eight hours a day or forty-eight hours a week, excluding certain farming occupations; *Bosley v. McLaughlin*, 236 U.S. 385 (1915), California eight-hour law extended to hospitals.
44. *Sligh v. Kirkwood*, 237 U.S. 52, 58–59 (1915).
45. Ibid., 59.
46. 234 U.S. 149 (1914).
47. 237 U.S. at 60. The quoted language came from *Bowman v. Chicago & Northwestern Railway Co.*, 125 U.S. 465, 489 (1888).
48. 237 U.S. at 57–58.
49. Ibid., 61–62.

The decay in the categories did not mean that the Court completely abdicated all controls over legislative enactments, even those in exercise of the police power. But when the justices turned to an old doctrine to invalidate a new law, the controversy was all the greater. The most celebrated example of that consequence, at least during the 1914 term, came in *Coppage v. Kansas*, a case decided without oral argument.[50] The Kansas statute at issue dated from 1903; it prohibited an employer from having as a condition of employment that each employee agree not to join a union. T. B. Coppage, the superintendent of a railway company, asked an employee to sign a statement that he had agreed to withdraw from membership in a union. When the employee refused to sign, Coppage fired him. Based on that action, Coppage was convicted of violating the statute. He then challenged his conviction as a violation of due process, in that it deprived him of his liberty to contract on whatever terms he chose.

Writing for six members of the Court, Justice Pitney explained that the case was governed by a 1908 decision of the Fuller Court, *Adair v. United States*.[51] In *Adair*, the Court had struck down a congressional act that prohibited similar "yellow dog" contracts between employer and employee. The Court reasoned that the congressional act violated the due process clause of the Fifth Amendment. *Adair* was based on the Court's perception of an equipoise in the relationship between employer and employee. Government could neither require an employer to hire an employee nor require an employee to work for an employer; both employee and employer had complete freedom to negotiate the terms of employment. In other words, the relationship was one of contract; that is, it was "private." With that principle in mind, Pitney could find no basis for distinguishing the result in *Coppage* under the Fourteenth Amendment's due process clause. "Granted the equal freedom of both parties to the contract of employment," Pitney asked rhetorically, "has not each party the right to stipulate upon what terms only he will consent to the inception, or to the continuance, of that relationship?"[52] There was a nineteenth-century gentility to Pitney's description, one that many would have said did not reflect the realities of employment in the twentieth century. In Pitney's mind, therefore, the question answered itself, with the result being that whatever reason one party might use to end a contract of employment could also be used as a condition for beginning the relationship. Thus, since an employer was free to discharge an employee for joining a union, the employer was free to require that a prospective employee promise not to join a union.

---

50. 236 U.S. 1 (1915).
51. 208 U.S. 161 (1908). For discussion of the actual use of yellow-dog contracts, as well as of legislative responses, see Daniel Ernst, "The Yellow-Dog Contract and Liberal Reform, 1917–1932," *Labor History* 30 (spring 1989): 251–74.
52. 236 U.S. at 12.

With the support of *Adair,* a precedent of recent vintage, the Court might well have ended its opinion without further explanation. More seemed to be required, however, in light of pressure from reformers to change both the reasoning and the result in cases such as *Adair.* Pitney acknowledged that "many" states had enacted similar laws; but, he added without seeming to appreciate the irony in the minds of some, he could not find any example in which the laws had "been judicially enforced" other than that of the Kansas court in *Coppage.*[53] Pitney therefore offered further explanation of the result. He began by narrowing the scope of the opinion, disclaiming any attempt to reach conduct suggested by the title of the act: "An Act to provide a penalty for coercing or influencing or making demands upon or requirements of employés, servants, laborers, and persons seeking employment."[54] Instead, in Pitney's view, Kansas sought to punish Coppage because he had insisted that an adult employee could "freely choose whether he would leave the employ of the Company or would agree to refrain from association with the union while so employed."[55] Pitney's use of the adverb "freely" must have been deliberate, for it reveals a critical part of the Court's view of the case. There could be no coercion, because the employee was free to choose whether to work for the employer. The Court implicitly appreciated the difference between its view and that of reformers (who did in fact use terms such as *coercive* to describe the relationship between employer and employee) in acknowledging that words were shifting in meaning: "[W]hen a party appeals to this court for the protection of rights secured to him by the Federal Constitution, the decision is not to depend upon the form of the state law, nor even upon its declared purpose, but rather upon its operation and effect as applied and enforced by the State."[56] Pitney emphasized his point a page later: "Nor can a State, by designating as 'coercion' conduct which is not such in truth, render criminal any normal and essentially innocent exercise of personal liberty or of property rights; for to permit this would deprive the Fourteenth Amendment of its effective force in this regard."[57] The consequence of not finding coercion was that the Court saw no support for the law in the police power of the state.

Pitney went beyond that conclusion to reject any support for the statute in what the Kansas Supreme Court had said was common knowledge, that there was an inequality of bargaining power between employees and employers. According to Pitney, that inequality was inevitable, being a natural con-

---

53. Ibid., 21. Pitney reported that a lower court in Ohio had upheld that state's law, but the result had been reversed.
54. The act is quoted in the Court's opinion, 236 U.S. at 6–7.
55. Ibid., 15.
56. Ibid.
57. Ibid., 16.

sequence of private property: "No doubt, wherever the right of private property exists, there must and will be inequalities of fortune; and thus it naturally happens that parties negotiating about a contract are not equally unhampered by circumstances. This applies to all contracts, and not merely to that between employer and employé. . . . And, since it is self-evident that, unless all things are held in common, some persons must have more property than others, it is from the nature of things impossible to uphold freedom of contract and the right of private property without at the same time recognizing as legitimate those inequalities of fortune that are the necessary result of the exercise of those rights."[58] With that thought in mind, Pitney had no difficulty reaffirming the conclusion that, in the absence of coercive conduct, government had no basis for interfering with natural exercises of human liberty, such as entering into contracts.

No contemporary would have failed to see Pitney's parenthetical, "unless all things are held in common," as a reference to socialism. The Socialist Party's successes in the national elections of 1910 and 1912, combined with victories in local elections in 1911 and the IWW-led strike of textile workers in Lawrence, Massachusetts, in 1912, had only heightened the fears of many.[59] By setting the Kansas statute on the side of socialism, Pitney showed that the Court's majority still stood on the side of nineteenth-century individualism. That divide was well captured in Herbert Croly's 1909 book, *The Promise of American Life*.[60] Termed "the most important book of its time" by one historian[61] and "the most systematic political treatise of American progressivism" by another,[62] Croly's book set out an agenda for resolving what Croly termed "grave national abuses."[63] In Croly's words, "a more highly socialized democracy is the only practical substitute on the part of convinced democrats for an excessively individualized democracy."[64]

Justices Holmes and Day wrote separate dissents. Holmes had dissented in *Adair* as well, but Day had joined the majority in the earlier opinion. In accord with opinions from his service on the Supreme Judicial Court of Massachusetts, Justice Holmes urged the Court to overrule *Adair*, reasoning that an employee might "not unnaturally . . . believe that only by belonging to a union can he secure a contract that shall be fair to him."[65] Regardless of the wisdom of such

---

58. Ibid., 17.
59. Painter, *Standing at Armageddon,* 259–64.
60. Herbert Croly, *The Promise of American Life* (New York: Macmillan, 1909).
61. Vincent P. DeSantis, *The Shaping of Modern America: 1877–1920,* 2d ed. (Wheeling, Ill.: Forum Press, 1989), 159.
62. Steven J. Diner, *A Very Different Age: Americans of the Progressive Era* (New York: Hill and Wang, 1998), 281.
63. Croly, *The Promise of American Life,* 20.
64. Ibid., 25.

a belief, it could at least be supported "by law in order to establish the equality of position between the parties in which liberty of contract begins."⁶⁶ In other words, Holmes took no position on the merits of the law; he merely agreed that a state legislature could take a position.

Day's dissent was more thorough, earning the support of Justice Hughes. Day agreed with the majority that the case posed a conflict between the state's police power and an individual's freedom. With thirteen other states having similar laws, he emphasized the importance of the decision, saying that the police power could be constrained only if exercised in a manner that was "arbitrary and capricious."⁶⁷ With agreement on the boundaries of the dispute, Day set about distinguishing *Adair* as a case that involved only a ban on dismissing an employee for belonging to a union. Since there was nothing in the Kansas statute that infringed an employer's power to discharge an employee, Day concluded that *Adair* did not control. Instead, the issue concerned the right of an employer to condition employment on a promise not to join a labor union. With all of the justices in agreement that employees had the right to join labor unions, Day concluded that the statute amounted to nothing more than "the protection of the exercise of a legal right, by preventing an employer from depriving the employé of it as a condition of obtaining employment."⁶⁸ In other words, the statute merely declared the public policy of the state to be opposed to agreements not to join labor unions. Such a declaration was no different from one opposing a promise to give up access to the courts; or, in one of the few judicial acknowledgments of the war in Europe, no different from one opposing a ban on employees joining the National Guard.⁶⁹ Day was moving toward envisioning the issue as one not of freedom of contract but of freedom of association, recognizing that employment had changed from the nineteenth century's face-to-face relationship to the twentieth century's relationship of groups—employers and unions.⁷⁰ Finally, Day disagreed with the Court on the critical point of coercion: When the stipulation was presented to the employee, "the one engaging to work, who may wish to preserve an independent right of action, as a condition of employment, is coerced to the signing of such an agreement against his will, perhaps impelled by the necessities of his situation."⁷¹

---

65. 236 U.S. at 26–27. Holmes referred to *Vegelahn v. Guntner,* 167 Mass. 92 (1896), and *Plant v. Woods,* 176 Mass. 492 (1900).
66. 236 U.S. at 27.
67. Ibid., 30.
68. Ibid., 33.
69. Ibid., 37.
70. For development of this thought, see Barry Cushman, "Doctrinal Synergies and Liberal Dilemmas: The Case of the Yellow-Dog Contract.," *The Supreme Court Review* (1992): 235–93.
71. 236 U.S. at 38.

Coppage revealed that there was still a limit to the reach of a state's police power. In *Coppage* the Court had found the limit in the liberty of contract guaranteed by the Fourteenth Amendment. As has been seen, the commerce clause set another limit. So, even though the justices continued to struggle with the starting and ending points for interstate commerce,[72] they still accepted that there was a time when the goods came to rest and thereby became subject to the state's police powers. Both the police power and the commerce clause were under increasing pressure to retain their viability as constitutional categories. In this term yet more pressure began to come from the different vocabulary of the Bill of Rights. Both the commerce clause and the police power belonged to the original structural portions of the Constitution. Even the concept of due process protecting liberty of contract could be seen as part of the original structure—the natural law obverse of the police power. But freedom of speech or of the press was different. They could not be said to inhere in the concept of government (as did the police power) or to belong to the heart of the structure of the federal system (as did the commerce power).[73] Instead, their protection depended upon the language of the First Amendment, language with which the Court as yet had little familiarity.

So it was that one of the most portentous of the Court's cases this term bound together the commerce clause, the police power, and the nascent concept of freedom of speech. For once, the Court found itself at the forefront of an issue. Ohio was only the second state to enact a statewide censorship of movies—Pennsylvania had preceded Ohio by two years.[74] The case, *Mutual Film Corporation v. Industrial Commission of Ohio,* involved a challenge to Ohio's 1913 act that created a state board of censors of motion pictures.[75] The key provision of the Ohio law was this: "Only such films as are in the judgment and

---

72. See, for example, *Illinois Central Railroad Co. v. Fuentes,* 236 U.S. 157, 163 (1915): "When freight actually starts in the course of transportation from one State to another it becomes a part of interstate commerce. The essential nature of the movement and not the form of the bill of lading determines the character of the commerce involved. And generally when this interstate character has been acquired it continues at least until the load reaches the point where the parties originally intended that the movement should finally end." *Pennsylvania Railroad Co. v. Clark Brothers Coal Mining Co.,* 238 U.S. 456 (1915), delivery FOB mine is interstate commerce.
73. The debate between the Federalists and the Antifederalists over the ratification of the Constitution *had* questioned whether the freedoms were inherent in the structure of government. The ratification of the Bill of Rights settled that phase of the debate.
74. Garth S. Jowett, "'A Capacity for Evil': The 1915 Supreme Court Mutual Decision," *Historical Journal of Film, Radio and Television* 9 (1989): 66.
75. 236 U.S. 230 (1915). The Court also decided two related cases on the same day. *Mutual Film Co. v. Industrial Commission of Ohio,* 236 U.S. 247 (1915). This case, involving the *Company,* an Ohio corporation, addressed the same issues as the main case, involving the *Corporation,* a Virginia corporation. *Mutual Film Corporation of Missouri v. Hodges,* 236 U.S. 248 (1915), similar statute from Kansas.

discretion of the board of censors of a moral, educational or amusing and harmless character shall be passed and approved by such board."[76] The law required that any film be approved by the board before being shown in Ohio. In the light of that requirement, the Court rejected the argument by the Mutual Film Corporation that the law interfered with interstate commerce. "There must be some time," Justice McKenna wrote for the unanimous Court, "when the films are subject to the law of the State, and necessarily when they are in the hands of the exchanges ready to be rented to exhibitors or have passed to the latter, they are in consumption, and mingled as much as from their nature they can be with other property of the State."[77]

Likewise, the Court rejected the argument that because the statute contained no standards it amounted to an improper delegation of legislative power. Once again referring to the ambiguity of distinctions, the Court repeated that although "administration and legislation are quite distinct powers, the line which separates exactly their exercise is not easy to define in words." With words thus losing their efficacy, the Court in some desperation turned to "illustrations,"[78] which, of course, was precisely what the early silent films had done. But all McKenna could provide was the hoary statement that a legislature declared policy while an administrative body found facts.

From those relatively sterile principles, however, the Court moved into unfamiliar territory to respond to the argument that the statute interfered with freedom of speech, as guaranteed by the Ohio state constitution: "Every citizen may freely speak, write, and publish his sentiments on all subjects, being responsible for the abuse of the right; and no law shall be passed to restrain or abridge the liberty of speech, or of the press."[79] The Court had not yet held that the First Amendment of the United States Constitution applied to the states. Thus, even though arguments of counsel pointed to the First Amendment,[80] the Court did not consider that argument. Under established precedents, the Court could consider questions of state constitutional law so long as they were part of a dispute properly before the Court on some other, federal ground.[81] In *Mutual Film* the federal ground was the question of whether the statute interfered with interstate commerce.

The lack of familiarity was evident both in the Court's dealing with the mechanism of film itself and in the Court's articulation of a principle of free speech. Consider, for example, this quaint description of the mechanism: "The film consists of a series of instantaneous photographs or positive prints

---

76. This was section 4 of the act of April 16, 1913, 103 Ohio Laws 399, quoted at 236 U.S. at 240.
77. 236 U.S. at 241.
78. Ibid., 245.
79. Ohio Constitution, sec. 11, quoted at 236 U.S. at 239 n. 1.
80. 236 U.S. at 231.
81. See, for example, *Ohio Tax Cases,* 232 U.S. 576, 586–87 (1914).

of action upon the stage or in the open. By being projected upon a screen with great rapidity there appears to the eye an illusion of motion."[82] The very fact that the Court thought it necessary to provide such a description suggests the novelty of the medium, in spite of the fact that in White's first full term as chief justice the Court had decided a case involving a copyright dispute about the movie *Ben Hur*.[83] In his opinion for the Court, Justice Holmes had written that "the Kalem Company, is engaged in the production of moving picture films, the operation and effect of which are too well known to require description. By means of them anything of general interest from a coronation to a prize fight is presented to the public with almost the illusion of reality—latterly even color being more or less reproduced."[84] Putting to one side the difference between Holmes's and McKenna's style, the change from the glib, self-assured description to the stumbling, technical description is but another small indicator of the change within the Court. Similarly, the state of film distribution is suggested by the fact that Mutual Film sold an average of fifty-six films a week in Ohio, representing some three hundred thousand dollars annually. Even more indicative of the place of the art in America was another film, one which opened in New York City between the time *Mutual Film* was argued on January 7, 1915, and the day the decision was announced, February 23. Originally titled *The Clansman* for its debut in Los Angeles on February 8, the movie was retitled *The Birth of a Nation* for its public opening in New York City on March 3.[85] The commercial success of the film is indicated by the fact that more people saw *The Birth of a Nation* than any other film, some 5 percent of the population.[86] President Wilson had a private showing at the White House, and justices of the Court saw it along with members of Congress at the Raleigh Hotel.[87] Directed by D. W. Griffith, the film displayed many of his trademark

---

82. 236 U.S. at 233.
83. *Kalem Co. v. Harper Brothers,* 222 U.S. 55 (1911).
84. Ibid., 60.
85. David A. Cook, *A History of Narrative Film* (New York: W. W. Norton, 1981), 77. See also Raymond Allen Cook, *Fire from the Flint: The Amazing Careers of Thomas Dixon* (Winston-Salem, N.C.: John F. Blair, 1968), 161–83; Thomas Cripps, *Slow Fade to Black: The Negro in American Film, 1900–1942* (New York: Oxford University Press, 1977), 41–69 (chapter entitled "The Year of *The Birth of a Nation*"); Michael Paul Rogin, *Ronald Reagan, the Movie: and Other Episodes in Political Demonology* (Berkeley: University of California Press, 1987), 190–235 (chapter on *The Birth of a Nation,* entitled "'The Sword Became a Flashing Vision'"); Fred Silva, ed., *Focus on "The Birth of a Nation"* (Englewood Cliffs, N.J.: Prentice-Hall, 1971).
86. Gerald R. Butters Jr., "*The Birth of a Nation* and the Kansas Board of Review of Motion Pictures: A Censorship Struggle," *Kansas History* 14 (1991): 9. For discussion of the debate over which film has earned the most profit, see Cook, *Fire from the Flint,* 237 n.18, 26.
87. Cook, *Fire from the Flint,* 169–73; John Hope Franklin, "'Birth of a Nation'—Propaganda as History," *Massachusetts Review* 40 (autumn 1979): 425; Arthur S. Link, *Wilson and the New Freedom* (Princeton, N.J.: Princeton University Press, 1956), 253.

innovations in the narrative film. Tragically, the blatant racism of the film overwhelmed the cinematographic artistry. The outburst of criticism, led by the NAACP, was the first occasion for that young organization to show it could mount a nationwide protest.

Not surprisingly, therefore, McKenna's opinion reflected a tone of rural gentility as it described the potential effects of this relatively new entertainment medium:

> But they may be used for evil, and against that possibility the statute was enacted. Their power of amusement and, it may be, education, the audiences they assemble, not of women alone nor of men alone, but together, not of adults only, but of children, make them the more insidious in corruption by a pretense of worthy purpose or if they should degenerate from worthy purpose. Indeed, we may go beyond that possibility. They take their attraction from the general interest, eager and wholesome it may be, in their subjects, but a prurient interest may be excited and appealed to. Besides, there are some things which should not have pictorial representation in public places and to all audiences. And not only the State of Ohio but other States have considered it to be in the interest of the public morals and welfare to supervise moving picture exhibitions. We would have to shut our eyes to the facts of the world to regard the precaution unreasonable or the legislation to effect it a mere wanton interference with personal liberty.[88]

Ironically, then, with novelty came assurance: the Court was confident about "the facts of the world" insofar as the effects of this new technology were concerned, while not so confident about a distinction between legislative and administrative powers. But novelty also brought a new denunciation—McKenna's use of *prurient* was the first occurrence of the word in opinions of the Supreme Court. The Court also feigned confidence about the freedom at issue: "We need not pause to dilate upon the freedom of opinion and its expression, and whether by speech, writing or printing. They are too certain to need discussion—of such conceded value as to need no supporting praise."[89] The issue, though, was whether "moving pictures" came within that freedom. "They, indeed, may be mediums of thought, but so are many things," wrote McKenna. Then he continued, "So is the theatre, the circus, and all other shows and spectacles, and their performances may be thus brought by the like reasoning under the same immunity from repression or supervision as the public press,—made the same agencies of civil liberty."[90]

---

88. 236 U.S. at 242.
89. Ibid., 243.
90. Ibid.

He then explained, making clear his view that movies were a part of urban America, as were the advertisements on the exterior of stages owned by the Fifth Avenue Coach Company:

> The first impulse of the mind is to reject the contention. We immediately feel that the argument is wrong or strained which extends the guaranties of free opinion and speech to the multitudinous shows which are advertised on the bill-boards of our cities and towns and which regards them as emblems of public safety, to use the words of Lord Camden, quoted by counsel, and which seeks to bring motion pictures and other spectacles into practical and legal similitude to a free press and liberty of opinion. The judicial sense supporting the common sense of the country is against the contention.[91]

In the end, the Court rejected the argument that movies were "like" the press. Instead, it chose a different but familiar metaphor:

> [T]he exhibition of moving pictures is a business pure and simple, originated and conducted for profit, like other spectacles, not to be regarded, nor intended to be regarded by the Ohio constitution, we think, as part of the press of the country or as organs of public opinion. They are mere representations of events, of ideas and sentiments published and known, vivid, useful and entertaining no doubt, but, as we have said, capable of evil, having power for it, the greater because of their attractiveness and manner of exhibition.[92]

Two other cases in this term also skirted issues associated with freedom of the press. One, *Fox v. Washington*,[93] was announced the same day as *Mutual Film*. The other, *Burdick v. United States*, had been announced a month earlier.[94] *Fox* involved a challenge to the constitutionality of a Washington state law punishing any publication that incited or had "a tendency to encourage or incite the commission of any crime, breach of the peace or act of violence."[95]

---

91. Ibid., 243–44.
92. Ibid., 244.
93. 236 U.S. 273 (1915).
94. 236 U.S. 79 (1915).
95. As quoted in the Court's opinion, the full text of the section read: "Every person who shall wilfully print, publish, edit, issue, or knowingly circulate, sell, distribute or display any book, paper, document, or written or printed matter, in any form, advocating, encouraging or inciting, or having a tendency to encourage or incite the commission of any crime, breach of the peace or act of violence, or which shall tend to encourage or advocate disrespect for law or for any court or courts of justice, shall be guilty of a gross misdemeanor" (236 U.S. at 275–76).

Jay Fox had published an article, "The Nude and the Prudes," which criticized unnamed people for interfering with a nudist camp. The article went on to call for a boycott of those people, with a promise of more information in future issues. The jury found Fox guilty of inciting individuals to violate a state law against indecent exposure. Fox did not raise the First Amendment issue, a fact that by itself said much about the status of constitutional argument. Instead, Fox contended that the statute violated his due process rights because it was imprecise and vague. The Court affirmed Fox's conviction, noting that the state supreme court had given the act the requisite specificity by construing it to apply "to encouraging an actual breach of law."[96] In that light, according to the Court, the person making the statement might be punished as an accomplice or even a principal in the illegal act.

The other case with hints of a First Amendment argument involved George Burdick, city editor for the *New York Tribune*. He published articles in the newspaper late in 1913 claiming that a former congressman, the president of United States Steel, and others had tried to evade customs duties by taking apart jewelry and importing the pieces as individual items. (Under the customs laws of the period, the duty on a single, large item might be 60 percent, while loose items would be subject to a duty of only 10 percent.)[97] The newspaper's allegations of fraud led to an investigation by a federal grand jury. When called to testify, Burdick refused, invoking his right against compulsory self-incrimination. He continued to refuse, even after the United States attorney arranged for a pardon from President Wilson, even though Burdick had not been charged with any crime. After Burdick refused to accept the pardon, the federal district court held him in contempt, fining him and jailing him until he agreed to testify. Burdick challenged his punishment, arguing that he should be able to invoke his right not to testify. The Court agreed, though the bulk of its opinion focused on the effect of an unaccepted pardon. Even so, the *New York Times* praised the decision for acknowledging the right of a reporter to withhold the names of sources.[98]

That the Court was in the early stages of dealing with application of the Bill of Rights to the states is nowhere better illustrated than in what was probably the single most notorious case of the term, if not of the decade, *Frank v. Mangum*.[99] In stark detail the case involved Leo Frank's challenge to his conviction for murdering a girl employed in his factory in Atlanta, Georgia.

---

96. 236 U.S. at 277. For a discussion of this case and the statute's enactment of the "bad tendency" test, see David M. Rabban, "The First Amendment in Its Forgotten Years," *Yale Law Journal* 90 (1981): 514–95.
97. See *United States v. Citroen*, 223 U.S. 407 (1912).
98. *New York Times,* January 27, 1915.
99. 237 U.S. 309 (1915). For general information, see Leonard Dinnerstein, *The Leo Frank Case* (New York: Columbia University Press, 1968).

But there was far more to the case than that. Frank, a Jew from New York, was also said to have sexually molested the fourteen-year-old white girl. Throughout the four-week trial, the courtroom was packed and the courthouse surrounded with spectators, all of whom appeared to be hostile to Frank. The judge was so apprehensive of violence that he suggested that the defendant not be present when the jury returned its verdict. Accordingly, both Frank and his attorney were not in the courtroom when the jury announced that it had found Frank guilty. Frank unsuccessfully challenged his conviction through the state courts, arguing that the mob's domination of the proceedings had deprived him of due process. After the state courts rejected his arguments, Frank petitioned a federal district court for a writ of habeas corpus. When that court denied the petition, he sought review in the Supreme Court. Only the appearance of a rare dissenting opinion (1 of but 11 this term, out of 273 opinions for the Court)[100] hints at the celebrity of the case. Otherwise, the Court's 7–2 vote suggests that the conclusion required nothing more than an application of accepted precedent. Indeed, Justice Pitney's opinion for the Court is a paean to the states, emphasizing the narrow scope of review under habeas corpus. He began with this explanation of the scope of that review: "Mere errors in point of law, however serious, committed by a criminal court in the exercise of its jurisdiction over a case properly subject to its cognizance, cannot be reviewed by habeas corpus. That writ cannot be employed as a substitute for the writ of error."[101] Of course, the Court had little incentive to provide an expansive interpretation of a statute when the result would be yet more cases added to an already overcrowded docket. Thus, the question as phrased by Pitney was a narrow one: Did the trial court lack jurisdiction to hear the case against Frank? By so framing the issue, Pitney made it virtually impossible for the challenge to succeed, for the grounds of challenge (intimidation by a mob and absence of Frank from the courtroom when the verdict was read) hardly fit the vocabulary of a challenge to jurisdiction, which related to the power of the court to hear the case. Further weakening Frank's chances was Pitney's view that the issue was not limited to the trial court—for the challenge implicated the entire state judicial system: "The rule stands upon a much higher plane, for it arises out of the very nature and ground of the inquiry into the proceed-

---

100. *Lankford v. Platte Iron Works Co.*, 235 U.S. 461 (1915); *American Water Softener Co. v. Lankford*, 235 U.S. 496 (1915); *Farish v. State Banking Board of the State of Oklahoma*, 235 U.S. 498 (1915); *Norfolk & Western Railway Co. v. Holbrook*, 235 U.S. 625 (1915); *Coppage v. Kansas*, 236 U.S. 1 (1915); *Pennsylvania Co. v. United States*, 236 U.S. 351 (1915); *United States v. Midwest Oil Co.*, 236 U.S. 459 (1915); *Frank v. Mangum*, 237 U.S. 309 (1915); *Cumberland Glass Manufacturing Co. v. De Witt and Co.*, 237 U.S. 447 (1915); *Kreitlein v. Ferger*, 238 U.S. 21 (1915); *Brand v. Union Elevated Railroad Co.*, 238 U.S. 586 (1915).
101. 237 U.S. at 326.

ings of the state tribunals, and touches closely upon the relations between the state and the Federal governments."[102] Thus, the issue of mob intimidation could not be limited to the effect on the trial court; instead, the issue had to be considered in light of the two-stage review afforded Frank—first by the trial court itself, then by the state supreme court. Based on examples of the state supreme court's having overturned verdicts on account of mob violence in the past, Pitney reasoned that the state court's review of Frank's case should be respected.

Holmes's dissent revealed his (and that of Justice Hughes, who joined him) disdain for the formalities of Pitney's opinion, as he explained in a graceful, if ultimately meaningless, statement near the beginning of his opinion: "[H]abeas corpus cuts through all forms and goes to the very tissue of the structure. It comes in from the outside, not in subordination to the proceedings, and although every form may have been preserved opens the inquiry whether they have been more than an empty shell."[103] He did, though, eventually identify the disagreement he had with the majority: "This is not a matter for polite presumptions; we must look facts in the face. Any judge who has sat with juries knows that in spite of forms they are extremely likely to be impregnated by the environing atmosphere. . . . Upon allegations of this gravity in our opinion it [the petition for *habeas corpus*] ought to be heard, whatever the decision of the state court may have been."[104] He concluded with a powerful reference to national conditions: "[I]t is our duty to act upon them [the facts] now and to declare lynch law as little valid when practiced by a regularly drawn jury as when administered by one elected by a mob intent on death."[105] Unfortunately, the reminder proved to be all too prescient. Two months after the Supreme Court's decision, the governor of Georgia commuted Frank's death sentence; then, two months later, a mob took Frank from the state penitentiary and hanged him.

Holmes's concept of rejecting forms in favor of substance was one with which the Court was experimenting throughout the term. Another case that illustrates the point, and supplies yet another tile in an emerging mosaic, is *United States v. Reynolds*.[106] The United States charged J. A. Reynolds with violating the federal anti-peonage act, which had been enacted in 1867 under the Thirteenth Amendment's prohibition of slavery and involuntary servitude.[107]

---

102. Ibid., 329.
103. Ibid., 346.
104. Ibid., 349.
105. Ibid., 350.
106. 235 U.S. 133 (1914).
107. Peonage Abolition Act, Act of March 2, 1867, ch. 187, 14 Stat. 546. See generally, Pete Daniel, *The Shadow of Slavery: Peonage in the South, 1901–1969* (Urbana: University of Illinois Press, 1972).

The origin of the charge lay in Reynolds's payment of a fine for a man charged with petit larceny. To repay the fine, the man had contracted to work for Reynolds at the rate of six dollars per month. In support of that system of payment and repayment by labor, Alabama law made it a crime to break a contract with someone who had paid a fine in such a case. Thus, if the man failed to complete his work for Reynolds, he could be convicted for breach of contract, which would bring on another cycle of fine, payment, and contract for work. It was that cycle the Court found to violate both the Thirteenth Amendment and the federal law. In the words of Justice Day, writing for the Court: "Looking then to the substance of things, and through the mere form which they have taken, we are to decide the question whether the labor of the convict, thus contracted for, amounted to involuntary service for the liquidation of a debt to the surety, which character of service it was the intention of the acts of Congress to prevent and punish. . . . Compulsion of such service by the constant fear of imprisonment under the criminal laws renders the work compulsory, as much so as authority to arrest and hold his person would be if the law authorized that to be done."[108]

To the extent that racial minorities would have seen *Reynolds* as a victory, the value would have been diminished by the Court's next decision. Announced immediately after *Reynolds* was *McCabe v. Atchison, Topeka & Santa Fe Railway Co.*,[109] in which the Court upheld Oklahoma's 1907 "Separate Coach Law." The law required all railroads operating in Oklahoma to "provide separate coaches or compartments, for the accommodation of the white and negro races," so long as the separate facilities were "equal in all points of comfort and convenience."[110] Since the state supreme court had held that the act applied only to intrastate commerce, the Court had no difficulty in concluding that the act could be sustained under *Plessy v. Ferguson*[111] and subsequent decisions. In dicta, however, the Court did offer a hint of hope by indicating that it was not prepared to accept mere formal inequality, for it rejected the lower court's support for a provision of the statute allowing railroads to haul "sleeping cars, dining or chair cars attached to their trains to be used exclusively by either white or negro passengers, separately but not jointly." The court of appeals had upheld that provision with the reasoning that limited demand by one race would justify the difference in service for these relatively luxurious accommodations. Justice Hughes's opinion for the unanimous Court rejected that reasoning as improperly subsuming individuals to groups:

---

108. 235 U.S. at 145–46.
109. 235 U.S. 151 (1914).
110. Ibid., 158; the statute is quoted in the Court's opinion.
111. 163 U.S. 537 (1896).

This argument with respect to volume of traffic seems to us to be without merit. It makes the constitutional right depend upon the number of persons who may be discriminated against, whereas the essence of the constitutional right is that it is a personal one. Whether or not particular facilities shall be provided may doubtless be conditioned upon there being a reasonable demand therefor, but, if facilities are provided, substantial equality of treatment of persons traveling under like conditions cannot be refused. It is the individual who is entitled to the equal protection of the laws, and if he is denied by a common carrier, acting in the matter under the authority of a state law, a facility or convenience in the course of his journey which under substantially the same circumstances is furnished to another traveler, he may properly complain that his constitutional privilege has been invaded.[112]

For once, nineteenth-century individualism offered protection, however minimal, for twentieth-century problems. Even so, the Court could provide no assistance for McCabe, for he had not shown any injury to himself from the enforcement of the act. Thus, the Court affirmed the dismissal of the complaint.

To the extent that *McCabe* offered little hope for protection of minorities, one decision at the end of the 1914–1915 term offered a bit more. In *Guinn and Beal v. United States*,[113] the Court declared unconstitutional an amendment to Oklahoma's original constitution. The amendment imposed a literacy test for voting but exempted anyone who was a lineal descendant of someone entitled to vote on January 1, 1866. The effect of this so-called grandfather clause was to exempt virtually all whites from the test, regardless of their literacy, while subjecting most other races to the vagaries of a literacy test that required them to read and write any section of the Oklahoma state constitution an election official might choose. Frank Guinn and J. J. Beal served as election officials in the 1910 congressional elections; in that capacity, they refused to allow certain black citizens to vote. As a result, the United States prosecuted them for violating a provision of the 1870 Ku Klux Klan Act. After being convicted, Guinn and Beal appealed their conviction to the circuit court of appeals, which in turn certified two questions to the Supreme Court.

In responding to those questions, Chief Justice White wrote on behalf of the unanimous Court. He held that the grandfather clause violated the Fifteenth Amendment to the Constitution. And, because the literacy test was an integral part of the Oklahoma constitutional amendment, it could not stand on its own.

---

112. 235 U.S. at 161–62.
113. 238 U.S. 347 (1915).

We have difficulty in finding words to more clearly demonstrate the conviction we entertain that this standard has the characteristics which the Government attributes to it than does the mere statement of the text. [True, the standard does not refer to race], but the standard itself inherently brings that result into existence since it is based purely upon a period of time before the enactment of the Fifteenth Amendment and makes that period the controlling and dominant test of the right of suffrage. . . . We say this because we are unable to discover how, unless the prohibitions of the Fifteenth Amendment were considered, the slightest reason was afforded for basing the classification upon a period of time prior to the Fifteenth Amendment. Certainly it cannot be said that there was any peculiar necromancy in the time named which engendered attributes affecting the qualification to vote which would not exist at another and different period unless the Fifteenth Amendment was in view.[114]

He ended with this rather strong conclusion for an ex-Confederate:

We are of opinion that neither forms of classification nor methods of enumeration should be made the basis of striking down a provision which was independently legal and therefore was lawfully enacted because of the removal of an illegal provision with which the legal provision or provisions may have been associated. We state what we hold to be the rule thus strongly because we are of opinion that on a subject like the one under consideration involving the establishment of a right whose exercise lies at the very basis of government a much more exacting standard is required than would ordinarily obtain where the influence of the declared unconstitutionality of one provision of a statute upon another and constitutional provision is required to be fixed.[115]

---

114. Ibid., 364–65.
115. Ibid., 366.

VI

THE 1915–1916 TERM

The 1915–1916 term confirmed what had begun in the previous term: the White Court had lost its youth. So, too, had the generation to which White and Holmes, the Court's leaders, belonged. As one observer saw the annual parade of the Grand Army of the Republic that fall, he noted that in "1865 it took two days for these soldiers to pass in review, in 1915 they passed by in less than two hours."[1] The energetic performance of White's first three terms had peaked in 1913–1914. The next term saw a modest drop of 7 percent in opinions for the Court. Now, in the 1915–1916 term, the number would drop another 10 percent. The reduction in output was at least in part the result of the illnesses of Justices Day and Lamar. Justice Day was absent from January 3, 1916, according to the official reports of the Supreme Court. He was therefore able to participate in at most eighty-seven of the Court's opinions, writing majority opinions in only eight.[2] Although Justice Day would recover and return for the 1916 term, Justice Lamar would not. At the end of the 1914 term, Lamar's wife had noted in her journal "that he was very tired." They spent the summer in White Sulphur Springs, West Virginia, as they usually did. Lamar had suffered a minor stroke early in September, but he was able to return to Washington. Unfortunately, he never recovered sufficiently to resume his role on the Court. He died January 2, 1916.[3] The other justices attempted to shoulder the extra burden that resulted from the absences of their colleagues, but they could not reach their usual standard. White (forty-one) and Holmes (forty-three) had, as usual, the greatest output of opinions for the Court, followed by Hughes (twenty-nine), McKenna (thirty-four), McReynolds (thirty), Pitney (thirty-four), and Van Devanter

---

1. Dunn, *From Harrison to Harding,* 290.

2. The Court's reports do not clearly indicate whether a particular justice participated in specific decisions. The number is based on those cases argued or submitted prior to January 3, 1916. He was named as the author of two opinions announced on January 10: *Northwestern Laundry v. City of Des Moines,* 239 U.S. 486 (1916), and *Southern Railway Co. v. Lloyd,* 239 U.S. 496 (1916).

3. Lamar, *The Life of Joseph Rucker Lamar,* 269–72; *New York Times,* October 12, 1915.

(twenty-four). McReynolds's prior service with the Justice Department continued to hamper his performance, since he recused himself from any case on which he had worked while with the department. In this term that amounted to almost forty of the announced opinions, roughly 15 percent of the cases.[4] In all cases represented by opinions, 90 percent were unanimous; of the twenty-six decisions that were not unanimous, only ten provoked written dissents.[5] No pattern emerges from those ten dissents. Seven were little more than statements of disagreement, ranging from a single sentence to a single page. The other three were only slightly longer. In short, even under the stress of being shorthanded the White Court remained remarkably cohesive.

Justice Lamar's death gave President Woodrow Wilson his second appointment to the Court. In light of the losses suffered in the 1914 elections, when the Democrats' majority in the House of Representatives was reduced from seventy-three to twenty-five, Wilson knew he would have to regain the support of Progressives if he hoped to defeat the Republican nominee in 1916, especially since the nominee almost certainly would not be weakened by the Taft-Roosevelt split.[6] Speculation had begun to focus on Justice Hughes, even though he had formally declared that he was not a candidate. Even so, with his reputation as a reformer he was attractive to many in the Republican Party.[7] Wilson's choice of Louis D. Brandeis to replace Lamar was in many ways the first act of his campaign for reelection. Wilson followed the nomination with a burst of legislative proposals. Their enactment meant that by election day in the fall virtually the entire Progressive platform became part of federal law.[8] Wilson could have done little more to attract the Progressives than nominating Brandeis, though the nomination shocked almost everyone. The *New York Times* referred to "the near-sensation caused by the nomination."[9]

---

4. Of the 243 cases with opinions, McReynolds participated in 205.
5. *Truax v. Raich,* 239 U.S. 33 (1915); *William Cramp and Sons Ship and Engine Building Co. v. United States,* 239 U.S. 221 (1915); *Mackenzie v. Hare,* 239 U.S. 299 (1915); *Northern Pacific Railway Co. v. Meese,* 239 U.S. 614 (1916); *Illinois Central Railroad Co. v. Messina,* 240 U.S. 395 (1916); *Detroit and Mackinac Railway Co. v. Michigan Railroad Commission and Fletcher Paper Co.,* 240 U.S. 564 (1916); *Northern Pacific Railway Co. v. Wall,* 241 U.S. 87 (1916); *United States v. Archer,* 241 U.S. 119 (1916); *American Well Works Co. v. Layne and Bowler Co.,* 241 U.S. 257 (1916); *Duel v. Hollins,* 241 U.S. 523 (1916).
6. Link, *Woodrow Wilson and the Progressive Era, 1910–1917,* 78.
7. See, for example, *New York Times,* March 26, 1915; May 5, 1915; August 19, 1915.
8. Link, *Woodrow Wilson and the Progressive Era, 1910–1917,* 229.
9. *New York Times,* January 29, 1916. On the nomination of Brandeis, see especially Alden L. Todd, *Justice on Trial: The Case of Louis D. Brandeis* (New York: McGraw-Hill, 1964); Melvin I. Urofsky, "Attorney for the People: The 'Outrageous' Brandeis Nomination," *Supreme Court Historical Society Yearbook* (1979): 8–19. On Brandeis in general, see Richard P. Adelstein, "Islands of Conscious Power: Louis D. Brandeis and the Modern Corporation," *Business History Review* 63 (1989): 614–56; Alexander M. Bickel, *The Unpublished Opinions of Mr. Justice Brandeis* (Chicago: University of Chicago Press, 1967); James McCauley Landis, "Mr. Justice Brandeis:

Born in Louisville, Kentucky, on November 13, 1856, Brandeis had by 1916 earned a nationwide reputation as an attorney for reform interests. He graduated from Harvard Law School at the top of his class in 1877 (having entered without a college diploma, though with the benefit of three years of travel and study in Europe). Soon after graduation he began practice in Boston with his classmate Samuel Warren. Their success allowed Brandeis to indulge his interest in being "the people's attorney."[10] In doing so, Brandeis followed the pattern of the Progressive movement—beginning with local interests, moving on to statewide issues, and finally concluding with national politics. Locally, for example, Brandeis successfully opposed the Boston Elevated Railroad in its efforts to control Boston's transportation system. He then moved to the state level, where he helped draft utilities laws and invented a plan for savings-bank life insurance. At the national level, Brandeis came to prominence for his defense of Oregon's statute limiting employment of women to ten hours a day in certain occupations.[11] His brief in that case, *Muller v. Oregon*,[12] drew on a wealth of nonlegal materials (more than one hundred pages of data compared to only two pages of judicial precedents) to show that the legislature had a basis for enacting the law. Brandeis himself explained his reason for using those materials: "In the past the courts have reached their conclusions largely deductively from preconceived notions and precedents. The method I have tried to employ in arguing cases before them has been inductive, reasoning from the facts."[13]

The other significant source for Brandeis's national reputation was more starkly politicized than his participation in *Muller*. Less than two years after the Court announced its decision in *Muller*, Brandeis agreed to serve as counsel for *Collier's Weekly* before a special congressional committee to investigate the so-called Pinchot-Ballinger Affair.[14] Gifford Pinchot was chief

---

A Law Clerk's View," *Publications of the American Jewish Historical Society* 46 (1957): 467–73; Mason, *Brandeis;* Philippa Strum, *Brandeis: Beyond Progressivism* (Lawrence: University Press of Kansas, 1993); Strum, *Louis D. Brandeis: Justice for the People;* Melvin I. Urofsky, *A Mind of One Piece: Brandeis and American Reform* (New York: Charles Scribner's Sons, 1971).

10. For a critical discussion of Brandeis's role in this capacity, see Clyde Spillenger, "Elusive Advocate: Reconsidering Brandeis as People's Lawyer," *Yale Law Journal* 105 (1996): 1445–535.

11. The statute applied to "any manufacturing, mechanical or mercantile establishment, laundry, hotel or restaurant." Act of February 25, 1907, ch. 200, General Laws of Oregon (1907). The 1907 act amended an earlier act by adding "manufacturing." See Act of February 20, 1903, General Laws of Oregon (1903), 148.

12. 208 U.S. 412 (1908). For an account of Brandeis's participation in the case, as well as that of Josephine Goldmark (Brandeis's sister-in-law) and Florence Kelley, on behalf of the National Consumers' League, see Strum, *Louis D. Brandeis: Justice for the People*, 114–31. See also Mason, *Brandeis*, 245–53.

13. Quoted in Strum, *Louis D. Brandeis: Justice for the People*, 124–25.

14. See Mason, *Brandeis*, 254–82; Strum, *Louis D. Brandeis: Justice for the People*, 132–40.

forester of the Department of Agriculture, an appointee of Theodore Roosevelt, and a staunch advocate of conservation. Richard Ballinger was President Taft's secretary of the interior, considerably less enthusiastic about conservation than was Pinchot. A simmering dispute between the two men came to a boil over allegations that Ballinger had improperly attempted to dispose of coal lands in Alaska. Although President Taft exonerated Ballinger, an article in *Collier's* magazine prompted a widespread call for further investigation. Congress responded by appointing a special investigating committee. In the end, the committee voted along party lines to support Ballinger; but in the almost five months of hearings Brandeis managed to show that Taft and his attorney general, George W. Wickersham, had intentionally misled the public about their investigation into the matter.

Brandeis carried his involvement in national politics into the 1912 presidential election. He at first supported Wisconsin's Senator Robert La Follette for the Republican nomination. When La Follette's campaign floundered, Brandeis shifted his support to the Democrats' nominee, Woodrow Wilson, in what Brandeis's biographer described as "Finding His Captain."[15] After the election, Wilson wanted to appoint Brandeis as attorney general, but he was dissuaded by opposition from business interests and from local party bosses in Massachusetts who were convinced Brandeis's Republican ties would harm their patronage rewards.[16] Nevertheless, Brandeis remained a confidant to Wilson throughout his first term as president, advising on important reform measures such as the Federal Reserve Act, the Clayton Antitrust Law, and the Federal Trade Commission. The respect Brandeis earned from his work with Wilson is nowhere better evidenced than in Wilson's speedy decision to nominate him to the Supreme Court. With support promised from progressive Republicans and from labor, Wilson announced the nomination on January 28, 1916. Twelve days later a five-man subcommittee of the Senate Judiciary Committee began hearings on the nomination. At the urging of the attorney general the committee took the unusual step of opening the hearings to the public.[17]

The story of the confirmation hearings on Brandeis's nomination is an oft-told one.[18] Brandeis found that his unique approach to public service now worked against him as opponents emerged from Boston and across the

---

15. The description is the title to chapter 24 in Alpheus T. Mason's masterful biography of Brandeis—*Brandeis: A Free Man's Life.*
16. In addition to the account in Mason's biography (385–94), see also Strum's *Louis D. Brandeis: Justice for the People,* 207.
17. Joseph P. Harris, *The Advice and Consent of the Senate* (Berkeley: University of California Press, 1953), 103.
18. In addition to Todd's encyclopedic *Justice on Trial* and Urofsky's "Attorney for the People," see Mason, *Brandeis,* 465–508; Strum, *Louis D. Brandeis: Justice for the People,* 291–300.

country. Although anti-Semitism played a part in the opposition, ultimately it was a minor one.[19] The major source of opposition came from those with an interest in preserving the status quo. They couched their opposition in terms of attacks on Brandeis's character and of allegations that he had acted unethically in representing certain clients. Brandeis himself did not appear before the committee. Indeed, he refused to make any public comment throughout the hearings, instead relying on others to respond to criticism. Brandeis did, though, personally manage his defense from his office in Boston.

At the instigation of George Wickersham—Taft's attorney general who had felt the brunt of Brandeis's attack during the investigation of Ballinger—six former presidents of the American Bar Association joined the incumbent president (for a total of seven out of the sixteen living ABA presidents)[20] in signing a communication to the Senate Judiciary Committee with this sweeping statement: "The undersigned feel under the painful duty to say to you in their opinion, taking into view the reputation, character and professional career of Mr. Louis D. Brandeis, he is not a fit person to be a member of the Supreme Court of the United States."[21] Among the seven signatures was that of former President Taft. More than fifty "citizens of Massachusetts," including the president of Harvard University, A. Lawrence Lowell, signed a petition asserting that Brandeis lacked the "judicial temperament and capacity" required of a justice.[22] Other, more specific attacks included criticism from Sidney Winslow, the president of United Shoe Machinery Company. Winslow charged that Brandeis had first represented the company, then later accused it of violating antitrust laws, using knowledge of its leases and tying arrangements he had gained while serving as its attorney.[23] Winslow also complained that Brandeis had used the knowledge to prepare his testimony in support of the Clayton Act. When pressed, how-

---

19. Brandeis would become the first Jewish justice. Todd could find no evidence to support a report that the first Jewish nominee was Judah P. Benjamin, who is reported to have declined President Fillmore's offer in 1853. Todd, *Justice on Trial,* 256.
20. Ibid., 161.
21. Quoted in ibid., 159. The ABA had no formal mechanism for evaluating nominees, though it would later develop one. See Joel B. Grossman, "The Role of the American Bar Association in the Selection of Federal Judges: Episodic Involvement to Institutionalized Power," *Vanderbilt Law Review* 17 (1964): 785–814, 790–91. The article became part of a book, Joel B. Grossman, *Lawyers and Judges: The ABA and the Politics of Judicial Selection* (New York: John Wiley & Sons, 1965).
22. Todd, *Justice on Trial,* 106; Mason, *Brandeis,* 472.
23. These were the same arrangements challenged in *United States v. Winslow,* 227 U.S. 202 (1913). For a discussion of the ethical issues involved in this and other charges against Brandeis, see John P. Frank, "The Legal Ethics of Louis D. Brandeis," *Stanford Law Review* 17 (1965): 683–709.

ever, Winslow could give no specific knowledge that Brandeis had gained; neither did he note that more than three years had elapsed between Brandeis's representation and his later actions.

Although there were other allegations against Brandeis, much of the opposition came from an aggrieved sense that he had not behaved as a "gentleman." It is tempting to say that the opposition complained that he had rejected the norms of the nineteenth-century bar in favor of that of the "expert" in the emerging twentieth century. Repeatedly, questioning disclosed that opponents' dislike arose because he had represented not a party to a dispute, but the "public." For example, one Boston lawyer who supported the nomination, Sherman Whipple, suggested that "if Mr. Brandeis had been a different sort of man, not so aloof, not so isolated, with more of the camaraderie of the bar," there would not have been the number of objections raised about him.[24] As a result, even a reformer such as Moorfield Storey, president of the NAACP and former president of the ABA, could respond to a question by saying that Brandeis's reputation was "that of a man who is an able lawyer, very energetic, ruthless in the attainment of his objectives, not scrupulous in the methods he adopts, and not to be trusted."[25] Countering the attacks on Brandeis were nine of the eleven faculty members of the Harvard Law School, including Roscoe Pound, who would soon be appointed dean.

The hearings came to a close on March 8, only to be reopened the next week to read the statement from the former ABA presidents and to take more testimony. The subcommittee reported on April 3, with a vote along party lines: the three Democrats in favor of the nomination; the two Republicans opposed. After further delay, the entire committee voted to reopen hearings, to allow yet more testimony. Finally, on May 24 the committee voted 10–8 in favor of Brandeis, again along party lines. A week later, Thursday, June 1, the Senate went into executive session. Thirty minutes later, the public learned that the Senate had confirmed Brandeis's nomination by a vote of 47–22. At the urging of a Court badly in need of help with a ballooning docket, Brandeis took the oath of office the following Monday, June 5.[26] The Court announced nineteen decisions that day and sixteen the next Monday before adjourning for the summer.

In between those Mondays, on Saturday, June 10th, Justice Hughes announced his resignation, effective immediately, to accept the Republican nomination for president. The nomination came as no surprise; there had been public speculation for months. But behind the scenes, Chief Justice White had intimated that he, too, might retire, saying to Hughes that if

---

24. Quoted in Todd, *Justice on Trial,* 118.
25. Quoted in ibid., 115; Mason, *Brandeis,* 480.
26. Urofsky and Levy, eds., *Letters of Louis D. Brandeis,* 6:210–11.

Hughes remained on the Court, Wilson was sure to appoint him as chief justice. Hughes remembered the conversation as concluding in this way: "'Why,' I [Hughes] said, 'President Wilson would never appoint me Chief Justice.' 'Well,' he [White] replied, 'he wouldn't appoint anyone else, as I happen to know.'"[27] To others, White was definite in his view that Hughes had made a mistake in resigning. Indiana Senator Thomas Watson recalled that he talked with White at the National Theater in Washington and asked about Hughes's decision. White's response was definite: "Watson, I think that it was a very grave mistake and one that will return to trouble us for years to come. In the future, fired by the ambition of being nominated for the presidency, some political-minded justices may be led to render political decisions instead of decisions based on principle, and that certainly would prove an undermining policy for such a judicial body. Justice Hughes is a very able man. He has made a fine record as a member of the Court and doubtless if elected to the presidency will grace that position because of his splendid capacity. Yet I look upon his nomination as a very great blunder and one from which we will be years in recovering."[28]

What seems clear is that with Brandeis Progressivism came to the Court. Even though his single vote could decide only the closest of cases, his intellect might sway other votes.[29] And, whatever the immediate results, his appointment portended future changes not unlike those already in place in other parts of the federal system. With the vacancy afforded by Hughes's resignation, Wilson sought to strengthen that single vote by nominating John Hessin Clarke on July 14, 1916. Only two years before, Wilson had appointed Clarke to the United States District Court for the Northern District of Ohio.[30] Clarke was born in Lisbon, Ohio (then New Lisbon), on September 18, 1857. He gradu-

---

27. Danelski and Tulchin, eds., *Autobiographical Notes of Charles Evans Hughes,* 180. McHargue also suggests that rumors of White's retirement had begun as early as 1916. He reports that the Department of Justice prepared a list of "Names Proposed for Vacancy on Supreme Court of the United States." The list is dated January 1, 1917. McHargue, "Appointments to the Supreme Court of the United States," 429.

28. James E. Watson, *As I Knew Them* (Indianapolis: Bobbs-Merrill Co., 1936), 163–64. The *New York Times,* which had so assiduously reported speculation that Hughes would succeed Fuller as chief justice, expressed a similar opinion; June 9, 1916; June 15, 1916; November 11, 1916 (comment after Hughes's defeat). For a contrary view, see "Hughes Not a Political Judge," *Nation* 102 (April 1916): 376.

29. See Strum, *Brandeis: Justice for the People,* 366–67.

30. Mason suggests that Brandeis may have played a role in suggesting Clarke's name to Wilson; Mason, *Brandeis,* 513. For an account of the nomination, see Burton J. Hendrick, "Another Radical for the Supreme Court," *World's Work* 33 (November 1916): 95. On Clarke in general, see David M. Levitan, "Jurisprudence of Mr. Justice Clarke," *Miami Law Quarterly* 7 (1952): 44–72; Hoyt Landon Warner, *The Life of Mr. Justice Clarke: A Testament to the Power of Liberal Dissent in America* (Cleveland: Western Reserve University Press, 1959); Carl Wittke, "Mr. Justice Clarke—A Supreme Court Justice in Retirement," *Mississippi Valley Historical Review* 36 (1949): 27–50.

ated from Western Reserve College in 1877, his achievement reflected by his election to Phi Beta Kappa. The next year he passed the bar examination, cum laude, after having studied in his father's law office. Not long afterward, Clarke moved to Youngstown, where he purchased a half interest in the local Democratic newspaper, the *Youngstown Vindicator*. He sold his interest in the newspaper after two years; but, in 1889 he reinvested in the paper to allow it to change from weekly to daily publication. In all, he practiced law in Youngstown for seventeen years, representing railroads and other corporations, all the while supporting Progressive causes such as civil-service reform, tariff reduction, and equal taxation. In 1896 he backed the "Gold" Democrats, in opposition to William Jennings Bryan's support for the free coinage of silver. Clarke's success as a trial lawyer contributed to an invitation to become a partner in a Cleveland law firm. He accepted the invitation, moving to Cleveland in 1897, where he continued to represent railroads and other corporations. He also continued to be active in the Democratic Party as a close ally of Cleveland's mayor, Tom L. Johnson—an alliance that earned Clarke a reputation as a radical.[31] From that friendship came Clarke's nomination for United States Senate by the Democratic state convention in 1903. Clarke's campaign supported Progressive causes, including the initiative and referendum, and abolition of the fellow-servant rule in industrial accident cases. In spite of Clarke's rhetorical skills, his cold personality failed to earn him votes. The Democrats suffered a crushing loss to the Republicans, ensuring that Clarke would not win election to the Senate. For a time after that defeat Clarke played a less prominent role in state politics. But in 1912 he campaigned actively for Wilson. In June 1913 he announced his candidacy for the United States Senate, in what would be the first direct election under the Seventeenth Amendment. Clarke's opponent for the Democratic nomination was a much better campaigner, so Clarke was not overly disappointed when Wilson nominated him to the federal district court, taking him out of the campaign. Once on the bench, Clarke's efficient handling of cases won the respect of the local bar and eliminated the backlog on the docket of a court whose volume of cases was exceeded only by those in New York and Chicago.[32] But he had little opportunity for impact on the law, since two years later Wilson nominated him to the Supreme Court. Unlike the inquiry for Brandeis, the Senate did not delay. In spite of Clarke's record as a Progressive, the Senate confirmed him by voice vote only ten days after receiving Wilson's nomination, no doubt speeded by the inquiry already made at the time of his appointment to the district court.[33] Clarke took the oath of office on

---

31. Hendrick, "Another Radical for the Supreme Court," 95–98; *Independent* 87 (July 24, 1916): 120; "Another Supreme Court 'Radical,'" *Literary Digest* 53 (July 1916): 240–41.
32. *Outlook* 113 (July 1916): 682–83.
33. See *New York Times,* July 15, 1916.

August 1, presumably to enable the Court to have his assistance as early as possible.

The Court's opinions during the 1915 term failed to match the stormy events surrounding Brandeis's nomination. Instead, the term saw the continuation of pressures on the Court to move away from old categories. Even though the justices continued to be called upon to review the legislation of earlier decades, this term seemed to have a particular focus on the response to the wave of immigration at the start of the century. More than eight million immigrants had entered the United States between 1900 and 1910, the largest number in any single decade in the nation's history.[34] One response to the stream of immigrants was to deny entry to anyone "likely to become a public charge."[35] One such denial eventually found its way to the Supreme Court, in *Gegiow v. Uhl.*[36] Ali Gegiow was one of a group of twenty Russian émigrés who had entered the United States in New York hoping to travel to Portland, Oregon. Immigration officials detained Gegiow and his group, pending deportation, on the ground that they would become public charges because there was little chance of aliens obtaining jobs in Portland. The justices refused to give the statute such a localistic interpretation. Instead, they reasoned that the likelihood of becoming a public charge referred to "permanent personal objections" to the individual immigrant, not to local conditions.[37] The phrase "likely to become a public charge" fell between "paupers" and "professional beggars" in the statute.[38] In so reasoning, the Court relied on a standard tenet of statutory interpretation, that all items in a list are to be construed together. But the import of the case went beyond mere rules of construction, for what the Court did was emphasize that immigrants were admitted to the nation, not to localities.

A week after announcing *Gegiow* the Court emphasized the nationalism of its decision. This second immigration case also resembled *Coppage,* which had been decided at the end of the previous term, in that both involved employment-at-will contracts. Under the accepted theory, "employment at will" meant that either the employer or the employee was free to terminate the contract at any time for any reason. Not surprisingly, such a theory lent

---

34. See George Brown Tindall and David E. Shi, *America: A Narrative History,* 4th ed. (New York: W. W. Norton & Co., 1984), 2:A37–38.

35. The quoted phrase is from the immigration act of February 20, 1907, ch. 1134, 34 Stat. 898, as amended by an Act of March 26, 1910, ch. 128, 36 Stat. 263.

36. 239 U.S. 3 (1915).

37. Ibid., 10.

38. The act declared "That the following classes of aliens shall be excluded from admission into the United States: All idiots, imbeciles . . . ; paupers; persons likely to become a public charge; professional beggars; persons afflicted with tuberculosis . . . ." Act of March 26, 1910, ch. 128, 36 Stat. 263.

itself to sweeping rhetoric about liberty and freedom. *Coppage* had not disappointed; and neither did the new opinion, *Truax v. Raich:* "[T]he right to work for a living in the common occupations of the community is of the very essence of the personal freedom and opportunity that it was the purpose of the [Fourteenth] Amendment to secure."[39] At issue in *Truax* was an Arizona law adopted by that model of Progressive electoral reform, the initiative.[40] The law mandated that any employer of more than five employees employ at least 80 percent "qualified electors or native-born citizens of the United States or some sub-division thereof."[41] William Truax owned a restaurant in which seven of his nine employees were neither native-born citizens nor qualified electors, among them Mike Raich, an Austrian. Upon being notified that he would be fired as soon as the law went into effect, Raich challenged the law as denying him equal protection. Even though he was an alien, Raich was entitled to the protection of the Fourteenth Amendment, whose language was not restricted to "citizens." Rather, the amendment prohibited a state from denying "to any person within its jurisdiction the equal protection of the laws."[42]

In a 7–1 decision the Court held that the Arizona law was unconstitutional. Justice McReynolds agreed that the act was invalid, but dissented because he thought the Eleventh Amendment barred the suit against a state. Writing for the majority, Justice Hughes noted that the case did not involve a claim to "the public domain, or of the common property or resources of the people of the State, the enjoyment of which may be limited to its citizens as against both aliens and the citizens of other States."[43] He also was careful to note "that the act is not limited to persons who are engaged on public work or receive the benefit of public moneys." Thus narrowed, the law fell within none of the established rules allowing discrimination through an exercise of the

---

39. 239 U.S. 33, 41 (1915).

40. The other core of Progressive electoral reform, the referendum, fared better in *Ohio ex rel. Davis v. Hildebrant,* 241 U.S. 565 (1916). This case involved referendum provisions added to the Ohio constitution in 1912, which gave voters the power to approve or disapprove any law enacted by the state legislature. In 1915 those procedures were used to disapprove of the legislature's drawing of lines for congressional districts. Some of those who disagreed with the outcome of the referendum sought a court order that the law be enforced; but both the Ohio Supreme Court and the United States Supreme Court upheld the action of the referendum, reasoning that there was no law to be enforced once the people acted to disapprove the law. Indeed, the Court even pointed to language in the congressional debates to show that when calling on the states to redistrict in light of the 1910 census, Congress had contemplated action by referendum as being equivalent to legislative action. 241 U.S. at 568–69.

41. The full text of the law is quoted in the Court's opinion, 239 U.S. at 35.

42. *The Nation* noted this point in its praise of the decision; *Nation* 101 (November 1915): 564.

43. 239 U.S. at 39–40.

state's police power. The Court had repeatedly written of the wide reach of the police power, but Hughes now cautioned that the power was not without limit. Adapting to Raich's argument, Hughes added this line to the personal-liberty chorus already quoted: "If [the right to work] could be refused solely upon the ground of race or nationality, the prohibition of the denial to any person of the equal protection of the laws would be a barren form of words."[44] He added to that thought the statement that the police power did not allow a state "to deny the lawful inhabitants, because of their race or nationality, the ordinary means of earning a livelihood."[45] But neither Hughes nor the Court was prepared to take the next step and conclude that Raich had an *individual* right to work. Instead, the Court took refuge in a more familiar structural part of the Constitution. Thus, Hughes turned to the principle that a state's police power could not conflict with national power. In the view of the Court, Arizona's statute did just that, interfering with the exclusive national power to control immigration. "The assertion of an authority to deny to aliens the opportunity of earning a livelihood when lawfully admitted to the State would be tantamount to the assertion of the right to deny them entrance and abode, for in ordinary cases they cannot live where they cannot work."[46] Having experienced difficulty with drawing lines throughout his tenure on the Court, Hughes showed no inclination to accept the state's argument that it should be allowed to fix the maximum employment of aliens at 20 percent of a workforce. To do that, Hughes concluded, would be to concede that the state could set the percentage at zero.

Hughes's cryptic reference in his *Truax* opinion to "persons who are engaged on public work" was explained four weeks later, when the Court announced its opinion in *Heim v. McCall*,[47] which had been argued just two days before *Truax*. The statute challenged in *Heim* was a 1909 New York law that required citizens to be given preference in employment on all public works projects. William E. Heim, a property owner and taxpayer in New York, challenged the statute as unconstitutional because it deprived employers of the freedom to choose their employees. He contended that contractors employed to extend the city's subway lines regularly hired a large number of Italians. Without that practice, he argued, the contracts could not be completed at the agreed-upon price. In the Court's opinion, the cost did not matter, for the state had complete control over its municipalities; thus the state could impose the requirement on contracts awarded by cities for public works. Writing for the Court, Justice McKenna pointed to a decision

---

44. Ibid., 41.
45. Ibid.
46. Ibid., 42.
47. 239 U.S. 175 (1915).

from the Fuller Court allowing a state to limit the hours of work on public contracts.[48] That case, he reasoned, was no different from this, with hours of work being of no significant difference from the kind of workers. In effect, the decision to employ for public works was as immune to federal judicial review as was the decision to permit the initiative or referendum.

The Court's strong emphasis on national power over immigration may well have been a reflection of the growing stress associated with the efforts by the United States to remain on the sidelines of the war in Europe. The sinking of the *Lusitania* in May 1915 raised tensions to the brink of war. But President Wilson declined to step over the brink, saying, "There is such a thing as a man being too proud to fight."[49] Later in the summer, Germany announced that it would no longer sink passenger ships without warning. The crisis had, however, given support to demands for increased spending to ensure the preparedness of the United States military forces. In November 1915, in the midst of *Gegiow, Truax,* and *Heim,* Wilson announced his support for a preparedness plan. That announcement provoked an outburst of criticism from Progressives, who saw the plan as supporting industrialists who would inevitably lead the nation into war. Other than the Court's emphatic language, little in these international cases suggested the ongoing war, much less the continuing involvement of the United States in Mexico and Central America. One exception was a laconic remark by Chief Justice White in *United States v. Hamburg-Amerikanische Packetfahrt-Actien Gesellschaft,* a case charging several companies with violating the Sherman Antitrust Act by combining to monopolize transatlantic steamship service.[50] The Court held that the case was moot, because steamship service had ended as a consequence of "the European war which is now flagrant—a matter of which we take judicial notice."[51] With that very modest exception, the Court made no explicit reference to the war. Nevertheless, the Court seemed intent on accentuating the national character of power, even if it meant depriving someone of the right to vote.[52] The person so deprived was Ethel Mackenzie, an American citizen by birth. In 1909 she married Gordon Mackenzie, a citizen of Great Britain. The couple continued to reside in California. Under the Citizenship Act of March 2, 1907, however, she took the nationality of her husband.[53] As a result, when she attempted to register to vote, state officials refused to allow her to do so. She challenged that refusal, arguing that

---

48. *Atkin v. Kansas,* 191 U.S. 207 (1903).
49. Link, *Woodrow Wilson and the Progressive Era,* 165
50. 239 U.S. 466 (1916).
51. Ibid., 475.
52. *Mackenzie v. Hare,* 239 U.S. 299 (1915).
53. Act of March 2, 1907, ch. 2534, 34 Stat. 1228.

Congress intended the statute to apply only to those who resided abroad. To construe the act to apply to her, she argued, would make the act unconstitutional.

Writing for the Court, Justice McKenna sided with the local election officials, reciting the familiar phrases: The statute was explicit and clear; to add conditions "would transcend judicial power." He declined to look to debates in Congress, writing that those debates were irrelevant: "Whatever was said in the debates on the bill or in the reports concerning it, preceding its enactment or during its enactment, must give way to its language, or, rather, all the reasons that induced its enactment and all of its purposes must be supposed to be satisfied and expressed by its words, and it makes no difference that in discussion some may have been given more prominence than others, seemed more urgent and insistent than others, presented the mischief intended to be remedied more conspicuously than others."[54]

Since the statute, as construed, deprived Mackenzie of her citizenship, McKenna turned to the argument that the statute was unconstitutional. Although expressing sympathy for her desire to retain her citizenship, McKenna could not accept her arguments. Once again the Court pointed to matters of national importance, indeed of international significance. In that venue the Court "should hesitate long before limiting or embarrassing such powers."[55] Here there was advance notice of the consequences of the marriage. Thus, in light of the potential international consequences, the case "involved more than personal considerations. As we have seen, the legislation was urged by conditions of national moment. . . . This is no arbitrary exercise of government. It is one which, regarding the international aspects, judicial opinion has taken for granted would not only be valid but demanded."[56]

One other passing reference to the war came in Justice McReynolds's opinion for the unanimous Court in *Butler v. Perry*.[57] Jake Butler challenged the constitutionality of a 1913 Florida law that required every "able-bodied male person over the age of twenty-one years, and under the age of forty-five years" to work on county roads for up to six ten-hour days each year. The statute allowed men to satisfy that requirement by providing a substitute or by paying a fixed sum to the county. When Butler refused to comply, he was convicted and sentenced to thirty days in jail. Butler contended that the statute violated the Thirteenth Amendment's ban on involuntary servitude as well as the Fourteenth Amendment's guarantee of due process and of

---

54. 239 U.S. at 308.
55. Ibid., 311.
56. Ibid., 312.
57. 240 U.S. 328 (1916).

equal protection. The Court rejected both contentions. McReynolds found long-standing—he called them "ancient"—precedents to support the conclusion that a state had "inherent power to require every able-bodied man within its jurisdiction to labor for a reasonable time on public roads near his residence without direct compensation. This is a part of the duty which he owes to the public."[58] McReynolds traced similar laws from eleventh-century England, through the colonies, and into nineteenth-century America, noting that as of 1889 twenty-seven states had statutes requiring work on public roads.[59]

In that light, the Thirteenth Amendment could not be seen as prohibiting a requirement of work on public roads. All that "the term involuntary servitude was intended to cover [was] those forms of compulsory labor akin to African slavery which in practical operation would tend to produce like undesirable results."[60] Thus, McReynolds concluded, with just the slightest glance toward events in Europe, the amendment "introduced no novel doctrine with respect of services always treated as exceptional, and certainly was not intended to interdict enforcement of those duties which individuals owe to the State, such as services in the army, militia, on the jury, etc. The great purpose in view was liberty under the protection of effective government, not the destruction of the latter by depriving it of essential powers."[61]

In sum, with almost insignificant exceptions, the Court went about its work as though unaffected by events outside the issues brought into its courtroom. As Chief Justice White said when welcoming Justice Clarke to the Court, "It is a great place, Judge, but we live in a cave."[62] In all likelihood the changes within the Court—which allowed for no decision during this term in which nine justices participated, and with 70 percent having fewer than eight justices—had a greater impact on the Court's disinclination to resolve important issues. That is further supported by the ten cases set for reargument at the beginning of the next term, the largest number at any time during White's tenure as chief justice.[63]

In the cases that it did decide, the Court continued to side with the national government on most questions of federalism. The creeping intru-

---

58. Ibid., 330.
59. Ibid., 330–32.
60. Ibid., 332.
61. Ibid., 333.
62. Quoted in Warner, *The Life of Mr. Justice Clarke,* 133n. 6.
63. The cases were these: *Pennsylvania Railroad Co. v. W. F. Jacoby & Co.,* 242 U.S. 89 (1916); *Pennsylvania Railroad Co. v. Sonman Shaft Coal Co.,* 242 U.S. 120 (1916); *Sim v. Edenborn,* 242 U.S. 131 (1916); *Alder v. Edenborn,* 242 U.S. 137 (1916); *Long Sault Development Co. v. Call,* 242 U.S. 272 (1916); *Clark Distilling Co. v. Western Maryland Railway Co.,* 242 U.S. 311 (1917); *Hawkins v. Bleakly,* 243 U.S. 210 (1917); *Paine Lumber Co., Ltd. v. Neal,* 244 U.S. 459 (1917); *Hitchman Coal & Coke Co. v. Mitchell,* 245 U.S. 229 (1917).

sion of national rules was evident in a case such as *Texas & Pacific Railway Co. v. Rigsby,* which held that the Safety Appliance Act applied even though the rail car on which the employee had been injured had been removed from interstate commerce for at least a month.[64] The injury occurred when a rung on a ladder (a grab iron) on a rail car failed, causing the employee to fall to the ground. The Court showed no inclination to use the cases which held that interstate commerce came to an end when goods, such as lightning rods, came to rest in the state. Instead, the Court sought the broadest remedial scope for the act. In the words of Justice Pitney: "We are therefore brought to the conclusion that the right of private action by an employee injured while engaged in duties unconnected with interstate commerce, but injured through a defect in a safety appliance required by the act of Congress to be made secure, has so intimate a relation to the operation of the Act as a regulation of commerce between the States that it is within the constitutional grant of authority over that subject."[65] There were, however, occasional exceptions, as shown by two cases involving the Federal Employers' Liability Act—*Shanks v. Delaware, Lackawanna & Western Railroad Co.*[66] and *Chicago, Burlington & Quincy Railroad Co. v. Harrington.*[67] In each case the Court avowed that it sought a "practical" approach, one which allowed for fuzziness at the edges of the concept, so long as the intent of Congress was met. Thus, in *Shanks* Justice Van Devanter wrote that the act "speaks of interstate commerce, not in a technical legal sense, but in a practical one better suited to the occasion."[68] Even though his language echoed that of Pitney in *Rigsby* ("closely related" vs. "intimate a relation"), Van Devanter concluded that the employee could not sue under the federal law. In *Harrington,* Justice Hughes quoted *Shanks* in support of the Court's conclusion that federal law did not apply. In one case the employee was injured while moving a piece of heavy equipment used to repair parts of locomotives that themselves would be used in interstate commerce; in the other case, the employee was moving coal from a storage track to a shed where it would be placed in bins for use by both intrastate and interstate trains.

A similar tilt toward national interests can be seen in *Atchison, Topeka & Santa Fe Railway Co. v. Harold,* a case involving the interpretation of a shipping document giving instructions for transporting goods.[69] The document, called a "bill of lading," set out the terms under which the railroad agreed to transport corn. When the corn was found to be damaged, both parties

---

64. 241 U.S. 33 (1916).
65. Ibid., 42.
66. 239 U.S. 556 (1916).
67. 241 U.S. 177 (1916).
68. 239 U.S. at 558.
69. 241 U.S. 371 (1916).

looked to the bill of lading to determine who should pay for the loss. The bill covered an interstate delivery, though the dispute involved only an intrastate segment of the total journey. As the Court noted, the intrastate bill of lading came at the end of an interstate shipment; accordingly, the entire shipment was considered to be an interstate one and therefore governed by federal statute, which sought a uniform rule.[70] Likewise, in a case that provoked one of the few written dissents of the term, the Court held that federal law governed a bill of lading that contained a provision requiring written notice of a claim for damages to cattle before they were removed from their destination or mingled with other cattle.[71] The cattle were shipped over two railroads from Montana to Chicago. Once they arrived in Chicago, they were sold before anyone gave notice of injury. The language at issue required that notification be given to an agent "of said company." The first railroad had no agent in Chicago; the second did. But, as noted, the shipper gave notice to no one. Under state law, the requirement of notice would have been invalid because of the absence of a representative of the first railroad. That is, under state law, the shipper had no obligation to give notice. Under federal law, however, the second carrier was the agent of the first. Thus, the shipper could have (and should have) given notice to the second railroad to satisfy the requirement of the bill of lading. By failing to give notice, the shipper lost its claim for damages.

McReynolds's dissent, joined by McKenna, did not disagree with the application of federal law. Rather, he thought the question had not been properly raised in the state courts; he therefore thought the Court lacked jurisdiction to hear the case. And, on the merits, he found the provision in the bill of lading to be so vague as to warrant invocation of the rule that it should be construed against the drafter, the railroad. He concluded his dissent with this stinging comment: "The construction placed upon [the bill of lading] by the state Supreme Court, when sitting within surroundings designed to stimulate clear thinking, is diametrically opposed to the one now adopted. In such circumstances it appears to me hardly reasonable to say that a stockman at a wayside Montana station was bound instantly to apprehend the true interpretation, notwithstanding any mental quickening which he may have received from a 'rough wind' and a

---

70. The federal statute was the Carmack Amendment to the Interstate Commerce Act. Act of June 29, 1906, ch. 3591, §7, 34 Stat. 584, 593. See also *New York, Philadelphia & Norfolk Railroad Co. v. Peninsula Produce Exchange*, 240 U.S. 34 (1916), Carmack Amendment construed to cover loss occasioned by delay in delivery as well as by damage to produce; *Georgia, Florida & Alabama Railway Co. v. Blish Milling Co.*, 241 U.S. 190 (1916), construction of bill of lading is a federal question; requirement of written notice of failure to make delivery is satisfied by telegram.

71. *Northern Pacific Railway Co. v. Wall*, 241 U.S. 87 (1916).

modest thermometer pointing to only 'seven or eight degrees below zero.'"[72]

In cases not involving a national interest, the Court was no less likely to side with what it perceived as public interests against those of individuals. Illustrative of that tendency was *Hadacheck v. Sebastian,* which involved a Los Angeles ordinance banning brick yards within certain parts of the city.[73] The ordinance was typical of efforts by Progressive reformers to use urban planning to combat the problems of cities. J. C. Hadacheck challenged his conviction for violating the act, which he characterized as an unconstitutional taking of his property, on which he had operated a brick yard since before the land was annexed by Los Angeles. In rejecting Hadacheck's argument, Justice McKenna supported the police power of the states with this strong language, hinting that he, if not the complete Court, was not entirely opposed to the changes brought by urban America:

> It is to be remembered that we are dealing with one of the most essential powers of government, one that is the least limitable. It may, indeed, seem harsh in its exercise, usually is on some individual, but the imperative necessity for its existence precludes any limitation upon it when not exerted arbitrarily. A vested interest cannot be asserted against it because of conditions once obtaining. . . . To so hold would preclude development and fix a city forever in its primitive conditions. There must be progress, and if in its march private interests are in the way they must yield to the good of the community. The logical result of petitioner's contention would seem to be that a city could not be formed or enlarged against the resistance of an occupant of the ground and that if it grows at all it can only grow as the environment of the occupations that are usually banished to the purlieus.[74]

Similar concern for "progress" came from the Court in response to suits for compensation for damages caused by flooding when the United States constructed levees on the Mississippi River. The construction had begun in 1883, under what was known as the Eads Plan. That plan envisioned using levees to force the water into a narrower channel, producing a more rapid flow that, in turn, would dig a deeper channel for navigation. The construc-

---

72. Ibid., 98.
73. 239 U.S. 394 (1915).
74. Ibid., 410. McKenna referred to a similar case, decided only the term before, in which the Court upheld an ordinance prohibiting livery stables within certain areas. *Reinman v. Little Rock,* 237 U.S. 171 (1915). Three weeks after announcing *Hadacheck,* the Court upheld a 1911 municipal ordinance that prohibited the emission of dense smoke in certain parts of a city, *Northwestern Laundry v. City of Des Moines,* 239 U.S. 486 (1916).

tion occupied private land both for the levees themselves and for the overflow caused by the higher water resulting from the location of the levees. A number of cases had reached the Court before White became chief justice; thus, there was little new in the decisions under White. The Court did, however, make it clear that it sided with the "progress" afforded by the levees, again through Justice McKenna: "Great problems confronted the National and state governments, great and uncertain natural forces were to be subdued or controlled, great disasters were to be averted; great benefits acquired. There might be liability to the individual; if so, the liability should be clear, the cause of it direct and certain."[75]

The suits concerning levees dealt with one part of the jurisprudence of takings—what constituted a "taking." Other cases in this term dealt with another part of the same jurisprudence—what constituted a "public" use. For example, a case from Alabama questioned whether a power company's taking of water to drive generators was a public use.[76] The Court's answer was brief, though expressed in the elegant obscurities of Holmes's prose: "In the organic relations of modern society it may sometimes be hard to draw the line that is supposed to limit the authority of the legislature to exercise or delegate the power of eminent domain. But to gather the streams from waste and to draw from them energy, labor without brains, and so to save mankind from toil that it can be spared, is to supply what, next to intellect, is the very foundation of all our achievements and all our welfare. If that purpose is not public we should be at a loss to say what is."[77]

The rest of the Court's term reflected the by now familiar hodgepodge of cases, few of which suggested lasting importance. In one series of cases, for instance, the Court reiterated that the Bill of Rights did not apply to the states, thereby allowing state juries in civil trials to return verdicts with less

---

75. *United States v. Archer,* 241 U.S. 119, 129 (1916). Pitney's dissent in this case contains a detailed description of the construction of the levees as well as a pained complaint about the Court's refusal to recognize the harm done to landowners. In *Cubbins v. Mississippi River Commission,* 241 U.S. 351 (1916), the Court held that a landowner could not recover for flooding caused by the construction of levees. For the Court, White relied upon precedents dating from the Code Napoleon, which held that all landowners had reciprocal rights to construct levees to protect their land from accidental and extraordinary flooding without incurring liability for flooding that might be caused by the construction.

76. *Mt. Vernon-Woodberry Cotton Duck Co. v. Alabama Interstate Power Co.,* 240 U.S. 30 (1916).

77. Ibid., 32. For another case dealing with taking water for hydroelectric purposes, see *Cuyahoga River Power Co. v. City of Akron,* 240 U.S. 462 (1916), Court remanded for additional proceedings to determine whether the power company had rights in the water supply. For cases dealing with irrigation and drainage districts as public uses, see *O'Neill v. Leamer,* 239 U.S. 244 (1915); *Houck v. Little River Drainage District,* 239 U.S. 254 (1915); *Myles Salt Co., Ltd. v. Board of Commissioners of the Iberia and St. Mary Drainage District,* 239 U.S. 478 (1916).

than unanimous votes.[78] In the first of those cases, *Minneapolis & St. Louis Railroad Co. v. Bombolis,* Chief Justice White hinted at the Court's surprise that the issue would raise so much argument by the railroads, who obviously wanted the tactical advantage of a unanimous jury in suits against them under the Federal Employer's Liability Act and other statutes. If the suits were brought in federal court, the Seventh Amendment required that the jury be unanimous; if the suits were brought in state court, as the statutes allowed, juries might be less than unanimous. White explained almost breathlessly that "it never entered the mind of anyone to suggest the new and strange view concerning the significance and operation of the Seventh Amendment which was urged in this case and the cases which were argued with it."[79] Nevertheless, he did devote several paragraphs to explaining why the amendment did not govern trials in state courts.

In other cases the Court upheld a state's exercise of its police power to regulate a variety of activities. For example, *Rast v. Van Deman & Lewis Co.* upheld the power of Florida to tax trading stamps.[80] The trading stamps were discount coupons or discount tokens wrapped with articles for sale to consumers. As the Court explained, the coupons and tokens could be redeemed either by a local merchant or by another party. Even though the redemptions often took place in interstate commerce, the Court had no difficulty in concluding that the retail sales within the state were not interstate commerce and were therefore subject to the state's police power. The retailers defended the coupons and tokens as nothing more than innocent advertising. In explaining why the Court did not accept that portrayal, Justice McKenna earned praise from Felix Frankfurter, who wrote to Holmes that McKenna's opinion gave Frankfurter "new strength in my belief in his perceptions in these constitutional questions, and it's so the fashion to sneer at him."[81] McKenna invoked the morality of a halcyon rural America:

> Advertising is merely identification and description, apprising of quality and place. It has no other object than to draw attention to the article to be sold, and the acquisition of the article to be sold constitutes the only inducement

---

78. *Minneapolis & St. Louis Railroad Co. v. Bombolis,* 241 U.S. 211 (1916); *St. Louis & San Francisco Railroad Co. v. Brown,* 241 U.S. 223 (1916); *Louisville & Nashville Railroad Co. v. Stewart,* 241 U.S. 261 (1916); *Chesapeake & Ohio Railway Co. v. Kelly,* 241 U.S. 485 (1916); *Chesapeake & Ohio Railway Co. v. Gainey,* 241 U.S. 494 (1916).
79. 241 U.S. at 218.
80. 240 U.S. 342 (1916).
81. Frankfurter to Holmes, March 22, 1916, Mennel and Compston, *Holmes and Frankfurter: Their Correspondence, 1912–1934,* (Hanover, N.H.: University Press of New England, 1996), 48. Frankfurter continued his praise of McKenna later in the year, writing: "He *does* seize the marrow of the big issues before the Court." Frankfurter to Holmes, December 21, 1916, ibid., 63.

to its purchase. The matter is simple, single in purpose and motive; its consequences are well defined, there being nothing ulterior; it is the practice of old and familiar transactions and has sufficed for their success.

The schemes of complainants have no such directness and effect. They rely upon something else than the article sold. They tempt by a promise of a value greater than that article and apparently not represented in its price, and it hence may be thought that thus by an appeal to cupidity lure to improvidence. This may not be called in an exact sense a "lottery," may not be called "gaming"; it may, however, be considered as having the seduction and evil of such, and whether it has may be a matter of inquiry, a matter of inquiry and of judgment that it is finally within the power of the legislature to make. Certainly in the first instance, and, as we have seen, its judgment is not impeached by urging against it a difference of opinion. . . . And it is not required that we should be sure as to the precise reasons for such judgment or that we should certainly know them or be convinced of the wisdom of the legislation.[82]

The Court followed that opinion with one upholding the power of North Dakota to regulate the size of containers in which lard was sold.[83] And, in a later opinion, the Court upheld Michigan's 1913 law regulating employment agencies.[84] The only exception to this list of cases upholding exercises of police power came in a holding that the District of Columbia did not have the power to compel a taxicab company to reveal rates charged on services provided through orders telephoned to its central garage.[85] The company was, in the language of the statute, a public utility insofar as it offered services to passengers at Union Station and insofar as it offered services at various hotels throughout the District. But calls to the garage were different in the eyes of the Court. They remained, like certain insurance, private contracts, as Holmes indicated by his citation of *German Alliance*. In his opinion for the Court, Holmes conceded that the case was not without difficulty: "Although I have not been able to free my mind from doubt the Court is of opinion that this part of the business is not to be regarded as a public utility. It is true that all business, and for the matter of that, every life in all its details, has a public aspect, some bearing upon the welfare of the community in which it is passed. But however it may have been in earlier days as to the common callings, it is assumed in our time that an invitation to the public to buy does not necessarily entail an obligation to sell."[86]

---

82. 240 U.S. at 365–66.
83. *Armour & Co. v. North Dakota*, 240 U.S. 510 (1916).
84. *Brazee v. Michigan*, 241 U.S. 340 (1916).
85. *Terminal Taxicab Co. v. Kutz*, 241 U.S. 252 (1916).
86. Ibid., 256.

VII

The 1916–1917 Term

When the justices assembled on October 9, they formed a full court for the first time in several years. The *New York Times* reported that all of the justices "looked ruddy and hearty after the Summer interval of recuperation."[1] This court would remain intact for the remaining five terms of White's tenure. One consequence of the recent interruptions in membership was that the justices faced eighteen cases set for reargument from a previous term, presumably to allow a full bench to resolve issues on which the justices were divided. A second consequence of changes in membership—though one to be felt in the future—was a significant drop in the percentage of unanimous opinions, down to just over 80 percent.[2] Chief Justice White's failing health may have contributed to an inability to forge unanimity. But he did seem able to maintain the justices' practice of not offering explanations for their disagreements: Of the forty-one cases in which there was a dissent, only fifteen had written dissents.[3] As in the past, there was no pattern to the dissents, either in issue or in author. Leadership within the Court also came from Justice Van Devanter. In spite of the fact that his "slow pen" continued to place him at the bottom in number of opinions for the Court (nineteen, versus White and Holmes, who led with twenty-nine each), Van Devanter was of considerable assistance during the justices' conferences.[4] He earned high praise from Brandeis, who said of Van Devanter, "He is inde-

---

1. *New York Times*, October 10, 1916.
2. Of the 214 opinions for the Court, 173 were unanimous, or 80.8 percent.
3. *Louisville & Nashville Railroad Co. v. United States*, 242 U.S. 60 (1916); *Detroit United Railway v. Michigan*, 242 U.S. 238 (1916); *Long Sault Development Co. v. Call*, 242 U.S. 272 (1916); *Caminetti v. United States*, 242 U.S. 470 (1917) ; *The Five Per Cent. Discount Cases*, 243 U.S. 97 (1917); *Owensboro, Kentucky v. Owensboro Water Works Co.*, 243 U.S. 166 (1917); *Wilson v. New*, 243 U.S. 332 (1917); *Motion Picture Patents Co. v. Universal Film Manufacturing Co.*, 243 U.S. 502 (1917); *New York Central Railroad Co. v. Winfield*, 244 U.S. 147 (1917); *Southern Pacific Co. v. Jensen*, 244 U.S. 205 (1917); *Western Oil Refining Co. v. Lipscomb*, 244 U.S. 346 (1917); *First National Bank of Bay City v. Fellows*, 244 U.S. 416 (1917); *Valdez v. United States*, 244 U.S. 432 (1917); *Paine Lumber Co., Ltd. v. Neal*, 244 U.S. 459 (1917); *Adams v. Tanner*, 244 U.S. 590 (1917).
4. Pusey, *Charles Evans Hughes*, 1:284. Praise for Van Devanter's role as a "task" leader continued under Chief Justice Taft, who succeeded White. Danelski, "The Influence of the

fatigable, on good terms with everybody, ready to help everybody, knows exactly what he wants and clouds over difficulties by fine phrases and deft language."[5]

The Court continued to be unable to hold its own against the flood of cases being brought to its docket—the *New York Times* headline for the first day of the term read "A Year Behind Its Work."[6] For the first time during the White Court, Congress had responded to those pressures, even though White still refused to use his office to lobby Congress. While serving as attorney general, McReynolds had been the principal drafter of an act that set the beginning of the Court's term a week earlier, on the first Monday in October instead of the second, as it had been since 1873.[7] That provision became effective in October 1917, so it provided no relief for the Court in the 1916–1917 term. Other parts of the act, however, took effect during the term, thereby giving the Court slight relief from certain kinds of disputes—eliminating the right to review in bankruptcy, trademark, and Federal Employers' Liability Act cases. An earlier act had allowed discretionary review in certain state cases.[8] The effect of these modest changes was to take some of the most tedious distinctions off the Court's mandatory docket. But the justices still had to consider many of those cases as petitions for certiorari. Although the legislation offered hope for the future, the immediate effect seemed to be a rush by lawyers to get cases onto the Court's docket before the restrictions became effective. The 658 cases filed during the term represented the largest percentage increase during the White Court; the twelve hundred cases on the Court's docket also represented the largest percentage increase in the same period.[9]

The Court wasted no time in dealing with the relief offered for its docket. In the first opinion announced during the term, Chief Justice White explained that the Court lacked jurisdiction to entertain a writ of error in the case—the Court had no discretion in cases properly brought under writs of error, it had to consider the merits of the case. The case came from the circuit court of appeals which had reviewed an opinion of the Supreme Court of the Territory of Hawaii, based solely on the amount in dispute. In that class of cases, White explained, review could be had in

---

5. Quoted in Strum, *Louis D. Brandeis: Justice for the People*, 369.
6. *New York Times,* October 10, 1916.
7. Act of September 6, 1916, ch. 448, 39 Stat. 726.
8. Act of December 23, 1914, ch. 2, 38 Stat. 790. For discussion of these changes, see Felix Frankfurter and James M. Landis, *The Business of the Supreme Court: A Study in the Federal Judicial System* (New York: Macmillan, 1928), 203–16.
9. Epstein et al., *The Supreme Court Compendium*, 2d ed., 72. In the 1912–1913 term, the Court had 1,201 cases on its docket; but that number represented a smaller percentage increase from the prior year.

the Supreme Court only by writ of certiorari, which was discretionary. He rebuffed all interpretations that would require review, pointing to the 1915 act: "Besides, as the remedy intended to be afforded by the Amendment of 1915 was evidently the restricting of the jurisdiction of this court to the end that the burden on its docket might be lightened, we cannot construe that amendment as frustrating the purpose which it was adopted to accomplish."[10] Likewise, later in the term the Court explained that controversies arising in bankruptcy could be reviewed only through the discretionary certiorari jurisdiction. This time it was Justice Day who expressed the Court's relief, writing that the 1915 act "manifested the purpose of Congress to relieve this court from the necessity of considering cases of this character, except when brought here by the writ of certiorari."[11]

As far as its certiorari jurisdiction was concerned, the Court was equally quick to provide instructions to counsel, though with a certain ambivalence and with remarkable kindness to overly diligent attorneys. Thus, early in the term the Court expressed its exasperation at having discovered that it had devoted parts of two days to hearing oral argument in a case that had been settled by the parties some twenty months earlier.[12] Writing for the Court, Justice McReynolds accepted that counsel had not intended to mislead the Court—even though the final decree had been based on an express compromise of the parties. In dismissing the writ as improvidently granted, the Court emphasized its dependence on the parties to reveal all the facts, at the same time giving rare insight into the workings of the Court:

> During the last term one hundred fifty-four petitions for certiorari were presented and acted upon. Because of recent legislation—Act of September 6, 1916, c. 448, 39 Stat. 726—their number hereafter may greatly increase. Such petitions go first to every member of the court for examination, and are then separately considered in conference. This duty must be promptly discharged. We are not aided by oral arguments and necessarily rely in an especial way upon petitions, replies and supporting briefs. Unless these are carefully prepared, contain *appropriate* references to the record and present with *studied accuracy, brevity and clearness* whatever is essential to ready and adequate understanding of points requiring our attention, the rights of interested parties may be

---

10. *Inter-Island Steam Navigation Co., Ltd. v. Ward,* 242 U.S. 1, 3–4 (1916). The Act of January 28, 1915, is printed at ch. 22, 38 Stat. 803.
11. *William R. Staats Co. v. Security Trust and Savings Bank,* 243 U.S. 121, 124 (1917).
12. *Furness, Withy & Co., Ltd. v. Yang-Tsze Insurance Association, Ltd.,* 242 U.S. 430 (1917).

prejudiced and the court will be impeded in its efforts properly to dispose of the causes which constantly crowd its docket.[13]

Examples of the need for relief abounded during the term, especially in cases involving the Federal Employers' Liability Act, cases that after October 6, 1916, could be reviewed only through a writ of certiorari. The Court's attempts at dealing with ever smaller pieces of the FELA puzzle showed precisely why these cases should be decided somewhere other than a *supreme* court.[14] For example, early in the term the Court held that a deceased employee had not lived long enough to warrant recovery for pain and suffering.[15] With that decision, the Court further calibrated its prior decisions on the same point, with the result being that "perhaps ten minutes" was not long enough, though just under two hours was;[16] and slightly more than half an hour was "close to the border line."[17]

Other examples came in less grotesque circumstances when the Court struggled to determine what constituted being involved in interstate commerce. In one decision, Justice Holmes wrote for the Court that it would be "extravagant" to hold that an intrastate trip was interstate commerce because it was the return leg of a round trip whose first leg carried cars traveling in interstate commerce.[18] On the same day, the Court held that an employee was not engaged in interstate commerce even though he would have been called to an interstate train had he not been injured when he alighted from an intrastate train to walk to the yardmaster's office for further orders.[19] That distinction was in keeping with the Court's holdings that logging was not interstate until the logs reached a common carrier.[20] By contrast, an employee *was* working in

---

13. 242 U.S. at 434 (emphasis in original). Three months later, Chief Justice White was a bit kinder in explaining another dismissal on account of the failure of counsel to provide an accurate statement of the facts. He reported that the Court had examined the record and found "that the question upon which the certiorari was prayed . . . does not arise on the record and is not open for consideration, and therefore (of course, we assume, through inadvertence of counsel) the petition for certiorari was rested upon a wholly unsubstantial and non-existing ground . . . ." *Tyrrell v. District of Columbia*, 243 U.S. 1, 4 (1917). In retirement, Justice Clarke confirmed that each justice separately considered each petition for certiorari; Clarke, "Methods of Work of the United States Supreme Court Judges," 401.
14. See Frankfurter and Landis, *The Business of the Supreme Court*, 208.
15. *Great Northern Railway Co. v. Capital Trust Co.*, 242 U.S. 144 (1916).
16. *Kansas City Southern Railway Co. v. Leslie*, 238 U.S. 599 (1915).
17. *St. Louis, Iron Mountain & Southern Railway Co. v. Craft*, 237 U.S. 648, 655 (1915).
18. *Illinois Central Railroad Co. v. Peery*, 242 U.S. 292 (1916).
19. *Erie Railroad Co. v. Welsh*, 242 U.S. 303 (1916).
20. *McCluskey v. Marysville & Northern Railway Co.*, 243 U.S. 36 (1917); *Bay v. Merrill & Ring Logging Co.*, 243 U.S. 40 (1917). Compare *Minneapolis & St. Louis Railroad Co. v. Winters*, 242 U.S. 353 (1917), not interstate commerce when working on engine once used in interstate commerce; *Lehigh Valley Railroad Co. v. Barlow*, 244 U.S. 183 (1917), not interstate commerce when unloading cars at rest for seventeen days after interstate movement.

interstate commerce when he left a task of inspecting cars moving on an interstate train to assist those injured in an accident in the rail yard.[21] And, the Court held that a person injured in the state of Washington while constructing a tunnel to be used by trains operating between Chicago and Seattle was not engaged in interstate commerce.[22] That decision was somewhat surprising in light of prior decisions holding that those employed on bridges used by interstate trains *were* engaged in interstate commerce. The distinction seemed to be that original construction was not interstate, whereas repairs of a facility in interstate use were.

The prospect of ending this Byzantine maze of distinctions under the FELA must have brought great joy to the Court. But, even as the justices glimpsed relief, they saw a different future in state workmen's compensation acts. The statutes represented yet a further development in attempts to deal with industrial accidents. The FELA, and similar state statutes, had abolished certain common-law defenses while requiring that employers be shown to be negligent before any recovery could be had. The typical workmen's compensation act, by contrast, eliminated the requirement of negligence; in return, employees could recover only the amount fixed by statute. As Professor Arthur McEvoy has shown, the workmen's compensation laws resulted from a redefinition of the category "accident," which in turn eliminated the requirement that workers show the "cause" of their injuries.[23]

In a series of eight cases reargued and decided in this term, the Court had to resolve the constitutionality of those state statutes both under the Fourteenth Amendment and under the supremacy clause.[24] The first in this series was *New*

---

21. *Southern Railway Co. v. Puckett*, 244 U.S. 571 (1917). See also *Erie Railroad Co. v. Winfield*, 244 U.S. 170 (1917), employee leaving rail yard at end of a day is engaged in interstate commerce.
22. *Raymond v. Chicago, Milwaukee & St. Paul Railway Co.*, 243 U.S. 43 (1917).
23. Arthur F. McEvoy, "The Triangle Shirtwaist Factory Fire of 1911: Social Change, Industrial Accidents, and the Evolution of Common-Sense Causality," *Law & Social Inquiry* 20 (spring 1995): 621–51.
24. The eight cases were *New York Central Railroad Co. v. White*, 243 U.S. 188 (1917), first argued February 29, and March 1, 1916, reargued February 1, 1917; *Hawkins v. Bleakly*, 243 U.S. 210 (1917), first submitted January 24, 1916, reargued December 20, 1916; *Mountain Timber Co. v. Washington*, 243 U.S. 219 (1917), first argued March 1, 2, 1916, reargued January 30, 1917; *New York Central Railroad Co. v. Winfield*, 244 U.S. 147 (1917), first argued February 29, and March 1, 1916, reargued February 1, 1917; *Erie Railroad Co. v. Winfield*, 244 U.S. 170 (1917), first argued March 1, 1916, reargued February 1, 2, 1917; *Southern Pacific Co. v. Jensen*, 244 U.S. 205 (1917), first argued February 28, 1916, reargued January 31, February 1, 1917; *Clyde Steamship Co. v. Walker*, 244 U.S. 255 (1917), first argued February 28, 1916, reargued January 30, February 1, 1917. There was one other workmen's compensation case this term, *Valley Steamship Co. v. Wattawa*, 244 U.S. 202 (1917), in which the Court upheld the Ohio law that prohibited employers who did not participate in the state's insurance fund from claiming the defenses of contributory negligence, fellow servant, and assumption of risk.

York Central Railroad Co. v. White.[25] The case involved an employee killed while working as a night watchman for the construction site of a station and tracks to be used in interstate commerce. Before reaching the issues concerning the statute's constitutionality, the Court quickly disposed of the claim that the employee had been engaged in interstate commerce—and therefore within the FELA rather than the state statute. Referring to the Washington tunnel case, Justice Pitney wrote for the unanimous Court that the night watchman's "work bore no direct relation to interstate transportation, and had to do solely with construction work."[26]

With that point behind him, Pitney turned to the constitutionality of the 1913 New York act.[27] The law defined certain occupations as hazardous and required that anyone employing persons in those occupations pay compensation according to a schedule in the act. (The schedule based compensation on the employee's average weekly wages and on the nature of the injury.) The payments followed any accident in the course of employment in a covered occupation, regardless of fault, which caused disability or death of an employee. The only exceptions were for injuries resulting from drunkenness or the intentional conduct of an employee. The act required employers to guarantee their ability to make the payments in one of two ways. Either they could provide proof of self-insurance or they could participate in an insurance plan, which might be through the state's insurance fund or through a private insurer authorized to provide workmen's compensation insurance in the state. There were other details to the law, but the outline is enough to show that Pitney was well justified in his understated observation that the "scheme of the act is so wide a departure from common-law standards respecting the responsibility of employer to employee that doubts naturally have been raised respecting its constitutional validity."[28]

The fundamental question was whether the Constitution protected those common-law standards from change by the state legislature. In translating the question into constitutional vocabulary, the companies made three arguments: (1) the statute deprived the employer of property without due process by imposing liability regardless of fault; (2) the employee lost

---

25. 243 U.S. 188 (1917). For discussion of these cases, see Robert E. Rodes Jr., "Due Process and Social Legislation in the Supreme Court—A Post Mortem," *Notre Dame Lawyer* 33 (December 1957): 5–33.

26. 243 U.S. at 192.

27. The act replaced one passed in 1910, which was held to violate the New York state constitution as well as the national constitution. *Ives v. South Buffalo Railway Co.*, 201 N.Y. 271 (1911). Following that decision, the people of New York amended the state constitution to permit laws of this type, and the state legislature enacted the law at issue in *White*. Justice Pitney summarized the law and its history in his opinion; 243 U.S. at 192–96.

28. 243 U.S. at 196.

the right to have damages based on injury rather than on the statutory schedule; and (3) both employer and employee lost the right to take the risks into account in their contract. Pitney acknowledged those arguments, but he never moved away from treating employer and employee as obverse sides of a single relationship. Ultimately, that image of reciprocity (quid pro quo, in the vocabulary of contract law) proved to be the cardinal point in the Court's decision to uphold the law.

Pitney drew on the nineteenth century in emphasizing the constitutional importance of the contractual relationship: "The close relation of the rules governing responsibility as between employer and employee to the fundamental rights of liberty and property is of course recognized."[29] But he just as quickly rejected any suggestion that the rules were immutable. "No person," he wrote, "has a vested interest in any rule of law entitling him to insist that it shall remain unchanged for his benefit." For support of that changing concept of liability, Pitney pointed to liability for violating statutes, of which the Safety Appliance Acts were examples; and he noted that the fellow-servant doctrine itself was less than a century old.[30] Even liability without fault was not a new concept.[31] He conceded that a state might go too far in altering the rules; but he was satisfied that that had not happened here, since the state had replaced one set of rules with another—thereby maintaining some semblance of give and take for both sides. In other words, the statute had maintained the nineteenth-century form of contract while providing a twentieth-century adaptation. That portrait disguised the subtle change effected by the statute. Even though Pitney had referred to "employer" and "employee" as singular, the statute treated them as collective concepts, with insurance providing intermediation between groups and individuals. Moreover, by treating injury to employees as part of the necessary cost of doing business, the statute had further depersonalized the worker, moving closer to the image of a worker being no different from a piece of machinery or any other element in production.[32] Even with Pitney's picture of apparent balance, the Court still had to determine whether the statute was "arbitrary and unreasonable, from the standpoint of natural justice."[33] With that phrase, Pitney brought the discussion back to the vocabulary of the Fourteenth Amendment.

Reducing the analysis to a fundamental economic point, Pitney observed that injury to employees was an inevitable part of conducting business. Fur-

---

29. Ibid., 197–98.
30. Ibid., 198–99. Pitney pointed to several antebellum cases as the origin of the fellow-servant rule.
31. Ibid., 204.
32. See John Fabian Witt, "The Transformation of Work and the Law of Workplace Accidents, 1842–1910," *Yale Law Journal* 107 (March 1998): 1492.
33. 243 U.S. at 202.

ther, showing that he could recognize an imbalance in the parties' relationship, he noted that only the employee would bear any physical loss. But, Pitney noted, economic loss could be shifted. And, since economic loss was as much a cost of doing business as was repairing machinery, he thought it "plain that, on grounds of natural justice, it is not unreasonable for the State, while relieving the employer from responsibility for damages measured by common-law standards and payable in cases where he or those for whose conduct he is answerable are found to be at fault, to require him to contribute a reasonable amount."[34] Once again subtle vocabulary changes masked vital shifts in meaning—equating employees with machinery made it almost impossible to envision employees engaging in meaningful contract negotiations with employers.

Pitney seemed to sense the shift. For his final task was to explain that upholding the law did not amount to a repudiation of the freedom of contract protected by *Coppage* and *Truax*.[35] He acknowledged that the New York law restricted freedom of contract; but he concluded that it was a permissible exercise of the state's police power to protect its citizens from harm. He offered no standard to test exercises of that power, other than the ubiquitous "reasonable." That the statute protected "human life or limb" may have made the decision palatable, but the restriction offered no limiting test for the reach of the state's police power. He quoted the "no man is an island" language from *Holden v. Hardy:* "The whole is no greater than the sum of all the parts, and when the individual health, safety, and welfare are so enforced or neglected, the State must suffer."[36]

The fragility of the Court's unanimity in *White* was emphasized by the 5–4 split in a third workmen's compensation decision announced on the same day, *Mountain Timber Co. v. Washington*.[37] (The Court was unanimous in the second case, *Hawkins v. Bleakly*, upholding Iowa's law, which allowed employers and employees to opt out of participation.)[38] Like its companion cases, *Mountain Timber* had been presented to the Court during the 1915–1916 term, then set for reargument in this term. At issue was a Washington statute that required all employers to participate in a state insurance fund, rather than giving them an option of self-insurance or private insurance as had the New York law. Washington mandated payments into the fund based on each employer's total payroll for the year, with those occupa-

---

34. Ibid., 203.
35. *Coppage v. Kansas,* 236 U.S. 1 (1915), struck down state laws prohibiting employers from requiring that employees not join unions; *Truax v. Raich,* 239 U.S. 33 (1915), struck down state law requiring that 80 percent of employees be qualified electors or native born.
36. 243 U.S. at 206–7, quoting *Holden v. Hardy,* 169 U.S. 366, 397 (1898).
37. 243 U.S. 219 (1917).
38. 243 U.S. 210 (1917).

tions designated as least dangerous being required to contribute 1.5 percent. The amount increased to 10 percent for the most dangerous occupation, powder works. The act provided for adjustments, even refunds, according to the experience of contributions and payments. The mandated contributions did not cause the Court any significant difficulty. Instead, the focus of the attack on the Washington statute was on its distribution of costs among members of a particular class of occupations, thereby taking the relationship yet a step further away from the one-to-one relationship imagined in nineteenth-century law. The result of that distribution was that employers had to contribute the fixed percentage to the fund regardless of their individual experience with loss. In short, the act created group liability rather than individual.

That distribution prompted a long examination by Pitney, again writing for the Court. To explore whether the law fulfilled a public purpose, justifying it as an exercise of the state's police power, Pitney drew on the shared images of veterans of wars. Although he recalled the American Civil War and the Spanish-American War, the imagery was made all the more poignant by the contemporaneous photographs from the war in Europe, where the German navy was resuming unrestricted submarine warfare and the German army was in the midst of constructing a defensive position known as the Hindenburg Line, at the time this decision was announced, March 6, 1917: "A familiar exercise of state power is the grant of pensions to disabled soldiers and to the widows and dependents of those killed in war. Such legislation usually is justified as fulfilling a moral obligation or as tending to encourage the performance of the public duty of defense."[39] With that piercing image in mind, Pitney posed a rhetorical question: "But is the State powerless to compensate, with pensions or otherwise, those who are disabled, or the dependents of those whose lives are lost, in the industrial occupations that are so necessary to develop the resources and add to the wealth and prosperity of the State?"[40] He answered his question with alacrity, showing the metaphorical path of common-law reasoning: "A machine as well as a bullet may produce a wound, and the disabling effect may be the same."[41] With the public purpose of the act thus affirmed, Pitney found little else to cause concern. He viewed the details of the act as no more than matters of discretion for the legislature in exercising its public function. In particular, he found nothing arbitrary or unreasonable about the requirement that employers share the costs of accidents within their common industry, especially in light of the fact that no employer could be entirely free from accident.

---

39. Ibid., 239–40.
40. Ibid., 240.
41. Ibid.

In a stunning exhibition of self-restraint, White, McKenna, Van Devanter, and McReynolds merely recorded their dissent. No one wrote to explain. They did, however, have a chance to explain when they found themselves in the majority in *Southern Pacific Co. v. Jensen*, the fourth of the workmen's compensation cases of the term.[42] *Jensen* was argued initially with *White*, then reargued with it; but the decision was delayed for more than two months, possibly indicating the difficulty of getting a majority or the need to allow Justice Pitney to compile the resources for his monumental dissent. In the end, Justice Day sided with the dissenters from *Mountain Timber*, leaving Holmes and Pitney to write dissents, with Brandeis and Clarke joining each dissent. *Jensen*, like *White*, involved a dispute over the New York workmen's compensation law. The critical difference between the two cases was that the employee in *Jensen* had been killed while unloading lumber from a steamship berthed in New York harbor. Southern Pacific, the owner of the steamship, challenged an award from the Workmen's Compensation Commission of New York. In addition to the arguments made in *White*, Southern Pacific argued that the New York law conflicted both with the Federal Employer's Liability Act and with general admiralty law. With respect to the first argument, Southern Pacific sought to bring its shipping activities within the FELA's definitional section, which made the statute applicable to "every common carrier by railroad."[43] Without reference to legislative history, McReynolds rejected the argument. The FELA, he wrote, applied only to "something having direct and substantial connection with railroad operations."[44] It was, he wrote, "unreasonable" to think that Congress had intended to change admiralty rules when a ship was owned by a railroad.

The second argument proved to be the most important, with a majority of the Court concluding that the presence of the ship in navigable waters meant that Congress's preeminent power over maritime law superseded the state law. The basis for their conclusion was yet another engagement in drawing lines—now between maritime and domestic law as opposed to interstate and intrastate commerce. But, according to McReynolds, the principles were the same.[45] As a result, since the deceased employee worked on a ship in navigable waters, his injuries occurred under maritime jurisdiction. The Court therefore reversed the state court's allowance of an award under New York's workmen's compensation law. McReynolds sought to buttress his conclusion with the suggestion of unacceptable consequences if New York were allowed to impose its law on ships entering its harbor. There would be a "destruction

---

42. 244 U.S. 205 (1917). There was a fifth case, decided on the basis of *Jensen*, since it also involved an injury on board a steamship while in New York harbor. *Clyde Steamship Co. v. Walker*, 244 U.S. 255 (1917).
43. 244 U.S. at 212, quoting the federal act.
44. Ibid., 213.
45. Ibid., 216–17.

of the very uniformity in respect to maritime matters which the Constitution was designed to establish; and freedom of navigation between the States and with foreign countries would be seriously hampered and impeded."[46]

Justice Holmes's dissent, joined by Brandeis and Clarke, includes two of his most memorable aphorisms. But the key point was that nothing in the Constitution or in federal law deprived a state of the power to mandate compensation for accidental injury. Neither did general principles of maritime law supersede state law. Maritime law, Holmes wrote, "is not a *corpus juris*—it is a very limited body of customs and ordinances of the sea."[47] He conceded that judges could change the maritime law; but their ability to do so was limited, "they can do so only interstitially; they are confined from molar to molecular motions."[48] When admiralty judges looked for rights, they had to look to "the common law or statutes of a State."[49] Even then the courts were restricted, for "[t]he common law is not a brooding omnipresence in the sky but the articulate voice of some sovereign or quasi-sovereign that can be identified; although some decisions with which I have disagreed seem to me to have forgotten the fact. It always is the law of some State."[50] So, if an admiralty court might adopt the common law or statute law of a state, then a state statute was not automatically inferior to general maritime rules. That was all the more true when the action was in a state court, where the state's law could be applied in the face of congressional silence.

Justice Pitney's dissent, which Brandeis and Clarke also joined, was considerably less ethereal than Holmes's opinion. Although Pitney agreed "substantially" with Holmes, he thought it "proper, in view of the momentous consequences of the decision, to present some additional considerations."[51] He viewed the majority as holding that state courts had to apply general maritime law, even when there was no act of Congress defining the duties owed by the employer. "This view," Pitney wrote, "is so entirely unsupported by precedent, and will have such novel and far-reaching consequences, that it ought not to be accepted without the most thorough consideration."[52] His thirty-page analysis of maritime jurisdiction was designed to show that "the States are at liberty to administer their own laws in their own courts when exercising a jurisdiction concurrent with that of

---

46. Ibid., 217. Congress quickly amended the statute to reverse the result announced by the Court. Act of October 6, 1917, ch. 97, 40 Stat. 395.
47. 244 U.S. at 220.
48. Ibid., 221.
49. Ibid.
50. Ibid., 222.
51. Ibid., 223.
52. Ibid., 225.

admiralty, and at liberty to change those laws by statute."[53] He based that conclusion on a wide-ranging examination of precedents, all designed to show that granting the power (that is, jurisdiction) to hear maritime cases did not require that the courts rely upon a fixed body of substantive law.

On the same day that it announced *Jensen*, the Court also further limited the reach of New York's workmen's compensation act by holding that the Federal Employers' Liability Act controlled recovery for all injuries (whether with or without fault) that occurred while a railroad employee was engaged in interstate commerce.[54] James Winfield, the injured employee, was struck in the eye by a pebble while tamping cross-ties as part of repairs being made on the railroad's tracks. He lost the use of his eye. All conceded that there was no fault or negligence. Thus, there would be no recovery under the FELA, which required proof that the employer was negligent. By contrast, the state law would have allowed an award to the employee. Writing for the Court, Justice Van Devanter echoed Justice McReynolds in *Jensen* in expressing concern for any outcome that would permit different rules to exist in different states: "Whether and in what circumstances railroad companies engaging in interstate commerce shall be required to compensate their employees in such commerce for injuries sustained therein are matters in which the Nation as a whole is interested and there are weighty considerations why the controlling law should be uniform and not change at every state line."[55] For support of that conclusion, McReynolds took the unusual step of quoting from congressional materials and referring to the president's message that accompanied the bill to Congress.[56] The requirement of universality meant that the FELA applied and limited recovery to instances of negligence; silence as to injury without negligence meant that there was to be no liability in those instances.

Justice Brandeis disagreed, so much so that the case "laid him low."[57] In this, his first dissent as a member of the Court, Brandeis inundated the reader with facts to explain why he drew a different conclusion from the silence of Congress. He could find nothing in the language of the act indicating that Congress meant to occupy the entire field, to the exclusion of the state's police power. Indeed, he pointed to the act's use of "in certain cases" in its title as supporting his conclusion that Congress did not intend to prevent states from providing an innovative remedy for employees injured without fault of the employer. Instead, he viewed the FELA as "emergency legislation," designed to deal with an "appalling" number of accidents to railroad

---

53. Ibid., 227.
54. *New York Central Railroad Co. v. Winfield*, 244 U.S. 147 (1917).
55. Ibid., 149.
56. Ibid., 150.
57. Urofsky, "The Brandeis-Frankfurter Conversations," 326.

employees.[58] In that light, the purpose of the federal statute was a narrow one, to restore recovery for injury caused by negligence in the face of the growth of common-law defenses of fellow servant, assumption of risk, and contributory negligence. In Brandeis's words, under the FELA "[t]he common-law liability for fault was to be restored by removing the abuses which prevented its full and just operation. . . . This limited purpose of the Employers' Liability Act precludes the belief that Congress intended thereby to deny to the States the power to provide compensation or relief for injuries not covered by the act."[59]

Brandeis's style, with footnotes and subheadings, provoked Harold Laski to complain to Justice Holmes. Laski wrote that he and Roscoe Pound had agreed "that if you could hint to Brandeis that judicial opinions aren't to be written in the form of a brief it would be a great relief to the world. Pound spoke rather strongly as to the advocate in B. being over-prominent in his decisions just as in his general philosophy."[60] Holmes replied, "What you say about the form of Brandeis's opinions had been remarked on by me to him before you wrote, if you refer to the form in a strict sense—the putting in of headings and footnotes—and on one occasion I told him that I thought he was letting partisanship disturb his judicial attitude. I am frank with him because I value him and think he brings many admirable qualifications to his work. In one case when he wrote a long essay on the development of employers' liability [Winfield, 244 US 147 (1917)] I told him that I thought it out of place and irrelevant to the only question: whether Congress had dealt with the matter so far as to exclude state action."[61]

If the FELA was not meant to change what Brandeis termed "the individualistic basis of right and of liability," then the state workmen's compensation acts were. To support that conclusion he invoked the studies of experts: "In the effort to remove abuses, a study had been made of facts; and of the world's experience in dealing with industrial accidents. That study uncovered as fiction many an assumption upon which American judges and lawyers had rested comfortably. The conviction became widespread, that our individualistic conception of rights and liability no longer furnished an adequate basis for dealing with accidents in industry. It was seen that no system of indemnity dependent upon fault on the employers' part could meet the situation."[62] But, as Brandeis noted, the study had not had an impact on the American states in 1908, when Congress enacted the FELA. That fact further

---
58. 244 U.S. at 162, 161.
59. Ibid., 164.
60. Laski to Holmes, January 13, 1918, Howe, *Holmes-Laski Letters*, 1:127.
61. Holmes to Laski, January 16, 1918, ibid., 128.
62. 244 U.S. at 164–65.

strengthened Brandeis's conviction that Congress had not intended to prevent the states from providing supplementary relief for their citizens. He rejected McReynolds's call for uniformity, noting that there was considerable diversity among the states in costs and other circumstances of living. Since states would ultimately bear the costs of caring for the injured, it was especially appropriate that they should be free to adapt remedial statutes to their particular conditions. Furthermore, Brandeis noted, the supposed uniformity in federal law was an illusion. He pointed to the ninety-three FELA cases on the Court's docket in October 1915, each of which he said involved close factual questions, often leading to inconsistent results.[63]

Brandeis's somewhat disingenuous characterization of the FELA as "emergency" legislation reflected the tone of the country shortly before the United States entered the war on April 6, 1917, some six weeks before the decision in *Winfield*. Brandeis and the other justices had joined members of Congress on April 2 to hear President Wilson request a declaration of war. Chief Justice White was the first on his feet to applaud Wilson's statement that the United States was to join the war "to make the world safe for democracy."[64] Wilson's speech followed Germany's decision to resume unrestricted submarine warfare on February 1, a day that fell in the middle of the four days devoted to argument of the FELA and workmen's compensation cases. At the end of February, the British government revealed the text of the Zimmerman telegram, in which the German foreign secretary offered Mexico the return of land in southwestern United States in exchange for Mexico's participation in the war on the side of Germany. Two weeks later the United States faced the imminent shutdown of all railroads in the country as the result of a labor dispute. The dispute had simmered for several months, with labor seeking higher wages and an eight-hour day in place of the then-standard ten-hour day. The previous summer, Congress had averted a national rail strike by rushing the Adamson Act into law.[65] The act, the "last major federal law of the progressive period," followed months of unsuccessful negotiation between railroad unions and owners.[66] Faced with the prospect of a nationwide strike, and unable to compel arbitration, President Wilson asked Congress for a law requiring an eight-hour day for railroad workers. Congress responded with a mandate that payment be based on an eight-hour day. To prevent a reduction in pay for

---

63. Ibid., 168n. 1.
64. Henry L. Stoddard, *As I Knew Them: Presidents and Politics from Grant to Coolidge* (New York: Harper & Brothers Publishers, 1927), 487; *New York Times,* May 20, 1921 (recollection of Chief Justice McCoy of the supreme court of the District of Columbia); Klinkhamer, *Edward Douglas White,* 63–64.
65. Act of September 3, 5, 1916, ch. 436, 39 Stat. 721. White quoted the relevant portions of the act in his opinion. *Wilson v. New,* 243 U.S. 332, 343–44 (1917).
66. Nugent, *From Centennial to World War: American Society, 1876–1917,* 185.

workers, Congress also mandated that no one receive less than currently received for a day's work. The result was that for many workers the ten-hour standard became an eight-hour one. To assuage the employers' concerns, Congress established a commission to study the costs of what was in effect an increase in wages. The commission's report could be the basis of additional legislation to authorize the Interstate Commerce Commission to increase rates to offset the increased costs. The effective date of the act was January 1, 1917. With the cooperation of all parties, a district court judge enjoined enforcement of the act, thereby allowing a direct appeal to the Supreme Court. The Court heard argument on January 8, 9, and 10, 1917. In the following months, labor leaders pressed their call for a strike. Under pressure from Wilson, on March 19 the railroads agreed to the terms set by the Adamson Act. Later the same day, the Court announced its opinion, in the case styled *Wilson v. New*.[67] One observer termed the opinion the most important that White wrote in his career and "probably the most important decision by the Supreme Court in the last three decades."[68] In what was the worst split of the term, Chief Justice White's "opinion of the Court" was weakened by the separate concurrence of Justice McKenna, the fifth member of the majority[69] Justices Day, Pitney, and

---

67. 243 U.S. 332 (1917).
68. Spring, "Two Chief Justices: Edward Douglass White and William Howard Taft," 169. See also, *Literary Digest* 54 (March 1917): 887.
69. The split was almost the worst of the White Court. Its only rival, to date, was *Wheeler v. Sohmer*, 233 U.S. 434 (1914), in which two opinions represented the five-man majority, thereby allowing Justice Holmes to announce only "the judgment of the court" (indicating that his opinion did not have the support of a majority of the justices). Ibid., 437. The issue in *Wheeler* was whether a state could impose an inheritance tax on negotiable documents located within its jurisdiction, even though the owner and the tangible property were outside the jurisdiction. Later, during the 1918–1919 term, there would be two other instances of a badly divided Court. In one, *Texas & Pacific Railway Co. v. Leatherwood*, 250 U.S. 478 (1919), there would again be no opinion for the Court. Justice Brandeis announced the judgment, with three justices joining him; two concurred; and three dissented, though without opinion. That case involved the much-discussed question of the effect of bills of lading containing restrictions on the right to sue for damages—bills of lading that covered transportation by more than one railroad. The other case, *Arizona Employers' Liability Cases*, 250 U.S. 400 (1919), continued the division so apparent during the 1916–1917 term, which was over efforts by states to redefine the liability of employers for injuries to employees. This last case did, however, produce an opinion of the Court (which indicates that five justices agreed), supplemented by a concurring opinion for three justices and opposed by two separate dissents on behalf of four justices.

Not until the 1919–1920 term would the Court again be so divided. In a curious little case, *The Mail Divisor Cases*, 251 U.S. 326 (1920), Justice Holmes again announced the "judgment" of the Court, with only White, Brandeis, and Clarke joining him. Pitney and McKenna agreed on a single concurring opinion; Day and Van Devanter dissented without an opinion; and McReynolds did not participate. At issue in that case was the proper method of computing the average weight of mail carried by trains during a specified period—thus the short title of

McReynolds each wrote a separate dissent; Justice Van Devanter joined Pitney and a part of Day's dissent.

In his usual reductionist style, White compressed the parties' arguments into two points: Whether Congress had the power to enact the type of legislation, and whether Congress had abused its power in enacting the specific legislation. Insofar as Congress's power was concerned, White described a dichotomy between the regulation of public businesses such as railroads and the respect owed to the "primarily private" relation of establishing wages.[70] But that portrayal quickly collapsed as he reacted to the crisis he envisioned from a failure of the employers and employees to agree—"the entire interruption of interstate commerce which was threatened, and the infinite injury to the public interest which was imminent."[71] Describing the crisis as one brought on "by the failure to exert the private right" of negotiating wages, he concluded that Congress had the power to act under the circumstances.[72] White's prose showed little of the press of the emergency he so obviously felt. It took him almost a hundred words to explain that the public interest could outweigh private interests in time of emergency: "This must be unless it can be said that the right to so regulate as to save and protect the public interest did not apply to a case where the destruction of the public right was imminent as the result of a dispute between the parties and their consequent failure to establish by private agreement the standard of wages which was essential; in other words that the existence of the public right and the public power to preserve it was wholly under the control of the private right to establish a standard by agreement."[73] He rejected as question begging the argument that an emergency could not create a power. Instead, "emergency may afford a reason for the exertion of a living power already enjoyed."[74] In short, Congress had the power to act to prevent a complete stoppage of interstate commerce, even if it meant constricting the heart of private contract—the setting of wages.

In response to the railroads' argument that the law deprived them of a reasonable rate of return by increasing costs without allowing an appropriate increase in rates, White's only response was a series of rhetorical questions, each of which must have been accompanied by a hint of panic in his

---

the cases. Holmes wrote sardonically to Frankfurter that the work put in on the case was "not thrilling." Holmes to Frankfurter, December 21, 1919, Mennel and Compston, *Holmes and Frankfurter: Their Correspondence,* 79. For background on *The Mail Divisor Cases,* see *New York Times,* January 16, 1917.
70. 243 U.S. at 347.
71. Ibid., 347–48.
72. Ibid., 348, 350 (where the phrase is "the failure to exercise the private right").
73. Ibid., 348.
74. Ibid.

voice when he announced the opinion: "What would be the value of the right to a reasonable rate if all movement in interstate commerce could be stopped as a result of a mere dispute between the parties or their failure to exert a primary private right concerning a matter of interstate commerce?";[75] and, What value would there be in the regulations "if there was no power to remedy a situation created by a dispute between employers and employees as to rate of wages, which if not remedied, would leave the public helpless, the whole people ruined and all the homes of the land submitted to a danger of the most serious character?"[76]

Having concluded that Congress had the power to enact the law, White devoted less attention to whether Congress had abused its power. He emphasized that Congress had fixed wages for only a short time, pending the results of the commission's investigation. For additional support, White adapted a technique from Brandeis, noting that the wage structure could not be abusive since it was already in place in approximately 15 percent of the industry. In sum, the statute's reasonableness was cinched by the recognition that all Congress had done was enact a form of compulsory arbitration.[77]

Justice McKenna's concurring opinion only indirectly confronted the issue that was so troublesome—that of regulating price, or wages. McKenna, who had struggled valiantly in *German Alliance Insurance Co. v. Lewis*,[78] now denied that the act was a wage law. Instead, he insisted, the statute dealt only with hours of service. Somewhat disingenuously he wrote:

> Nothing is fixed but the time of service—the hours which shall be deemed a day's work—the number to be eight. All else—compensation and conditions—is left to contract . . . .
>
> The distinction between what is left to the parties and what is fixed by the law is real. There is certainly a difference between the prescription of the time of service and the prescription of compensation for the service, and the difference is observed in the speech and conduct of men; it is observed in the regulations of legislation. It has never been supposed that the agitation for an eight-hour day for labor or the legislation which has responded to it, was intended to fix or did fix the rate of wages to be paid.[79]

Then he conceded that there was a relationship between hours and wages: "Of course, in a sense, the two things are related. The time of service and the price of service may be said to be the reciprocals of each other—each the

---

75. Ibid., 350.
76. Ibid., 351.
77. Ibid., 351, 359.
78. 233 U.S. 389 (1914).
79. Ibid., 361.

price of the other.... But, as I have said, in the practice of men and in the examples of legislation, regulation of one is not regarded as the regulation of the other."[80] As though he was not quite convinced, he repeated the point later in his short opinion: "I have only to point out that it is the sense of the practical world that prescribing the hours of labor is not prescribing the wages of labor, and Congress has kept the purposes distinct."[81]

Justice Day dissented on the basis of a single point: Congress's inability to determine a fair wage for employees (as evidenced by the appointment of a commission) showed that the wage was arbitrary.[82] He conceded that Congress had the power to fix wages; but the due process clause required that Congress investigate before it legislated. He was not prepared to allow Congress to delegate to experts such a critical part of the employment relationship. To impose costs without first being sure that the costs were appropriate amounted "to the taking of the property of one and giving it to another in violation of the spirit of fair play and equal right which the Constitution intended to secure in the due process clause."[83]

Although Justices Pitney and Van Devanter agreed with Day's analysis of due process, they did not accept his conclusion that Congress could regulate wages. Consequently, they joined in a separate dissent, written by Pitney. In that dissent, Pitney emphasized that the law regulated wages, not hours. The only reference to hours, he pointed out, was as a standard for pay; there was no limit on hours, no penalty for exceeding eight hours in a day. As such, in his view, the act was "a regulation not of commerce but of the internal affairs of the commerce carriers."[84] In another phrase, he explained that there was no power to regulate employment that was "a matter of private bargaining between the parties, in which each has a constitutional right to exact such terms as he may deem proper."[85] In that light, he spurned White's rationale that the failure of the parties to reach an agreement authorized Congress to act. In Pitney's view, "A failure to agree is not a waiver but an exercise of the right—as much so as the making of an agreement."[86] He scorned the suggestion that the act would improve the efficiency of the railroads, describing the argument as "altogether fanciful."[87]

Justice McReynolds's three-paragraph dissent was devoid of explanation for his conclusion that the power to regulate commerce did not include the

---

80. Ibid., 361–62.
81. Ibid., 362.
82. Ibid., 368–69.
83. Ibid., 370.
84. Ibid., 377.
85. Ibid., 381.
86. Ibid., 387.
87. Ibid., 380.

power to regulate wages. He did, though, conclude with a somewhat sinister suggestion that from the Court's opinion "it follows as of course" that Congress had the power to set maximum wages as well as minimum, to require compulsory arbitration, and "to take measures effectively to protect the free flow of such commerce against any combination, whether of operatives, owners, or strangers."[88]

Three weeks later, the Court announced its decision in *Bunting v. Oregon*.[89] Argued at the end of the week following argument in *Wilson*, *Bunting* involved a challenge to a 1913 Oregon law that set ten hours as the maximum anyone could work in a day. The statute did allow for certain emergencies and for an additional three hours in a single day, but for those hours the statute mandated that the employee be paid overtime. The state indicted F. O. Bunting for requiring an employee to work thirteen hours in a single day in the Lakeview Flouring Mills, without paying overtime or coming within one of the other statutory exceptions. Capturing the distinction that had proved so powerful in the past, Bunting challenged the statute as a wage law and therefore a denial of due process. In the alternative, if the statute was viewed as an hours-of-service law, Bunting contended that it was a denial of equal protection, since it applied only to mills, factories, and manufacturing establishments. Brandeis originally oversaw the defense of the statute, along with his sister-in-law Josephine Goldmark—the same team that had successfully defended another Oregon statute in *Muller v. Oregon*. Once Brandeis joined the Court, Oregon engaged Felix Frankfurter to present the oral argument. In his argument, Frankfurter emphasized the statistics compiled by Progressive reformers, saying that the legislature was fully justified in passing the statute. Justice Holmes suggested that the argument placed the statute in what "may be called the penumbra of the police power." To that suggestion White responded with concern, "Let us take care that the penumbra does not darken our light." But Frankfurter spurned the imagery, saying that "the mass of evidence we offer throws so much light that we are not even in the region of the penumbra."[90]

Writing for the 5–3 Court, McKenna again rejected the contention that the law was a wage law. "To assent to this," he wrote, "is to ascribe to the legislation such improvidence of expression as to intend one thing and effect another, or artfulness of expression to disguise illegal purpose."[91] He accepted at face value the statute's own declaration that it was unhealthy to work more than ten hours a day in any of the covered occupations. But McKenna also

---

88. Ibid., 389.
89. 243 U.S. 426 (1917).
90. Mary D. Hopkins, "Human Conservation and the Supreme Court," *Survey* 36 (May 1916): 221. (*Bunting* was first argued April 18, 1916, then set for reargument in January 1917.)
91. 243 U.S. at 435.

acknowledged that there was "a certain verbal plausibility" in the suggestion that the statute regulated wages.[92] Even so, he concluded, "the plausibility disappears upon reflection. The provision for overtime is permissive, in the same sense that any penalty may be said to be permissive. Its purpose is to deter by its burden and its adequacy for this was a matter of legislative judgment under the particular circumstances."[93] Those "particular circumstances" threatened to undo the Court's move toward accepting national regulation for the economy. Here, accepting the state's defense of the law, the Court could not know local conditions, only the state's legislature and courts could have that knowledge.[94]

McKenna also acknowledged the imprecision of regulation, writing that "the constitutional validity of legislation cannot be determined by the degree of exactness of its provisions or remedies. New policies are usually tentative in their beginnings, advance in firmness as they advance in acceptance. They do not at a particular moment of time spring full-perfect in extent or means from the legislative brain. Time may be necessary to fashion them to precedent customs and conditions and as they justify themselves or otherwise they pass from militancy to triumph or from question to repeal."[95] By upholding the Oregon law, as applied to an employee in a flour mill, the Court effectively overruled *Lochner* without referring to the earlier case.[96]

White's emphasis on the extraordinary circumstances in *Wilson* was a reminder of another of his opinions this same term, *Clark Distilling Co. v. Western Maryland Ry. Co.*, upholding the 1913 Webb-Kenyon Act.[97] The act was the first temperance law of nationwide application passed by Congress, marking the prohibition movement's successful shift from local to national politics.[98] The act prohibited the interstate shipment of alcohol when its use was illegal in the state to which it was shipped.[99] The silence of the only two dissenters (Holmes and Van Devanter) from White's opinion belied the controversy that followed the act. Holmes himself regretted that he had not written a dissent, though he "thought the law should be construed more narrowly to avoid awkward doubts."[100] White only hinted at the controversy when

---

92. Ibid., 436.
93. Ibid.
94. Ibid., 437.
95. Ibid.
96. See David P. Currie, "The Constitution in the Supreme Court: 1910–1921," *Duke Law Journal* 1985:1130.
97. 242 U.S. 311 (1917).
98. Chambers, *The Tyranny of Change: America in the Progressive Era, 1900–1917*, 134–35; James H. Timberlake, *Prohibition and the Progressive Movement, 1900–1920* (Cambridge, Mass.: Harvard University Press, 1963), 159.
99. Act of March 1, 1913, ch. 90, 37 Stat. 699.
100. Holmes to Frankfurter, January 13, 1917, Mennel and Compston, *Holmes and Frankfurter: Their Correspondence*, 66.

he referred to "opinions adverse to the power of Congress to enact the law . . . in other departments of the government."[101] In fact, the attorney general issued an opinion that the bill was unconstitutional; and President Wilson vetoed it.[102] Congress, however, promptly overrode the veto. West Virginia almost as promptly sought an injunction to prevent railroads from bringing liquor into the state in violation of its 1913 prohibition act.

White's opinion moved quickly past questions about the constitutionality of the state law. The only genuine issue was whether the Webb-Kenyon Act was constitutional. White emphasized that the act itself did not ban personal use of alcohol, it only offered national support for states that chose to ban importation for that use. Pointing to the "exceptional nature of the subject here regulated," White wrote that there could be no doubt about the power of Congress to ban alcohol from interstate commerce, citing cases involving lottery tickets and prostitutes.[103] Thus, in his analysis, the issue was whether Congress had the power to regulate commerce in liquor in a manner short of prohibition, especially when the manner allowed for variable results depending upon the law of each state. White's inclination toward the apocalyptic was evident in his assertion that if the power to regulate meant only the power to prohibit, then "the existence of government under the Constitution would be no longer possible."[104] Then, ignoring the call for uniformity in *Winfield,* White wrote that the attempt to require uniformity was an attempt to add what was not in the Constitution.[105] Indeed, rather than being a defect, the act's deference to the states was a sign of respect for the "dual system of government," as shown by Congress's structuring its regulation "to produce coöperation between the local and national forces of government to the end of preserving the rights of all."[106]

The final argument against the statute amounted to a rebuttal of White's optimistic portrayal—the statute portended putting all objects of interstate commerce under the control of the states. Rather than admit

---

101. 242 U.S. at 325.

102. Opinion of the Attorney General, 30 Op. A. G. 88 (February 28, 1913); Veto Message of the President (February 28, 1913), *Congressional Record,* 62d Cong., 3d sess., vol. 49, pt. 5: 4291. White cites both in his opinion, 242 U.S. at 325. The Court later upheld the act against a challenge to the vote to override the president's veto. *Missouri Pacific Railway Co. v. Kansas,* 248 U.S. 276 (1919). The Wilson administration's dislike of the act is further suggested by the failure of anyone from the administration to appear before the Court to defend the act. Instead, the Anti-Saloon League's Wayne Wheeler argued the case on behalf of West Virginia.

103. *Lottery Case (Champion v. Ames),* 188 U.S. 321 (1903); *Hoke v. United States,* 227 U.S. 308 (1913).

104. 242 U.S. at 326.

105. Ibid., 327.

106. Ibid., 331.

that Congress might do just that, under its plenary power over interstate commerce, White chose to emphasize the special nature of liquor. Like lottery tickets and prostitutes (and adulterated food as well), liquor had an inherent quality that subjected it to special regulation. He concluded his opinion with the comment that "the exceptional nature of the subject here regulated is the basis upon which the exceptional power exerted must rest and affords no ground for any fear that such power may be constitutionally extended to things which it may not, consistently with the guarantees of the Constitution, embrace."[107] No doubt, White would have invoked "common experience" to support the "exceptional nature" of liquor. Certainly nothing in the opinion suggested that White had relied on experts or other fact finders.

White's repeated use of prostitution as an analogy to support the Webb-Kenyon Act reflected the presence of *Caminetti v. United States*[108] on the Court's docket at the same time as *Clark Distilling*. In fact, the two cases had been argued only a week apart in November 1916 before being decided on consecutive Mondays in January 1917. *Caminetti* involved the prosecution of two men, F. Drew Caminetti and Maury Diggs, for taking two high-school girls with them from Sacramento, California, to Reno, Nevada. The evidence pointed to a consensual relationship between the pairs, with no suggestion that there was a commercial motive to the travel. Caminetti was the son of the commissioner of immigration under President Wilson; Diggs was the former state architect for California. The celebrity attached to the case came from the fact that each man was well connected politically and from allegations that then-Attorney General McReynolds had succumbed to political pressure. McReynolds had ordered the trial delayed so that Caminetti's father could complete an assignment in Washington, D.C., in time to travel to California for the trial.[109] Rather than revealing an invidious motive, the postponement more likely revealed the political naïveté of the then newly appointed attorney general. Whatever the validity of the charges, McReynolds did not participate in the case when it reached the Supreme Court.

Before the Court, however, the sole question was whether the Mann Act was limited to commercialized vice. Writing for the Court's majority, Justice Day portrayed the issue in familiar, neutral phrases:

> It is elementary that the meaning of a statute must, in the first instance, be sought in the language in which the act is framed, and if that is plain,

---

107. Ibid., 332.
108. 242 U.S. 470 (1917).
109. See Bond, *I Dissent*, 44–47; Hendrick, "James C. McReynolds," 31–32; Schimmel, "The Judicial Policy of Mr. Justice McReynolds," 112ff.; "The Attorney-General in Hot Water," *Literary Digest* 47 (July 1913): 39–41.

and if the law is within the constitutional authority of the law-making body which passed it, the sole function of the courts is to enforce it according to its terms. . . .

Where the language is plain and admits of no more than one meaning the duty of interpretation does not arise and the rules which are to aid doubtful meanings need no discussion. . . . There is no ambiguity in the terms of this act. . . .

Statutory words are uniformly presumed, unless the contrary appears, to be used in their ordinary and usual sense, and with the meaning commonly attributed to them.[110]

Here, the act punished the interstate transportation of "any woman or girl for the purpose of prostitution or debauchery, or for any other immoral purpose."[111] Although Day conceded that the "immoral purpose would be more culpable in morals and attributed to baser motives if accompanied with the expectation of pecuniary gain,"[112] that fact did not invalidate Congress's attempt to punish the lesser act as well as the greater.

Day rejected all attempts to narrow that meaning of the act's language. That the act gave itself the title White-Slave Traffic Act had no bearing: "If the words are plain, they give meaning to the act, and it is neither the duty nor the privilege of the courts to enter speculative fields in search of a different meaning."[113] Likewise rejected were congressional reports: "[W]hen words are free from doubt they must be taken as the final expression of the legislative intent, and are not to be added to or subtracted from by considerations drawn from titles or designating names or reports accompanying their introduction, or from any extraneous source. In other words, the language being plain, and not leading to absurd or wholly impracticable consequences, it is the sole evidence of the ultimate legislative intent."[114]

Justice McKenna dissented, even though he had written the Court's unanimous opinion in *Hoke v. United States,* which upheld the constitutionality of the Mann Act.[115] Now, joined by White and Clarke, he refused to accept the application of the act to anything other than commercial activities. He suggested that the majority had succumbed to emotion; and he urged that the judiciary "should not shut its eyes to the facts of the world and assume not to know what everybody else knows. And everybody knows that there is a difference between the occasional immoralities of men and

---

110. 242 U.S. at 485–86.
111. The statute is quoted in Justice Day's opinion. Ibid., 488 n. 1.
112. 242 U.S. at 486.
113. Ibid., 490.
114. Ibid.
115. 227 U.S. 308 (1913).

women and that systematized and mercenary immorality epitomized in the statute's graphic phrase 'White-slave traffic.'"[116] He described Day's principle of statutory construction as having "attractive and seemingly disposing simplicity."[117] McKenna placed special emphasis on the phrase "any other immoral practice,"[118] which he asserted could not have the sweeping meaning it would be given in ordinary usage, covering "every form of vice, every form of conduct that is contrary to good order."[119] Just why it could not, McKenna never explained; but he used that self-discovered ambiguity to launch an inquiry into the purpose of the statute. In essence, McKenna followed the same path trod by White in his "rule of reason" opinions. Both justices found that "every" could not possibly mean "*every*"; instead, each statute required a reasonable construction. For an answer, he found it appropriate to look at various congressional materials, though reports were to be favored over statements made during debate: "The representations of the latter may indeed be ascribed to the exaggerations of advocacy or opposition. The report of a committee is the execution of a duty and has the sanction of duty."[120] In keeping with this breadth of search for meaning was his otherwise surprising admission that "the words of the statute should be construed to execute it [the purpose of the statute]," and, he added, the words "may be so construed even if their literal meaning be otherwise."[121] After referring to cases to support his rule, he added in its support:

> It not only rescues legislation from absurdity (so far the opinion of the court admits its application), but it often rescues it from invalidity, a useful result in our dual form of governments and conflicting jurisdictions. It is the dictate of common sense. Language, even when most masterfully used, may miss sufficiency and give room for dispute. Is it a wonder there-

---

116. 242 U.S. at 502.
117. Ibid., 496.
118. The actual text of the statute was this: "That any person who shall knowingly transport or cause to be transported, or aid or assist in obtaining transportation for, or in transporting, in interstate or foreign commerce, or in any Territory or in the District of Columbia, any woman or girl for the purpose of prostitution or debauchery, or for any other immoral purpose, or with the intent and purpose to induce, entice, or compel such woman or girl to become a prostitute or to give herself up to debauchery, or to engage in any other immoral practice . . . shall be deemed guilty of a felony." Justice Day emphasized the earlier phrase "any other immoral purpose"; Justice McKenna emphasized the latter, "any other immoral practice." Although the provisions are distinct, and a careful reader might find cause to distinguish the two phrases, no one on the Court suggested a distinction; the two phrases were treated as equals.
119. 242 U.S. at 497.
120. Ibid., 499.
121. Ibid., 500.

fore, that when used in the haste of legislation, in view of conditions perhaps only partly seen or not seen at all, the consequences, it may be, beyond present foresight, it often becomes necessary to apply the rule? And it is a rule of prudence and highest sense. It rescues from crudities, excesses and deficiencies, making legislation adequate to its special purpose, rendering unnecessary repeated qualifications and leaving the simple and best exposition of a law the mischief it was intended to redress. Nor is this judicial legislation. It is seeking and enforcing the true sense of a law notwithstanding its imperfection or generality of expression.[122]

McKenna's cautionary essay in *Caminetti* suggests a certain respect for the police powers of the states, powers which would be infringed by the Court's reading of the Mann Act as covering noncommercial, immoral acts. That suggestion is all the more intriguing in light of his repeated emphasis on the malleability of meaning and the need to adapt to changing conditions. Those two traits found support in his opinions for the Court upholding states' "Blue Sky" laws,[123] which required registration of all dealers in securities.[124] In the first of the opinions, *Hall v. Geiger-Jones*, McKenna berated attorneys for doing nothing more than pitting the state's police power against the mandates of the Fourteenth Amendment. Everyone, McKenna wrote, should understand that the police power could limit the exercise of rights guaranteed by the Fourteenth Amendment. "Such are the declarations of the cases," he added, "become platitudes by frequent repetition and many instances of application."[125]

The state's power to regulate intrastate trades in corporate stock was equal to the already upheld power to regulate the sale of products labeled "ice cream."[126] Both cases rested on "the power of the State to prevent frauds and impositions." The one difference was that ice cream was tangible, which allowed

---

122. Ibid., 501.
123. McKenna explained the origin of the term in this way: "The name that is given to the law indicates the evil at which it is aimed, that is, to use the language of a cited case, 'speculative schemes which have no more basis than so many feet of "blue sky"'; or, as stated by counsel in another case, 'to stop the sale of stock in fly-by-night concerns, visionary oil wells, distant gold mines and other like fraudulent exploitations'"; 242 U.S. at 550.
124. The opinions came in three decisions, announced the same day: *Hall v. Geiger-Jones Co.*, 242 U.S. 539 (1917) (Ohio); *Caldwell v. Sioux Falls Stock Yards Co.*, 242 U.S. 559 (1917) (South Dakota); *Merrick v. N. W. Halsey & Co.*, 242 U.S. 568 (1917) (Michigan). Also in this term, the Court upheld licensing of private detectives, *Lehon v. City of Atlanta*, 242 U.S. 53 (1916); automobiles, *Kane v. New Jersey*, 242 U.S. 160 (1916); medical practitioners, *Crane v. Johnson*, 242 U.S. 339 (1917); and optometrists, *McNaughton v. Johnson*, 242 U.S. 344 (1917).
125. 242 U.S. at 549.
126. *Hutchinson Ice Cream Co. v. Iowa*, 242 U.S. 153 (1916), Brandeis's opinion for a unanimous Court upholds state's requirement of a minimum butterfat content of 12 percent in products sold as "ice cream."

a test of the product; securities, by contrast, were intangible, thus requiring regulation of parties involved in the trades.[127]

In the final opinion of this trilogy McKenna paused as though reflecting on the dramatic changes considered by the Court in this one term. Unlike some of his brethren, he at least seemed comfortable with those changes:

> Every new regulation of business or conduct meets challenge and, of course, must sustain itself against challenge and the limitations that the Constitution imposes. But it is to be borne in mind that the policy of a State and its expression in laws must vary with circumstances. . . . It may be that constitutional law must have a more fixed quality than customary law . . . . This, however, does not mean that the form is so rigid as to make government inadequate to the changing conditions of life, preventing its exertion except by amendments to the organic law.[128]

McKenna carried that view forward, at the end of the term, when he dissented from the Court's holding that a state could not prohibit employment agencies from charging fees to prospective employees. The case, *Adams v. Tanner*,[129] involved a Washington law enacted through that state's initiative procedure during a period of particularly high unemployment.[130] *The New Republic* summarized the Progressive critique of private employment agencies: "The private employment agency has for years been recognized as one of the sore points of irritation in the industrial machine. It preys on the ignorant and the unskilled, exacting its tribute when the stress of unemployment renders them defenseless. It charges extortionate fees and performs services which are often illusory."[131] Following that critique, the magazine pointed to the closeness of recent votes in the Court on reform legislation. Then the magazine concluded: "If the Employment Agencies law is contrary to due process, no new social legislation can be considered safe in the hands of the Supreme Court."[132] Late in the 1915–1916 term the Court had unanimously held that a state could impose a license fee on employment agencies.[133] As Justice McReynolds had explained, "The general nature of the business is

---

127. 242 U.S. at 552.
128. *Merrick v. N. W. Halsey & Co.*, 242 U.S. at 586–87.
129. 244 U.S. 590 (1917).
130. The initiative measure passed in 1914; Brandeis notes that there was high unemployment in Washington between 1913 and 1915; 244 U.S. at 613.
131. *The New Republic*, 11 (June 1917): 234.
132. Ibid., 235.
133. *Brazee v. Michigan*, 241 U.S. 340 (1916). The act also imposed other restrictions on employment agencies, the most significant of which was a ban on sending applicants to employers who had not requested help.

such that unless regulated many persons may be exposed to misfortunes against which the legislature can properly protect them."[134] In *Adams*, however, McReynolds found that the state had gone too far. Echoing the language of *Caminetti*, McReynolds wrote that "there is nothing inherently immoral or dangerous to public welfare in acting as paid representative of another to find a position in which he can earn an honest living."[135] That abuses might occur did not warrant the state's "destruction of one's right to follow a distinctly useful calling in an upright way."[136]

In dissent, McKenna contented himself with a single sentence, saying that the law was constitutional under decisions of the Court.[137] Brandeis, in only the second dissenting opinion of his inaugural term on the Court, produced a brief, complete with titles, subtitles, and footnotes filled with legislative and other studies of employment agencies. In addition, he added his first citation to a law review, one of the earliest such citations in the history of the Supreme Court.[138] In the end, he concluded, statutes of this sort were no different from employers' liability acts, in that both shifted certain costs to the employers.

Outside the circle of employers' liability disputes, the Court found yet other issues, none the less critical, and few the less divisive. Some few of these other cases involved similar issues of division of power between the state and federal governments. One of those cases was *Louisville & Nashville Railroad Co. v. United States,* in which the Court declined to uphold an ICC order that the railroad share its terminal facility in Nashville with another railroad.[139] In spite of the complexity of the facts, which ordinarily would have led the Court to defer to an administrative agency, the Court held that the Interstate Commerce Act itself prohibited the commission from issuing an order to share terminal facilities. The act provided that it should "not be construed as requiring any such common carrier to give the use of its tracks or terminal facilities to another carrier engaged in like business."[140] Writing for the 5–4 Court, Justice Holmes explained that the terminal facility in Nashville fell within that provision even though ownership was shared by two railroads and a separate terminal company. To the suggestion that his reasoning offered an opportunity to evade the jurisdiction of the ICC, Holmes responded with a familiar obser-

---

134. 241 U.S. at 343.
135. 244 U.S. at 593.
136. Ibid., 594.
137. Ibid., 597.
138. Strum, *Brandeis: Justice for the People,* 363–64; Michael L. Closen and Robert J. Dzielak, "The History and Influence of the Law Review Institution," *Akron Law Review* 30 (1996): 26–27. Justice White is credited with the first citation of a law review, in his dissent in *Trans-Missouri Freight,* 166 U.S. 290 (1897).
139. 242 U.S. 60 (1916).
140. The language is from section 3 of the act, quoted at 242 U.S. at 73.

vation: "But the very meaning of a line in the law is that right and wrong touch each other and that anyone may get as close to the line as he can if he keeps on the right side."[141]

In other instances, the Court continued to struggle with state regulations of railroad traffic. The Court upheld both a state's rules concerning long- and short-haul provisions in intrastate commerce,[142] and a state's regulation of railroad headlights, in the absence of rules from the ICC.[143] Likewise, a municipality was allowed to order a railroad to remove a spur line of track when there was no contract between the municipality and the railroad.[144] And, in yet another pair of cases, the Court upheld orders that a railroad bear the expenses of constructing a bridge over a new drainage ditch and that a different railroad pay to enlarge the span of its bridge across the Ohio River.[145]

In writing of changed circumstances, three cases, each affected by the First World War, brought changes unlike any the Court had seen in recent years. The first of this trio of cases to be decided was *The Steamship Appam*.[146] The ship was one which had been captured on the high seas by a German cruiser in January 1916. On account of the state of war between Britain and Germany, the German officers decided to take the captured ship to the United States, then neutral, rather than risk trying to run the British blockade. The ship arrived at Hampton Roads, Virginia, on February 1; the next day the German ambassador informed the United States State Department that the ship planned to remain in port until further notice. The British owners of the ship and of the cargo then began proceedings to reclaim their property. Between the oral argument in the case and the Court's decision, relations between the United States and Germany worsened, largely due to Germany's resumption of submarine warfare and the discovery of the Zimmerman telegram. In a decision announced a month before the United States entered the war, the Court unanimously sided with the British owners.

---

141. 242 U.S. at 74.
142. *Missouri Pacific Railway Co. v. McGrew Coal Co.*, 244 U.S. 191 (1917).
143. *Vandalia Railroad Co. v. Public Service Commission of Indiana*, 242 U.S. 255 (1916).
144. *Seaboard Air Line Railway v. City of Raleigh*, 242 U.S. 15 (1916). In another decision the Court emphasized that contract could not be used to hamper the state's police powers. *Puget Sound Traction, Light & Power Co. v. Reynolds*, 244 U.S. 574 (1917). The contract cases proved to be the most troublesome, with the Court being other than unanimous in three of the other four such cases. In the only unanimous example of these cases this term, *Seton Hall College v. Village of South Orange*, 242 U.S. 100 (1916), the Court could find no contract under which the village had contracted to exempt certain land belonging to the college from taxes. Although the village offered an exemption, the college did nothing in return; thus there could be no contract.
145. *Lake Shore & Michigan Southern Railway Co. v. Clough*, 242 U.S. 375 (1917); *Louisville Bridge Co. v. United States*, 242 U.S. 409 (1917).
146. 243 U.S. 124 (1917).

The Court held that bringing the ship into a United States port was a violation of principles of neutrality, which justified the exercise of jurisdiction by the United States courts. It followed, the Court reasoned, that the appropriate sanction for that violation was restitution of the ship and its cargo to its owners.[147]

Horn v. Mitchell also involved Germany and Britain.[148] Werner Horn claimed to be an officer in the German army; he sought a writ of habeas corpus to free him from custody on a charge of illegally transporting explosives from New York to Maine. The explosives were needed for his attempt to blow up a bridge in Canada, with which he was also charged. After a federal district court denied Horn's petition, he appealed to the court of appeals. That court affirmed the denial. When Horn took his case to the Supreme Court, Justice Pitney announced that there was no statute that gave the Court jurisdiction to hear an appeal from the circuit court. Yet again, the vocabulary of judicial decision separated the Court from the idiom of daily life.

The most significant of the cases involving the war was *The Kronprinzessin Cecilie*.[149] The ship, owned by a German corporation, had sailed on July 28, 1914, from New York for Germany (via England), with a cargo of gold and almost nineteen hundred passengers. The ship turned back near midnight on July 31, after the ship's master learned of Austria's declaration of war against Serbia, and of the preparations for war by Germany. The master testified that the ship's supply of fuel would have allowed him to go no further and still be able to return to North America. The ship reached port in Maine, avoiding British ships supposed to be around New York; upon arrival in port, the master returned the gold to its owners. The owners sued for damages for failure to deliver the gold to the consignees. The critical issue was whether the master was justified in abandoning the journey, knowing only of the *likelihood* of war. In terms of contract law, the issue was whether the master had an excuse for his failure to comply with the terms of the contract. Writing for the Court, Justice Holmes held that the master "acted as a prudent man" and did not have to wait for the outbreak of war before turning back.[150] Holmes further explained that "the master is not to be put in the wrong by nice calculations that if all went well he might have delivered the gold and escaped capture by the margin of a few hours."[151] In other words, the Court adapted contract law to accept the uncertainties of the situation.

---

147. Ibid., 156.
148. 243 U.S. 247 (1917).
149. 244 U.S. 12 (1917).
150. Ibid., 24. Justices Clarke and Pitney dissented, saying only that they agreed with the reasoning of the majority of judges in the circuit court.
151. Ibid.

A month earlier, Holmes had found himself on the losing side of a Court vote in *Motion Picture Patents Co. v. Universal Film Manufacturing Co.*[152] In this case, the Court finally put together a majority to overrule the plurality opinion upholding tying arrangements in *Henry v. A. B. Dick Co.*[153] *Motion Picture Patents* presented a by now familiar set of facts: A patent holder seeking to use the patent to justify requiring all users of the patented device to agree to some further condition, whether it be to use certain products or to sell at fixed prices. As Justice Clarke explained in his majority opinion, the case "presented anew the inquiry, which is arising with increasing frequency in recent years, as to the extent to which a patentee or his assignees is authorized by our patent laws to prescribe by notice attached to a patented machine the conditions of its use and the supplies which must be used in the operation of it, under pain of infringement of the patent."[154] After surveying the Court's decisions interpreting the patent law, Clarke announced that the right to "use" the patented device did not extend to "materials or supplies not described in the patent and not by its terms made a part of the thing patented."[155] Accordingly, the Court overruled *A. B. Dick*.

Justice Holmes wrote a dissent in which he was joined by McKenna and Van Devanter. He repeated the analysis he had penned in earlier cases, based on the premise that a patent holder had the right to keep the patented device from the public. With that right granted, Holmes could not understand why the patent holder might not "keep it out of use unless the licensee, or, for the matter of that, the buyer, will use some unpatented thing in connection with it."[156]

---

152. 243 U.S. 502 (1917).
153. 224 U.S. 1 (1912).
154. 243 U.S. at 509.
155. Ibid., 514.
156. Ibid., 519.

VIII

THE 1917–1918 TERM

In the sixteen weeks of the Court's vacation during the summer of 1917, the country moved rapidly toward full wartime mobilization. On June 15, at the beginning of the vacation, Congress passed the Espionage Act, which punished a variety of "disloyal" acts and allowed the postmaster general to exclude a wide range of materials from the mails.[1] Just over a month later the War Industries Board emerged from a maze of administrative agencies and became responsible for coordinating the various committees created to oversee the production requirements of military procurement. In August Congress passed the Lever Food and Fuel Control Act, which gave the president power to fix prices and promote wartime production.[2] Then, just before the Court reassembled, the federal government staged coordinated raids throughout the country on offices of the radical labor organization the Industrial Workers of the World (IWW). Responses to the wartime emergency continued into the fall, with the War Revenue Act and the Trading with the Enemy Act coming the same week as the Court's opening of term.[3]

In their personal lives the justices experienced the shortages that came from the war.[4] In the spring, White was distraught over the Germans' shelling of Paris from a distance of over seventy-five miles. The shelling continued for almost a week before Good Friday 1918, when a shell landed on a church, killing seventy-five and wounding ninety.[5] One evening shortly after the bombardment began, Vice President Thomas Marshall encountered White walking down New Jersey Avenue. As Marshall later told the story, White "would walk a few steps, take off his hat, look around him and

---

1. Act of June 15, 1917, ch. 30, 40 Stat. 217.
2. Act of August 10, 1917, ch. 53, 40 Stat. 276.
3. War Revenue Act, Act of October 3, 1917, ch. 63, 40 Stat. 300; Trading with the Enemy Act, Act of October 6, 1917, ch. 106, 40 Stat. 411.
4. See, for example, Holmes to Einstein, December 20, 1917, and January 23, 1918, Peabody, *The Holmes-Einstein Letters*, 156, 157.
5. For accounts of the shelling and the efforts to locate the German guns, see *New York Times*, March 24, 1918; March 25, 1918; March 26, 1918; March 30, 1918; March 31, 1918; April 1, 1918.

seemingly mutter something to himself." When Marshall caught up with White, he asked, "Mr. Chief Justice, are you overruling *nunc pro tunc* a petition for rehearing that has not yet been filed?" The response from a "dazed" White was a series of questions: "Is civilization going down in barbarism? Will not these German guns shoot across the channel, destroy Great Britain and lay the world in ruins? Has all the long, long fight for civilization come to naught?"[6]

Professionally, however, the Court would remain outside the vortex of the military activities only until the eve of its break for Christmas. Then, with the *Selective Draft Law Cases,* the Court would begin reviewing issues arising from the war—a review that would last for the remainder of White's term and beyond.[7] These cases had much the same effect on the Court as the war itself had on other governmental institutions—a speeding up of changes already begun. And, just as was true for other institutions, the speed produced uneven results, sometimes successful, sometimes stumbling. Because those changes point so clearly to the further increases in national power during the 1930s, it is tempting to concentrate on the cases involving these "modern" issues in anticipation of the next great constitutional revolution in the 1930s. Moreover, because the cases at last brought the Court fully into the Progressives' debate about the proper role of the national government, the decisions offer an intellectual excitement not present in yet another line-drawing exercise over the application of the Federal Employers' Liability Act, or in a further iteration of principles of appellate procedure. To concentrate solely on these wartime cases, however, would be to misread the pulse of the Court; for, in spite of the harbingers for the future, these cases came amidst a mind-numbing parade of pedestrian cases.

A good example of the mix of future excitement and routine comes from the first major decision day of the 1917–1918 term, Monday, November 5. Of course, nothing the Court did would have the impact of the Bolshevik revolution in Russia, which occurred on the next two days. By a different meter, however, the announcement of seventeen decisions (all but one unanimous) made that day one of the most productive of the entire term.[8] Nestled in the midst of the day was an opinion that would become one of the most

---

6. Marshall, *Recollections of Thomas R. Marshall,* 337.
7. 245 U.S. 366 (1918).
8. The largest output came on March 4, 1918, when the Court announced thirty-three decisions. Other days were closer to November 5 in number: twenty-three on December 12 and May 5; twenty-one on April 15; and twenty on June 3. The only other day with more than eight decisions was January 7, with thirteen.

The exception to unanimity was *Fidelity & Columbia Trust Co. v. City of Louisville,* 245 U.S. 54 (1917), in which White dissented without writing an opinion.

parsed decisions of the White Court, *Buchanan v. Warley*,[9] in which the Court unanimously struck down Louisville, Kentucky's residential segregation law. As will be discussed more fully below, the decision offered a ray of hope to a minority community wracked by lynchings and economic despair. Following generations would discover the difficulties of making that ray shine brighter; but their efforts and their agenda should not allow the decision to assume greater importance than it deserves. Looking first at the other cases on the Court's docket provides a better perspective for the *Buchanan* decision in its own time as well as for the future.

On November 5, Chief Justice White set the theme for the day with his two decisions. One involved prominent terms of the Court's vocabulary, *eminent domain* and *contract;* the other illustrated the stranglehold of minutia on the Court's docket. The first of White's opinions resolved a dispute over the power of the city of Philadelphia to take land owned by a hospital.[10] The hospital argued that it had given up land in 1854 in return for a promise by the state that no streets would be opened through the hospital's remaining land without its consent. With that exchange, no one could contest that the hospital had a contract right, akin to a veto power, to prevent unwanted streets. And, of course, the hospital retained ownership rights in its real property. Thus, when the city initiated the process required to take yet more hospital land for new streets, the hospital conceded that the city could use its power of eminent domain to take the land; but the hospital argued that the contracts clause of the Constitution prohibited interference with the separate contract right that required the hospital's consent to any new street. The ingenious argument met with no success, even though it appealed to one of the most significant words in the Court's vocabulary: *contract.* In affirming decisions of the lower courts, White reasserted the long-standing principle that governments could not contract away their ability to exert governmental powers.[11]

White's second opinion on November 5 illustrated the other side of the Court's docket, the mundane. But it also illustrated how the Court was not yet free from the nation's past, for the case involved a dispute over an 1841 survey of some 850 acres in Arkansas. In a typically prolix opinion, White held that a mistake could be corrected in the survey, even after seventy years.[12]

Following White came McKenna, with four opinions. Three of the opinions concerned the same issue—the power of the ICC to compel officers of

---

9. 245 U.S. 60 (1917).
10. *Contributors to the Pennsylvania Hospital v. City of Philadelphia,* 245 U.S. 20 (1917).
11. 245 U.S. at 23.
12. *Lee Wilson & Co. v. United States,* 245 U.S. 24 (1917).

railroad corporations to testify about the use of political contributions to prevent competition.[13] The officers refused to testify, claiming that the questions were purely political and had nothing to do with the running of the railroads. The Court rejected those claims, pointing to the broad powers conferred on the ICC and to the Court's traditional reluctance to construe statutes to restrict those powers. Writing for the unanimous Court, McKenna seemed a bit bemused: "We find it difficult to treat counsel's argument as seriously as they urge it. The expenditures of the carriers essentially concern their business."[14] But he concluded with this somewhat biting observation: "Abstractly speaking, we are not disposed to say that a carrier may not attempt to mould or enlighten public opinion, but we are quite clear that its conduct and the expenditures of its funds are open to inquiry. If it may not rest inactive and suffer injustice, it may not on the other hand use its funds and its power in opposition to the policies of government. Beyond this generality it is not necessary to go."[15]

McKenna's final opinion for the day involved interpretation of the Bankruptcy Act, as it applied to the cash surrender value of a life insurance policy.[16] The decision itself involved a relatively straightforward interpretation of the language of the statute—the Court held that the trustee in bankruptcy could reach the cash surrender value. But the fact that the lower courts had each reached different conclusions illustrated the discomfort with which courts in general dealt with the growing insurance industry, as evidenced by the Court's opinion in the *German Alliance* case in 1911.

The same kind of uncertainty was evident in the next opinion announced by the Court, *Fidelity & Columbia Trust Co. v. City of Louisville*, written by Holmes.[17] The issue in *Fidelity* concerned the power of a municipality to tax property belonging to one of its citizens but held in another state. In this case, a resident of Louisville had a bank account in St. Louis, where he had once lived. The Court conceded that Missouri could tax the property, but that did not prevent another state from also imposing a tax.

---

13. *Smith v. Interstate Commerce Commission,* 245 U.S. 33 (1917); *Smith v. Interstate Commerce Commission,* 245 U.S. 47 (1917); *Jones v. Interstate Commerce Commission,* 245 U.S. 48 (1917). The Court had already dealt with the issue in *United States v. Louisville & Nashville Railroad Co.,* 236 U.S. 318 (1915), in which the Court held that a resolution by only one house of Congress, here the Senate, could not enlarge the powers of the ICC to investigate. Thus, in that case, the Court held that the ICC could require railroads to produce accounts, but could not require production of correspondence. The Court reprinted the entire Senate resolution (dated November 6, 1913), 236 U.S. at 324–26 n. 1, which was the same resolution involved in the opinions announced on November 5, 1917.
14. 245 U.S. at 45.
15. Ibid., 46.
16. *Cohen v. Samuels,* 245 U.S. 50 (1917).
17. 245 U.S. 54 (1917).

The Kentucky tax, the Court reasoned, was a personal tax, imposed "for the general advantages of living within the jurisdiction."[18] Accordingly, a state could measure its tax by the overall wealth of the person involved, even when that measure included property in other states.

Next in seniority after Holmes came Day, who had three decisions to announce. Two involved questions of appellate review that had been answered frequently in the past.[19] Day's third opinion was *Buchanan v. Warley*, the tenth decision announced that day. Day's opinion for the Court came just six months after the second oral argument and almost nineteen months after the first.[20] The reargument and delay suggested that there was more difficulty in reaching consensus than the Court's unanimity might have suggested.[21] Further suggestions of the case's significance came from the seven amicus briefs. Among those briefs was a pair of opposing briefs, one from the city of Baltimore, the other from the Baltimore branch of the NAACP, reflecting the ongoing struggle over Baltimore's attempts to require segregated housing. The city's 1910 ordinance was the first in the nation; the Baltimore branch of the NAACP had successfully challenged it and its successor. The city's third attempt was before Maryland's highest court, pending a decision in *Buchanan*.[22] The case itself involved a challenge to Louisville's 1914 ordinance, with the title "An ordinance to prevent conflict and ill-feeling between the white and colored races in the City of Louisville, and to preserve the public peace and promote the general welfare by making reasonable provisions requiring, as far as practicable, the use of separate blocks for residents, places of abode and places of assembly by white and colored people respectively."[23] The essence of the law was that a member of either race could not move into a house in a block the majority of whose houses were occupied by members of the other race.

After failing in their efforts to prevent passage of the ordinance, the Louisville chapter of the NAACP enlisted help from the national office to fund a challenge. William Warley, who was black and head of the local NAACP, con-

---

18. Ibid., 58.
19. *Ex parte Park & Tilford*, 245 U.S. 82 (1917), mandamus cannot be used to review a decision a statute made final in the lower court; *Gauzon v. Compañia General De Tabacos De Filipinas*, 245 U.S. 86 (1917), application of mortgage law of Philippines.
20. At the time of the first oral argument, April 1916, the Court had only seven members, with Lamar having died three months earlier and Day himself being ill.
21. For discussion of a dissent Justice Holmes wrote but did not announce, see Bickel and Schmidt, *History of the Supreme Court of the United States: The Judiciary and Responsible Government, 1910–21*, 804–10.
22. George C. Wright, "The NAACP and Residential Segregation in Louisville, Kentucky, 1914–1917," *Kentucky Historical Society Register* 78 (1980): 44. The Maryland court later declared its state law unconstitutional, relying on *Buchanan*. *Jackson v. State*, 132 Md. Ct. App. 311, 103 A. 910 (1918).
23. Quoted in 245 U.S. at 70.

tracted to buy a lot from Charles Buchanan, who was white and a local real estate dealer opposed to the ordinance. To emphasize that the purchase was contrived to challenge the ordinance, Warley wrote to Buchanan stating that he planned to use the lot to construct a residence and specifying that he should not be required to accept the purchase unless the municipal ordinances allowed him to live in the residence. When Warley ostensibly refused to complete the purchase, Buchanan sued for specific performance of the contract. Warley's defense was a standard invocation of doctrine that the contract was illegal because of the ordinance and therefore unenforceable. Buchanan's response was that the ordinance itself was unconstitutional, a violation of the Fourteenth Amendment's due process, equal protection, and privileges and immunities clauses. Thus, as one historian has written with decided understatement, the NAACP had "developed an unusual case"—with a white man (Buchanan) attacking the ordinance with the support of the NAACP; on the other side was a black man (Warley), represented by Louisville's city attorney, supporting the ordinance.[24]

After the Kentucky courts upheld the ordinance, the NAACP announced that its president, Moorfield Storey, would join Buchanan's lawyer in presenting the case to the Supreme Court. Storey, who had opposed Brandeis's nomination, would now be arguing before the justice. This was only the second appearance of the NAACP before the Court. The first had been its amicus brief in *Guinn and Beal v. United States,* involving the challenge to Oklahoma's grandfather clause.[25] Good lawyers that they were, they invoked all of the shibboleths of laissez-faire in attacking this interference with freedom of contract—*Truax v. Raich, Lochner v. New York,* and the *Slaughter-House Cases,* to name but a few.[26] In short, they presented their argument in a language with which the justices were thoroughly familiar. The opponents also chose familiar language—that of police powers, and introduced a wealth of information to support their contention that the ordinance was reasonable—not unlike what another Louisville citizen, Brandeis, had done in support of other police powers in *Muller v. Oregon.*[27]

Justice Day's richly textured opinion for the Court well illustrates how precariously the Court balanced between the old and the new. He accepted

---

24. Wright, "The NAACP and Residential Segregation in Louisville, Kentucky," 47.
25. Kenneth W. Goings, *"The NAACP Comes of Age": The Defeat of Judge John J. Parker* (Bloomington: Indiana University Press, 1990), 13–14.
26. *Truax v. Raich,* 239 U.S. 33 (1915), using freedom of contract, invalidated law requiring 80 percent of employees to be citizens; *Lochner v. New York,* 198 U.S. 45 (1905), freedom of contract impermissibly bound by New York law limiting the hours of work of bakers; *Slaughter-House Cases,* 16 Wall. (83 U.S.) 36 (1872), Fourteenth Amendment held to have no bearing on states' right to protect contract right of its citizens.
27. 208 U.S. 412 (1908).

the proffered vocabulary of contract, the old, characterizing the dispute as one involving Buchanan's right to contract to sell his property. In opposition was the similarly familiar doctrine of police power. Even so, Day showed no sympathy for the ordinance's racialism. He characterized the ordinance as being "based wholly upon color; simply that and nothing more." And he described that basis as a "drastic measure."[28] In that light, the case involved not merely a contract right to sell to the world at large. Instead, Day viewed the statute as one that attempted to interfere with the contract right solely on the basis of the race of one party to the contract. He followed that view with a survey of the Civil War amendments and cases decided under them, along with the various congressional acts designed to enforce the amendments. At each stage in his survey, Day emphasized the intent to protect the right of blacks to equality of treatment. To be sure, Day adhered to the linguistic distinction between "social" rights, which were not protected, and "property" rights, which were. Accordingly, he ended his survey with this remark: "The Fourteenth Amendment and these statutes enacted in furtherance of its purpose operate to qualify and entitle a colored man to acquire property without state legislation discriminating against him solely because of color."[29]

Day also acknowledged the racial problems in the country at large, possibly referring to the early moves of the Wilson administration to segregate federal departments or to the continuing wave of lynchings in the country.[30] "That there exists a serious and difficult problem arising from a feeling of race hostility which the law is powerless to control, and to which it must give a measure of consideration, may be freely admitted. But its solution cannot be promoted by depriving citizens of their constitutional rights and privileges."[31] Although Day's language resonated with the same sense of futility that had marked Justice Brown's opinion in *Plessy v. Ferguson*,[32] Day (and the entire Court) now seemed less willing to accept the justification for the ordinance. They pointed critically to the inconsistency between the ordinance's purported goal of racial purity and the permission granted to employ blacks as servants in homes owned by whites. Day then returned to the relative comfort of the vocabulary of contract, reiterating that the true effect of the ordinance was to interfere with the freedom to dispose of prop-

---

28. 245 U.S. at 73.
29. Ibid., 79.
30. See Nancy J. Weiss, "The Negro and the New Freedom: Fighting Wilsonian Segregation," *Political Science Quarterly* 84 (1969): 61–79; reprinted in *Race, Law and American History, 1700–1990*, vol. 4, *The Age of Jim Crow: Segregation from the End of Reconstruction to the Great Depression*, ed. Paul Finkelman (New York: Garland, 1992), 545–63; Link, *Woodrow Wilson and the Progressive Era*, 63–66; Link, *Wilson and the New Freedom*, 243–52.
31. 245 U.S. at 80–81.
32. 163 U.S. 537 (1896).

erty as the owner saw fit.[33] Upon learning of the decision, Warley wrote to Oswald Garrison Villard, publisher of both the *New York Evening Post* and the *Nation,* and first chairman of the NAACP's board of directors: "I cannot help thinking it is the most important decision that has been made since the *Dred Scott* case, and happily this time it is the right way."[34] The national office of the NAACP asked that all branches arrange a celebration for the decision.[35] The joy was destined to be short lived, however; supporters of segregated housing soon found an alternative to city ordinances, turning to private contracts with restrictive covenants in deeds to prevent sales to those of certain races.

Following Day's opinions came two each by Van Devanter, McReynolds, and Clarke, with a single opinion by Brandeis. Van Devanter's opinions seemed to reflect his increasing relegation to simple opinions without dissent to accommodate his inability to keep up with the pace of opinion writing. The first case looked back to an 1865 treaty with the Omaha Indians as part of the basis of deciding which of two members of the tribe was entitled to forty acres in Nebraska.[36] The other case reached the Court for the fourth time, with the result that even Van Devanter was moved to complain "that the [prior] rulings were right, so clearly so that the appeal seems to be without reasonable justification, and therefore to have been taken for delay."[37] McReynolds's two opinions provoked a similar show of impatience. One dispute involved what McReynolds described as "notable and repeated successful efforts to avoid payment" of bonds issued by a county.[38] As a result, the Court upheld an order that the county officials collect the taxes necessary to repay the bonds. Brandeis's single opinion, like the earlier one by McKenna, involved only a simple question of interpreting the Bankruptcy Act.[39]

Clarke's two opinions each involved a nice question of statutory construction, though neither suggested great significance, even though the Court had chosen to review the first case by granting a writ of certiorari.

---

33. For further discussion of this case, see William Cohen, *At Freedom's Edge: Black Mobility and the Southern White Quest for Racial Control, 1861–1915* (Baton Rouge: Louisiana State University Press, 1991); Randall Kennedy, "Race Relations Law and the Tradition of Celebration," *Columbia Law Review* 86 (1986): 1622–61.

34. Quoted in William B. Hixson Jr., "Moorfield Storey and the Struggle for Equality," *Journal of American History* 55 (1988): 551; reprinted in *Civil Rights in American History: Major Historical Interpretations,* ed. Kermit Hall (New York: Garland, 1987).

35. Charles Flint Kellogg, *NAACP: A History of the National Association for the Advancement of Colored People* (Baltimore: Johns Hopkins Press, 1967), 187.

36. *United States v. Chase,* 245 U.S. 89 (1917).

37. *Eichel v. United States Fidelity & Guaranty Co.,* 245 U.S. 102, 105 (1917).

38. *Hendrickson v. Apperson,* 245 U.S. 105, 113 (1917); *Hendrickson v. Creager,* 245 U.S. 115 (1917).

39. *Kelley v. Gill,* 245 U.S. 116 (1917).

That case, *Scharrenberg v. Dollar Steamship Co.*,[40] involved a 1907 congressional act that prohibited encouraging alien contract laborers to immigrate to the United States.[41] The allegation was that the steamship company had hired a Chinese sailor in Shanghai to sail to the United States, where he joined the crew of another vessel that would return him to Shanghai. The Supreme Court agreed with the lower courts that the conduct did not amount to a violation of the law. The critical words in the statute were "laborers" and immigration "into the United States." As Clarke noted, "In familiar speech a 'seaman' may be called a 'sailor' or a 'mariner,' but he is never called a 'laborer.'"[42] Moreover, the movement of the sailor from a British vessel to one registered in the United States could not be said to be a coming into the United States. The second of Clarke's opinions originated in a request by Illinois that a person be extradited from New York.[43] The case required little of the Court other than to note that the extradition clause of the Constitution should be construed liberally and that review by habeas corpus did not involve a full inquiry into the facts of the case.

Taken together, these seventeen cases captured the Court on the cusp of its encounter with the First World War and, in a very real sense, with the future. Three of the cases drew the Court's attention to a past with which its members would have been quite familiar. The cases involved land claims, treaties with Indians, and even the Civil War itself. More recent events involving the power of the Interstate Commerce Commission, the construction of the 1898 Bankruptcy Act, and the extent of states' power to tax provided no significant challenge, and even prompted signs of impatience over the relative insignificance of the cases. In several instances even the attorneys themselves seemed to be groping for a new vocabulary in which to describe their arguments. Of all the cases, *Buchanan* best captured a portrait of a court poised in its search to replace the dialect of the past.

Other cases throughout the term called attention to the Court's having entered more completely into the contemporaneous world. For example, in one of the first decisions announced during the term, the Court upheld the power of a state regulatory commission to order railroads to provide special tickets for regular travelers.[44] The words used to describe the tickets, "commutation tickets," have an archaic quality to them; but a glimpse of the future was evident in Day's opinion for the Court:

---

40. 245 U.S. 122 (1917).
41. Act of February 20, 1907, ch. 1134, 34 Stat. 898, as amended by Act of March 26, 1910, ch. 128, 36 Stat. 263.
42. 245 U.S. at 126.
43. *Biddinger v. Commissioner of Police of the City of New York*, 245 U.S. 128 (1917).
44. *Pennsylvania Railroad Co. v. Towers*, 245 U.S. 6 (1917). There were three dissenting votes—White, McKenna, and McReynolds—but none wrote an opinion to explain his dissent.

The service rendered the commuter, carrying little baggage and riding many times on a single ticket for short distances, is of a special character and differs from that given the single-way passenger.

It is well known that there have grown up near to all the large cities of this country suburban communities which require this peculiar service, and as to which the railroads have themselves, as in this instance, established commutation rates. . . .

On the strength of these commutation tariffs, it is a fact of public history that thousands of persons have acquired homes in city suburbs and nearby towns in reliance upon this action of the carriers in fixing special rates and furnishing particular accommodations suitable to the traffic.[45]

One such suburb was Douglaston, a part of the borough of Queens, New York. Justice Clarke described Douglaston as "a rapidly growing settlement of three hundred and thirty houses, of an average cost of $7,500."[46] For such a growing community, the state's public service commission could order a gas company to extend its lines to provide service. Similarly, in *Wells v. Roper* the Court upheld a statute authorizing the postmaster general to purchase "wagons or automobiles" for an "experiment" in delivering mail in Washington, D.C.[47] In another case, the Court learned of a dispute between a South Dakota city and a telephone company that wanted to install "the Automatic System" to permit subscribers to call any other subscriber within the system.[48]

These demographic shifts began to push changes in the law with an increasing momentum. Thus, the Court acknowledged an evolution toward allowing greater opportunity for excuse from performing obligations under a contract: "The modern cases may have abated somewhat the absoluteness of the older ones in determining the scope of the undertaking by the literal meaning of the words alone."[49] Similarly, there were new rules concerning admissibility of testimony, with Justice Clarke asserting that "the dead hand of the common-law rule of 1789 should no longer be applied."[50] He explained the development as occurring "under dominance of the convic-

---

45. Ibid., 12.
46. *New York ex rel. New York & Queens Gas Co. v. McCall*, 245 U.S. 345 (1917).
47. 246 U.S. 335 (1917).
48. *City of Mitchell v. Dakota Central Telephone Co.*, 246 U.S. 396 (1918).
49. *Day v. United States*, 245 U.S. 159, 161 (1917).
50. *Rosen v. United States*, 245 U.S. 467, 471 (1918). Justices Van Devanter and McReynolds dissented from this part of the opinion, though they did not write to explain their reasons. The Court's statement should be contrasted with Holmes's opinion for the Court in *Gardiner v. William S. Butler & Co., Inc.*, 245 U.S. 603, 605 (1918): "But the law as to leases is not a matter of logic in vacuo; it is a matter of history that has not forgotten Lord Coke."

tion of our time that the truth is more likely to be arrived at by hearing the testimony of all persons of competent understanding who may seem to have knowledge of the facts involved in a case, leaving the credit and weight of such testimony to be determined by the jury or by the court."[51] The "Brandeis brief" had come to the law of evidence. In short, newness brought with it new meanings for words and even new methods for determining those meanings. As Holmes would write early in 1918, "A word is not a crystal, transparent and unchanged, it is the skin of a living thought and may vary greatly in color and content according to the circumstances and the time in which it is used."[52]

Words also played an important part in the Court's decisions under the food and drug laws. In *Weeks v. United States,* for example, the Court held that a producer could be convicted of misbranding a product even though the label was not false.[53] Oscar J. Weeks had shipped in interstate commerce a product labeled as lemon oil when it was in fact a mixture of alcohol and citral.[54] Similarly, the Court upheld an indictment charging that the label "Compound Ess Grape" was misleading because there was no grape product in the substance.[55] The Court refused to permit a seller to add the word "compound" to its label and thereby avoid prosecution. As Justice McReynolds explained, "The statute enjoins truth; this label exhales deceit."[56]

But the Court was not quite ready to accept that all words were malleable. For statutes, in particular, the justices continued to show an especial respect, refusing to look behind the words of the statute to find guides for meaning. As already noted, the Court found meaning for words such as *income* and phrases such as "into the United States" in the common reckoning or familiar speech.[57] In addition, the Court reversed an award of damages to a seven-year-old child who had lost a leg when he tried to recover a marble under a railroad car.[58] The state statute barred recovery by "any person" injured while "walking, standing or playing on any railroad." Writing

---

51. 245 U.S. at 471.
52. *Towne v. Eisner,* 245 U.S. 418 (1918). Holmes was referring to the definition of *income,* a word that appeared both in the Sixteenth Amendment to the Constitution and in the Income Tax Law of 1913, Act of October 3, 1913, ch. 16, 38 Stat. 114. The unanimous Court held that a stock dividend was not income. The Court also considered the definition of *income* in *Lynch v. Turrish,* 247 U.S. 221 (1918), increase in value of property is not income; *Southern Pacific Co. v. Lowe,* 247 U.S. 330 (1918), dividends from wholly owned company are not income; *Lynch v. Hornby,* 247 U.S. 339 (1918), cash dividend is income.
53. 245 U.S. 618 (1918).
54. Citral is a liquid derived from lemon-grass oil and used as a flavoring.
55. *United States v. Schider,* 246 U.S. 519 (1918).
56. Ibid., 522.
57. *Scharrenberg v. Dollar Steamship Co.,* 245 U.S. 122, 126 (1917); *Lynch v. Hornby,* 247 U.S. 339, 344 (1918).
58. *Erie Railroad Co. v. Hilt,* 247 U.S. 97 (1918).

for the Court, Holmes explained that "the word 'playing' sufficiently indicates that [the statute] had minors in view, even if the absoluteness of the opening phrase 'any person' were not enough."[59]

There was, however, at the end of the term a breach of the practice, even as it regarded statutes.[60] The United States had initiated a suit to cancel a grant of land to a railroad, contending that the railroad had misrepresented the land when it applied for the grant. The railroad's rejoinder pointed to a federal statute that it said barred the United States from bringing the action. The problem the Court faced was that the final clause in the statute appeared to conflict with prior clauses. To resolve the problem, the Court turned to legislative sources, while disclaiming any interest other than in discovering what was already "common knowledge":

> It is not our purpose to relax the rule that debates in Congress are not appropriate or even reliable guides to the meaning of the language of an enactment.... But the reports of a committee, including the bill as introduced, changes made in the frame of the bill in the course of its passage, and statements made by the committee chairman in charge of it, stand upon a different footing, and may be resorted to under proper qualifications.... The remarks of Mr. Lacey, and the amendment offered by him, in response to an objection urged by another member during the debate, were in the nature of a supplementary report of the committee; and as they related to matters of common knowledge they may very properly be taken into consideration as throwing light upon the meaning of the proviso; not for the purpose of construing it contrary to its plain terms, but in order to remove any ambiguity by pointing out the subject-matter of the amendment.[61]

The comfort with "common experience" as the basis for interpreting words spilled over into other problems confronting the Court. More often than not, common experience meant primarily the experiences of the judges; so, it is not surprising that disagreements could arise over that experience, especially among judges of different generations. And these disagreements, too, helped move the Court away from certainty about a shared, common past. The most revealing discussion of that disagreement came in yet another of the cases that asked the Court to decide whether a grant of a corporate franchise was perpetual. The argument usually arose whenever a government tried to impose a new regulation on a corporation; the corpo-

---

59. Ibid., 100.
60. *United States v. St. Paul, Minneapolis & Manitoba Railway Co.*, 247 U.S. 310 (1918).
61. Ibid., 318.

ration would respond that the new regulation amounted to an infringement of contract rights inherent in its perpetual charter. That pattern emerged when the commissioners of Stark County, Ohio, attempted to cancel a charter granted to a railroad. By threatening cancellation, the commissioners hoped to force a reduction in rates.[62] Although the state supreme court interpreted the charter as being subject to cancellation by either party, the Supreme Court disagreed. The charter had no statement of duration; thus the contract required interpretation. Writing for the six-man majority, McReynolds explained that it "would be against common experience to conclude that rational men wittingly invested large sums of money in building a railroad subject to destruction at any moment by mere resolution of county commissioners."[63] Here again, the language of the Court contained a nuanced shift from the vision of contract as an exchange to that of contract as reliance. Justice Day had even used the word reliance in describing the commuters who moved to suburbs expecting the continuation of reduced rates for their rail travel into the city.

Justice Clarke disagreed. He took issue with McReynolds's invocation of common experience, writing that, had the charter contained a word such as *perpetual,* the county commissioners would have rejected it out of hand. Indeed, he invoked the concept with a diametrically different conclusion: "That it would be against common experience to conclude that rational men would wittingly invest their money in a railroad constructed under a grant determinable by the action of county commissioners is reasoning which it seems is more persuasive with courts than with investors or men of affairs. To reason upon what is reasonable is always uncertain and often misleading, but in this case we have ascertained facts to guide us."[64] Pointing to examples from Massachusetts, Wisconsin, and the District of Columbia, Clarke's "facts" trumped McReynolds's "common experience." Not surprisingly, Brandeis joined Clarke in his invocation of the new century against the old.

Three months later, the Court split 7–2 over whether an ordinance awarded a perpetual franchise. The majority held that it did.[65] Once again, Clarke dissented (again with Brandeis joining), unable to agree that what he termed "an obscurely worded clause of a single sentence"[66] was "the language men would use who were intending to grant perpetual rights in city streets."[67] For the first time, however, he suggested an audience for his dissent—the future: "Fully realizing the futility, for the present, of dissenting

---

62. *Northern Ohio Traction & Light Co. v. Ohio,* 245 U.S. 574 (1918).
63. Ibid., 585.
64. Ibid., 592.
65. *City of Covington v. South Covington & Cincinnati Street Railway Co.,* 246 U.S. 413 (1918).
66. Ibid., 423.
67. Ibid., 420.

from what seems to me to be an unfortunate extension of the doctrine of [an earlier case], I deem it my duty to record my dissent, with the hope for a return to the sound, but now seemingly neglected, doctrine," which would require that any claim of private right against the public be supported by "express terms."[68]

Not surprisingly, Brandeis himself also backed an appeal to facts rather than to common experience. His statement came in an opinion explaining why he concurred in the Court's reiteration that a patent holder could not use the patent to insist that any resale of the patented item must be at a fixed price.[69] As was his style, Brandeis made the point succinctly: "Whether a producer of goods should be permitted to fix by contract, express or implied, the price at which the purchaser may resell them, and if so, under what conditions, is an economic question. To decide it wisely it is necessary to consider the relevant facts, industrial and commercial, rather than established legal principles."[70]

With such a clearly formed position, Brandeis's inability to participate in *United States v. United Shoe Machinery Co.*, announced two months later, proved critical.[71] McReynolds also recused himself, leaving the Court with only seven members to deal with one of the decade's most important antitrust cases. After an initial failure against United Shoe five years earlier,[72] the government persisted in its effort to break up the company's control over machines used to assemble shoes. This new case was argued for four days in March 1917, then reargued for three in January 1918. When the decision was finally announced, the Court split 4–3, with the plurality siding with United Shoe. The government had charged United Shoe with violating the Sherman Act through combinations with and acquisitions of other companies that made machines used in manufacturing shoes. United Shoe responded that its size resulted from nothing more than the legitimate use of its patents, along with the superiority of its machinery. The particular use of patents involved leasing machinery with requirements that the lessee use the machine in combination only with other machines from United Shoe. (These were the leases Brandeis had defended while representing United Shoe.)[73] In the eyes of Justice McKenna, writing for the four-man plurality, "the leases are simply bargains, not different from others, moved upon calculated considerations, and, whether provident or improvident, are enti-

---

68. Ibid., 423.
69. *Boston Store of Chicago v. American Graphophone Co.*, 246 U.S. 8 (1918).
70. Ibid., 27–28.
71. 247 U.S. 32 (1918).
72. *United States v. Winslow*, 227 U.S. 202 (1913).
73. Mason, *Brandeis*, 214–19.

tled nevertheless to the sanctions of the law." Then, as though he recognized that the doctrine was losing vitality through repeatedly being invoked against newer arguments, he added: "We have said this, indeed, with iteration, but sometimes propositions which have become postulates have to be justified to meet objections, which, if they do not deny their existence, tend to bring them into question."[74]

The differences in common experience proved to be critical in four other cases decided during the term: *Hitchman Coal & Coke Co. v. Mitchell*,[75] *Selective Draft Law Cases*,[76] *Toledo Newspaper Co. v. United States*,[77] and *Hammer v. Dagenhart*.[78] The legal issue in *Hitchman* arose out of the by now typical pattern of efforts by a union to organize a group of workers. Here, the workers were miners employed by Hitchman Coal in a West Virginia coal mine. The company required its employees to sign contracts in which they promised not to join unions, reminding employees that anyone who joined a union would be fired, which, as the Court's majority would repeat, was "a part of the constitutional rights of personal liberty and private property."[79] When Hitchman learned that John Mitchell, as president of the United Mine Workers, planned to unionize the mine, it obtained an injunction against interfering with the employment relation between Hitchman and its employees. Once again, the vocabulary of the argument was contract. Thus, when Pitney wrote the opinion for the 6–3 Court, he could point out that the union's attempts to get the miners to join the union were contrary to the contracts they had signed.[80]

The dissenting trio, Brandeis, Holmes, and Clarke, also drew on contract, but with a very different view. Brandeis wrote that claiming an interference with economic liberty was of no assistance—every contract was a restriction on liberty, a point White had emphasized in his "rule of reason" opinions.[81] The ques-

---

74. 247 U.S. at 66. The United States would finally win a decree against United Shoe in 1922, in the Supreme Court's first decision under section 3 of the Clayton Act, which made tying agreements illegal. *United Shoe Machinery Corp. v. United States*, 258 U.S. 451 (1922).
75. 245 U.S. 229 (1917).
76. 245 U.S. 366 (1918). *Jones v. Perkins*, 245 U.S. 390 (1918), was decided along with the other cases. Jones, who was in prison for failing to register for the draft, sought a writ of habeas corpus. The Court rejected the petition, noting that habeas corpus could not be used prior to trial, especially since all the constitutional questions had been resolved in a preceding decision.
77. 247 U.S. 402 (1918). The Supreme Court overruled *Toledo* in *Nye v. United States*, 313 U.S. 33 (1941).
78. 247 U.S. 251 (1918).
79. 245 U.S. at 251.
80. Pitney thought the point so important that he included it in his opinion twice. 245 U.S. at 245, 248.
81. Ibid., 270–71. He would make the same point in an antitrust opinion three months later. *Board of Trade of the City of Chicago v. United States*, 246 U.S. 231, 238 (1918): "But the legality

tion, therefore, was whether the goal of the agreement was legal. For Brandeis there was no doubt that union membership was a legal goal, and efforts to achieve that goal could not properly be branded as "coercive": "The employer is free either to accept the agreement or the disadvantage. Indeed, the plaintiff's whole case is rested upon agreements secured under similar pressure of economic necessity or disadvantage. If it is coercion to threaten to strike unless plaintiff consents to a closed union shop, it is coercion also to threaten not to give one employment unless the applicant will consent to a closed non-union shop."[82] Brandeis's description of all contract as "coercive" was very much in the mainstream of emerging twentieth-century jurisprudence.[83]

The *Selective Draft Law Cases* brought together the past with the present, with an ex-Confederate soldier (White) writing a stirring opinion defending the draft as an exercise of the powers granted to Congress to declare war, to raise an army, and to do all that was necessary and proper to support the war and the army. During oral argument one of the attorneys challenging the act suggested that the people had never approved the war. White cut him off, saying, "I don't think your statement has anything to do with the legal arguments and should not have been said to this court. It is a very unpatriotic statement to make."[84] Not surprisingly, White's response to arguments against the statute was typically dismissive: "As the mind cannot conceive an army without the men to compose it, on the face of the Constitution the objection that it does not give power to provide for such men would seem to be too frivolous for further notice."[85] Moreover, reminding everyone of the then current world war, and the need for the United States to be seen as an equal on the world stage, he reported that almost every nation in the world authorized a draft, as had every government from colonial times to 1861. It was in that year, according to White's classic circumlocution, "that mutterings of the dread conflict which was to come began to be heard."[86] Without referring to the "North" or to the

---

of an agreement or regulation cannot be determined by so simple a test, as whether it restrains competition. Every agreement concerning trade, every regulation of trade, restrains. To bind, to restrain, is of their very essence. The true test of legality is whether the restraint imposed is such as merely regulates and perhaps thereby promotes competition or whether it is such as may suppress or even destroy competition." To apply that test, Brandeis wrote, courts must look at facts, the history, and the reasons for adopting the rule.

82. 245 U.S. at 271. For discussion of the concept of *coercion* in the context of labor decisions, see Cushman, "Doctrinal Synergies and Liberal Dilemmas: The Case of the Yellow-Dog Contract," 248–55.

83. See, for example, Roscoe Pound, "Liberty of Contract," *Yale Law Journal* 18 (May 1909): 454–87.

84. *New York Times,* December 14, 1917.

85. 245 U.S. at 377.

86. Ibid., 385.

"South," White made his meaning clear when he wrote that it "would be childish to deny the value of the added strength which was thus afforded" to the North by the draft.[87] Then, as though drawing the South into the world of nations, he buttressed his argument by an oblique reference to "events in another environment."[88] The Confederacy, too, had adopted a draft (though there was no reference to the draft having added strength to that army). Thus aided by history and his own logic, White concluded that the law was constitutional.

The *Selective Draft Law Cases* began the calendar year of 1918 with strong reinforcement of national power, at least when directed internationally. Five months later, at the close of the term, the Court produced an equally strong rebuke against the domestic exercise of national power, in *Hammer v. Dagenhart*.[89] In *Hammer* the Court held the Child Labor Act of 1916 to be unconstitutional. The essence of the act was a prohibition of shipment in interstate commerce of any goods manufactured by children.[90]

Writing for the 5–4 Court, Day explained that the prohibition exceeded Congress's powers over interstate commerce. He acknowledged that the Court had given the federal government a long series of victories in regulating commerce, even when there was a strong moral component to the regulation. With laws banning the interstate commerce of lottery tickets, putrid food, alcohol, and women transported for immoral purposes, there seemed to be ample precedent for the child-labor law, as supporters of the law were quick to point out.[91] But Day rejected the suggestion that the cases supported a power to ban "ordinary commodities" from interstate commerce. On the contrary, he explained, the cases "rest upon the character of the particular subjects dealt with and the fact that the scope of governmental authority, state or national, possessed over them is such that the authority to prohibit is as to them but the exertion of the power to regulate."[92] Day struggled to make clear the point that had been subsumed in many of the earlier opinions: Common experience understood that there was something inherently evil or immoral in the products regulated, whether they be lottery tickets, putrid eggs, or liquor.

---

87. Ibid., 387.
88. Ibid., 388.
89. 247 U.S. 251 (1918). See Stephen B. Wood, *Constitutional Politics in the Progressive Era: Child Labor and the Law* (Chicago: University of Chicago Press, 1968).
90. Known as the Keating-Owen Act, the statute covered all work by children under fourteen; for children between the ages of fourteen and sixteen, the act affected their products only if they had worked more than eight hours in a day, or more than six days a week, or before 6 a.m. or after 7 p.m. Act of September 1, 1916, ch. 432, 39 Stat. 675.
91. For example, see, *The New Republic* 12 (September 1917): 186–88.
92. 247 U.S. at 270.

The Court's majority could not say the same for products manufactured by child labor, indeed, in Day's words, "The goods shipped are of themselves harmless."[93]

Staying well within the vocabulary of precedents, Day went on to declare that the evil associated with child labor had ended when the goods entered interstate commerce. In particular, he wrote that "the mere fact that they were intended for interstate commerce transportation does not make their production subject to federal control under the commerce power."[94] He was, of course, correct in his reliance on precedent—"commerce" did not begin until there was "actual delivery to a common carrier for transportation."[95] For support of that long-standing principle, Day pointed to the nature of the federal system: "The maintenance of the authority of the States over matters purely local is as essential to the preservation of our institutions as is the conservation of the supremacy of the federal power in all matters entrusted to the Nation by the Federal Constitution."[96] He ended his opinion with a vision of the apocalypse worthy of Chief Justice White: "The far reaching result of upholding the act cannot be more plainly indicated than by pointing out that if Congress can thus regulate matters entrusted to local authority by prohibition of the movement of commodities in interstate commerce, all freedom of commerce will be at an end, and the power of the States over local matters may be eliminated, and thus our system of government be practically destroyed."[97]

Holmes's dissent gathered the support of McKenna, Brandeis, and Clarke. He rejected the argument that a state's police power could interfere with Congress's exercise of its power over interstate commerce. Reflecting his deference to the people's voice as expressed through the legislature, Holmes wrote that it did "not matter whether the supposed evil precedes or follows the transportation. It is enough that in the opinion of Congress the transportation encourages the evil."[98] He even went so far as to imply support for opposition to child labor: "But if there is any matter upon which civilized countries have agreed—far more unanimously than they have with regard to intoxicants and some other matters over which this country is now emotionally aroused—it is the evil of premature and excessive child labor. I should have thought that if we were to introduce our own moral conceptions where in my opinion they do not belong, this was preëminently a case for upholding the exercise of all its powers by the United States."[99]

---

93. Ibid., 272.
94. Ibid.
95. Ibid.
96. Ibid., 275.
97. Ibid., 276.
98. Ibid., 279–80.
99. Ibid., 280.

Supporters of the Child Labor Law were stunned by the Court's decision. They had anticipated that the Court would uphold the act, continuing the line of cases that had begun with the successful ban on lottery tickets. One of the original sponsors of the bill, Oklahoma's Senator Robert Owen, was so irate that he proposed abolishing the judiciary.[100] Once tempers cooled, Congress responded by levying an excise tax of 10 percent on profits from the sale of products manufactured by child labor. The tax was part of the larger War Revenue Bill signed by President Wilson in February 1919, almost immediately after he returned from the negotiations in Paris to end the First World War and to establish the League of Nations.[101] The Court would later declare that act unconstitutional as well.[102]

The final case in the quartet that explored the meaning of common experience was *Toledo Newspaper,* which arose out of a long-standing dispute over the fares charged by street railways in Toledo. The newspaper *(The Toledo News-Bee)* sided with the city, criticizing both the railway and its creditors who sought to enjoin a city ordinance ordering lower fares. As the dispute dragged on, the newspaper continued to publish articles, enlarging its criticism to include the federal district judge who enjoined enforcement of the statute. The judge's response was to cite the newspaper for contempt and impose a fine. Both the Circuit Court of Appeals for the Sixth Circuit and the Supreme Court upheld the judge's actions.

Chief Justice White wrote the opinion for the Court, which divided 5–2, with Day and Clarke not participating.[103] As was typical of his opinions, White provided no quotation from the newspaper articles that provoked the district judge.[104] White's was not a style that emphasized facts. Instead, he contented himself with generalized descriptions of the articles' efforts to influence the judge by alleging that any order siding with the railway would produce such disrespect for him and his court that the public would refuse to follow the order. The appellate court had upheld the actions, on the ground that there were facts sufficient to support a conclusion that the newspaper had attempted to intimidate the judge. With the issue thus presented

---

100. *New York Times,* June 19, 1918. Owen had earlier proposed eliminating the power of federal courts to declare acts of Congress unconstitutional. See Robert L. Owen, "Withdrawing Power from Federal Courts to Declare Acts of Congress Void," U.S. Senate. 1917. 64th Cong., 2d sess., S. Doc. 737 (address delivered in Oklahoma City, Oklahoma, January 27, 1917); *New York Times,* January 9, 1917 (proposed joint resolution).
101. Act of February 24, 1919, ch. 18, tit. 12, 40 Stat. 1057, 1138.
102. *Bailey v. Drexel Furniture Co.,* 259 U.S. 20 (1922).
103. Holmes attributed their recusals to their relationship with the trial court judge. Holmes to Pollock, June 14, 1918, Howe, *Holmes-Pollock Letters,* 267.
104. There are lengthy quotations in the district court's opinion. *United States v. Toledo Newspaper Co.,* 220 F. 458 (N.D. Ohio 1915).

as one of sufficiency of the evidence, White thought the conclusion was inevitable, "since no other course, under the statement, is possible compatibly with the sacred obligation of courts to preserve their right to discharge their duties free from unlawful and unworthy influences and, in doing so, if need be, to clear from the pathway leading to the performance of this great duty all unwarranted attempts to pervert, obstruct or distort judgment."[105]

The one addition to the familiar path of review was the newspaper's argument that the citation for contempt violated the freedom of the press. But White would have none of that argument, portraying it as amounting to "the contention that the freedom of the press is the freedom to do wrong with impunity and implies the right to frustrate and defeat the discharge of those governmental duties upon the performance of which the freedom of all, including that of the press, depends."[106]

Holmes dissented, joined by Brandeis. Like White, Holmes devoted little attention to the actual text printed in the newspaper. He mentioned that the paper had "published news, comment and cartoons"; he summarized the articles but described in particular only one editorial cartoon.[107] He combined that summary of the facts with an analysis of the statute that authorized judges to punish by contempt the "misbehavior of any person in their presence, or so near thereto as to obstruct the administration of justice."[108] He thought the statute required something more than a possibility for obstructing the court; there had to be an actual obstruction. Here, he expected a federal judge "to be a man of ordinary firmness of character," and he found "it impossible to believe that such a judge could have found in anything that was printed even a tendency to prevent his performing his sworn duty."[109] Thus, without reference to the First Amendment, Holmes concluded that the facts did not warrant summary trial for contempt.

---

105. 247 U.S. at 416.
106. Ibid., 419.
107. Ibid., 422, 424–25.
108. Ibid., 423.
109. Ibid., 424.

IX

THE 1918–1919 TERM

On September 7, 1918, a month before the justices began their new term, a soldier in Company B, 42d Infantry, reported for sick call at Camp Devens, Massachusetts. By the time the Court's term ended, in June 1919, some 675,000 Americans had died from influenza and the related pneumonia. That number exceeded the total number of battle deaths in the United States military in all wars in the twentieth century.[1] The Court's only response to the epidemic was to adjourn early once during the fall. As Holmes explained to Sir Frederick Pollock, "it was not thought right to require lawyers to come, often across the continent, to a crowded and infected spot."[2] The Court also adjourned on January 6, 1919, immediately after learning of the death of former President Roosevelt. The decision to adjourn without taking any other action that day was unprecedented in the memory of those closely associated with the Court.[3] In spite of those interruptions, the Court managed to hand down 229 opinions during the term, bringing an end to the downward slide in number of opinions written each term. The justices even managed to increase slightly the percentage of opinions without dissent.[4] But this would be the last such achievement by the Court. In the final two terms, the number of opinions, as well as the percentage of unanimous ones, would decline.

---

1. Alfred W. Crosby, *America's Forgotten Pandemic: The Influenza of 1918* (Cambridge: Cambridge University Press, 1989), 5, 206–7.
2. Holmes to Pollock, October 31, 1918, Howe, *Holmes-Pollock Letters,* 1:270.
3. *New York Times,* January 7, 1919.
4. Of the 229 opinions for the Court, 197 were unanimous, or 86 percent. Of the thirty-two cases in which there was a dissent, sixteen had written dissents: *Ruddy v. Rossi,* 248 U.S. 104 (1918); *Cleveland-Cliffs Iron Co. v. Arctic Iron Co.,* 248 U.S. 178 (1918); *Sandberg v. McDonald,* 248 U.S. 185 (1918); *Neilson v. Rhine Shipping Co.,* 248 U.S. 205 (1918); *International News Service v. The Associated Press,* 248 U.S. 215 (1918); *The Hebe Co. v. Shaw,* 248 U.S. 297 (1919); *United States v. Hill,* 248 U.S. 420 (1919); *Detroit United Railway v. City of Detroit,* 248 U.S. 429 (1919); *Bank of California v. Richardson,* 248 U.S. 476 (1919); *United States v. Doremus,* 249 U.S. 86 (1919); *Webb v. United States,* 249 U.S. 96 (1919); *Baltimore & Ohio Railroad Co. v. Leach,* 249 U.S. 217 (1919); *Union Tank Line Co. v. Wright,* 249 U.S. 275 (1919); *Arizona Employers' Liability Cases,* 250 U.S. 400 (1919); *Erie Railroad Co. v. Shuart,* 250 U.S. 465 (1919); *Southern Pacific Co. v. Bogert,* 250 U.S. 483 (1919).

As a result, for the final five terms of the White Court, the justices would average 211 opinions per term, compared with almost 270 in the first five terms. There was a similar change in the unanimity of the Court: For the first half of White's tenure as chief justice, 90 percent of all opinions were unanimous; for the last half, 81 percent were.

With this term, the Court's continuing struggle with words came to a head. Nothing better illustrated the ongoing strain than a trio of opinions announced in succession on December 23, 1918: *Sandberg v. McDonald*,[5] *Neilson v. Rhine Shipping Co.*,[6] and *International News Service v. The Associated Press*.[7] *Sandberg* and *Neilson* each involved a United States law that prohibited paying seamen in advance of their having earned the wages.[8] Not unlike the antipeonage statutes, and resembling state regulations of employment agencies, this provision aimed at preventing seamen from being always in debt to a ship owner or other person to whom they had assigned their wages.[9] The dispute in *Sandberg* arose when sailors, in accord with the statute and with maritime practice, sought payment of half of the wages they had earned on the first leg of their voyage. The sailors, who were not citizens of the United States, made the demand while their British-registered ship was in port in Mobile, Alabama, having sailed there from Dublin, Ireland, where the sailors had first boarded the ship. The ship's master met the demand, but deducted amounts advanced to the sailors before they sailed. After leaving the ship, the sailors sued in federal court for the amounts deducted. In support of their claim, they pointed to this language in the statute: "[T]his section shall apply as well to foreign vessels while in waters of the United States, as to vessels of the United States."[10]

Writing for the 5–4 Court, Justice Day explained that the master was entitled to deduct the advance payments, which were legal under British law. The Court read the clause identified by the sailors as meaning only that the statute applied to contracts made while the vessels were in United States waters. Day therefore reiterated, even strengthened, the Court's presumption against the extraterritorial application of United States law, first announced in 1909.[11] Day wrote that legislation "is presumptively territorial and confined to limits over which the law-making power has jurisdic-

---

5. 248 U.S. 185 (1918).
6. 248 U.S. 205 (1918).
7. 248 U.S. 215 (1918).
8. The provision was contained in the Seaman's Act of 1915, ch. 153, 38 Stat. 1164. It is quoted in the Court's opinion, 248 U.S. at 192–93. For the background to the act and its effect on existing maritime treaties, see Link, *Woodrow Wilson and the Progressive Era*, 61–63.
9. See 248 U.S. at 193–94.
10. Ibid., 193.
11. See *American Banana Co. v. United Fruit Co.*, 213 U.S. 347 (1909) (Holmes for the Court).

tion."[12] To declare void contracts made elsewhere, the Court reasoned, would be futile, since the foreign countries would continue to enforce the contracts. Day found further support for his conclusion in the fact that the statute made it a criminal offense to pay in advance. "Congress," he wrote, "certainly did not intend to punish criminally acts done within a foreign jurisdiction; a purpose so wholly futile is not to be attributed to Congress."[13] Day therefore concluded that the contractual provisions of the statute were to be given a similarly restrictive application. He ended his opinion by acknowledging that he had looked at references to reports and proceedings in Congress concerning the act. But he had found "nothing in them, so far as entitled to consideration, which requires a different meaning to be given the statute."[14]

Neilson presented the same issue, though with a sufficiently different background to make the decision more difficult to reach. Paul Neilson was a sailor on a ship registered in the United States. He joined the crew in Buenos Aires, where, in accord with local custom, he signed a note, payable to the shipping master, for a month's wages, twenty-five dollars. In effect, the master served the same role as an employment agency in the United States— charging part or all of the first month's wages in return for finding the position. Acting in accord with consular regulations, the United States consul noted the agreement and directed the master to honor the note.[15] When the ship arrived in New York, Neilson invoked the Seaman's Act of 1915 in an attempt to recover the advance.

Once again Day wrote the opinion for the 5–4 Court. Because he found that *Sandberg* controlled, he added no further analysis of the statute. He deplored the fact that the holding meant that United States ships could obtain crews in Buenos Aires only by complying with the local custom of working through agents who required a month's wages as a commission. "But," Day added, "we are unable to discover that in passing this statute Congress intended to place American shipping at the great disadvantage of this inability to obtain seamen when compared with the vessels of other nations which are manned by complying with local usage."[16]

Justice McKenna dissented in both cases, joined by Holmes, Brandeis, and Clarke. He emphasized what he termed the "universality" of the language prohibiting the payment of advances.[17] In the supposed consequences

---

12. 248 U.S. at 195.
13. Ibid., 196.
14. Ibid., 197.
15. Justice McKenna quotes a portion of the consular regulation in his dissent in *Neilson*. 248 U.S. at 214.
16. 248 U.S. at 213.
17. Ibid., 200.

of applying the language, he professed to have no interest. Instead, he wrote with a curious combination of humility and bravado: "Ours is the simple service of interpretation, and there is no reason to hesitate in its exercise because of supposed consequences."[18] He supplemented that comment by recalling that all conceded "that the words of the sections are grammatically broad enough to include all seamen, foreign as well as American, and advances and contracts, wherever made."[19] Of course, the ship owners had argued that regardless of the language, Congress intended to reach only American sailors. McKenna's rejoinder to their limited construction was the most revealing part of his dissent: "The contention would take us from the certainty of language to the uncertainties of construction dependent upon the conjecture of consequences; take us from the deck to the sea, if we may use a metaphor suggested by our subject. Language is the safer guide, for it may be defined; consequences brought forward to modify its meaning may be in fact and effect disputed."[20] His assurance about the certainty of words was even more explicit in his short dissent in *Neilson*, when he responded to arguments that his interpretation would imprison United States ships in foreign ports, where the only escape could come through violating the law. The statute, McKenna wrote, was clear; if applications had "the embarrassment depicted by counsel, the appeal must be to Congress, which no doubt will promptly correct the improvidence, if it be such, of its legislation. We have already expressed our view of the control of the language of the law and that it is a barrier against alarms and fault-finding."[21]

Even though Brandeis joined both of these dissents, his view of language was markedly different from McKenna's. McKenna recognized a certainty in language; but that recognition was not a rejection of change, for he acknowledged movement in society as well as in law. Brandeis, too, perceived change; indeed, among the justices he was the exemplar of change. But change extended to language, which offered him little of the certainty found by McKenna. Instead, Brandeis looked to facts for information about meaning. The most significant consequence of that difference was that McKenna would retain a larger role for the courts in dealing with language. Brandeis, by contrast, was the prototypical Progressive: He would defer to the opportunities of legislators, as well as administrators and other experts, to find the facts on which meaning could be based.

Nowhere was that difference better illustrated than in the case that followed *Neilson* on December 23, *International News Service v. The Associated Press.*[22]

---

18. Ibid., 201.
19. Ibid., 202.
20. Ibid.
21. Ibid., 215.
22. 248 U.S. 215 (1918).

The Court, in an opinion by Pitney, upheld an injunction against the International News Service prohibiting it from copying AP reports from the AP's own bulletins and from the early editions of newspapers that subscribed to the AP's services. The AP sought the injunction after the INS, which was controlled by William Randolph Hearst's syndicate, pirated AP reports of war activities. The British government had earlier banned the INS from using cables from Britain, and elsewhere on the continent.[23] Complaints about the INS dated to reports about the Easter Uprising in Ireland in May 1916. Two months later, the INS reported on a British naval defeat in terms not approved by the censor.[24] Repeated transgressions led to the ban in October.[25] As the Court explained, most news reports came from foreign sources through New York; from there, the AP distributed reports to subscribers throughout the country. Taking advantage of time zones and irregularities in telegraph services, the INS could often copy an AP report in New York and send it to a western newspaper before it could be received by an AP subscriber in the same location. There was an element of pride in human achievement when Pitney wrote that the distribution could occur because "in speed the telegraph and telephone easily outstrip the rotation of the earth."[26] The invisibility of the information sent by those technologies made resolution of the legal issue all the more difficult. "News" was not capable of being copyrighted—the events themselves were not the creation of human effort. Nevertheless, copyright remained as a vital analogy in AP's argument—much like copyright and patent had served in cases such as *Dr. Miles Medical* and *A. B. Dick*. In place of copyright as a rubric of law, the AP based its claim on unfair competition. Even so, Pitney struggled to define the ephemeral property right claimed by the AP:

> We are dealing here not with restrictions upon publication but with the very facilities and processes of publication. The peculiar value of news is in the spreading of it while it is fresh; and it is evident that a valuable property interest in the news, as news, cannot be maintained by keeping it secret. . . . That business consists in maintaining a prompt, sure, steady, and reliable service designed to place the daily events of the world at the breakfast table of the millions at a price that, while of trifling moment to each reader, is sufficient in the aggregate to afford compensation for the cost of gathering and distributing it, with the added profit so necessary as an incentive to effective action in the commercial world.[27]

---

23. Oliver Gramling, *AP: The Story of News* (New York: Farrar and Rinehart, Inc., 1940), 263, 285.
24. *New York Times*, June 28, 1916.
25. *New York Times*, October 11, 1916.
26. 248 U.S. at 238.
27. Ibid., 235.

The INS contended that once the AP published a report it abandoned any claim to it. Pitney rejected that argument, characterizing the AP's publication as being "for limited purposes" of informing the public through its subscribers; the publication did not give a competitor the right to sell the information, representing it as its own. The key lay in the competitive use of the news; anyone could distribute gratuitously. Thus, Pitney concluded for the Court, the injunction should prohibit the INS from copying the AP stories for so long as they had commercial value to any of its subscribers.

Justice Brandeis was the lone dissenter.[28] Ironically, much in this opinion was a near repudiation of his seminal work on the right to privacy.[29] In arguing for recognition of a "right" to privacy in 1890, he had applauded the judicial expansion of the concept of property. Now, however, he argued for a limitation on the reach of judges in reforming the law: "The knowledge for which protection is sought in the case at bar is not of a kind upon which the law has heretofore conferred the attributes of property; nor is the manner of its acquisition or use nor the purpose to which it is applied, such as has heretofore been recognized as entitling a plaintiff to relief."[30] Responding to Pitney's difficulty in defining the claim to protection, Brandeis noted that it was the form or arrangement of ideas for which protection was sought, not the content. For that claim the common law afforded no protection. He referred to a contemporaneous English case for support, one in which a court declined to enjoin a photographer from publishing photographs of a dog show. The English court reasoned that the organizer of the show had no right to control the photographs, since they had been taken without the photographer going onto the property where the show was held.[31] With that case in mind, Brandeis concluded: "If, when the plaintiff creates the event recorded, he is not entitled to the exclusive first publication of the news (in that case a photograph) of the event, no reason can be shown why he should be accorded such protection as to events which he simply records and transmits to other parts of the world, though with great expenditure of time and money."[32] Brandeis followed his restrictive reading of precedents to the conclusion that the INS obtained the

---

28. Justice Clarke did not participate, according to the *New York Times*, "because he is himself a newspaper publisher [of the *Youngstown Vindicator*]." *New York Times*, December 24, 1918. Justice Holmes concurred with Justice Pitney's opinion, but would narrow the injunction to prohibit only the unacknowledged use of AP's reports. Thus, in his view, the INS should be permitted to use those reports, so long as it acknowledged the source. Justice McKenna joined Holmes's opinion.
29. Samuel Warren and Louis Brandeis, "The Right to Privacy," *Harvard Law Review* 4 (1890): 193–220.
30. 248 U.S. at 251.
31. *Sports and General Press Agency, Ltd. v. "Our Dogs" Publishing Co., Ltd.*, [1916] 2 K.B. 880.
32. 248 U.S. at 255–56.

reports legally and that it and its subscribers were "merely using [the AP's] product without making compensation." "That," he continued, "they have a legal right to do; because the product is not property, and they do not stand in any relation to the Associated Press, either of contract or of trust, which otherwise precludes such use."[33] Even though he conceded that the INS's conduct was unjust, he saw no basis for the courts to respond; instead, the matter was for legislative response, but only after investigation of the facts. His explanation is worth quoting at some length, for it amounts to a credo for the twentieth century's jurisprudence, now replacing that of the nineteenth:

> The great development of agencies now furnishing country-wide distribution of news, the vastness of our territory, and improvements in the means of transmitting intelligence, have made it possible for a news agency or newspapers to obtain, without paying compensation, the fruit of another's efforts and to use news so obtained gainfully in competition with the original collector. The injustice of such action is obvious. But to give relief against it would involve more than the application of existing rules of law to new facts. It would require the making of a new rule in analogy to existing ones. The unwritten law possesses capacity for growth; and has often satisfied new demands for justice by invoking analogies or by expanding a rule or principle. This process has been in the main wisely applied and should not be discontinued. Where the problem is relatively simple, as it is apt to be when private interests only are invoked, it generally proves adequate. But with the increasing complexity of society, the public interest tends to become omnipresent; and the problems presented by new demands for justice cease to be simple. Then the creation or recognition by courts of a new private right may work serious injury to the general public, unless the boundaries of the right are definitely established and wisely guarded. In order to reconcile the new private right with the public interest, it may be necessary to prescribe limitations and rules for its enjoyment; and also to provide administrative machinery for enforcing the rules. It is largely for this reason that, in the effort to meet the many new demands for justice incident to a rapidly changing civilization, resort to legislation has latterly been had with increasing frequency.[34]

In short, for Brandeis words had meaning insofar as they had a basis in fact. For words depending upon complex facts for meaning, courts lacked the ability to compile a concordance; instead, only legislatures had the requisite competence.

---

33. Ibid., 260.
34. Ibid., 262–63.

Throughout the term the Court teetered between the two approaches, reflecting the tension between words as part of a known lexicon, or common experience, and words as objects to be discovered. Ever so gradually the balance was tipping toward Brandeis, and his view that words were malleable, subject to having different meanings in different contexts, contexts that might not be known to judges. One particularly good example of that tension came in the Court's opinions dealing with contracts for transport of goods. The outbreak of the war had produced a series of dramatic changes, many of which had significant impact on the performance of contracts. As a result, any number of parties sought relief from what had become burdensome obligations under contracts. Although the Supreme Court had recognized an expanded doctrine of excuse in *The Kronprinzessin Cecilie*,[35] it remained less than generous in granting relief from the obligations of a contract.[36] For example, in *Allanwilde Transport Corp. v. Vacuum Oil Co.* the Court refused to order repayment of freight charges when the United States government barred sailing vessels (though not steamships) from leaving port, on account of the threat posed by German submarines.[37] The vessel sailed September 11, 1917, but had to return to port when a storm caused a leak in its hull. Not knowing of the government's order, issued September 28, the vessel returned to New York. When it was denied permission to leave after making repairs, the shippers had to obtain another carrier. They then sought a refund of the freight charges already paid. McKenna's opinion for the Court offered only an abrupt conclusion: The shipping contract specifically provided that prepaid freight was not refundable. With that provision in mind, there was no need to consider whether the government's order was foreseeable—the parties must have bargained for that provision along with other terms in the contract.[38]

The Court reached a similar result in *Columbus Railway, Power & Light Co. v. City of Columbus*, a case in which the railway claimed an exemption from limits imposed by the city on its fares.[39] The railway operated under franchises

---

35. 244 U.S. 12 (1917).
36. The Court did direct that proceedings in a lawsuit by a British company against an Austro-Hungarian company be postponed until the end of the war, when communication could resume between the attorney in New York and the client in Europe. *Watts, Watts & Co., Ltd. v. Unione Austriaca di Navigazione*, 248 U.S. 9 (1918).
37. 248 U.S. 377 (1919).
38. The Court reached similar results in the two cases reported immediately following *Allanwilde*. *International Paper Co. v. The Schooner "Gracie D. Chambers,"* 248 U.S. 387, 392 (1919) ("It was for the parties to consider them, and to accept their estimate is not to do injustice but accord to each the due of the law determined by their own judgment and convention, which represented, we may suppose, what there was of advantage or disadvantage as well in the rates as in the risks."); *Standard Varnish Works v. Steamship "Bris,"* 248 U.S. 392 (1919) (prepaid freight not to be repaid even in the absence of the word "irrevocable").
39. 249 U.S. 399 (1919).

awarded in 1901, the terms of which obligated the railway to sell eight tickets for twenty-five cents. In July 1918, the War Labor Board ordered a more than 50-percent increase in the wages for the railway's employees. When the city refused to alter the franchises, the railway surrendered its charter. And, in a pre-emptive move, the railway sought to enjoin the city from compelling it to perform. The railway claimed that it had the right to raise its fares to recoup the higher costs that resulted from the required increase in wages. The Court rejected the claim, holding that the railway was bound by the contract it had with the city. The Court insisted on taking the franchise as a whole contract, with profit or loss to be determined over the full twenty-five-year period. Accordingly, the railway had no ground for arguing that the rates were so low as to amount to a denial of due process. Instead, the railway based its argument on basic contract principles—the need for equitable relief in light of the changed circumstances, pointing to *The Kronprinzessin Cecilie* for support. But the Court found no support for relief, even though it conceded that the parties had not anticipated the outbreak of war, much less the action of the War Labor Board. The key fact remained that there was no showing that the contract would be unprofitable for the twenty-five-year duration of the contract. Thus, as Justice Day explained, on behalf of the Court, when the words of the contract were clear, "Unforeseen difficulties will not excuse performance. Where the parties have made no provision for a dispensation, the terms of the contract must prevail."[40]

The irony in *Columbus Railway* was the reversal of positions with respect to the ordinance. Typically, companies argued that ordinances were contracts, perpetual ones, which insulated them against changes mandated by municipalities. Here, however, the city turned the ordinance against the company through insisting that its terms be enforced even in the face of significantly changed circumstances. Although one argument was made in the vocabulary of the Constitution and the other in the language of private contracts, both shared the premise that changed circumstances should justify a change in the relationship between the parties. The very fact that parties would once have agreed to fixed terms showed the change in circumstances. For, as Holmes noted in another case decided this term, "The charter contracts in question are of a kind that goes back to the time when railroads were barely beginning and that would not likely to be repeated."[41] Even so, the Court continued its consistent pattern of holding cities to their bargains, just as it did railroads and other parties.[42]

---

40. Ibid., 412.
41. *Central of Georgia Railway Co. v. Wright*, 248 U.S. 525, 527 (1919).
42. In addition to *Central of Georgia*, see *Georgia v. Trustees of the Cincinnati Southern Railway*, 248 U.S. 26 (1918).

At the end of the term, the Court displayed considerably less sympathy for an ordinance that actually *reduced* rates.[43] The Court criticized the parties for allowing the litigation to continue for over a decade (the city originally ordered a reduction in rates in 1906). Even so, the Court remanded the case for evidence concerning the effect of the rates under wartime conditions, saying: "It is a matter of common knowledge that, owing principally to the world war, the costs of labor and supplies of every kind have greatly advanced since the ordinance was adopted, and largely since this cause was last heard in the court below. And it is equally well known that annual returns upon capital and enterprise the world over have materially increased, so that what would have been a proper rate of return for capital invested in gas plants and similar public utilities a few years ago furnishes no safe criterion for the present or for the future."[44]

The wartime context provided at least one other example of a doctrine having unanticipated results. In one of the most discussed decisions of the White Court, *Schenck v. United States*,[45] the Court unanimously upheld convictions for violating the Espionage Act of 1917.[46] The indictment charged that Charles Schenck, general secretary of the Socialist Party, had coordinated the mailing of some fifteen thousand copies of a leaflet to men who had been drafted. The leaflet called on each recipient to challenge the draft, which the leaflet asserted violated the Constitution. According to Holmes, who wrote the opinion of the Court, Schenck and his codefendant did not deny that a jury might find that the intent of the leaflet was to encourage recipients to obstruct the process of conscription.[47] So framed, the issue faced by the Court was whether the First Amendment protected efforts to obstruct the draft during wartime. Here, then, the context of the leaflet's words had especial significance, as Holmes wrote: "We admit that in many places and in ordinary times the defendants in saying all that was said in the circular would have been within their constitutional rights. But the character of every act depends upon the circumstances in which it is done."[48] He continued with one of his best-known aphorisms:

---

43. *Lincoln Gas & Electric Light Co. v. City of Lincoln*, 250 U.S. 256 (1919).
44. Ibid., 268.
45. 249 U.S. 47 (1919). On the same day that the Court announced its opinion in *Schenck*, Justice Brandeis also announced an opinion for a unanimous Court holding that no substantial federal question was presented in a challenge to another conviction under the Espionage Act. *Sugarman v. United States*, 249 U.S. 182 (1919). Brandeis explained that the objections were insignificant because they pointed to the judge's charge to the jury, which was substantially what the defendant had requested.
46. Act of June 15, 1917, ch. 30, 40 Stat. 217.
47. 249 U.S. at 51.
48. Ibid., 52.

The most stringent protection of free speech would not protect a man in falsely shouting fire in a theatre and causing a panic. It does not even protect a man from an injunction against uttering words that may have all the effect of force. . . . The question in every case is whether the words used are used in such circumstances and are of such a nature as to create a clear and present danger that they will bring about the substantive evils that Congress has a right to prevent. It is a question of proximity and degree. When a nation is at war many things that might be said in time of peace are such a hindrance to its effort that their utterance will not be endured so long as men fight and that no Court could regard them as protected by any constitutional right.[49]

A week later Holmes seemed to retreat from some of his language in *Schenck*. In *Frohwerk v. United States* he again wrote for a unanimous Court in upholding a conviction under the Espionage Act.[50] Once again the Court saw the issue as one of the sufficiency of the evidence to support the conviction; and, given that low barrier, the Court again found that the verdict should be sustained. As Holmes explained, it was "impossible to say that it might not have been found that the circulation of the paper was in quarters where a little breath would be enough to kindle a flame and that the fact was known and relied upon by those who sent the paper out."[51] But Holmes backed away from the suggestion in *Schenck* that war might justify greater restrictions on freedom of speech: "It may be that all this might be said or written even in time of war in circumstances that would not make it a crime. We do not lose our right to condemn either measures or men because the Country is at war."[52]

Holmes also wrote the Court's opinion in the companion case to *Frohwerk*—*Debs v. United States*.[53] Eugene V. Debs, the three-time Socialist candidate for president, was by far the most prominent person convicted for violating the Espionage Act. The occasion for his arrest was a speech in Canton, Ohio, on June 16, 1918. The speech seemed to invite prosecution, with its defense of other Socialists already in jail for violating the act and its encouragement of those in the audience to oppose the war. At his trial, Debs would not let his lawyers contest the charges against him; instead, he told the jury, "I have been accused of obstructing the war. I admit it."[54] Holmes added little to his opinion

---

49. Ibid. For a discussion of the evolution of the "clear and present danger" test see David M. Rabban, "The Emergence of Modern First Amendment Doctrine," *University of Chicago Law Review* 50 (1983): 1205–1355.
50. 249 U.S. 204 (1919).
51. Ibid., 209.
52. Ibid., 208.
53. 249 U.S. 211 (1919).
54. Quoted by Holmes in ibid., 214.

in *Frohwerk*, recalling the long-standing legal doctrine that if words had a particular effect, then their speaker intended the effect.[55] Holmes wrote Sir Frederick Pollock that Debs, "a noted agitator, was rightly convicted of obstructing the recruiting service so far as the law was concerned."[56] Then Holmes added:

> I wondered that the Government should press the case to a hearing before us, as the inevitable result was that fools, knaves, and ignorant persons were bound to say he was convicted because he was a dangerous agitator and that obstructing the draft was a pretence. How it was with the Jury of course I don't know, but of course the talk is silly as to us. There was a lot of jaw about free speech, which I dealt with somewhat summarily in an ealier [sic] case—*Schenck* v. *U.S.* . . . also *Frohwerk* v. *U.S.* . . . As it happens I should go farther probably than the majority in favor of it, and I daresay it was partly on that account that the C.J. assigned the case to me.[57]

Even though Holmes thought little of the issue in *Debs*, others apparently thought much of it. Within a month Holmes would write to Lewis Einstein, "Just now I am receiving some singularly ignorant protests against a decision that I wrote sustaining a conviction of Debs, a labor agitator, for obstructing the recruiting service. They make me want to write a letter to ease my mind and shoot off my mouth; but of course I keep a judicial silence."[58] Late in April 1919 a postal clerk discovered one of what would prove to be thirty-six bombs addressed to Holmes and others, including the attorney general and the secretary of labor.[59] Police and postal authorities speculated that there was a conspiracy of International Workers of the World (IWW, or "wobblies") and Bolsheviks, intent on having the bombs explode the same day across the country.[60] Also that May Day, riots broke out in some twenty-five cities in conjunction with demonstrations by radical groups. Holmes associated the bomb with his opinion in *Debs*, writing to Harold Laski, "I suppose it was the Debs incident that secured me the honor of being among those destined to receive an explosive machine, stopped in the Post Office as you may [have] seen. It shows a want of intelligence in the senders."[61] Even to the bomb, Holmes's response was brusque, this time writing to Einstein: "I haven't thought much about it

---

55. Ibid., 216.
56. Holmes to Pollock, April 5, 1919, Howe, *Holmes-Pollock Letters*, 2:7.
57. Ibid.
58. Holmes to Einstein, April 5, 1919, Peabody, *Holmes-Einstein Letters*, 184.
59. Robert K. Murray, *Red Scare: A Study of National Hysteria, 1919–1920* (1955; New York: McGraw-Hill Book Company, 1964), 68–71.
60. *New York Times*, May 1, 1919.
61. Holmes to Laski, May 1, 1919, Howe, *Holmes-Laski Letters*, 1:199.

except when reminded by letters, for, as I said to my wife, if I worried over all the bullets that have missed me I should have a job."[62]

In spite of Holmes's apparent retreat from the broad language of *Schenck,* the Court clearly responded generously to demands for executive power to deal with the wartime emergency. In *McKinley v. United States,* for example, the Court needed only a memorandum opinion to uphold a federal law empowering the secretary of war to suppress prostitution "within such distance as he may deem needful" of any military base.[63] Jacob McKinley was convicted of violating the regulation by operating a house of prostitution within the five-mile distance set by the secretary. According to Day, "That Congress has the authority to raise and support armies and to make rules and regulations for the protection of the health and welfare of those composing them, is too well settled to require more than the statement of the proposition."[64]

The Court resolved more momentous war-related issues later, on the penultimate Monday of the term. In a series of cases, the justices affirmed the federal government's takeover of the nation's trains, telegraphs, telephones, and shipping. Then, for good measure, a week later the Court upheld the takeover of the marine cable system. Appropriately for issues of such consequence, Chief Justice White took it upon himself to write the Court's opinion in all but one of the cases. He began with *Northern Pacific Railway Co. v. North Dakota,* which held that the federal takeover of the railroads precluded state railroad commissions from setting rates even for intrastate traffic.[65] The president assumed control of the railroads by proclamation of December 26, 1917.[66] After reciting the history of the takeover, White did little more than pose a rhetorical question. How could any conclusion other than that the federal power was supreme be reached, he asked, given the conjunction of national legislative and executive action in creating "one control, one administration, one power for the accomplishment of the one purpose"?[67] For further support he turned to what he termed "the complete and undivided character of the war power of the United States." To interpret that power as being subject to "the continuance of a state power limiting and controlling the national authority was but to deny its existence."[68]

---

62. Holmes to Einstein, May 22, 1919, Peabody, *Holmes-Einstein Letters,* 186.
63. 249 U.S. 397 (1919).
64. Ibid., 399. He cited only the *Selective Draft Law Cases* to support that proposition.
65. 250 U.S. 135 (1919).
66. 40 Stat. 1733. He relied on powers granted under an act of August 29, 1916, ch. 418, 39 Stat. 619, 645. Congress provided for payment to the railroads under the Federal Control Act of March 21, 1918, ch. 25, 40 Stat. 451.
67. 250 U.S. at 148.
68. Ibid., 149, 150.

With the sweep of the war power thus described, White had little difficulty in confirming a similar power over telephone and telegraph systems.[69] Once the president assumed control of those systems, they operated as an agency of the national government. As such, the states lacked power to regulate even intrastate rates. To all arguments that the president's exercise of the power given him was unwarranted, White responded that because at most the argument showed "a mere excess or abuse of discretion in exerting a power given, it is clear that [the contention] involves considerations which are beyond the reach of judicial power."[70]

Even in cases not directly involving the war power the Court seemed clearly influenced by the national mobilization when it faced yet more disputes requiring it to balance the powers of the national and state governments. Attempts to regulate alcoholic beverages continued to bedevil the Court as the country lurched toward complete prohibition. In this term the Court saw those principles extended to the regulation of narcotics. First, though, in January 1919 the Court construed the Reed Amendment, which barred the importation of liquor into any state that prohibited the manufacture or sale of liquor.[71] Echoing the dispute over the Mann Act (the White-Slave Traffic Act), the trial court had concluded that the Reed Amendment applied only to importation for commercial use—after all, Congress derived its power from a "commerce" clause. Thus the trial court dismissed an indictment against a man who brought liquor from Kentucky into West Virginia for personal use. West Virginia's own laws allowed the importation of up to a quart of liquor for personal use. Even so, the Supreme Court held that a state's law could not restrict Congress's power over interstate commerce, a power that extended to prohibition of certain products. Justice Day's otherwise quite ordinary opinion for the Court prompted a unique pairing in dissent. For the only time during his service on the Court, Justice Clarke joined a written dissent by Justice McReynolds. Their agreement is all the more notable in light of the fact that McReynolds seemed to go out of his way to make Clarke's life miserable.[72] In

---

69. *Dakota Central Telephone Co. v. South Dakota*, 250 U.S. 163 (1919); *Kansas v. Burleson*, 250 U.S. 188 (1919); *Burleson v. Dempcy*, 250 U.S. 191 (1919); *Macleod v. New England Telephone & Telegraph Co.*, 250 U.S. 195 (1919). In each case, Justice Brandeis was the lone dissenter, without written opinion.

By Joint Resolution of July 16, 1918, ch. 154, 40 Stat. 904, Congress authorized the president to take control of the nation's telephone, telegraph, marine cable, and radio systems. The president took control of the telephone and telegraph systems by proclamation dated July 22, 1918, 40 Stat. 1807, authorizing the postmaster general to exercise the authority granted to the president.

70. 250 U.S. at 184.

71. *United States v. Hill*, 248 U.S. 420 (1919). The Reed Amendment was part of the Post Office Appropriation Act of March 3, 1917, ch. 162, §5, 39 Stat 1058, 1069.

72. Acheson, *Morning and Noon*, 76.

their view, the Reed Amendment was "a direct intermeddling with the State's internal affairs." In so exceeding federal power, the amendment opened "possibilities for partial and sectional legislation which may destroy proper control of their own affairs by the several States."[73] McReynolds went on to suggest that there could be no limit to Congress's powers under the majority's reasoning. "If Congress may deny liquor to those who live in a State simply because its manufacture is not permitted there," he asked, "why may not this be done for any suggested reason, e.g., because the roads are bad or men are hanged for murder or coals are dug."[74]

When the subject matter of Congress's regulation changed to heroin in *United States v. Doremus,* the Court likewise upheld the exercise of power, but only by a 5–4 vote.[75] Unlike liquor, Congress chose to regulate heroin indirectly, by requiring that all those who sold the drug register with the commissioner of Internal Revenue and pay a token tax of one dollar annually. The act also required that the drug be sold only to buyers who had an order form issued by the commissioner; sellers had to maintain records of each transaction.[76] Under the act the United States charged Dr. C. T. Doremus with failing to use the requisite form when Doremus supplied five hundred tablets of heroin for the purpose of satisfying the recipient's drug habit. This statute depended upon Congress's power to tax, not upon its control over interstate commerce. With that source in mind, the district court held the statute unconstitutional, as an improper invasion of powers reserved to the states. In a generous opinion, the Court reversed, holding that the statute was constitutional.

Writing for the Court, Justice Day explained that the only restriction on Congress's power to impose excise taxes was that they be geographically uniform;[77] the courts had no authority to add additional restrictions. Subject to that limitation, Congress had complete discretion over the choice of subjects taxed; no court could inquire into the motives behind the choice. "If the legislation enacted has some reasonable relation to the exercise of the taxing authority conferred by the Constitution, it cannot be invalidated because of the supposed motives which induced it."[78] With that principle in mind, in spite of the apparent insignificance of the registration tax, Day announced that the Court could not say that the requirements of registration and record keeping had nothing to do with the collection of the tax. As a result, he concluded that the statute was constitutional.

---

73. 248 U.S. at 428.
74. Ibid.
75. 249 U.S. 86 (1919).
76. Harrison Narcotic Drug Act of December 17, 1914, ch. 1, 38 Stat. 785.
77. The restriction is contained in section 8 of article 1 of the Constitution: "all duties, imposts and excises shall be uniform throughout the United States."
78. 249 U.S. at 93.

Chief Justice White dissented, joined by McKenna, Van Devanter, and McReynolds. Instead of writing an opinion, however, White simply stated that he agreed with the court below that Congress had exceeded its powers by attempting "to exert a power not delegated, that is, the reserved police power of the States."[79]

When the Court turned from challenges to the exertion of national power to consider challenges to the exercise of state power, it was also quite cordial to the states. For example, the Court upheld rates set by a state railroad commission on the transportation of timber from forest to mill. The Court noted that the timber came to rest at the mill, where it was stored on average for five months. Even though 95 percent of the lumber would eventually be shipped in interstate commerce, there was no intention to transport the timber anywhere else until after it was processed at the mill.[80]

The Court was equally solicitous of administrative regulations restricting the use that could be made of certain words on product labels. For example, the Court upheld an Ohio statute prohibiting the sale of "condensed milk unless it has been made from . . . unadulterated . . . milk, from which the cream has not been removed."[81] The statute further required a minimum percentage of milk solids. The company challenging the statute sold a product labeled "Hebe A Compound of Evaporated Skimmed Milk and Vegetable Fat Contains 6% Vegetable Fat, 24% Total Solids." The company argued that because its product was wholesome, the statute should not be construed to restrict its sales. The Court disagreed. It read the statute as prohibiting the sale of condensed skimmed milk. According to the Court, Hebe did not avoid that prohibition by adding coconut oil. Indeed, the addition only served to make the cheaper product "more like the dearer and better one and thus at the same time more available for a fraudulent substitute."[82] Holmes conceded that the label truthfully disclosed the product's ingredients, but that mattered little, since "the consumer in many cases never sees it." He even went so far as to assert that by including a statement that Hebe could be used for "Coffee and Cereals For Baking and Cooking," the label represented the product as condensed milk. Even with such an extraordinary construction, the statute passed constitutional muster, since the Court could not say that it was arbitrary.

Other words that mattered included *sausage* and *Creamo*. Of a federal regulation of the use of the term *sausage*, Justice Clarke wrote for the Court: "Few purchasers read long labels, many cannot read them at all, and the act of Con-

---

79. Ibid., 95.
80. *Arkadelphia Milling Co. v. St. Louis Southwestern Railway Co.*, 249 U.S. 134, 151 (1919).
81. *The Hebe Company v. Shaw*, 248 U.S. 297 (1919).
82. Ibid., 303.

gress having committed to the head of the department, constantly dealing with such matters, the discretion to determine as to whether the use of the word 'sausage' in a label would be false and deceptive or not, under such circumstances as we have here, this court will not review, and the Circuit Court of Appeals should not have reviewed and reversed the decision of the Secretary of Agriculture."[83] The Court accepted with similar alacrity the federal government's ban on the use of *Creamo* once the manufacturer eliminated all cream in the product. As the Court observed, the company's assertion that the name was a valuable asset only further supported the conclusion that the name was misleading.[84]

Other decisions of the Court proved equally hospitable to state regulations. The Court allowed a Virginia city to discharge raw sewage into a bay even though the pollution destroyed oyster beds leased from the state by individuals. The Court refused to permit the contract for lease to prevent the state from "using its legislative power to sanction one of the very most important public uses of water already partly polluted."[85] In contrast to that sanction of pollution, the Court upheld a state's ban on the shipment of wild birds outside the state.[86] In this case, Brandeis explained for the Court that the Federal Migratory Bird Act[87] had not occupied the entire field. Instead, it only regulated the seasons during which the birds could be hunted. Showing unusual solicitousness for the state's police power, Brandeis invoked a principle that an "intent to supersede the exercise by a State of its police powers is not to be implied unless the act of Congress fairly interpreted is in actual conflict with the law of the State."[88]

The decision that best represented the line drawing by the White Court was announced on the last day of the term, in the *Arizona Employers' Liability Cases*.[89] Argument in the five cases decided under that title had occurred in January 1918 and April 1919. In June 1919 Justice Pitney announced the opinion of the Court; Justice Holmes (joined by Brandeis and Clarke) concurred, with an opinion describing additional reasons for his conclusion. White, McKenna, Van Devanter, and McReynolds dissented, with opinions by McKenna and McReynolds explaining their reasons. Two years earlier, Pitney had written all three of the Court's opinions upholding workmen's compensation laws in New York, Iowa, and Washington.[90] Only the opinion involving Washington's law,

---

83. *Houston v. St. Louis Independent Packing Co.*, 249 U.S. 479, 487 (1919).
84. *Brougham v. Blanton Manufacturing Co.*, 249 U.S. 495, 502 (1919).
85. *Darling v. City of Newport News*, 249 U.S. 540, 544 (1919).
86. *Carey v. South Dakota*, 250 U.S. 118 (1919).
87. Act of March 4, 1913, ch. 145, 37 Stat. 828.
88. 250 U.S. at 122.
89. 250 U.S. 400 (1919).
90. *New York Central Railroad Co. v. White*, 243 U.S. 188 (1917) (New York); *Hawkins v. Bleakly*, 243 U.S. 210 (1917) (Iowa); *Mountain Timber Co. v. Washington*, 243 U.S. 219 (1917) (Wash

which mandated that each industry share the costs of industrial accidents, had provoked disagreement; and, even then, White, McKenna, Van Devanter, and McReynolds simply noted their dissent, without providing an explanation.

The cause of the unusual division in the Arizona cases was the imposition of liability without fault, but only in occupations designated by the legislature as "especially dangerous and hazardous."[91] The Arizona law was all the more uncommon because it had been mandated by provisions in the state's first constitution. The statute allowed an employee to elect to have any suit tried before a jury, without any limitation on the amount of recovery, though the employer would be allowed to assert the defense of contributory negligence or assumption of risk. (As was usual with workmen's compensation laws, that defense would not be available if the employee sought only the limited, statutory remedy.) Justice Holmes originally had the assignment of writing the opinion for the Court.[92] But because some justices objected to a draft opinion, Pitney drew the task of holding the majority together.[93] As Holmes explained in a letter to Sir Frederick Pollock: "To my wonder four were the other way, and my opinion was thought too strong by some of the majority, so that Pitney spoke for the Court and I concurred, with what I had to say—Brandeis and Clarke only with me. I pointed out that even in what was supposed to be the Constitutional principle of basing liability on fault it meant that a man had to take the risk of deciding the way the jury would decide—in doubtful cases."[94]

In explaining the Court's decision, Pitney recited all of the by now familiar incantations about the Court's lack of interest in the wisdom of a statute; the wide range of discretion left to states, subject only to a determination whether the statute was arbitrary and unreasonable; and the equally wide freedom of states to change the law. Pitney then turned to address the question that divided the Court: Whether there was a basis outside the statutory law for saying that there should be no liability without fault. He narrowed the issue by noting that the statute allowed only compensatory damages, not punitive; therefore, as Pitney explained, there was no question of imposing punishment without fault. The question then, was where the losses associated with industrial employment should fall. He fairly summarized the pre-

---

ington). During the 1918–1919 term, Pitney had also written the opinion for the unanimous Court upholding the Texas workmen's compensation law. *Middleton v. Texas Power & Light Co.*, 249 U.S. 152 (1919).

91. Justice McReynolds quoted the relevant statutory provisions in his dissent. 250 U.S. at 443–46 n. 1.

92. For discussion of the drafting of the opinions in this case, see Bickel, *The Unpublished Opinions of Mr. Justice Brandeis*, 61–76.

93. Holmes to Pollock, June 17, 1919, Howe, *Holmes-Pollock Letters*, 2:14; Acheson, *Morning and Noon*, 67–68.

94. Holmes to Pollock, June 17, 1919, Howe, *Holmes-Pollock Letters*, 2:15

vailing rule, which imposed the risks on the employee, subject to being shifted by proof of the employer's negligence; added to that balance were the doctrines associated with assumption of risk, the fellow servant rule, and contributory negligence. But, lest anyone begin to think that these were something resembling rules of natural law, Pitney reminded his audience that "it is to be borne in mind that the matter of the assumption of the risks of employment and the consequences to flow therefrom has been regulated time out of mind by the common law, with occasional statutory modifications."[95] Reflecting something of Holmes's relativism, he wrote that the rules were "no more than rules of law, deduced by the courts as reasonable and just, under the conditions of our civilization, in view of the relations existing between employer and employee *in the absence of legislation.*"[96] Then, in a puzzling aside, he added that the Fourteenth Amendment did not deprive a state of power to change the rules, so long as the change was not arbitrary and unreasonable, "and in defiance of natural justice."[97] Pitney said nothing more of "natural justice"; instead, his opinion focused on the reasonableness of the statute. That reasonableness arose because the act imposed the costs of accidents on the employer, who was in a position to take those costs into account by adjusting other parts of the business's economy, such as wages, selling price, and conditions of work.

In the remains of what had once been the draft majority opinion, Holmes added a few ruminations about the statute to explain "additional reasons" for his agreeing with Pitney. The key point was Holmes's emphasis on the fact that the statute shifted the costs for both injury and pain to the employer, as Holmes thought it should. As he explained his stark theory of economic competition: "If a business is unsuccessful it means that the public does not care enough for it to make it pay. If it is successful the public pays its expenses and something more. It is reasonable that the public should pay the whole cost of producing what it wants and a part of that cost is the pain and mutilation incident to production. By throwing that loss upon the employer in the first instance we throw it upon the public in the long run and that is just."[98]

McKenna's dissent was marked by a forthright acknowledgment that he thought the Court had extended precedents too far beyond the reasoning

---

95. 250 U.S. at 421.
96. Ibid. (Pitney's italics.)
97. Ibid., 421–22.
98. Ibid., 433. Holmes's references to consumers' desires and wants contained hints of an emerging economic analysis, *marginalism*. Although the concept would rival Darwiniansim for influence in legal and other areas, the concept never captured the minds of the justices on the White Court. For a discussion of both concepts, see Herbert Hovenkamp, "The Marginalist Revolution in Legal Thought," *Vanderbilt Law Review* 46 (March 1993): 305–59.

of the other workmen's compensation cases: "The present case certainly comes after those cases and has that symptom of being their sequence." But he thought this case was "a step beyond them. I hope it is something more than timidity, dread of the new, that makes me fear that it is a step from the deck to the sea—the metaphor suggests a peril in the consequences."[99] His concern was that acceptance of this statute would mean that there was no limit to the imposition of liability without fault, pointing to the inclusion of the unqualified category "manufacturing" in the existing statute.[100] He was equally candid in identifying the source of his disagreement as an aphorism so true as to be accepted by all who heard it: "It seems to be of the very foundation of right— of the essence of liberty as it is of morals—to be free from liability if one is free from fault."[101] Plainly, the source of his aphorism was the life of rural America:

> We know things are in change—have changed—and a mark of it is that the drift of public opinion, and of legislation following opinion, is to alter the relation between employer and employee and to give to the latter a particular distinction, relieve him from a responsibility which would seem to be, and which until lately it has been the sense of the world to be, as much upon him as upon his employer, not in dependence, not as a mark of subservience, but as an obligation of his freedom, and, therefore as a consequence, that where he has liberty of action he has responsibility for action. In a word, the drift of opinion and legislation now is to set labor apart and to withdraw it from its conditions and from the action of economic forces and their consequences, give it immunity from the pitilessness of life. . . . In what legislation the drift (it is persuasion in some) may culminate cannot now be predicted, but it is very certain that, whatever it be, the judgment now delivered will be cited to justify it. Will it not be said that if one right of an employer can be made to give way, why not another?[102]

Justice McReynolds's dissent had the marks of a draft originally written for a majority opinion. (He, after all, had written the Court's opinion in the one case to invalidate a state workmen's compensation law, *Southern Pacific Co. v. Jensen,* in which the Court held that federal maritime law superseded the state statute as it applied to seamen.)[103] Unlike Pitney's generic opinion,

---

99. 250 U.S. at 434. McKenna had used the image of stepping from the deck to the sea in his opinion for the Court in *Sandberg v. McDonald,* 248 U.S. 185, 202 (1918) (statutory ban on payment of seamen's wages in advance).
100. 250 U.S. at 437.
101. Ibid., 436.
102. Ibid., 438.
103. 244 U.S. 205 (1917). This was a 5–4 decision, with Justice Day providing the swing vote, as he did in the cases from Arizona.

McReynolds began with a statement of facts from one of the cases; he then quoted all of the relevant state constitutional and statutory provisions, along with portions of opinions from the Arizona courts. He followed that recital by summarizing the statute as one "which undertakes, in the absence of fault, to impose upon all employers (individual and corporate) engaged in enterprises essential to the public welfare, not subject to prohibition by the States and often not attended by any extraordinary hazard, an unlimited liability to employees for damages resulting from accidental injuries—including physical and mental pain."[104] He then identified the characteristic of the law that made it arbitrary, in the vocabulary of jurisprudence under the Fourteenth Amendment: In return for that unlimited liability, the employer received nothing. That absence of an exchange pointed to the critical word for McReynolds, *contract*.[105] He referred to *Adair* and *Coppage* as articulating the protection afforded freedom of contract by the Constitution. This statute, in his view, infringed that right.

---

104. 250 U.S. at 449.
105. Ibid., 450, 452 (no quid pro quo).

X

THE 1919–1920 TERM

When the Court assembled for the 1919–1920 term on October 7, President Wilson had only the week before suffered the stroke that would incapacitate him for the remainder of his term; steelworkers were on strike for the right to organize and for an eight-hour day; and Cincinnati was one victory away from winning the World Series against a Chicago team led by "Shoeless" Joe Jackson. The term would see the smallest number of opinions (177) of any term under White as chief justice. There would also be the smallest percentage of unanimous opinions (66 percent),[1] and the largest number of cases with written dissents (twenty-three).[2] The reasons for the drop in output are not easy to determine. Part of the reduction can be attributed to White's increasingly poor health.[3] His hearing continued to deteriorate, and cataracts had so impaired his eyesight that he could no longer cross streets alone.[4] The 1916 term had been the last in which he kept pace with Holmes in number of opinions written. White's total output of majority opinions for his final two years on the Court, this term and the next, was less than his lowest output in any *single* term prior to 1916. White's health may also have made him a less efficient manager of the

---

1. Of the 177 opinions for the Court, 117 were unanimous, or 66.1 percent.
2. *Maxwell v. Bugbee*, 250 U.S. 525 (1919); *Pennsylvania Railroad Co. v. Public Service Commission*, 250 U.S. 566 (1919); *Abrams v. United States*, 250 U.S. 616 (1919); *Evans v. National Bank of Savannah*, 251 U.S. 108 (1919); *St. Louis, Iron Mountain & Southern Railway Co. v. United States*, 251 U.S. 198 (1920); *Jacob Ruppert, A Corp. v. Caffey*, 251 U.S. 264 (1920); *United States v. United States Steel Corp.*, 251 U.S. 417 (1920); *Schaefer v. United States*, 251 U.S. 466 (1920); *Eisner v. Macomber*, 252 U.S. 189 (1920); *Pierce v. United States*, 252 U.S. 239 (1920); *Manners v. Morosco*, 252 U.S. 317 (1920); *South Covington & Cincinnati Street Railway Co. v. Kentucky*, 252 U.S. 399 (1920); *Cincinnati, Covington & Erlanger Railway Co. v. Kentucky*, 252 U.S. 408 (1920); *United States v. Simpson*, 252 U.S. 465 (1920); *Hull v. Philadelphia & Reading Railway Co.*, 252 U.S. 475 (1920); *United States v. Reading Co.*, 253 U.S. 26 (1920); *Knickerbocker Ice Co. v. Stewart*, 253 U.S. 149 (1920); *Calhoun v. Massie*, 253 U.S. 170 (1920); *Evans v. Gore*, 253 U.S. 245 (1920); *Ohio Valley Water Co. v. Ben Avon Borough*, 253 U.S. 287 (1920); *National Prohibition Cases*, 253 U.S. 350 (1920); *F. S. Royster Guano Co. v. Commonwealth of Virginia*, 253 U.S. 412 (1920); *Federal Trade Commission v. Gratz*, 253 U.S. 421 (1920).
3. See Holmes to Einstein, May 20, 1921, Peabody, *Holmes-Einstein Letters*, 195.
4. Acheson, *Morning and Noon*, 60.

Court's time. Part of the reduction may also be attributed to the success of the jurisdictional changes made in 1916—the Court averaged some fifty fewer opinions each year thereafter.[5] Those numbers do not, of course, mean that there was less work for the justices; the changes merely shifted their work from preparing opinions to considering petitions for certiorari. It also seems likely that the jurisdictional changes meant that the issues presented for argument were more difficult—many of the easier cases could no longer be brought to the Court; and, presumably, the justices would use their somewhat greater control over the docket to select more important cases for argument. The greater difficulty is suggested by the low percentage of unanimous opinions (by far the lowest of the White Court) and by the high number of dissenting opinions (again, by far the highest of White's tenure).[6] In addition, thirteen cases were argued this term but carried over to the next for decision. Finally, the division within the Court reveals how close the justices had at last come to turning the corner toward the modern America. But the immediate cause of the increased difficulty was a specific group of cases, combining a series of Progressive legislative measures with special measures occasioned by the war. Given the divisions those measures had provoked within American society in general, it is not surprising that they caused division within the Court.

No cases better illustrate this culmination of events than do the *National Prohibition Cases*.[7] Announced on the last day of the term, the decision in these seven cases dealt with a series of challenges to the Eighteenth Amendment and to the Volstead Act, which Congress passed to enforce the amendment.[8] By its own terms, the amendment took effect on January 16, 1920, a year after its ratification. In attempting to enforce a national police power, Congress struggled against more than a century of precedent that held that the states were primarily, if not exclusively, responsible for protecting the health and morals of their citizens. The White Court had permitted encroachment on that principle—the Mann Act and various federal regulations of alcohol being the best examples. But the Court had balked when Congress attempted to regulate child labor. It is therefore not surprising

---

5. In the first five full terms of the White Court, the average number of opinions per year was 267.8; in the final five full terms, the average was 211.

6. The percentage of unanimous opinions (66.1) was considerably below the next lowest, 80.8 percent for the 1916–1917 term. The number of written dissents, twenty-six, was likewise higher than the next highest, twenty, also during the 1916–1917 term. Comparison of the number of opinions for the Court in each term makes the difference even starker: In 1916–1917 there were 214 opinions; in 1919–1920, there were only 177.

7. 253 U.S. 350 (1920).

8. The amendment was declared ratified on January 28, 1919, 40 Stat. 1941; the Volstead Act passed over President Wilson's veto on October 28, 1919, ch. 85, 41 Stat. 305.

that the first two sections of the amendment itself reflected the tensions, almost to the point of incoherence: "After one year from the ratification of this article the manufacture, sale, or transportation of intoxicating liquors within, the importation thereof into, or the exportation thereof from the United States and all territory subject to the jurisdiction thereof for beverage purposes is hereby prohibited. The Congress and the several States shall have concurrent power to enforce this article by appropriate legislation." Rather than empower Congress to enact legislation, section 1 of the amendment expressly declared a ban on "intoxicating" liquor. Empowerment came from section 2; but the empowerment was of *both* state and national governments. Thus, beyond the task of defining *intoxicating* was the more troublesome issue of defining *concurrent*. The complexity of the issue so badly divided the justices that no one could produce an opinion for the Court. Instead, Justice Van Devanter "announced the conclusion of the court."[9] After quoting Article 5 of the Constitution (which describes the procedure for amendment) and the Eighteenth Amendment, Van Devanter announced a seriatim list of eleven conclusions. He finished with the disposition of the seven cases without providing any reasoning to support the conclusions. In those conclusions the Court announced that the amendment was part of the Constitution, having been properly ratified, and that the Volstead Act was constitutional, even in its reach to liquors with as little as 0.5 of 1 percent of alcohol. It is not known whether Van Devanter's slow pen prevented him from writing anything more in the almost ten weeks since oral argument or whether the majority (Van Devanter, Holmes, Day, Pitney, and Brandeis) truly could not agree on reasons. Van Devanter wrote only twelve opinions for the Court this term, though this was the only "opinion" with less than a seven-man majority. Since the Court announced seventy-one opinions in the final ten weeks of its term, it seems likely that no other justice had the time to take the assignment from Van Devanter. And it seems equally likely that the Court did not want to delay a decision in so controversial a case. Plus, the nature of the opinion shows signs of the skill for which Van Devanter was so respected in conference. Here it seems that his conference summary became the published product. The texture of the disagreements became apparent only in the separate opinions of the justices who did not join Van Devanter's announcement for the Court.

    Chief Justice White, who had begun his career as chief justice with a determination to stop "this dissenting business," must have been deeply hurt by his inability to produce a more respectable result. A sense of failure is evident in the opening sentence of his opinion: "I profoundly regret that in a case of this magnitude, affecting as it does an amendment to the Constitu-

---

9. 253 U.S. at 384.

tion dealing with the powers and duties of the national and state governments, and intimately concerning the welfare of the whole people, the court has deemed it proper to state only ultimate conclusions without an exposition of the reasoning by which they have been reached."[10] He then shifted from the collective "court" to the personal in explaining "that the greater the perplexities the greater the duty devolving upon me to express the reasons" for the conclusions. Turning to the amendment, he conceded that the "mere" words of section 2 would defeat the enforcement of section 1, by requiring that states enact laws before any congressional enactment could be enforced. But, White added in his familiar stratagem, if the words "be read in the light of the cardinal rule which compels a consideration of the context" then any "confusion will be seen to be only apparent."[11] The solution was one that reflected the gradual erasure of state lines throughout White's tenure. The amendment allowed Congress to define the offending beverages. The words *concurrent power* captured much of the constitutional debate of the past half century as the nation had struggled with the meaning of a federal system in an increasingly integrated economy.[12] White acknowledged that purpose as an effort to accommodate Congress's powers "to the dual system of government existing under the Constitution."[13] The difficulty lay in finding a way to effect the suggestion that section 2 required that any enforcement of the prohibition authorized by the first section be through joint legislative action by the national and state governments. Were that suggestion accepted, the Volstead Act would be unconstitutional, since no state had ratified its provisions. White, in his inimitable way, wrote that such a suggestion was impossible to accept. His explanation of how Congress and the states would work together portrayed a sweeping effect for the first section, obliterating at last the faded lines that defined the states, and acknowledging a power that operated "throughout the length and breadth of the United States, without reference to state lines or the distinctions between state and federal power."[14] According to White, that power would become effective through combining Congress's legislative power with the administrative agencies of the state and national governments.

Justice McReynolds's three-sentence concurrence encapsulated what must have been the reaction of many when he confessed that he had no idea what the amendment meant. He concurred with the Court's conclusions, but he

---

10. Ibid., 388.
11. Ibid., 390.
12. For discussion of the states' rights arguments behind this section, see Richard F. Hamm, "Southerners and the Shaping of the Eighteenth Amendment, 1914–1917," *Georgia Journal of Southern Legal History* 1 (1991): 81–107.
13. 253 U.S. at 391.
14. Ibid.

preferred to be free to consider the "multitude of questions" that would follow from the "bewilderment" the amendment created.[15]

Justices McKenna and Clarke each wrote a separate dissent, though each focused on the "concurrent power" language of section 2. With candor, and tongue in cheek, McKenna began by admitting that he could not be sure of the nature of his disagreement with the majority: "I am, however, at a loss how, or to what extent, to express the grounds for this action. The court declares conclusions only, without giving any reasons for them. The instance maybe wise—establishing a precedent now, hereafter wisely to be imitated. It will undoubtedly decrease the literature of the court if it does not increase lucidity. However, reasons for the conclusions have been omitted, and my comment upon them may come from a misunderstanding of them, their present import and ultimate purpose and force."[16] Even so, he agreed with White that the key issue lay in finding the meaning of the words in section 2. The United States had argued that the words envisioned "separate and independent action" by the state and national governments; in the event of conflict, the congressional enactment would be supreme, as it always was. McKenna's response to that argument was unusually blunt for him: "I contest the assertions and oppose to them the common usage of our language, and the definitions of our lexicons, general and legal. . . . Opposing laws are not concurring laws, and to assert the supremacy of one over the other is to assert the exclusiveness of one over the other, not their concomitance."[17] He pointed to the fact that for both Congress and the states, the power to enforce prohibition came from the amendment. To him that common source meant the actions had to be equal. In other areas of constitutional law, Congress's powers were supreme because they alone derived from the Constitution. For prohibition, by contrast, both state and federal governments derived their powers from the same source. Thus, after carefully considering the language of the amendment, McKenna could reach but one conclusion, "that there must be united action between the States and Congress, or, at any rate, concordant and harmonious action."[18]

Clarke agreed with McKenna's conclusion that the amendment required joint action by state and national legislatures. And, alluding to the divisions within American society over prohibition, he suggested that the requirement might actually have a beneficial effect: "It would, to a great extent, relieve Congress of the burden and the general government of the odium to be derived from the antagonism which would certainly spring from enforcing, within States, federal laws which must touch the daily life of the people very intimately

---

15. Ibid., 392.
16. Ibid., 393.
17. Ibid., 396–97.
18. Ibid., 405.

and often very irritatingly."[19] To that sanguine prediction, Clarke added that the Volstead Act was unconstitutional insofar as it declared certain liquors to be intoxicating when, in fact, they were not. The power under the amendment was not as great as that under Congress's war powers. He concluded with a cautionary, and clearly atavistic, reminder of the need to preserve the federal system:

> In the *Slaughter-House* [16 Wall. 36], and other cases, this court was urged to give a construction to the Fourteenth Amendment which would have radically changed the whole constitutional theory of the relations of our state and federal governments by transferring to the general government that police power, through the exercise of which the people of the various States theretofore regulated their local affairs in conformity with the widely differing standards of life, of conduct and of duty which must necessarily prevail in a country of so great extent as ours, with its varieties of climate, of industry and of habits of the people. But this court, resisting the pressure of the passing hour, maintained the integrity of state control over local affairs to the extent that it had not been deliberately and clearly surrendered to the general government, in a number of decisions which came to command the confidence of the generation active when they were rendered and which have been regarded by our succeeding generation as sound and wise and highly fortunate for our country.
>
> The cases now before us seem to me to again present questions of like character to, and of not less importance than, those which were presented in those great cases, and I regret profoundly that I cannot share in the disposition which the majority of my associates think should be made of them.[20]

Coming at the end of the term, the *National Prohibition Cases* capped an exhausting eight months of struggle with similar issues. Clarke's reference to a link between prohibition and the war power was natural in light of the Court's opinion in *Jacob Ruppert v. Caffey,* decided five months earlier.[21] In this case a divided Court (5–4) had upheld the War-Time Prohibition Act, which virtually prohibited the production of "intoxicating beverages." Although termed a "war-time" measure, the act was actually passed November 21, 1918, ten days after the armistice ended the First World War. Attempting to eke the most out of its war powers, Congress declared that the act would remain in effect "until the termination of demobilization, the date

---

19. Ibid., 408.
20. Ibid., 411.
21. 251 U.S. 264 (1920).

of which shall be determined and proclaimed by the President."[22] The act also left to administrative action the definition of "intoxicating beverages." Subsequently, the definition covered beverages with as little as 0.5 of 1 percent alcohol by volume. In October 1919, the Volstead Act enacted that definition into law.[23]

Justice Brandeis wrote a sweeping opinion for the Court's majority. In a conflation that rejected Clarke's concerns for preserving the states, Brandeis virtually equated Congress's war powers to the states' police powers. He provided an encyclopedic listing of state statutes and court opinions to show that the only way to enforce prohibition was to ban all liquor. Dean Acheson, Brandeis's law clerk this term, declared that the footnotes "established a world's record to that time" and, he added cleverly, they "constituted 57 per centum of the opinion by volume."[24] In his opinion, Brandeis would not concede that there was a limit to the ability of Congress to exercise its power in an effective manner. Thus, the definition of *intoxicating* was an appropriate choice to make the law effective. Moreover, he dismissed the argument that the ban on liquor amounted to a taking of the property of those who already had liquor in their possession. The ban "was no appropriation of private property, but merely a lessening of value due to a permissible restriction imposed upon its use."[25] Of course, for those who held the liquor for resale, the value was "lessened" to zero.

Justice McReynolds dissented, joined by Day and Van Devanter. (Clarke dissented alone, without an opinion.) Less willing than the majority to accept the declaration of Congress on face value, McReynolds asked: "Can it be truthfully said, in view of the well-known facts existing on October 28, 1919, [the date of the Volstead Act] that general prohibition immediately after that day of the sale of non-intoxicating beer theretofore lawfully manufactured, could afford any direct and appreciable aid in respect of the war declared against Germany and Austria?"[26] Apprehensive of stacking implied powers upon implied powers, he would deny Congress the power, prior to the Eighteenth Amendment, to prohibit the sale and manufacture of liquor.

It is important to recognize that the 5–4 vote in *Ruppert* followed a unanimous opinion upholding the War-Time Prohibition Act itself. Decided just three weeks earlier, *Hamilton v. Kentucky Distilleries & Warehouse Co.* involved a narrower question—whether a ban on removing distilled spirits from

---

22. Act of November 21, 1918, ch. 212, 40 Stat. 1045. The act is quoted in the Court's opinion. 251 U.S. at 279.
23. Act of October 28, 1919, ch. 85, 41 Stat. 305.
24. Acheson, *Morning and Noon*, 79.
25. 251 U.S. at 303.
26. Ibid., 309.

bonded warehouses was a taking of property that required compensation.[27]

The Court upheld the act, noting that Congress had given more than six months' notice of the effective date of the ban.

It is also critical to recognize that these prohibition cases, with their sweeping affirmance of Congress's powers during, and even after, war, produced results quite different from other contemporaneous cases. These other cases involved prosecutions under the Espionage and Sedition Acts. Beginning on the eve of the first anniversary of the armistice, these other cases were intertwined with the prohibition decisions. One of the first of these cases was *Abrams v. United States,* in which the Court affirmed Jacob Abrams's conviction for violating the Espionage Act.[28] The charges originated with some five thousand leaflets which Abrams and four others distributed in late August 1918, with one version printed in English, another in Yiddish. Because *Schenck* and other cases had established the constitutionality of the Espionage Act, Abrams's challenge to his conviction was limited to a review of the evidence, with Abrams contending that the trial judge should have dismissed the indictment for lack of sufficient evidence. Responding to that contention, Justice Clarke quoted portions of the two circulars in his majority opinion. The English-language circular, with the title "The Hypocrisy of the United States and her Allies," criticized President Wilson and the United States for sending troops to Russia. (The United States, along with more than a dozen other nations, had sent troops to Russia after the Bolshevik revolution. The ostensible purpose was to protect Allied supplies; but the clear intent was to side with the forces opposing Lenin.) According to Clarke, the most inflammatory sentences were these:

> The Russian Revolution cries: Workers of the World! Awake! Rise! Put down your enemy and mine!
>   Yes! friends, there is only one enemy of the workers of the world and that is CAPITALISM.

As Clarke interpreted the language, it was "clearly an appeal to the 'workers' of this country to arise and put down by force the Government of the United States which they characterize as their 'hypocritical,' 'cowardly' and 'capitalistic' enemy."[29]

The circular printed in Yiddish focused on the events in Russia, saying of the United States involvement: "Workers, our reply to the barbaric inter-

---

27. 251 U.S. 146 (1919).
28. 250 U.S. 616 (1919). On the same day the Court announced *Abrams,* it also announced *Stilson v. United States,* 250 U.S. 583 (1919), in which it upheld two convictions for violating the Espionage Act. Both the majority and the two dissenters (Holmes and Brandeis) dealt only briefly with the challenges to the convictions.
29. 250 U.S. at 620.

vention has to be a general strike!" Clarke annotated other parts of the circular with his own comments, emphasizing that even if a goal of the circulars had been to aid the Russian revolution, the suggested means of attaining the goal was the "defeat of the war program of the United States." The call for a general strike brought special condemnation from Clarke, leading to his conclusion that "the plain purpose of their propaganda was to excite, at the supreme crisis of the war, disaffection, sedition, riots, and, as they hoped, revolution."[30]

Holmes dissented, joined by Brandeis. In the eight months since his majority opinion in *Schenck*, Holmes had been pressed to modify his views, with special pressure coming from friends at Harvard such as Zechariah Chafee and Harold Laski, and federal district judge Learned Hand.[31] Holmes also reacted against the excesses of federal prosecution of dissenters during the period. He had, for example, written this to Sir Frederick Pollock shortly after the oral argument in *Abrams:* "I hope that we have heard the last, or nearly the last, of the Espionage Act cases. Some of our subordinate Judges seem to me to have been hysterical during the war. It is one of the ironies that I, who probably take the extremest view in favor of free speech, (in which, in the abstract, I have no very enthusiastic belief, though I hope I would die for it), that I should have been selected for blowing up. I don't understand the Government pressing those cases . . . but that is not my business."[32]

The previous nine months had seen a general strike in Seattle in February 1919, just before *Schenck*. Then, in April, postal officials discovered the mail bombs. The summer and fall witnessed riots in cities across the nation, followed by a Boston police strike in September. November brought the first of the raids against radical organizations, led by Attorney General A. Mitchell Palmer.[33] Three days after that initial raid, Holmes announced his dissent in *Abrams*, which is seen by many as his first attempt to modify the views he expressed in *Schenck*.[34] Holmes did not, however, retreat from the rule of law announced in *Schenck*, for here he wrote that "the United States constitutionally may punish speech that produces or is intended to produce a clear and imminent danger that it will bring about forthwith certain substantive evils that the United States constitutionally may seek to prevent."[35] Then he added,

---

30. Ibid., 623.
31. Among the most useful discussions of *Abrams* and of Holmes's evolution are Richard Polenberg, *Fighting Faiths: The Abrams Case, the Supreme Court, and Free Speech* (New York: Viking, 1987); and Fred Ragan, "Justice Oliver Wendell Holmes, Jr., Zechariah Chafee, Jr. and the Clear and Present Danger Test for Free Speech: The First Year, 1919," *Journal of History* 58 (June 1971): 24–45. See also Jeremy Cohen, "*Schenck v. United States:* A Clear and Present Danger to the First Amendment" (Ph.D. diss., University of Washington, 1983).
32. Holmes to Pollock, October 26, 1919, Howe, *Holmes-Pollock Letters*, 2:28–29.
33. See Murray, *Red Scare: A Study in National Hysteria*.
34. See White, *Justice Oliver Wendell Holmes*, 436–37.
35. 250 U.S. at 627.

in language remarkably similar to that used in the *Prohibition Cases,* "The power undoubtedly is greater in time of war than in time of peace because war opens dangers that do not exist at other times."[36] And, as he added at the end of his opinion, "Only the emergency that makes it immediately dangerous to leave the correction of evil counsels to time warrants making any exception to the sweeping command" of the First Amendment.[37]

Where Holmes strove to distinguish himself from the majority was in the reading of the offending language. To support his view, Holmes quoted from the circulars, though not to the length Clarke had done. But unlike Clarke, he could find no evidence of an attack on the form of government in the United States. He conceded that there was material that urged a reduction in the production of munitions; but, in the critical part of his dissent, he denied that the language evidenced any intent to hinder the war effort. The statute required the intent; Clarke had used the standard test, writing, "Men must be held to have intended, and to be accountable for, the effects which their acts were likely to produce."[38] Holmes acknowledged the standard and admitted its appropriateness in other contexts. But, when a statute implicated the First Amendment, he suggested that a more stringent standard should apply, both for determining intent and for assessing the likely effects. He asserted that there was a distinction between an intent to halt involvement in Russia and an intent to hamper the United States war effort. His concluding description of the effect of these circulars is classic: "Now nobody can suppose that the surreptitious publishing of a silly leaflet by an unknown man, without more, would present any immediate danger that its opinions would hinder the success of the government arms or have any appreciable tendency to do so."[39]

Putting aside all legal niceties, in *Abrams* Holmes said in public what he had been writing in private—that the government had overstepped in deciding to prosecute. "Even if I am technically wrong and enough can be squeezed from these poor and puny anonymities to turn the color of legal litmus paper," then only nominal punishment was appropriate, not the twenty years to which they had been sentenced. Moreover, he wrote one of his most famous statements of relativism, linking competition in ideas to competition between patented devices for success in the marketplace:

> But when men have realized that time has upset many fighting faiths, they may come to believe even more than they believe the very foundations of

---

36. Ibid., 627–28.
37. Ibid., 630–31.
38. Ibid., 621.
39. Ibid., 628.

their own conduct that the ultimate good desired is better reached by free trade in ideas—that the best test of truth is the power of the thought to get itself accepted in the competition of the market, and that truth is the only ground upon which their wishes safely can be carried out. That at any rate is the theory of our Constitution. It is an experiment, as all life is an experiment. Every year if not every day we have to wager our salvation upon some prophecy based upon imperfect knowledge. While that experiment is part of our system I think that we should be eternally vigilant against attempts to check the expression of opinions that we loathe and believe to be fraught with death, unless they so immediately threaten immediate interference with the lawful and pressing purposes of the law that an immediate check is required to save the country."[40]

Argued with *Abrams,* but not decided until four months later, was *Schaefer v. United States,* which also involved numerous charges of violating the Espionage Act.[41] Peter Schaefer and other defendants, who published a German-language newspaper in Philadelphia, stood accused of printing false reports of news in an attempt to obstruct recruiting and otherwise aid the enemies of the United States. Illustrating how fact specific the cases had become, as well as how finely balanced some of them were, Clarke joined Holmes and Brandeis in dissent. The fact-specific nature of the cases makes them less useful than they might be for precedent, though it did seem to encourage the justices to flights of rhetoric. Moreover, the flights seemed to epitomize the attempts to work out the nature of the protection afforded to speech and to the press.

Thus, in *Schaefer* the Court reversed the convictions of two defendants, while affirming those of three. In the midst of McKenna's opinion for the Court was evidence of the struggle to make the transition from the vocabulary of the past to the emerging vocabulary of the future. McKenna seemed to sense an anachronism to some of his remarks, for he paused to offer this comment: "If it be said this comment is but the expression of commonplaces, we reply that commonplaces are sometimes necessary to be brought forward lest earnestness or interest disregard them and urge too far the supervising power of the court, which, we repeat, is subordinate to that of the jury on questions of fact and certainly 'a rule of reason' cannot be asserted for it upon a mere difference in judgment."[42] He took that link to White's antitrust opinions and reached yet further into the past by appealing to another icon of the Court's

---

40. Ibid., 630.
41. 251 U.S. 466 (1920).
42. Ibid., 476. Two terms earlier McKenna had written a similar statement: "We have said this, indeed, with iteration, but sometimes propositions which have become postulates have to be justified to meet objections, which, if they do not deny their existence, tend to bring them into question." *United States v. United Shoe Machinery Co.,* 247 U.S. 32, 66 (1918).

jurisprudence, "liberty": "Free speech is not an absolute right and when it or any right becomes wrong by excess is somewhat elusive of definition. However, some admissions may be made. That freedom of speech and of the press are elements of liberty all will acclaim."[43] The final sentence is especially important, for it suggests a link to the liberty of the past; but it also hints at something to come, for liberty is protected not by the First Amendment, but by the Fifth and Fourteenth Amendments. If McKenna's intimation was followed, the First Amendment would apply to the states through the Fourteenth Amendment. That train of reasoning would not, however, be accepted by the Court until 1925, in *Gitlow v. New York*.[44]

Dissenting were both Brandeis and Clarke, with Holmes joining Brandeis. Brandeis accepted the *Schenck* test, describing it as a "rule of reason."[45] But, as had been so evident in the past, *his* reason was determined largely by a careful analysis of facts. Where the majority quoted excerpts from the newspapers, Brandeis quoted entire articles, even going so far as to provide side-by-side English and German columns to show what he said were errors in translation. Once again, the difference lay in the implications to be drawn from the facts, a point made clear in Clarke's dissent: "To me it seems simply a case of flagrant mistrial, likely to result in disgrace and great injustice, probably in life imprisonment for two old men, because this court hesitates to exercise the power, which it undoubtedly possesses, to correct, in this calmer time, errors of law which would not have been committed but for the stress and strain of feeling prevailing in the early months of the late deplorable war."[46]

The stylistic differences reappeared in the final Espionage Act case of the term, *Pierce v. United States*.[47] Clinton H. Pierce, and three others, had been convicted of conspiring to cause insubordination in the military through the distribution of copies of a Socialist pamphlet, "The Price We Pay." Writing for the majority, Justice Pitney explained that the pamphlet was "too long to be quoted in full."[48] He therefore relied on excerpts to establish that there was sufficient evidence on which the jury could base a conviction. Justice Brandeis responded directly to Pitney's statement, writing, "In order to determine whether the leaflet furnishes any evidence to establish any of the above enumerated elements of the offences charged, the whole leaflet must necessarily be read."[49] He then devoted eight pages of

---

43. 251 U.S. at 474.
44. 268 U.S. 652 (1925).
45. 251 U.S. at 482.
46. Ibid., 501.
47. 252 U.S. 239 (1920).
48. Ibid., 245.
49. Ibid., 256.

the *United States Reports* to reprinting the two-thousand-word pamphlet. To supplement the text, he added two facts: that the author was "an Episcopal clergyman and a man of sufficient prominence to have been included in the 1916–1917 edition of 'Who's Who in America'"; and that the defendants had not distributed the pamphlet until a judge in another district held that the pamphlet did not violate the law.[50] The first "fact" seemed at best irrelevant—other than insofar as possession of position implied that one would not seek to destroy that position; the second at least bore on the true intent of the parties. In the end, though, Brandeis portrayed the pamphlet as part of the normal process of change within a democratic system, not as a challenge to the system: "The fundamental right of free men to strive for better conditions through new legislation and new institutions will not be preserved, if efforts to secure it by argument to fellow citizens may be construed as criminal incitement to disobey the existing law—merely, because the argument presented seems to those exercising judicial power to be unfair in its portrayal of existing evils, mistaken in its assumptions, unsound in reasoning or intemperate in language. No objections more serious than these can, in my opinion, reasonably be made to the arguments presented in 'The Price We Pay.'"[51]

Brandeis's call for recognition of the process of change recurred in a case argued the week after he announced his dissent in *Pierce*. Instead of the First Amendment, however, this case involved the right to trial by jury guaranteed by the Seventh Amendment. The case, Ex parte *Peterson,* grew out of a suit to recover the price of coal delivered.[52] Because of the complex claims and counterclaims, the trial judge appointed an auditor to sift through the evidence and provide a report. The plaintiff contended that the use of the auditor deprived him of his right to a jury trial, since the auditor would usurp the jury's responsibility to find the facts. The Court divided 6–3 in affirming the use of the auditor. Brandeis recounted a long history of special advisers being used in complex cases. From that history he deduced the conclusion that federal judges had an inherent power to appoint auditors—no doubt, much like the power of legislators to appoint experts in the form of administrative agencies. But even with that historical precedent, Brandeis thought it important to emphasize the need for flexibility in responding to change:

> The command of the Seventh Amendment that "the right of trial by jury shall be preserved" does not require that old forms of practice and procedure be retained. . . . It does not prohibit the introduction of new meth-

---

50. Ibid., 253–54.
51. Ibid., 273.
52. 253 U.S. 300 (1920).

ods for determining what facts are actually in issue, nor does it prohibit the introduction of new rules of evidence. Changes in these may be made. New devices may be used to adapt the ancient institution to present needs and to make of it an efficient instrument in the administration of justice. Indeed, such changes are essential to the preservation of the right. The limitation imposed by the Amendment is merely that enjoyment of the right of trial by jury be not obstructed, and that the ultimate determination of issues of fact by the jury be not interfered with.

In so far as the task of the auditor is to define and simplify the issues, his function is, in essence, the same as that of pleading. The object of each is to concentrate the controversy upon the questions which should control the result. . . . No one is entitled in a civil case to trial by jury unless and except so far as there are issues of fact to be determined.[53]

Of course, change was precisely what the Court had been dealing with throughout White's tenure. Gradually the Court had begun to explore the fabric of the Bill of Rights as more and more cases redirected its attention away from the structural portions of the Constitution. There is therefore more than a little discordance in the fact that the strongest affirmation of change came from a dispute over a structural component, in Holmes's opinion for the Court in *Missouri v. Holland*.[54] In response to a 1916 treaty between the United States and Great Britain (which acted for Canada),[55] Congress passed the Migratory Bird Treaty Act of 1918.[56] By establishing a federal program for regulation of migratory birds, the law appeared to depart sharply from the Court's recent approval of state regulation of the killing of migratory birds—under the rubric of the police power.[57] Now, as had been true for the *Prohibition Cases,* the Court blurred state lines and legal vocabulary by approving the federal government's exercise of a police power. Thus, in contrast to the Court's prior holdings, Holmes explained that the new federal law drew its authority from the treaty, which by virtue of the Constitution was superior to any state law. Then in an exercise of legerdemain surprising even for Holmes's pen, he suggested that a treaty might

---

53. Ibid., 309–10. Two terms earlier Clarke had expressed a similar thought concerning rules of evidence. *Rosen v. United States,* 245 U.S. 467, 471 (1918).
54. 252 U.S. 416 (1920). For discussion of the case, see Charles A. Lofgren, "*Missouri v. Holland* in Historical Perspective," *The Supreme Court Review* (1975): 77–122; Clement E. Vose, "State against Nation: The Conservation Case of *Missouri v. Holland,*" 16 *Prologue* (winter 1984): 233–47.
55. Act of July 3, 1918, ch. 128, 40 Stat. 755.
56. Convention with Great Britain for the Protection of Migratory Birds, August 16, 1916, 39 Stat. 1702 (1916); Migratory Bird Treaty Act of 1918, Act of July 3, 1918, ch. 128, 40 Stat. 755.
57. *Heim v. McCall,* 239 U.S. 175 (1915), upholding state law barring shipment of game out of state; *Patsone v. Pennsylvania,* 232 U.S. 138 (1914), upholding state law prohibiting aliens from hunting game.

even support legislation in *excess* of the Constitution itself: "It is obvious that there may be matters of the sharpest exigency for the national well being that an act of Congress could not deal with but that a treaty followed by such an act could, and it is not lightly to be assumed that, in matters requiring national action, 'a power which must belong to and somewhere reside in every civilized government' is not to be found."[58] The notion of a power exercised by "every civilized government" recalled the sequence of war-powers cases, which allowed that the United States should have the powers necessary to support its newly acquired leading role on the world stage.[59] Holmes's image of an adaptive constitution was even more flexible than that offered by Brandeis; and in language Frankfurter described as "thrilling," Holmes wrote:

> [W]e may add that when we are dealing with words that also are a constituent act, like the Constitution of the United States, we must realize that they have called into life a being the development of which could not have been foreseen completely by the most gifted of its begetters. It was enough for them to realize or to hope that they had created an organism; it has taken a century and has cost their successors much sweat and blood to prove that they created a nation. The case before us must be considered in the light of our whole experience and not merely in that of what was said a hundred years ago. The treaty in question does not contravene any prohibitory words to be found in the Constitution. The only question is whether it is forbidden by some invisible radiation from the general terms of the Tenth Amendment. We must consider what this country has become in deciding what that Amendment has reserved.[60]

Of course, what the country had become was precisely the subject of the continuing debate. But it was clear, at least for a number of the justices, that the United States had become a prominent actor in the world arena. From that perception they drew the conclusion that the Constitution should be interpreted to permit a continuation of that role. Holmes's resolution of the question of the nation's power was not unlike his "clear and present danger" test for speech: "We see nothing in the Constitution that compels the Government to sit by while a food supply is cut off and the protectors of our forests and our crops are destroyed. It is not sufficient to rely upon the

---

58. *Missouri v. Holland,* 252 U.S. at 433 (1920). The quotation is from *Andrews v. Andrews,* 188 U.S. 14, 33 (1903), full faith and credit clause applied to enforcement of divorce decree.

59. See, for example, *Selective Draft Law Cases,* 245 U.S. 366 (1918).

60. 252 U.S. 433–34. Frankfurter to Holmes, May 15, 1920, Mennel and Compston, *Holmes and Frankfurter: Their Correspondence,* 89.

States. The reliance is vain, and were it otherwise, the question is whether the United States is forbidden to act."[61]

To be sure, the Court was not always so receptive to change. For example, it grudgingly deferred to the city of Shreveport, Louisiana, in upholding an ordinance requiring that street cars have crews of two. Ostensibly relying on the principle that local communities knew local needs better than federal judges, Justice Clarke nevertheless suggested a certain conservatism, if not longing, when he wrote for the Court that a lone crew member "could not render such assistance as is often necessary to infirm or crippled or very young passengers, or to those encumbered with baggage or bundles, and it would not be difficult to suggest emergencies of storm or accident in which a second man might be of first importance to the safety and comfort of passengers."[62]

The most extreme example of deferring to local communities came in *Green v. Frazier,* in which the Court upheld North Dakota's 1919 law creating an industrial commission to operate a wide range of agricultural-related enterprises, from a bank to grain mills and elevators.[63] This exercise of "public" power in what had, at least for a time, been a "private" function was yet another example of the Progressive tendency to move from regulation of industry to co-option.

Similar progressions could be seen in other fields as well, with workmen's compensation statutes continuing to be a prime example. At the beginning of the term, the Court upheld a 1916 amendment to New York's workmen's compensation statute to cover serious disfigurement of the face or head.[64] The employer objected that any award of damages would be a denial of due process because it lacked relation to the employee's job performance and because the computation was left to the discretion of a compensation committee without being based on the average wage, as was true for all other injuries. The Court rejected both arguments, saying that there was no constitutional reason that limited a state to considering only impairment of job performance. Moreover, even if that were the only criterion allowable, the Court thought it likely that disfigurement would have an effect on earning capacity.[65] Again, however, the differ-

---

61. 252 U.S. at 435.
62. *Sullivan v. City of Shreveport,* 251 U.S. 169, 172 (1919).
63. 253 U.S. 233 (1920). As Justice Pitney observed in his majority opinion, the closest example of a comparable exercise of the police power was *Jones v. City of Portland,* 245 U.S. 217 (1917), in which the Court had upheld a state law allowing municipalities to sell fuel.
64. *New York Central Railroad Co. v. Bianc,* 250 U.S. 596 (1919). At the end of the previous term, in his concurring opinion in the *Arizona Employers' Liability Cases,* 250 U.S. 400 (1919), Holmes had suggested that "it is reasonable that the public should pay the whole cost of producing what it wants and a part of that cost is the pain and mutilation incident to production. By throwing that loss upon the employer in the first instance we throw it upon the public in the long run and that is just." 250 U.S. at 433.
65. 250 U.S. at 601–2.

ence between affirmance and rejection was small. Thus, by a vote of 7–2, the Court reiterated that a state's law could not cover an injury that occurred on board a ship at harbor.[66] Congress then amended federal law in an effort to allow states to extend workmen's compensation laws to maritime injuries.[67] The Court responded by holding that the Constitution did not permit such an extension that would expose shippers to the uncertainties of varying state laws.[68] As Justice McReynolds explained for the 5–4 Court, the object of the grant of control over maritime law "was to commit direct control to the Federal Government; to relieve maritime commerce from unnecessary burdens and disadvantages incident to discordant legislation; and to establish, so far as practicable, harmonious and uniform rules applicable throughout every part of the Union."[69] With that mandate of uniformity, Congress could not delegate its legislative power to the states. McReynolds distinguished the Webb-Kenyon Act, which declared that alcoholic beverages were subject to state regulation even when they moved in interstate commerce—the unique nature of liquor justified that action.[70]

Holmes himself was not averse to using an argument for uniformity, as he did in *Pennsylvania Railroad Co. v. Public Service Commission*.[71] There he held that the combination of two federal regulations superseded a state law that set the minimum width for the rear platform of the last car on a train. One set of regulations came from the post office; the other from the ICC. "The subject-matter in this instance is peculiarly one that calls for uniform law and in our opinion regulation by the paramount authority has gone so far that the statute of Pennsylvania cannot impose the additional obligation in issue here."[72]

When the subject changed from employee safety to segregation of passengers, the Court showed less concern for uniformity. Thus, in *South Covington & Cincinnati Street Railway Co. v. Kentucky* the Court upheld Kentucky's separate car law.[73] As interpreted by the commonwealth's supreme court, the

---

66. *Peters v. Veasey*, 251 U.S. 121 (1919).
67. Act of October 6, 1917, ch. 97, 40 Stat. 395.
68. *Knickerbocker Ice Co. v. Stewart*, 253 U.S. 149 (1920).
69. 253 U.S. at 164. The Court used similar language in striking down a state law which imposed penalties on telegraph companies for late delivery of messages. *Western Union Telegraph Co. v. Boegli*, 251 U.S. 315, 316 (1920).
70. Act of March 1, 1913, ch. 90, 37 Stat. 699. Holmes dissented, joined by Pitney, Brandeis, and Clarke. In this term, 1919–1920, the Court upheld the Reed Amendment, which barred importation of liquor into a state that prohibited the sale or manufacture of liquor, even when the importation was for personal use. *United States v. Simpson*, 252 U.S. 465 (1920).
71. 250 U.S. 566 (1919).
72. Ibid., 569. Clarke dissented alone, based on a careful analysis of the facts and an emphasis on the need for the conductor to have the rear platform to permit boarding a moving train.
73. 252 U.S. 399 (1920).

law applied only to intrastate travel; and it required either separate cars for the races or "a good and substantial wooden partition" to separate the compartments of a single car.[74] Even though the railway company operated cars between Cincinnati, Ohio, and South Covington, Kentucky, the Court accepted the lower court's disingenuous conclusion that the law applied only to the routes in Kentucky. The conclusion that there was at most "only incidental effect on interstate commerce" was based on the "necessity, under our system of government, to preserve the power of the States within their sovereignties [and] to prevent the power from intrusive exercise within the National sovereignty." Thus, the Court continued, "an interurban railroad company deriving its powers from the State, and subject to obligations under the laws of the State, should not be permitted to exercise the powers given by the State, and escape its obligations to the State under the circumstances presented by this record, by running its coaches beyond the state lines."[75] Possibly the Court's deference to the states came in an attempt to soften the blow from *Missouri v. Holland,* decided the same day. Or, it may simply be true that the decision reflects the Court's continuing unwillingness to move actively away from the "separate but equal" doctrine of *Plessy.*

Justice Day dissented, joined by Van Devanter and Pitney. He pointed to his earlier opinion for the Court in which he had held that this same line was involved in interstate commerce.[76] Here, there would be an inevitable burden on interstate commerce, since the route consisted of a single car traveling between points in Ohio and Kentucky. Moreover, Day emphasized, Ohio had a different law, thereby subjecting the same car to inconsistent rules.[77]

The final area of change concerned the widening sweep of taxes to provide funds needed for the growth of government at all levels. For states, the Court barely upheld the extension of inheritance taxation to nonresidents who owned property within the state imposing the tax.[78] The states did have to be careful to allow the nonresidents some semblance of equal treatment;[79] but the Court strongly endorsed the power of states to tax property that received the protection of state laws:

---

74. Ibid., 400.
75. Ibid., 404.
76. *South Covington & Cincinnati Street Railway Co. v. City of Covington,* 235 U.S. 537 (1915).
77. 252 U.S. at 407.
78. *Maxwell v. Bugbee,* 250 U.S. 525 (1919) (5–4 decision).
79. *Travis v. Yale & Towne Manufacturing Co.,* 252 U.S. 60 (1920) (New York's 1919 income tax law declared unconstitutional insofar as it allowed exemptions for residents but not for nonresidents).

In our system of government the States have general dominion, and, saving as restricted by particular provisions of the Federal Constitution, complete dominion over all persons, property, and business transactions within their borders; they assume and perform the duty of preserving and protecting all such persons, property, and business, and, in consequence, have the power normally pertaining to governments to resort to all reasonable forms of taxation in order to defray the governmental expenses. . . . In well-ordered society, property has value chiefly for what it is capable of producing, ... That the State, from whose laws property and business and industry derive the protection and security without which production and gainful occupation would be impossible, is debarred from exacting a share of those gains in the form of income taxes for the support of the government, is a proposition so wholly inconsistent with fundamental principles as to be refuted by its mere statement. That it may tax the land but not the crop, the tree but not the fruit, the mine or well but not the product, the business but not the profit derived from it, is wholly inadmissible.[80]

The end of the term saw several of the justices depart more tired than usual, as evidenced by Holmes's note to Frankfurter: "The poor Chief was heroic this term but dreadfully hampered and my last news was that the operation on his eyes must be postponed to the autumn. He seemed very sad as we said goodbye. McKenna was on the train coming up and very pleasant, as usual. Van Devanter also showed a deal of grit. He was suffering badly from lumbago etc., but put through the 18th amendment and the main burden, shared by Pitney, of the private war between Texas, Oklahoma and the U.S. Pitney also looked worn, but it seemed a relief to him to lay his opinions on one side and do this business."[81]

---

80. *Shaffer v. Carter*, 252 U.S. 37, 50–51 (1920). See also *Maguire v. Trefry*, 253 U.S. 12 (1920), upholds tax on income from trust held in another state; *Cream of Wheat Co. v. County of Grand Forks*, 253 U.S. 325 (1920), upholds tax on corporate property outside the state.
81. Holmes to Frankfurter, June 22, 1920, Mennel and Compston, *Holmes and Frankfurter: Their Correspondence*, 94.

XI

THE FINAL TERM

October 4, the first day of the Court's new term, fell between two events important both in symbol and in fact. On September 16 a bomb exploded on Wall Street, killing forty-three people and wounding some two hundred more. As tragic as the incident was, it proved to be the last incident of unrest that had begun early in 1919. More indicative of the future was the presidential election early in November. Republican Warren Harding became the first presidential candidate to give a speech over the radio; and Pittsburgh's KDKA became the first radio station to provide a live broadcast of election returns. Those returns showed that Harding had received the largest electoral total to date, along with 60 percent of the popular vote. Shadowing that success was the vote for the Socialist candidate, Eugene Debs, in his fourth and final campaign. Although his vote total was higher than in 1912, the percentage of the vote dropped sharply. Harding's campaign for a "return to normalcy" carried the day, marking an end to two tumultuous decades of reform.

    As would be expected, the Court's docket had no immediate reflection of the campaign. Nevertheless, the Court did continue its move into the modern world, complete with cultural icons and changing constitutional doctrine. Of the cases argued this term, the first to be decided was *Western Union Telegraph Co. v. Speight*.[1] It well illustrates, if not defines, the final term of the White Court. Addie Speight originally sued in state court to recover damages for mental anguish caused by an error in transmitting these words: "Father died this morning. Funeral tomorrow, 10:10 a.m." The telegram correctly repeated the words, but it showed the wrong date of sending— January 23 instead of January 24. Thus, when Speight received the telegram on January 24 and saw the date of January 23, she thought she had missed the funeral. One aspect of the case illustrates the reach of technology—the sender used the telegraph, not the telephone, to transmit an important message between two towns in North Carolina, Greenville and Rosemary, which

---

1. 254 U.S. 17 (1920).

were less than a day's travel apart. That technology was not, however, ubiquitous—Western Union sent the message through its normal route, from Greenville to Richmond, Virginia; then to Norfolk, Virginia; then Roanoke Rapids, North Carolina, from where it would be delivered to Rosemary. This was hardly the service Justice Pitney had so glowingly described in *International News Service* two years earlier. Another aspect of the case shows the continuing difficulty of giving meaning to federalism—the rule of law depended upon whether the company's actions were characterized as interstate or intrastate; yet the commercial activity ignored state boundaries. The rule of law revealed yet a third aspect of the case—state law, in this case statutory law, recognized mental suffering as a basis for recovery; federal common law did not,[2] even as Freud's theories were coming into prominence.

Holmes's opinion for the Court mentioned none of the rich symbolism of the case. Instead, the opinion presented only a bland statement that Western Union had used the most efficient routing available. In light of the reasonableness of the routing, the conclusion followed that the transmission was interstate commerce; and, therefore, Speight could not recover for mental anguish.

The first month of this term afforded other glimpses of emerging technology. Two decisions announced with *Speight* involved patents for scaffolding. The newer technology allowed for construction of taller buildings by hanging scaffolding from the building's frame rather than requiring that the scaffolding rest on the ground. The merits of the disputes are not important; but an almost casual comment by Pitney is significant. In discussing the different types of scaffolding, Pitney wrote, "We may refer to our own observation of the first forms of scaffolding."[3] In an era well aware that sending a telegram less than a hundred miles could involve three or more intermediate stages, the judges of the nation's highest court could call on their common, personal experience for information about scaffolding—just as they could be confident that a letter addressed to Albert B. Guilfuss would be delivered in Milwaukee, or a letter to C. Ferger would be delivered in Indianapolis.

But there were signs of continuing change, and at an increasing rate. For example, two weeks after the telegraph and scaffolding opinions, the Court returned briefly to the regulation of automobiles. By now the experiment with motor vehicles for delivery of the mail had expanded beyond the District of Columbia. One consequence was that postal drivers encountered

---

2. The White Court had upheld the common law's denial of recovery for mental anguish in *Southern Express Co. v. Byers*, 240 U.S. 612 (1916), suit for late arrival of burial clothes.

3. *New York Scaffolding Co. v. Liebel-Binney Construction Co.*, 254 U.S. 24, 26 (1920). The companion case involved scaffolding used to construct Chicago's Blackstone Hotel and later the city hall. *New York Scaffolding Co. v. Chain Belt Co.*, 254 U.S. 32 (1920).

state laws requiring licensing of drivers. When Maryland convicted a federal driver of driving without a license, he challenged the conviction.[4] As was true with the other decisions announced early in this term, the Court devoted little time to explanation. Instead, it simply announced that a state could not require a license of a federal driver. To do so, Holmes explained, was not unlike a state taxing the federal government; both acts threatened to make the national government subservient to the state. Holmes conceded that a federal driver would have to obey local laws regulating the "mode of turning at the corners of streets," but any greater intrusion by the states would be unconstitutional.[5]

The week before the Maryland case, the Court heard argument in one of the term's two cases involving use of the police powers to conserve natural resources. This first case involved a 1919 Wyoming statute that placed restrictions on burning natural gas without using it for heat.[6] The Court upheld the conservation law, saying simply: "[W]e do not think that the State was required by the Constitution of the United States to stand idly by while these resources were disproportionately used, or used in such way that tended to their depletion, having no power of interference."[7] In the other conservation case the Court even more readily upheld a heavy tax imposed only on fishers of herring, to preserve the supplies of that fish off the coast of Alaska. As Holmes quipped in his opinion for the unanimous court, the Constitution had "known protective tariffs for a hundred years."[8] While these two exercises of the police power met with the Court's approval, the justices were not prepared to involve themselves on the side of conservation. When New York sought an injunction against New Jersey's dumping of raw sewage into the Passaic River, which flowed into New York harbor, the Court declined. Observing that some nine hundred million gallons of sewage entered the bay daily, the Court concluded that New Jersey's sewage could not make any difference. In place of judicial remedies, the Court urged the parties to negotiate with each other toward a cooperative solution.[9]

---

4. *Johnson v. Maryland*, 254 U.S. 51 (1920). The post office was not alone in experimenting with automobiles. When the District of Columbia passed an ordinance restricting interest charged by a pawnbroker, one enterprising entrepreneur moved his office across the Potomac to Virginia but kept his storage facility in the district; he offered free automobile service between the two locations. The ingenuity proved to be for naught, as the Court affirmed his conviction for violating the district's ordinance. *Horning v. District of Columbia*, 254 U.S. 135 (1920) (The 5–4 vote was the result of disagreement about the propriety of the judge's charge to the jury, with the majority holding that it was a harmless error.)
5. 254 U.S. at 56.
6. *Walls v. Midland Carbon Co.*, 254 U.S. 300 (1920).
7. Ibid., 324.
8. *Alaska Fish Salting & By-Products Co. v. Smith*, 255 U.S. 44, 48 (1921).
9. *New York v. New Jersey & Passaic Valley Sewerage Commissioners*, 256 U.S. 296 (1921).

A month after argument in the Maryland driver's license case, the Court heard argument in yet another of the cases involving challenges to a state's police powers. In this case a railroad challenged an order that it eliminate fifteen grade crossings in Paterson, New Jersey, at a cost of some two million dollars. Once again, the decision seemed relatively easy, though three members of the Court dissented from Holmes's opinion.[10] Protection of the public from danger, as Holmes explained, was "one of the most obvious cases of the police power, or to put the same proposition in another form, the authority of the railroads to project their moving masses across thoroughfares must be taken to be subject to the implied limitation that it may be shut down whenever and so far as the safety of the public requires." To the argument that the cost might bankrupt the railroad, Holmes showed no sympathy: "That the States might be so foolish as to kill a goose that lays golden eggs for them, has no bearing on their constitutional rights."[11] The Court deferred to the states as having better knowledge of the danger posed by specific crossings; that deference found support in the greater protection due the public, especially with the advent of automobiles: "Grade crossings call for a necessary adjustment of two conflicting interests—that of the public using the streets and that of the railroads and the public using them. Generically the streets represent the more important interest of the two. There can be no doubt that they did when these railroads were laid out, or that the advent of automobiles has given them an additional claim to consideration."[12]

The automobile would come to provide faster, personal transportation; just as the telephone would provide immediate communication without the intervention of messages sent at intervals along serpentine routes. The automobile could also provide greater opportunity for illicit activities. It was not surprising, therefore, that on the eve of the Roaring Twenties, the Court heard its first case involving an automobile used to violate the nation's Prohibition laws.[13] Acting under an 1866 law, the United States sought to enforce the forfeiture of the automobile—a Hudson, valued at eight hun-

---

10. *Erie Railroad Co. v. Board of Public Utility Commissioners*, 254 U.S. 394 (1921). White, Van Devanter, and McReynolds dissented without opinion. Justice McKenna joined White and McReynolds in dissenting from an opinion that upheld the exercise of police power to order a bridge company to add a roadway for vehicles to its bridge across the Niagara River from the United States to Canada. *International Bridge Co. v. New York*, 254 U.S. 126 (1920). Although this case was argued twice, in December 1919 and in October 1920, none of the dissenters wrote an opinion.

11. 254 U.S. at 410.

12. Ibid. Similar concerns about safety led the Court to refuse to prevent the city of Dallas from cooperating with a railroad to remove tracks from a street that had grown to considerable importance as Dallas grew from a population of 35,000 in 1890 to almost 160,000 in 1920. *Armour & Co. v. City of Dallas*, 255 U.S. 280 (1921).

13. *J. W. Goldsmith, Jr.-Grant Co. v. United States*, 254 U.S. 505 (1921).

dred dollars—because it had been used to store almost sixty gallons of whiskey for which the tax imposed by the federal government had not been paid. (The law related to concealment of goods for the purpose of avoiding a tax.) Complicating the case was the fact that the person charged with violating the law was not the owner of the car. Not surprisingly, therefore, the corporate owner challenged the forfeiture as a violation of due process, since the corporation had not been involved in any criminal activity. The Court had little difficulty resolving the dispute. Justice McKenna's opinion did admit to some distress in accepting the forfeiture of property whose owner neither participated in nor knew of the illegal activity. Even so, the law was clear in imposing a kind of guilt on the property, leaving to the owner the obligation to police the use.

The automobile and Prohibition would become increasingly prominent in the nation's life over the next decade. For the White Court, though, the cases presented only the first intimations of issues to come. Thus, the Court held that the government could not penalize the storage of liquor for personal use when the liquor had been lawfully owned at the time the Volstead Act was passed.[14] Likewise, the Court upheld the Eighteenth Amendment itself as well as federal statutes enacted to enforce it.[15] The challengers to the amendment argued that Congress had acted improperly in imposing a time limit on ratification, the first time Congress had done so.[16] The Court held that Congress had not exceeded its authority, reasoning that setting a time limit was but a detail of the power to choose the mode of ratification.[17]

Obviously, the automobile had raised questions of federalism, just as had the telegram that wound its way across southeastern Virginia before being delivered in North Carolina. Not all of these issues were so easily resolved; indeed, they proved to be the most divisive of the term. In what is seen as the most portentous opinion of the term, if not of the entire White Court, Brandeis himself linked the federalism of the commerce clause with

---

14. *Street v. Lincoln Safe Deposit Co.*, 254 U.S. 88 (1920). For the Volstead Act see Act of October 28, 1919, ch. 85, 41 Stat. 305. One estimate said that as much as thirty million gallons of whiskey was stored in bonded warehouses in Kentucky. The Court held that a tax on the removal of that whiskey was a violation of the Kentucky state constitution. *Dawson v. Kentucky Distilleries & Warehouse Co.*, 255 U.S. 288 (1921).

15. *Williams v. United States*, 255 U.S. 336 (1921). This opinion merely reaffirmed the Court's holdings in *Clark Distilling Co. v. Western Maryland Railway Co.*, 242 U.S. 311 (1917), and *United States v. Hill*, 248 U.S. 420 (1919).

16. *Dillon v. Gloss*, 256 U.S. 368 (1921).

17. In dictum, the Court commented that it was "untenable" to suggest that any one of the four amendments still pending could become a part of the Constitution. 256 U.S. at 374–75. That view proved false when Congress accepted the ratification of the Twenty-seventh Amendment in 1992, based on Michigan's ratification of an amendment first proposed in 1789. 106 Stat. 5145.

the federalism of the Bill of Rights. *Gilbert v. Minnesota* involved a challenge to the first state sedition law to reach the Court.[18] The 1917 Minnesota law had made it illegal "to advocate or teach by word of mouth or otherwise that men should not enlist in the military or naval forces of the Unites States or the state of Minnesota."[19] The indictment charged that Joseph Gilbert, an organizer for the Non-partisan League, had violated the law by making this statement while the United States was at war with Germany: "We are going over to Europe to make the world safe for democracy, but I tell you we had better make America safe for democracy first. . . . If this is such a great democracy, for Heaven's sake why should we not vote on conscription of men. We were stampeded into this war by newspaper rot to pull England's chestnuts out of the fire for her. I tell you if they conscripted wealth like they have conscripted men, this war would not last over forty-eight hours."[20]

Gilbert challenged his conviction on two grounds: first, that the states lacked power to legislate concerning sedition, in light of congressional legislation; and, second, that the state statute violated his freedom of speech. He based his first argument on Congress's war powers, reasoning that because the state of Minnesota had neither power to declare war nor power to raise an army, it had no power to prevent interference with activities related to war. Writing for the Court, McKenna suggested that the statute might well be upheld by resort to the familiar vocabulary of the police power—as an exercise of that power to promote civil order. The suggestion found support in the fact that some who attended Gilbert's public speech objected strongly to his remarks, thereby raising the specter of a breach of the peace. As McKenna noted laconically, "And such is not an uncommon experience."[21] But McKenna adventured beyond the police power into the more difficult border between the states and the nation to deny the premise for Gilbert's argument. McKenna sought to describe the intertwined interests of the state and nation in this way: "The United States is composed of the States, the States are constituted of the citizens of the United States, who are also citizens of the States, and it is from these citizens that armies are raised and wars waged, and whether to victory and its benefits, or to defeat and its calamities, the States as well as the United States are intimately concerned."[22] "Cold and technical reasoning in its minute consideration may indeed insist on a separation of the sovereignties and resistance in each to any cooperation from the other, but there is opposing demonstration in the fact that this country is one composed of many and must on occasions be ani-

---

18. 254 U.S. 325 (1920).
19. Quoted in ibid., 326.
20. Quoted in ibid., 327.
21. Ibid., 331.
22. Ibid., 329.

mated as one and that the constituted and constituting sovereignties must have power of coöperation against the enemies of all."[23] Seen in that view, the Minnesota law did nothing more than complement the national one.

Of Gilbert's argument that the statute deprived him of free speech, McKenna had less to say. It mattered not whether the source of the right was the state or the federal constitution, it might even be "natural and inherent."[24] Whatever the source, in cases such as *Schenck, Frohwerk, Debs,* and *Abrams,* the Court had already decided that the right was not absolute. With those cases in mind, the Court had no difficulty concluding that Gilbert's comments showed an intention to impede enlistment.

Justice McKenna's opinion drew the support of five other members of the Court. Of the remaining three, Holmes announced that he concurred in the result, without writing an opinion. White used a single sentence to explain that he dissented on the ground that the congressional laws had occupied the entire field. Brandeis wrote a separate dissent. He began by pouncing on the Court's almost offhand suggestion that the statute could be sustained as an exercise of the police power, freed from the justification afforded by a state of war. Such an application, Brandeis warned, would reach anyone teaching pacifism to a single person regardless of the relationship between the people. Invoking a hypothetical image, he continued: "Thus the statute invades the privacy and freedom of the home. Father and mother may not follow the promptings of religious belief, of conscience or of conviction, and teach son or daughter the doctrine of pacifism. If they do any police officer may summarily arrest them."[25] Of course, Gilbert's public speech to the Non-partisan League had none of the characteristics of this tranquil portrait of a family gathering. But by his suggestive use of the "privacy and freedom" of the home, Brandeis had again enlisted the image of castles and copses that he had used to such effect in his writing on privacy thirty years before. With that image secured, he once again moved into uncharted territory as he struggled to explain how the First Amendment's ban on Congress's interference with freedom of speech could reach a state's action.

Touching the key rubrics of the Fourteenth Amendment, Brandeis wrote that the Minnesota law "affects directly the functions of the Federal Government. It affects rights, privileges and immunities of one who is a citizen of the United States; and it deprives him of an important part of his liberty. These are rights which are guaranteed protection by the Federal Constitution; and they are invaded by the statute in question."[26] The ease

---

23. Ibid.
24. Ibid., 332.
25. Ibid., 335–36.
26. Ibid., 336.

with which Brandeis moved from "functions" of government to "rights" of citizens may suggest to a later reader that Brandeis intended to concentrate on the rights. But this statement came early in the Court's struggle to define the place of rights in the constitutional sphere. In 1920 not even Brandeis was prepared to stand solely on the "rights" side of constitutional argument. Instead, he shifted gently back toward the structural side of the dialogue, moving from "privileges and immunities" and "liberty" to the right of the people to assemble for the purpose of petitioning Congress on matters of national importance. The Minnesota statute inevitably interfered with that right, at least in Brandeis's opinion. Then, as though swept up in Holmes's rhetoric from *Abrams,* Brandeis added: "Like the course of the heavenly bodies, harmony in national life is a resultant of the struggle between contending forces. In frank expression of conflicting opinion lies the greatest promise of wisdom in governmental action; and in suppression lies ordinarily the greatest peril. There are times when those charged with the responsibility of Government, faced with clear and present danger, may conclude that suppression of divergent opinion is imperative; because the emergency does not permit reliance upon the slower conquest of error by truth. And in such emergencies the power to suppress exists."[27] But that power belonged to Congress insofar as speech might affect the nation's military. To support his argument that states could not interfere with the national government in this area, Brandeis recalled *Johnson v. Maryland,* the case which held that a state could not require that a driver for the post office have a state license. A state could no more require a license of a federal driver than it could usurp Congress's power over enlistments for the army and navy. Brandeis would reach that conclusion whether Congress had enacted a specific statute or not, "because by omitting to make regulations Congress signifies its intention that, in this respect, the action of the citizen shall be untrammelled."[28] In this case, however, he had no need to rely on silence, for Congress had enacted the Espionage Act, which Brandeis viewed as showing exclusive federal control in the area.

To that conclusion from the structural part of the Constitution, Brandeis added a final paragraph. Accepting that there was no need to address the question whether the Minnesota statute violated Gilbert's freedom of speech, Brandeis nonetheless added that he had "difficulty in believing that the liberty guaranteed by the Constitution, which has been held to protect against state denial the right of an employer to discriminate against a workman because he is a member of a trade union, . . . the right of a business man to conduct a private employment agency . . . or to contract outside the

---

27. Ibid., 338.
28. Ibid., 342.

State for insurance of his property . . . does not include liberty to teach, either in the privacy of the home or publicly, the doctrine of pacifism; so long, at least, as Congress has not declared that the public safety demands its suppression. I cannot believe that the liberty guaranteed by the Fourteenth Amendment includes only liberty to acquire and to enjoy property."[29] In making that suggestion, Brandeis elaborated on a more subtle statement made by McKenna in *Schaefer v. United States* the term before.[30] Through his further elaboration Brandeis inaugurated the debate about whether the strictures of the Bill of Rights, written to apply only to Congress, also applied to the states, through the words of the Fourteenth Amendment.[31] In the succinct phrase of Zechariah Chafee, this opinion was the "first glimmer of the new day."[32]

Brandeis recited the litany of "liberty of contract" cases again in his dissent in *United States ex rel. Milwaukee Social Democratic Publishing Co. v. Burleson*.[33] Unlike *Gilbert, Burleson* involved a sanction under federal law, though both cases aimed at restricting speech or publication of material deemed inimical to the United States war effort. The sanction in *Burleson* was revocation of second-class mailing privileges for *The Milwaukee Leader*, as permitted under the Espionage Act of 1917. Writing for the Court, Justice Clarke explained that the basis for the action was the repeated publication of comment very much like that for which Gilbert was convicted—articles declaring "that the war was unjustifiable and dishonorable on our part, a capitalistic war, which had been forced upon the people by a class, to serve its selfish ends."[34] Clarke then summarized the effect of the articles, along with the consequent absence of protection for them under the First Amendment: "These publications were not designed to secure amendment or repeal of the laws denounced in them as arbitrary and oppressive, but to create hostility to, and to encourage violation of, them. Freedom of the press may protect criticism and agitation for modification or repeal of laws, but it does not extend to protection of him who counsels and encourages the violation of the law as it exists. The Constitution was adopted to preserve our Government, not to serve as a protecting screen for those who while claiming its privileges seek to destroy it."[35] With no constitutional protection for the articles, the only remaining question was whether the postmaster general had the power to revoke the

---

29. Ibid., 343.
30. 251 U.S. 466 (1920).
31. For more on this debate, see Michael Kent Curtis, *No State Shall Abridge: The Fourteenth Amendment and the Bill of Rights* (Durham, N.C.: Duke University Press, 1986); William Nelson, *The Fourteenth Amendment: From Political Principle to Judicial Doctrine* (Cambridge, Mass.: Harvard University Press, 1988).
32. Zechariah Chafee, Jr., *Free Speech in the United States* (New York: Atheneum, 1969), 285–98.
33. 255 U.S. 407 (1921).
34. Ibid., 413.
35. Ibid., 414.

mailing privilege entirely, or whether he was obligated to deny it issue by issue. The answer for the Court lay in practicalities; it would be impossible, Clarke announced, for postal authorities to screen each issue of the newspaper. Moreover, he found the succession of articles, extending over five months, to provide ample support for concluding that the paper was unlikely to change its content in the future.

Brandeis dissented, contending that the right to distribute newspapers through the mail was akin to the contract right protected in cases such as *Adair, Coppage,* and *Allgeyer.* By depriving the paper of the right to reduced postal rates, the postmaster general had effectively imposed a punishment that grew daily, as the costs of increased rates mounted.[36]

Brandeis's call for protection of the sanctity of the home and of private spaces[37] found greater support in three other opinions during the term, all involving the exclusionary rule. In the first of this trio of cases, *Gouled v. United States,* a unanimous Court sharply criticized military officials for deception in gaining access to an office.[38] The army suspected Felix Gouled and others of conspiring to defraud the United States through contracts for clothing and equipment. To collect evidence, military officials ordered an acquaintance of Gouled to pretend to visit his office. While there, the acquaintance took several documents, one of which was introduced in Gouled's trial. Writing for the Court, Justice Clarke pointed to a trio of decisions in which the Court had developed an exclusionary rule against the use as evidence in a criminal prosecution of property obtained through an unreasonable search.[39] He summarized the holdings of those cases in language remarkably similar to what Brandeis had written in *Gilbert:* "The effect of the decisions cited is: that such rights are declared to be indispensable to the 'full enjoyment of personal security, personal liberty and private property'; that they are to be regarded as of the very essence of constitutional liberty; and that the guaranty of them is as important and as imperative as are the guaranties of the other fundamental rights of the individual citizen,—the right, to trial by jury, the writ of *habeas corpus* and to due process of law."[40] Although *Gouled* involved the federal government, that language revealed that the entire Court was willing to consider yet more rights as belonging within the definition of "liberty."

---

36. Ibid., 432–34.
37. See *Green v. Frazier,* 253 U.S. 233 (1920), discussion of "public" functions in light of North Dakota's sweeping reform of industrial commission.
38. 255 U.S. 298 (1921).
39. Two of the cases belonged to the White Court—*Weeks v. United States,* 232 U.S. 383 (1914); *Silverthorne Lumber Co. v. United States,* 251 U.S. 385 (1920). The third was *Boyd v. United States,* 116 U.S. 616 (1886).
40. 255 U.S. at 304.

Clarke went on to summarize the protections afforded by the Fourth and Fifth Amendments against using force, threats, or coercion to gain entry to a house or office and then search it. Given those protections, he wrote, "it is impossible to successfully contend that a like search and seizure would be a reasonable one if only admission were obtained by stealth instead of by force or coercion."[41] He then returned to language reminiscent of Brandeis's when he concluded: "The security and privacy of the home or office and of the papers of the owner would be as much invaded and the search and seizure would be as much against his will in the one case as in the other, and it must therefore be regarded as equally in violation of his constitutional rights."[42] Any decisions to the contrary he dismissed as "unsound," without bothering to cite them.[43]

Justice Clarke also wrote the opinion for the unanimous Court in the second of the three cases, *Amos v. United States*,[44] announced the same day as *Gouled*. Lawrence Amos challenged his conviction for violating parts of the Prohibition law; he particularly challenged the use of evidence obtained from a search of his home. The government contended that its revenue officers had permission to search from "a woman who said she was his wife." (It is not clear from Clarke's opinion whether she really was Amos's wife.) The Court ordered Amos's conviction be reversed, without considering whether a wife could waive her husband's constitutional rights, "for it is perfectly clear that under the implied coercion here presented, no such waiver was intended or effected."[45] Clarke did not specify the source of the "implied coercion," other than what would have come from the revenue officers identifying themselves and saying that they had come to search for evidence of violation of the revenue laws.

In spite of the strong support for the Fourth Amendment in *Gouled* and in *Amos*, a majority of the Court could not be persuaded to extend the rule to encompass searches made by private individuals without the government's knowledge. Thus, in *Burdeau v. McDowell*, the Court declined to order the United States to return papers to a defendant charged with fraudulent use of the mails.[46] An officer of J. C. McDowell's employer had searched his office, later turning papers from the office over to a parent corporation; the parent corporation then delivered the papers to the Justice Department. Writing for the Court, Justice Day summarized the facts and the rules associated with the Fourth Amendment before concluding that nothing in the Constitution required the government to return the papers.

---

41. Ibid., 305.
42. Ibid., 305–6.
43. Ibid., 306.
44. 255 U.S. 313 (1921).
45. Ibid., 317.
46. 256 U.S. 465 (1921).

Justice Brandeis, joined by Holmes, dissented. The brevity of this opinion, unsupported by careful analysis of the principles, again suggests that Brandeis was in the early stages of working out his own position. For the moment, he was content to rest on the common-law principle that had the stolen papers been in the possession of a thief, a court would have ordered their return. The government, he wrote, should not occupy "an exceptional position." He concluded with a plea similar to that in *Gilbert:* "Respect for law will not be advanced by resort, in its enforcement, to means which shock the common man's sense of decency and fair play."[47]

Two other attempts to extend federal judicial power to protect rights met with not even the hint of success afforded by Brandeis's dissents. Both cases involved federal statutory law. One, *United States v. Wheeler,*[48] arose out of an indictment charging, in the austere language of the law, a conspiracy to deprive some 221 people of rights guaranteed them as citizens; the other, *Newberry v. United States,*[49] involved an attempt to apply the Federal Corrupt Practices Law to primary elections for Congress. In each of these cases, the Court resorted to its concern for the place of states in the federal system.

Wheeler involved an indictment of twenty-five men, all charged with conspiring to violate the civil rights of the more than two hundred "Wobblies" who had been herded onto a train in July 1917 and taken from Bisbee, Arizona, into the desert near Hermanas, New Mexico, where they were left with only minimal supplies of food or water.[50] Sheriff Harry C. Wheeler had personally led a band of newly created deputies in rounding up some twelve hundred men in response to union activities that had closed Bisbee's copper mines. The suspected Wobblies found meager shelter at an army camp, where officers discovered that few of the men were aliens, much less enemy aliens, as alleged by Sheriff Wheeler. Under pressure from labor and political leaders, the Wilson administration charged Wheeler and others with violating the rights of those removed. The trial judge dismissed the indictment, reasoning that the defendants' actions were solely within the power of the states to punish. The Supreme Court affirmed. The United States had argued that inherent in the Constitution's creation of a single, national government was a right of each citizen to freedom of movement among the states. Because the right belonged to national citizenship, Congress could protect it by legislation.

---

47. Ibid., 477.
48. 254 U.S. 281 (1920).
49. 256 U.S. 232 (1921).
50. See Melvyn Dubofsky, *We Shall Be All: A History of the Industrial Workers of the World,* 2d ed. (Urbana: University of Illinois Press, 1988), 385–87; Philip Taft, "The Bisbee Deportation," *Labor History* 13 (winter 1972): 3–40; Richard White, *"It's Your Misfortune and None of My Own": A History of the American West* (Norman: University of Oklahoma Press, 1991), 290–96.

The argument failed to persuade the Court. Writing for all but Justice Clarke, Chief Justice White explained that the 1870 Civil Rights Act could not reach so far. The Constitution gave no power to the national government to protect the privileges and immunities it sought to guarantee: "The Citizens of each State shall be entitled to all Privileges and Immunities of Citizens in the several States."[51] Instead, the protection was left to the states, except when a state itself discriminated. Then, the federal government would have a role to play. But in no case would the conduct of individuals justify a governmental response.[52]

The other case, *Newberry*, involved a more recent federal statute, one passed in 1910 and amended in 1911.[53] The original act had restricted the amount of money candidates for Congress could spend in their election campaigns; the amendment applied the restriction to primary elections as well as general elections. Supporters of the statute pointed to Article 1, section 4 of the Constitution for Congress's authority to enact such a provision: "The Times, Places and Manner of holding Elections for Senators and Representatives, shall be prescribed in each State by the Legislature thereof, but the Congress may at any time by Law make or alter such Regulations, except as to the Places of chusing [*sic*] Senators."

According to the charges against Truman H. Newberry, he spent more than $100,000 in 1918 to secure his nomination and election to the United States Senate, defeating Henry Ford. Under the statute, candidates could spend no more than $3,750. Represented by former justice Charles Evans Hughes, Newberry successfully challenged his conviction. In what was the oddest configuration for a five-vote majority of the White Court, four justices each wrote a separate opinion explaining that the conviction should be reversed.

Writing for this bare majority of the Court, McReynolds emphasized that "primaries" were not part of "elections," pointing to the fact that they were unknown in the eighteenth century, when the Constitution was adopted. He thought that definition applied both to the text of the Constitution and to the Seventeenth Amendment, which provided for the direct election of senators by the people. Beyond the textual argument, McReynolds emphasized one of his favorite points, that to permit Congress to regulate primaries "would interfere with purely domestic affairs of the State and infringe upon liberties reserved to the people."[54]

---

51. U.S. Constitution, art. 4, sec. 2.
52. 254 U.S. at 298.
53. Act of June 25, 1910, ch. 392, 36 Stat. 822, as amended by Act of August 19, 1911, ch. 33, 37 Stat. 25.
54. 256 U.S. at 258.

The fifth vote for McReynolds's opinion came from McKenna, who joined only the interpretation of the statute; he expressed no opinion about Congress's power under the Seventeenth Amendment.

In what would prove to be his last written opinion, Chief Justice White explained that he thought the conviction should be reversed because of an error in the instructions to the jury. For there to be a violation of the statute, in White's view, the candidate must do something more than continue his campaign after learning that the spending limits had been exceeded, even if not caused by him. White supported that conclusion with an unusually comprehensive account of the legislative history of the statute. He could not, however, agree with the constitutional analysis in McReynolds's opinion. In the "time, place and manner" provision, White saw a grant of power for both state and national government—indeed, the *only* grant of power concerning congressional elections. As a consequence, given the common language of "time" and "manner," anything that states could do under their grant, Congress could do under its. To hold that a "primary" was subject to state regulation but not congressional was, in White's word, "suicidal,"[55] especially in light of the "necessary and proper" clause that gave Congress the power it needed to carry out its delegated powers. He showed a similar disdain for the argument that a primary was different from the subsequent election, drawing one last time on common knowledge: "The influence of who is nominated for elective office upon the result of the election to fill that office is so known of all men that the proposition may be left to destroy itself by its own statement."[56] Frankfurter saw in this "vigorous nationalist dissent" the "characteristic" trait of White's jurisprudence.[57]

Justice Pitney also wrote a separate opinion, in which Brandeis and Clarke joined. Insofar as the trial was concerned, Pitney reached a conclusion similar to that of White—the judge had erroneously instructed the jury concerning the amount of participation by the candidate in order to support a conviction. On the constitutional question, Pitney's opinion reached the same conclusion as had White's, but he touched on more provisions. Unlike White, Pitney did not rely solely on the "time, place and manner" provision; instead, he looked to all of the constitutional provisions concerning selection of members of Congress. Since that selection was a federal function, both state and national power must come from the Constitution; as a consequence, if Congress lacked power over primaries, then so did the states. But Pitney's response to that conclusion was comically abrupt: "It is said primaries were unknown when the

---

55. Ibid., 262.
56. Ibid., 263.
57. Frankfurter to Holmes, May 20, 1921, Mennel and Compston, *Holmes and Frankfurter: Their Correspondence*, 114.

Constitution was adopted. So were the steam railway and the electric telegraph."[58] The simple fact, in his view, was that primaries and general elections were so closely related as to be a single process. If Congress lacked the power to reach primaries, "the result would be to leave the general Government destitute of the means to insure its own preservation without governmental aid from the States, which they might either grant or withhold according to their own will. This would render the Government of the United States something less than supreme in the exercise of its own appropriate powers; a doctrine supposed to have been laid at rest forever by the decisions of this court in . . . the time of Chief Justice Marshall and since."[59]

Although the efforts to broaden the reach of those two federal statutes met with no success, two new statutes did find sympathy with the Court. Both involved rent control statutes, one in the District of Columbia, the other in New York. The district's 1919 act declared that it was required by the necessities of war. Under the act, tenants could continue their tenancy beyond a lease's existing term, so long as they continued to pay the agreed-upon rent. The law allowed the landlord to appeal to a special commission to seek an increase in rent; and the law allowed the landlord to take possession of any premises needed for personal or family use, so long as the landlord gave the tenant advance notice of at least thirty days. The law would be effective for only two years. In *Block v. Hirsh,* the Court upheld the law by a 5–4 vote.[60] The Court also upheld the New York law by the same 5–4 division, with neither side making significant additions to their opinions in *Block.*[61]

Writing for the majority in *Block,* Holmes began his opinion much like he had done in *Schenck,* by emphasizing the emergency facing the nation, then adding, "and the question is whether Congress was incompetent to meet it in the way in which it has been met by most of the civilized countries of the world."[62] Answering the question was relatively easy for Holmes, who offered an almost breathtaking series of analogies. He began with the broadest concept, writing that regulation was allowed because "circumstances have clothed the letting of buildings in the District of Columbia with a public interest so great as to justify regulation by law. Plainly circumstances may so change in time or so differ in space as to clothe with such an interest what at other times or in other places would be a matter of purely private concern."[63] Then he

---

58. 256 U.S. at 282.
59. Ibid., 281.
60. 256 U.S. 135 (1921).
61. *Marcus Brown Holding Co., Inc. v. Feldman,* 256 U.S. 170 (1921).
62. 256 U.S. at 155. He returned to that point at the end of his opinion: "It is enough that we are not warranted in saying that legislation that has been resorted to for the same purpose all over the world, is futile or has no reasonable relation to the relief sought." Ibid., 158.
63. Ibid., 155.

moved quickly to the police power, which, once extended to regulation of the height of buildings, could surely extend to regulation of the rent charged. And, finally, he suggested that the law was little different from other wartime measures designed to prevent excess profits, or from the ordinary prohibition of usury.[64]

Justice McKenna dissented, writing for himself and White, Van Devanter, and McReynolds. McKenna began with a sweeping assertion of his own to counter Holmes's, saying that the law was "contrary to every conception of leases that the world has ever entertained, and of the reciprocal rights and obligations of lessor and lessee."[65] To that, he added his own view of Armageddon with this more direct response to Holmes's invocation of the world's electorate: "Have conditions come, not only to the District of Columbia, embarrassing the Federal Government, but to the world as well, that are not amenable to passing palliatives, so that socialism, or some form of socialism, is the only permanent corrective or accommodation? It is indeed strange that this court, in effect, is called upon to make way for it and, through the instrument of a constitution based on personal rights and the purposeful encouragement of individual incentive and energy, to declare legal a power exerted for their destruction."[66]

For McKenna and the other dissenters, property was second only to personal security in the pantheon of rights; yet this statute struck at the heart of property by depriving owners of control of its use. The differences between his opinion and that of Holmes were so fundamental that he could do little other than counter Holmes, platitude for platitude. Most revealing of the chasm that separated the opposing views was McKenna's warning about the war being used as a justification for the emergency measure. The chasm was all the more distinct on account of McKenna's having written this statement earlier in the same term: "To assert that the first steps of a policy make it immutable, is to assert that imperfections and errors in legislation become constitutional rights. This is a narrow conception of sovereignty."[67] Now, however, faced with the rent control laws, McKenna warned in the simple language of a coded password, "Withstand beginnings."[68] In the end, though, words failed him; McKenna found that it was "not possible to express the possession or exercise of more unbounded or irresponsible power."[69] It mattered not that the statute professed to be limited to two years; for, as McKenna noted, if the statute could

---

64. Ibid., 155–57.
65. Ibid., 159.
66. Ibid., 162–63.
67. *Thornton v. Duffy*, 254 U.S. 361, 369 (1920), Court approved a change in Ohio's workmen's compensation law.
68. 256 U.S. at 160.
69. Ibid., 167.

set its own limits at two years, it could do it for longer. He concluded with his own vision, phrased in the elliptical terms appropriate to apocalyptic literature: If government could destroy these contracts related to property, then it could also destroy the "contracts made by the National Government in the necessity or solicitude of the conduct of the war . . . . if one contract can be disregarded in the public interest every contract can be; patriotic honor may be involved in one more than in another, but degrees of honor may not be attended to—the public interest being regarded as paramount."[70]

Dean Acheson, a former law clerk to Brandeis, wrote to Felix Frankfurter of McKenna's opinion: "What did you think of McKenna's panic-stricken utterances of Monday last? If he doesn't stop this business of using the bench as a confessional we are apt to learn something about the judicial process before he gets through. [Several earlier decisions] and now this, have given us pretty nearly everything except his views on marriage and big league baseball."[71] Frankfurter responded to Holmes, more critical of McKenna than usual, referring to McKenna's "naive absolutes," then adding that McKenna "certainly baffles predictability."[72] Holmes agreed, responding to Frankfurter, "McKenna, as you say, is unpredictable."[73]

---

70. Ibid., 168–69.
71. Acheson to Frankfurter, April 20, 1921, *Among Friends: Personal Letters of Dean Acheson*, eds. David C. McLellan and David C. Acheson (New York: Dodd, Mead & Co., 1980), 12.
72. Frankfurter to Holmes, April 25, 1921, Mennel and Compston, *Holmes and Frankfurter: Their Correspondence*, 111.
73. Holmes to Frankfurter, April 30, 1921, Mennel and Compston, *Holmes and Frankfurter: Their Correspondence*, 112.

Conclusion

Near the end of the 1920 term Justice Holmes wrote to Sir Frederick Pollock, describing Chief Justice White's health: "[T]he poor old boy is the object of nothing but sympathy just now. He has stuck to his work (I think unwisely) in the face of illness—cataracts on his eyes that have blinded one of them, and very great deafness. But he has gone to the hospital and was to have an operation performed at 11:30 today, I was told (not on his eyes). I hope that it is not serious but feel no assurance till I hear the result. His infirmities have made the work harder for others, and I imagine that he has suffered much more than he has told."[1] Unfortunately, the operation was not a success, and White died shortly thereafter, on May 19.

White's death, like his appointment, brought no significant change to the Court. He came from within the Court, thereby affording no opportunity for a symbolic change of "command." Likewise, he left from within the Court, without having shown an inclination to use the office of chief justice to lobby Congress or otherwise seek benefit for the Court. During White's tenure as chief justice, the Court for the most part ratified the decisions reached by the executive and legislative branches at both the national and the state level. Only on rare occasions had the Court placed a distinctive mark on a dispute. Possibly the best-known occasion from the early years of the White Court was the development of the "rule of reason" in antitrust cases. That doctrine proved to be part of a larger attempt by the Court to accommodate the law to growing appreciation for the inherent uncertainty of language. Holmes's dissent in *Abrams,* near the end of White's service, was more direct—"all life is an experiment." Indeed, it seems that for most of the previous decade the Court itself had been engaged in an experiment. It tested old doctrines for suitability in new circumstances. Later, it had experimented with rubrics such as police power and commerce, as well as liberty; when each was found wanting, the Court

---

1. Holmes to Pollock, May 18, 1921, Howe, *Holmes-Pollock Letters,* 1:68. See also Holmes to Laski, May 27, 1921, Howe, *Holmes-Laski Letters,* 1:338; Holmes to Einstein, May 20, 1921, Peabody, *Holmes-Einstein Letters,* 195.

began to test newer categories as it followed the rest of the nation into a modern world.

In the end, the final sentence of Willa Cather's 1918 novel, *My Ántonia*, captured the justices' struggle: "Whatever we had missed, we possessed together the precious, the incommunicable past."[2] For the justices of the older generation the past was indeed precious. That they found it impossible to communicate that past to the younger generation proved to be their singular failure.

That White left no jurisprudential monument should be seen as neither a negative comment nor a surprise. White presided over a Court moving from rural to urban America. In that service, he had been a good friend to most, if not all, of the members of the Court. Appropriately, therefore, the final word should be left to Holmes, who wrote simply, "I shall miss him a good deal personally."[3]

---

2. Quoted in C. Barry Chabot, *Writers for the Nation: American Literary Modernism* (Tuscaloosa: University of Alabama Press, 1997), 66.

3. Holmes to Einstein, May 20, 1921, Peabody, *Holmes-Einstein Letters*, 195.

APPENDIX

Table of Cases

Abrams v. United States, 250 U.S. 616 (1919)
Adair v. United States, 208 U.S. 161 (1908)
Adams v. City of Milwaukee, 228 U.S. 572 (1913)
Adams v. Tanner, 244 U.S. 590 (1917)
Alaska Fish Salting & By-Products Co. v. Smith, 255 U.S. 44 (1921)
Alder v. Edenborn, 242 U.S. 137 (1916)
Allanwilde Transport Corp. v. Vacuum Oil Co., 248 U.S. 377 (1919)
Allen v. St. Louis, Iron Mountain & Southern Railway Co., 230 U.S. 553 (1913)
Allgeyer v. Louisiana, 165 U.S. 578 (1897)
Aluminum Company of America v. Ramsey, 222 U.S. 251 (1911)
American Banana Co. v. United Fruit Co., 213 U.S. 347 (1909)
American Railroad Company of Porto Rico v. Birch, 224 U.S. 547 (1912)
American Security and Trust Co. v. Commissioners of the District of Columbia, 224 U.S. 491 (1912)
American Water Softener Co. v. Lankford, 235 U.S. 496 (1915)
American Well Works Co. v. Layne and Bowler Co., 241 U.S. 257 (1916)
Amos v. United States, 255 U.S. 313 (1921)
Andrews v. Andrews, 188 U.S. 14 (1903)
Arizona Employers' Liability Cases, 250 U.S. 400 (1919)
Arkadelphia Milling Co. v. St. Louis Southwestern Railway Co., 249 U.S. 134 (1919)
Armour & Co. v. City of Dallas, 255 U.S. 280 (1921)
Armour & Co. v. North Dakota, 240 U.S. 510 (1916)
Atchison, Topeka & Santa Fe Railway Co. v. Harold, 241 U.S. 371 (1916)
Atchison, Topeka & Santa Fe Railway Co. v. O'Connor, 223 U.S. 280 (1912)
Athanasaw v. United States, 227 U.S. 326 (1913)
Atkin v. Kansas, 191 U.S. 207 (1903)
Atlantic Coast Line Railroad Co. v. Georgia, 234 U.S. 280 (1914)
Atlantic Coast Line Railroad Co. v. Riverside Mills, 219 U.S. 186 (1911)
B. Altman & Co. v. United States, 224 U.S. 583 (1912)

Bailey v. Drexel Furniture Co., 259 U.S. 20 (1922)
Baltic Mining Co. v. Massachusetts, 231 U.S. 68 (1913)
Baltimore & Ohio Railroad Co. v. Interstate Commerce Commission, 221 U.S., 612 (1911)
Baltimore & Ohio Railroad Co. v. Leach, 249 U.S. 217 (1919)
Bank of California v. Richardson, 248 U.S. 476 (1919)
Banker Brothers Co. v. Pennsylvania, 222 U.S. 210 (1911)
Barrett v. Indiana, 229 U.S. 26 (1913)
Bartell v. United States, 227 U.S. 427 (1913)
Bauer & Cie v. O'Donnell, 229 U.S. 1 (1913)
Bay v. Merrill & Ring Logging Co., 243 U.S. 40 (1917)
Bennett v. United States, 227 U.S. 333 (1913)
Beutler v. Grand Trunk Junction Railway Co., 224 U.S. 85 (1912)
Biddinger v. Commissioner of Police of the City of New York, 245 U.S. 128 (1917)
Block v. Hirsh, 256 U.S. 135 (1921)
Board of Trade of the City of Chicago v. United States, 246 U.S. 231 (1918)
Bobbs-Merrill Co. v. Straus, 210 U.S. 339 (1908)
Boise Artesian Hot and Cold Water Co., Ltd. v. Boise City, 230 U.S. 84 (1913)
Booth v. Indiana, 237 U.S. 391 (1915)
Bosley v. McLaughlin, 236 U.S. 385 (1915)
Boston Store of Chicago v. American Graphophone Co., 246 U.S. 8 (1918)
Bowman v. Chicago & Northwestern Railway Co., 125 U.S. 465 (1888)
Boyd v. United States, 116 U.S. 616 (1886)
Bradley v. City of Richmond, 227 U.S. 477 (1913)
Brand v. Union Elevated Railroad Co., 238 U.S. 586 (1915)
Brazee v. Michigan, 241 U.S. 340 (1916)
Breese & Dickerson v. United States, 226 U.S. 1 (1912)
Brougham v. Blanton Manufacturing Co., 249 U.S. 495 (1919)
Browning v. City of Waycross, 233 U.S. 16 (1914)
Buchanan v. Warley, 245 U.S. 60 (1917)
Bunting v. Oregon, 243 U.S. 426 (1917)
Burdeau v. McDowell, 256 U.S. 465 (1921)
Burdick v. United States, 236 U.S. 79 (1915)
Burleson v. Dempcy, 250 U.S. 191 (1919)
Butler v. Perry, 240 U.S. 328 (1916)
Caldwell v. Sioux Falls Stock Yards Co., 242 U.S. 559 (1917)
Calhoun v. Massie, 253 U.S. 170 (1920)
Caminetti v. United States, 242 U.S. 470 (1917)
Camp v. Boyd, 229 U.S. 530 (1913)
Carey v. South Dakota, 250 U.S. 118 (1919)
Central of Georgia Railway Co. v. Wright, 248 U.S. 525 (1919)

Champion v. Ames, see *Lottery Case*
Chesapeake & Ohio Railway Co. v. Conley, 230 U.S. 513 (1913)
Chesapeake & Ohio Railway Co. v. Gainey, 241 U.S. 494 (1916)
Chesapeake & Ohio Railway Co. v. Kelly, 241 U.S. 485 (1916)
Chicago, Burlington & Quincy Railroad Co. v. Harrington, 241 U.S. 177 (1916)
Chicago, Burlington & Quincy Railway v. United States, 220 U.S. 559 (1911)
Chicago Dock and Canal Co. v. Fraley, 228 U.S. 680 (1913)
Chicago, Indianapolis and Louisville Railway Co. v. United States, 219 U.S. 486 (1911)
Chicago, Rock Island & Pacific Railway Co. v. Hardwick Farmers Elevator Co., 226 U.S. 426 (1913)
Cincinnati, Covington & Erlanger Railway Co. v. Kentucky, 252 U.S. 408 (1920)
Citizens' Telephone Co. of Grand Rapids v. Fuller, 229 U.S. 322 (1913)
City and County of Denver v. New York Trust Co., 229 U.S. 123 (1913)
City of Covington v. South Covington & Cincinnati Street Railway Co., 246 U.S. 413 (1918)
City of Mitchell v. Dakota Central Telephone Co., 246 U.S. 396 (1918)
City of Owensboro v. Cumberland Telephone & Telegraph Co., 230 U.S. 58 (1913)
City of Sault Ste. Marie v. International Transit Co., 234 U.S. 333 (1914)
Clark Distilling Co. v. Western Maryland Railway Co., 242 U.S. 311 (1917)
Cleveland-Cliffs Iron Co. v. Arctic Iron Co., 248 U.S. 178 (1918)
Clyde Steamship Co. v. Walker, 244 U.S. 255 (1917)
Cohen v. Samuels, 245 U.S. 50 (1917)
Collins v. Texas, 223 U.S. 288 (1912)
Columbus Railway, Power & Light Co. v. City of Columbus, 249 U.S. 399 (1919)
Connolly v. Union Sewer Pipe Co., 184 U.S. 540 (1902)
Contributors to the Pennsylvania Hospital v. City of Philadelphia, 245 U.S. 20 (1917)
Coppage v. Kansas, 236 U.S. 1 (1915)
Coyle v. Smith, 221 U.S. 559 (1911)
Crane v. Johnson, 242 U.S. 339 (1917)
Cream of Wheat Co. v. County of Grand Forks, 253 U.S. 325 (1920)
Crozier v. Fried. Krupp Aktiengesellschaft, 224 U.S. 290 (1912)
Cubbins v. Mississippi River Commission, 241 U.S. 351 (1916)
Cumberland Glass Manufacturing Co. v. De Witt and Co., 237 U.S. 447 (1915)
Cuyahoga River Power Co. v. City of Akron, 240 U.S. 462 (1916)
Dakota Central Telephone Co. v. South Dakota, 250 U.S. 163 (1919)
Darling v. City of Newport News, 249 U.S. 540 (1919)
Dawson v. Kentucky Distilleries & Warehouse Co., 255 U.S. 288 (1921)
Day v. United States, 245 U.S. 159 (1917)
Debs v. United States, 249 U.S. 211 (1919)

Delaware, Lackawanna & Western Railroad Co. v. United States, 231 U.S. 363 (1913)
Delk v. St. Louis and San Francisco Railroad, 220 U.S. 580 (1911)
Detroit and Mackinac Railway Co. v. Michigan Railroad Commission and Fletcher Paper Co., 240 U.S. 564 (1916)
Detroit United Railway v. City of Detroit, 248 U.S. 429 (1919)
Detroit United Railway v. Michigan, 242 U.S. 238 (1916)
Diaz v. United States, 223 U.S. 442 (1912)
Dillon v. Gloss, 256 U.S. 368 (1921)
Dr. Miles Medical Co. v. John D. Park & Sons Co., 220 U.S. 373 (1911)
Dreier v. United States, 221 U.S. 394 (1911)
Duel v. Hollins, 241 U.S. 523 (1916)
Duplex Printing Press Co. v. Deering, 254 U.S. 443 (1921)
Eastern Cherokees, In re, 220 U.S. 83 (1911)
Eichel v. United States Fidelity & Guaranty Co., 245 U.S. 102 (1917)
Eisner v. Macomber, 252 U.S. 189 (1920)
Employers' Liability Cases, 207 U.S. 463 (1908)
Erie Railroad Co. v. Board of Public Utility Commissioners, 254 U.S. 394 (1921)
Erie Railroad Co. v. Hilt, 247 U.S. 97 (1918)
Erie Railroad Co. v. Shuart, 250 U.S. 465 (1919)
Erie Railroad Co. v. Welsh, 242 U.S. 303 (1916)
Erie Railroad Co. v. Winfield, 244 U.S. 170 (1917)
Evans v. Gore, 253 U.S. 245 (1920)
Evans v. National Bank of Savannah, 251 U.S. 108 (1919)
F. S. Royster Guano Co. v. Commonwealth of Virginia, 253 U.S. 412 (1920)
Farish v. State Banking Board of the State of Oklahoma, 235 U.S. 498 (1915)
Federal Trade Commission v. Gratz, 253 U.S. 421 (1920)
Fidelity & Columbia Trust Co. v. City of Louisville, 245 U.S. 54 (1917)
Fifth Avenue Coach Co. v. City of New York, 221 U.S. 467 (1911)
First National Bank of Bay City v. Fellows, 244 U.S. 416 (1917)
Five Per Cent. Discount Cases, 243 U.S. 97 (1917)
Flint v. Stone Tracy Co., 220 U.S. 107 (1911)
Fox v. Washington, 236 U.S. 273 (1915)
Frank v. Mangum, 237 U.S. 309 (1915)
Frohwerk v. United States, 249 U.S. 204 (1919)
Furness, Withy & Co., Ltd. v. Yang-Tsze Insurance Association, Ltd., 242 U.S. 430 (1917)
Galveston, Harrisburg & San Antonio Railway Co. v. Wallace, 223 U.S. 481 (1912)
Gardiner v. William S. Butler & Co., Inc., 245 U.S. 603 (1918)
Garrett v. Louisville & Nashville Railroad Co., 235 U.S. 308 (1914)

TABLE OF CASES 269

Gauzon v. Compañia General De Tabacos De Filipinas, 245 U.S. 86 (1917)
Gegiow v. Uhl, 239 U.S. 3 (1915)
Georgia, Florida & Alabama Railway Co. v. Blish Milling Co., 241 U.S. 190 (1916)
Georgia v. Trustees of the Cincinnati Southern Railway, 248 U.S. 26 (1918)
German Alliance Insurance Co. v. Lewis, 233 U.S. 389 (1914)
Gilbert v. Minnesota, 254 U.S. 325 (1920)
Gitlow v. New York, 268 U.S. 652 (1925)
Gompers v. Bucks Stove & Range Co., 221 U.S. 418 (1911)
Gouled v. United States, 255 U.S. 298 (1921)
Grand Trunk Western Railway Co. v. City of South Bend, 227 U.S. 544 (1913)
Grannis v. Ordean, 234 U.S. 385 (1914)
Great Northern Railway Co. v. Capital Trust Co., 242 U.S. 144 (1916)
Green v. Frazier, 253 U.S. 233 (1920)
Greenleaf Johnson Lumber Co. v. Garrison, 237 U.S. 251 (1915)
Guinn and Beal v. United States, 238 U.S. 347 (1915)
Hadacheck v. Sebastian, 239 U.S. 394 (1915)
Hall v. Geiger-Jones Co., 242 U.S. 539 (1917)
Hamilton v. Kentucky Distilleries & Warehouse Co., 251 U.S. 146 (1919)
Hammer v. Dagenhart, 247 U.S. 251 (1918)
Harris v. United States, 227 U.S. 340 (1913)
Hawkins v. Bleakly, 243 U.S. 210 (1917)
Heaton-Peninsular Button-Fastener Co. v. Eureka Specialty Co., 77 F. 288 (6th Cir. 1896)
Hebe Co. v. Shaw, 248 U.S. 297 (1919)
Heim v. McCall, 239 U.S. 175 (1915)
Hendrickson v. Apperson, 245 U.S. 105 (1917)
Hendrickson v. Creager, 245 U.S. 115 (1917)
Henry v. A. B. Dick Co., 224 U.S. 1 (1912)
Hipolite Egg Co. v. United States, 220 U.S. 45 (1911)
Hitchman Coal & Coke Co. v. Mitchell, 245 U.S. 229 (1917)
Hoke v. United States, 227 U.S. 308 (1913)
Holden v. Hardy, 169 U.S. 366 (1898)
Horn v. Mitchell, 243 U.S. 247 (1917)
Horning v. District of Columbia, 254 U.S. 135 (1920)
Houck v. Little River Drainage District, 239 U.S. 254 (1915)
Houston, East & West Texas Railway Co. v. United States, see *Shreveport Rate Cases*
Houston v. St. Louis Independent Packing Co., 249 U.S. 479 (1919)
Hull v. Philadelphia & Reading Railway Co., 252 U.S. 475 (1920)
Hutchinson v. City of Valdosta, 227 U.S. 303 (1913)
Hutchinson Ice Cream Co. v. Iowa, 242 U.S. 153 (1916)

Illinois Central Railroad Co. v. Behrens, 233 U.S. 473 (1914)
Illinois Central Railroad Co. v. Fuentes, 236 U.S. 157 (1915)
Illinois Central Railroad Co. v. Messina, 240 U.S. 395 (1916)
Illinois Central Railroad Co. v. Peery, 242 U.S. 292 (1916)
Inter-Island Steam Navigation Co., Ltd. v. Ward, 242 U.S. 1 (1916)
International Bridge Co. v. New York, 254 U.S. 126 (1920)
International News Service v. The Associated Press, 248 U.S. 215 (1918)
International Paper Co. v. The Schooner "Gracie D. Chambers," 248 U.S. 387 (1919)
Ives v. South Buffalo Railway Co., 201 N.Y. 271 (1911)
J. W. Goldsmith, Jr.-Grant Co. v. United States, 254 U.S. 505 (1921)
J. W. Perry Co. v. City of Norfolk, 220 U.S. 472 (1911)
Jackson v. State, 132 Md. Ct. App. 311, 103 A. 910 (1918)
Jacob Ruppert, A Corp. v. Caffey, 251 U.S. 264 (1920)
Jacobs v. Beecham, 221 U.S. 263 (1911)
Johnson v. Maryland, 254 U.S. 51 (1920)
Jones v. City of Portland, 245 U.S. 217 (1917)
Jones v. Interstate Commerce Commission, 245 U.S. 48 (1917)
Jones v. Perkins, 245 U.S. 390 (1918)
Kalem Co. v. Harper Brothers, 222 U.S. 55 (1911)
Kane v. New Jersey, 242 U.S. 160 (1916)
Kansas City Southern Railway Co. v. Leslie, 238 U.S. 599 (1915)
Kansas v. Burleson, 250 U.S. 188 (1919)
Kelley v. Gill, 245 U.S. 116 (1917)
Kiernan v. Portland, 223 U.S. 151 (1912)
Knickerbocker Ice Co. v. Stewart, 253 U.S. 149 (1920)
Knott v. St. Louis, Kansas City & Colorado Railroad Co., 230 U.S. 512 (1913)
Knott v. St. Louis Southwestern Railway Co., 230 U.S. 509 (1913)
Kreitlein v. Ferger, 238 U.S. 21 (1915)
Kronprinzessin Cecilie, The, 244 U.S. 12 (1917)
Lake Shore & Michigan Southern Railway Co. v. Clough, 242 U.S. 375 (1917)
Lankford v. Platte Iron Works Co., 235 U.S. 461 (1915)
Lapina v. Williams, 232 U.S. 78 (1914)
Lee Wilson & Co. v. United States, 245 U.S. 24 (1917)
Lehigh Valley Railroad Co. v. Barlow, 244 U.S. 183 (1917)
Lehon v. City of Atlanta, 242 U.S. 53 (1916)
Lewis v. Frick, 233 U.S. 291 (1914)
Lewis Publishing Co. v. Morgan, 229 U.S. 288 (1913)
Lewis Publishing Co. v. Wyman, 228 U.S. 610 (1913)
Light v. United States, 220 U.S. 523 (1911)
Lincoln Gas & Electric Light Co. v. City of Lincoln, 250 U.S. 256 (1919)

Lochner v. New York, 198 U.S. 45 (1905)
Long Sault Development Co. v. Call, 242 U.S. 272 (1916)
Lottery Case [Champion v. Ames] 188 U.S. 321 (1903)
Louisville & Nashville Railroad Co. v. Mottley, 219 U.S. 467 (1911)
Louisville & Nashville Railroad Co. v. Stewart, 241 U.S. 261 (1916)
Louisville & Nashville Railroad Co. v. United States, 242 U.S. 60 (1916)
Louisville Bridge Co. v. United States, 242 U.S. 409 (1917)
Ludwig v. Western Union Telegraph Co., 216 U.S. 146 (1910)
Luther v. Borden, 7 How. (48 U.S.) 1 (1849)
Lynch v. Hornby, 247 U.S. 339 (1918)
Lynch v. Turrish, 247 U.S. 221 (1918)
Mackenzie v. Hare, 239 U.S. 299 (1915)
Macleod v. New England Telephone & Telegraph Co., 250 U.S. 195 (1919)
Madera Water Works v. Madera, 228 U.S. 454 (1913)
Maguire v. Trefry, 253 U.S. 12 (1920)
Mail Divisor Cases, 251 U.S. 326 (1920)
Manners v. Morosco, 252 U.S. 317 (1920)
Marbury v. Madison, 1 Cranch (5 U.S.) 137 (1803)
Marcus Brown Holding Co., Inc. v. Feldman, 256 U.S. 170 (1921)
Maxwell v. Bugbee, 250 U.S. 525 (1919)
McCabe v. Atchison, Topeka & Santa Fe Railway Co., 235 U.S. 151 (1914)
McCluskey v. Marysville & Northern Railway Co., 243 U.S. 36 (1917)
McCulloch v. Maryland, 4 Wheat. (17 U.S.) 316 (1819)
McGowan v. Parish, 228 U.S. 312 (1913)
McKinley v. United States, 249 U.S. 397 (1919)
McNaughton v. Johnson, 242 U.S. 344 (1917)
Merrick v. N. W. Halsey & Co., 242 U.S. 568 (1917)
Metropolis Theatre Co. v. City of Chicago, 228 U.S. 61 (1913)
Meyer v. Wells, Fargo & Co., 223 U.S. 298 (1912)
Middleton v. Texas Power & Light Co., 249 U.S. 152 (1919)
Miller v. Wilson, 236 U.S. 373 (1915)
Minneapolis & St. Louis Railroad Co. v. Bombolis, 241 U.S. 211 (1916)
Minneapolis & St. Louis Railroad Co. v. Winters, 242 U.S. 353 (1917)
Minnesota Rate Cases, 230 U.S. 352 (1913)
Missouri v. Holland, 252 U.S. 416 (1920)
Missouri Pacific Railway Co. v. Castle, 224 U.S. 541 (1912)
Missouri Pacific Railway Co. v. Kansas, 248 U.S. 276 (1919)
Missouri Pacific Railway Co. v. McGrew Coal Co., 244 U.S. 191 (1917)
Missouri Rate Cases, 230 U.S. 474 (1913)
Motion Picture Patents Co. v. Universal Film Manufacturing Co., 243 U.S. 502 (1917)

Mt. Vernon-Woodberry Cotton Duck Co. v. Alabama Interstate Power Co., 240 U.S. 30 (1916)
Mountain Timber Co. v. Washington, 243 U.S. 219 (1917)
Muller v. Oregon, 208 U.S. 412 (1908)
Munn v. Illinois, 94 U.S. 113 (1876)
Mutual Film Co. v. Industrial Commission of Ohio, 236 U.S. 247 (1915)
Mutual Film Corporation v. Industrial Commission of Ohio, 236 U.S. 230 (1915)
Mutual Film Corporation of Missouri v. Hodges, 236 U.S. 248 (1915)
Mutual Loan Co. v. Martell, 222 U.S. 225 (1911)
Myles Salt Co., Ltd. v. Board of Commissioners of the Iberia and St. Mary Drainage District, 239 U.S. 478 (1916)
National Phonograph Co. v. Schlegel, 128 F. 733 (8th Cir. 1904)
National Prohibition Cases, 253 U.S. 350 (1920)
Neilson v. Rhine Shipping Co., 248 U.S. 205 (1918)
New York Central & Hudson River Railroad Co. v. Carr, 238 U.S. 260 (1915)
New York Central Railroad Co. v. Bianc, 250 U.S. 596 (1919)
New York Central Railroad Co. v. White, 243 U.S. 188 (1917)
New York Central Railroad Co. v. Winfield, 244 U.S. 147 (1917)
New York ex rel. New York & Queens Gas Co. v. McCall, 245 U.S. 345 (1917)
New York Life Insurance Co. v. Deer Lodge County, 231 U.S. 495 (1913)
New York Life Insurance Co. v. Head, 234 U.S. 149 (1914)
New York, Philadelphia & Norfolk Railroad Co. v. Peninsula Produce Exchange, 240 U.S. 34 (1916)
New York Scaffolding Co. v. Chain Belt Co., 254 U.S. 32 (1920)
New York Scaffolding Co. v. Liebel-Binney Construction Co., 254 U.S. 24 (1920)
New York v. New Jersey & Passaic Valley Sewerage Commissioners, 256 U.S. 296 (1921)
Newberry v. United States, 256 U.S. 232 (1921)
Norfolk & Suburban Turnpike Co. v. Virginia, 225 U.S. 264 (1912)
Norfolk & Western Railway Co. v. Holbrook, 235 U.S. 625 (1915)
North Carolina Railroad Co. v. Zachary, 232 U.S. 248 (1914)
Northern Ohio Traction & Light Co. v. Ohio, 245 U.S. 574 (1918)
Northern Pacific Railway Co. v. Meese, 239 U.S. 614 (1916)
Northern Pacific Railway Co. v. North Dakota, 250 U.S. 135 (1919)
Northern Pacific Railway Co. v. Trodick, 221 U.S. 208 (1911)
Northern Pacific Railway Co. v. Wall, 241 U.S. 87 (1916)
Northern Pacific Railway Co. v. Washington, 222 U.S. 370 (1912)
Northwestern Laundry v. City of Des Moines, 239 U.S. 486 (1916)
Nye v. United States, 313 U.S. 33 (1941)
Ocean Steam Navigation Co., Ltd. v. Mellor, 233 U.S. 718 (1914)
Ohio ex rel. Davis v. Hildebrant, 241 U.S. 565 (1916)

Ohio Tax Cases, 232 U.S. 576 (1914)
Ohio Valley Water Co. v. Ben Avon Borough, 253 U.S. 287 (1920)
Old Colony Trust Co. v. City of Omaha, 230 U.S. 100 (1913)
Omaha & Council Bluffs Street Railway Co. v. Interstate Commerce Commission, 230 U.S. 324 (1913)
O'Neill v. Leamer, 239 U.S. 244 (1915)
Oregon Railroad & Navigation Co. v. Campbell, 230 U.S. 525 (1913)
Owensboro, Kentucky v. Owensboro Water Works Co., 243 U.S. 166 (1917)
Pacific States Telephone and Telegraph Co. v. Oregon, 223 U.S. 118 (1912)
Paine Lumber Co., Ltd. v. Neal, 244 U.S. 459 (1917)
Park & Tilford, Ex parte, 245 U.S. 82 (1917)
Patsone v. Pennsylvania, 232 U.S. 138 (1914)
Pedersen v. Delaware, Lackawanna & Western Railroad Co., 229 U.S. 146 (1913)
Pennsylvania Co. v. United States, 236 U.S. 351 (1915)
Pennsylvania Railroad Co. v. Clark Brothers Coal Mining Co., 238 U.S. 456 (1915)
Pennsylvania Railroad Co. v. Public Service Commission, 250 U.S. 566 (1919)
Pennsylvania Railroad Co. v. Sonman Shaft Coal Co., 242 U.S. 120 (1916)
Pennsylvania Railroad Co. v. Towers, 245 U.S. 6 (1917)
Pennsylvania Railroad Co. v. W. F. Jacoby & Co., 242 U.S. 89 (1916)
Peters v. Veasey, 251 U.S. 121 (1919)
Peterson, Ex parte, 253 U.S. 300 (1920)
Philadelphia, Baltimore & Washington Railroad Co. v. Schubert, 224 U.S. 603 (1912)
Pierce v. United States, 252 U.S. 239 (1920)
Pipe Line Cases, 234 U.S. 548 (1914)
Plant v. Woods, 176 Mass. 492 (1900)
Plessy v. Ferguson, 163 U.S. 537 (1896)
Port Richmond & Bergen Point Ferry Co. v. Board of Chosen Freeholders of Hudson County, 234 U.S. 317 (1914)
Porto Rico v. Rosaly Y Castillo, 227 U.S. 270 (1913)
Puget Sound Traction, Light & Power Co. v. Reynolds, 244 U.S. 574 (1917)
Pullman Co. v. Kansas, 216 U.S. 56 (1910)
Purity Extract and Tonic Co. v. Lynch, 226 U.S. 192 (1912)
Quong Wing v. Kirkendall, 223 U.S. 59 (1912)
Rail & River Coal Co. v. Yaple, 236 U.S. 338 (1915)
Railroad Commission of Louisiana v. Texas & Pacific Railway Co., 229 U.S. 336 (1913)
Rainey v. W. R. Grace & Co., 231 U.S. 703 (1914)
Rast v. Van Deman & Lewis Co., 240 U.S. 342 (1916)
Raymond v. Chicago, Milwaukee & St. Paul Railway Co., 243 U.S. 43 (1917)
Reinman v. Little Rock, 237 U.S. 171 (1915)

Rosen v. United States, 245 U.S. 467 (1918)
Rosenthal v. New York, 226 U.S. 260 (1912)
Ruddy v. Rossi, 248 U.S. 104 (1918)
St. Louis & San Francisco Railroad Co. v. Brown, 241 U.S. 223 (1916)
St. Louis, Iron Mountain & Southern Railway Co. v. Craft, 237 U.S. 648 (1915)
St. Louis, Iron Mountain & Southern Railway Co. v. Edwards, 227 U.S. 265 (1913)
St. Louis, Iron Mountain & Southern Railway Co. v. United States, 251 U.S. 198 (1920)
St. Louis, Iron Mountain & Southern Railway Co. v. Wynne, 224 U.S. 354 (1912)
Sandberg v. McDonald, 248 U.S. 185 (1918)
Savage v. Jones, 225 U.S. 501 (1912)
Schaefer v. United States, 251 U.S. 466 (1920)
Scharrenberg v. Dollar Steamship Co., 245 U.S. 122 (1917)
Schenck v. United States, 249 U.S. 47 (1919)
Schlemmer v. Buffalo, Rochester & Pittsburg Railway, 220 U.S. 590 (1911)
Schmidinger v. City of Chicago, 226 U.S. 578 (1913)
Seaboard Air Line Railway v. City of Raleigh, 242 U.S. 15 (1916)
Second Employers' Liability Cases, 223 U.S. 1 (1912)
Selective Draft Law Cases, 245 U.S. 366 (1918)
Sena v. American Turquoise Co., 220 U.S. 497 (1911)
Seton Hall College v. Village of South Orange, 242 U.S. 100 (1916)
Seven Cases of Eckman's Alternative v. United States, 239 U.S. 510 (1916)
Shaffer v. Carter, 252 U.S. 37 (1920)
Shanks v. Delaware, Lackawanna & Western Railroad Co., 239 U.S. 556 (1916)
Shreveport Rate Cases [Houston and Texas Railway v. United States], 234 U.S. 342 (1914)
Silverthorne Lumber Co. v. United States, 251 U.S. 385 (1920)
Sim v. Edenborn, 242 U.S. 131 (1916)
Sioux Remedy Co. v. Cope, 235 U.S. 197 (1914)
Slaughter-House Cases, 16 Wall. (83 U.S.) 36 (1872)
Sligh v. Kirkwood, 237 U.S. 52 (1915)
Smith v. Hitchcock, 226 U.S. 53 (1912)
Smith v. Interstate Commerce Commission, 245 U.S. 33 (1917)
Smith v. Interstate Commerce Commission, 245 U.S. 47 (1917)
Smoot v. Heyl, 227 U.S. 518 (1913)
South Covington & Cincinnati Street Railway Co. v. City of Covington, 235 U.S. 537 (1915)
South Covington & Cincinnati Street Railway Co. v. Kentucky, 252 U.S. 399 (1920)
Southern Express Co. v. Byers, 240 U.S. 612 (1916)
Southern Pacific Co. v. Bogert, 250 U.S. 483 (1919)
Southern Pacific Co. v. Campbell, 230 U.S. 537 (1913)

TABLE OF CASES

Southern Pacific Co. v. Interstate Commerce Commission, 219 U.S. 433 (1911)
Southern Pacific Co. v. Jensen, 244 U.S. 205 (1917)
Southern Pacific Co. v. Kentucky, 222 U.S. 63 (1911)
Southern Pacific Co. v. Lowe, 247 U.S. 330 (1918)
Southern Railway Co. v. Lloyd, 239 U.S. 496 (1916)
Southern Railway Co. v. Puckett, 244 U.S. 571 (1917)
Southern Railway Co. v. Reid, 222 U.S. 424 (1912)
Southern Railway Co. v. United States, 222 U.S. 20 (1911)
Sports and General Press Agency, Ltd. v. "Our Dogs" Publishing Co., Ltd., [1916] 2 K.B. 880
Stalker v. Oregon Short Line Railroad Co., 225 U.S. 142 (1912)
Standard Oil Co. of New Jersey v. United States, 221 U.S. 1 (1911)
Standard Sanitary Manufacturing Co. v. United States, 226 U.S. 20 (1912)
Standard Stock Food Co. v. Wright, 225 U.S. 540 (1912)
Standard Varnish Works v. Steamship "Bris," 248 U.S. 392 (1919)
Steamship Appam, The, 243 U.S. 124 (1917)
Stilson v. United States, 250 U.S. 583 (1919)
Stratton's Independence, Ltd. v. Howbert, 231 U.S. 399 (1913)
Street v. Lincoln Safe Deposit Co., 254 U.S. 88 (1920)
Sugarman v. United States, 249 U.S. 182 (1919)
Sullivan v. City of Shreveport, 251 U.S. 169 (1919)
Sy Joc Lieng v. Gregorio Sy Quia, 228 U.S. 335 (1913)
Taylor v. Columbian University, 226 U.S. 126 (1912)
Terminal Taxicab Co. v. Kutz, 241 U.S. 252 (1916)
Texas & New Orleans Railroad Co. v. Sabine Tram Co., 227 U.S. 111 (1913)
Texas & Pacific Railway Co. v. Leatherwood, 250 U.S. 478 (1919)
Texas & Pacific Railway Co. v. Rigsby, 241 U.S. 33 (1916)
Thames and Mersey Marine Insurance Company, Ltd. v. United States, 237 U.S. 19 (1915)
Thornton v. Duffy, 254 U.S. 361 (1920)
Toledo Newspaper Co. v. United States, 247 U.S. 402 (1918)
Towne v. Eisner, 245 U.S. 418 (1918)
Travis v. Yale & Towne Manufacturing Co., 252 U.S. 60 (1920)
Truax v. Raich, 239 U.S. 33 (1915)
Tyrrell v. District of Columbia, 243 U.S. 1 (1917)
Union Tank Line Co. v. Wright, 249 U.S. 275 (1919)
United Shoe Machinery Corp. v. United States, 258 U.S. 451 (1922)
United States ex rel. Milwaukee Social Democratic Publishing Co. v. Burleson, 255 U.S. 407 (1921)
United States v. A. Schrader's Son, Inc., 252 U.S. 85 (1920)
United States v. American Tobacco Co., 221 U.S. 106 (1911)

United States v. Anderson, 228 U.S. 52 (1913)
United States v. Antikamnia Chemical Co., 231 U.S. 654 (1914)
United States v. Archer, 241 U.S. 119 (1916)
United States v. Chase, 245 U.S. 89 (1917)
United States v. Chavez, 228 U.S. 525 (1913)
United States v. Citroen, 223 U.S. 407 (1912)
United States v. Colgate & Co., 250 U.S. 300 (1919)
United States v. Curtiss-Wright Export Corp., 299 U.S. 304 (1936)
United States v. Delaware & Hudson Co., 213 U.S. 366 (1909)
United States v. Doremus, 249 U.S. 86 (1919)
United States v. E. C. Knight Co., 156 U.S. 1 (1895)
United States v. Erie Railroad Co., 220 U.S. 275 (1911)
United States v. Freight Association, 166 U.S. 290 (1897)
United States v. Goelet, 232 U.S. 293 (1914)
United States v. Grimaud, 220 U.S. 506 (1911)
United States v. Hamburg-Amerikanische Packetfahrt-Aktien Gesellschaft, 239 U.S. 466 (1916)
United States v. Hammers, 221 U.S. 220 (1911)
United States v. Hill, 248 U.S. 420 (1919)
United States v. Holte, 236 U.S. 140 (1915)
United States v. Johnson, 221 U.S. 488 (1911)
United States v. Joint Traffic Association, 171 U.S. 505 (1898)
United States v. Lehigh Valley Railroad Co., 220 U.S. 257 (1911)
United States v. Lexington Mill & Elevator Co., 232 U.S. 399 (1914)
United States v. Louisville & Nashville Railroad Co., 236 U.S. 318 (1915)
United States v. Midwest Oil Co., 236 U.S. 459 (1915)
United States v. Mosley, 238 U.S. 383 (1915)
United States v. Reading Co., 253 U.S. 26 (1920)
United States v. Reynolds, 235 U.S. 133 (1914)
United States v. St. Paul, Minneapolis & Manitoba Railway Co., 247 U.S. 310 (1918)
United States v. Schider, 246 U.S. 519 (1918)
United States v. Simpson, 252 U.S. 465 (1920)
United States v. Société Anonyme des Anciens Etablissements Cail, 224 U.S. 309 (1912)
United States v. Toledo Newspaper Co., 220 F. 458 (N.D. Ohio 1915)
United States v. Trans-Missouri Freight Association, 166 U.S. 290 (1897)
United States v. United Shoe Machinery Co., 247 U.S. 32 (1918)
United States v. United States Steel Corp., 251 U.S. 417 (1920)
United States v. Wheeler, 254 U.S. 281 (1920)
United States v. Winslow, 227 U.S. 202 (1913)

United States Express Co. v. Minnesota, 223 U.S. 335 (1912)
Valdez v. United States, 244 U.S. 432 (1917)
Valley Steamship Co. v. Wattawa, 244 U.S. 202 (1917)
Vandalia Railroad Co. v. Public Service Commission of Indiana, 242 U.S. 255 (1916)
Vegelahn v. Guntner, 167 Mass. 92 (1896)
Virtue v. Creamery Package Manufacturing Co., 227 U.S. 8 (1913)
Walls v. Midland Carbon Co., 254 U.S. 300 (1920)
Watts, Watts & Co., Ltd. v. Unione Austriaca di Navigazione, 248 U.S. 9 (1918)
Webb v. United States, 249 U.S. 96 (1919)
Weeks v. United States, 232 U.S. 383 (1914)
Weeks v. United States, 245 U.S. 618 (1918)
Wells v. Roper, 246 U.S. 335 (1917)
West v. Kansas Natural Gas Co., 221 U.S. 229 (1911)
Western Oil Refining Co. v. Lipscomb, 244 U.S. 346 (1917)
Western Union Telegraph Co. v. Boegli, 251 U.S. 315 (1920)
Western Union Telegraph Co. v. Brown, 234 U.S. 542 (1914)
Western Union Telegraph Co. v. Kansas, 216 U.S. 1 (1910)
Western Union Telegraph Co. v. Speight, 254 U.S. 17 (1920)
Westinghouse Electric & Mfg. Co. v. Wagner Electric Mfg. Co., 225 U.S. 604 (1912)
Weyerhaeuser v. Hoyt, 219 U.S. 380 (1911)
Wheeler v. City and County of Denver, 229 U.S. 342 (1913)
Wheeler v. Sohmer, 233 U.S. 434 (1914)
William Cramp and Sons Ship and Engine Building Co. v. United States, 239 U.S. 221 (1915)
William R. Staats Co. v. Security Trust and Savings Bank, 243 U.S. 121 (1917)
Williams v. United States, 255 U.S. 336 (1921)
Wilson v. New, 243 U.S. 332 (1917)
Wilson v. United States, 221 U.S. 361 (1911)
Yazoo & Mississippi Valley Railroad Co. v. Greenwood Grocery Co., 227 U.S. 1 (1913)

SELECTED BIBLIOGRAPHY

Abraham, Henry J. *Justices and Presidents: A Political History of Appointments to the Supreme Court.* 3d ed. New York: Oxford University Press, 1992.
Abraham, Henry J., and Edward M. Goldberg. "A Note on the Appointment of Justices of the Supreme Court of the United States." *American Bar Association Journal* 46 (1960): 147–50, 219–22.
Acheson, Dean. *Morning and Noon.* Boston: Houghton Mifflin Co., 1965.
Adelstein, Richard P. "Islands of Conscious Power: Louis D. Brandeis and the Modern Corporation." *Business History Review* 63 (1989): 614–56.
Aichele, Gary J. *Oliver Wendell Holmes, Jr.: Soldier, Scholar, Judge.* Boston: Twayne Publishers, 1989.
"Another Supreme Court 'Radical.'" *Literary Digest* 53 (July 1916): 240–41.
Arnold, Peri. "The Intellectual Roots of the Progressive Era Presidency." *Miller Center Journal* 1 (spring 1994): 25–33.
"The Attorney-General in Hot Water." *Literary Digest* 47 (July 1913): 39–41.
Baker, Liva. *The Justice from Beacon Hill: The Life and Times of Oliver Wendell Holmes.* New York: Harper Collins, 1991.
Baldwin, Elbert F. "The Supreme Court Justices." *Outlook* 97 (January 1911): 160.
Barker, Charles E. *With President Taft in the White House.* Chicago: A. Kroch and Son, 1947.
Belknap, Michal R. "Mr. Justice Pitney and Progressivism." *Seton Hall Law Review* 16 (1986): 381–426.
Beth, Loren P. *John Marshall Harlan: The Last Whig Justice.* Lexington: University Press of Kentucky, 1992.
———. "Justice Harlan and the Chief Justiceship, 1910." *Supreme Court Historical Society Yearbook* (1983) 6: 73–79.
———. *The Development of the American Constitution, 1877–1917.* New York: Harper & Row, 1971.
———. "Justice Harlan and the Uses of Dissent." *American Political Science Review* 49 (1955): 1085–1104.
Bickel, Alexander M. "Mr. Taft Rehabilitates the Court." *Yale Law Journal* 79 (November 1969): 1–45.
———. *The Unpublished Opinions of Mr. Justice Brandeis.* Chicago: University Chicago Press, 1967.

Bickel, Alexander M., and Benno C. Schmidt Jr. *History of the Supreme Court of the United States: The Judiciary and Responsible Government, 1910–21.* New York: Macmillan, 1984.

Biddle, Francis. *A Casual Past.* Garden City, N.Y.: Doubleday, 1961.

Birkby, Robert H. "Teaching Congress How to Do Its Work: Mr. Justice McReynolds and Maritime Torts." *Congressional Studies* 8 (1981): 11–20.

Blaisdell, Doris Ariane. "The Constitutional Law of Mr. Justice McReynolds." Ph.D. diss., University of Wisconsin, 1954.

Blaustein, Albert P., and Roy M. Mersky. *The First One Hundred Justices: Statistical Studies on the Supreme Court of the United States.* Hamden, Conn.: Archon Books, 1978.

Bond, James E. *I Dissent: The Legacy of Chief Justice James Clark McReynolds.* Fairfax, Va.: George Mason University Press, 1992. ("Chief Justice" is a misprint.)

Bowen, Catherine Drinker. *Yankee from Olympus: Justice Holmes and His Family.* Boston: Little, Brown, 1944.

Breed, Alan R. "Mahlon Pitney: His Life and Career, Political and Judicial." B.A. thesis, Princeton University, 1932.

Brill, Abraham A. "The Introduction and Development of Freud's Work in the United States." *American Journal of Sociology* 45 (November 1939): 318–25.

Broderick, Francis L. *Progressivism at Risk: Electing a President in 1912.* New York: Greenwood Press, 1989.

Buenker, John D. "The Progressive Era: A Search for Synthesis." *Mid-America* 51 (1969): 175–93.

Butler, Charles Henry. *A Century at the Bar of the Supreme Court of the United States.* New York: G. P. Putnam's Sons, 1942.

Butt, Archibald W. *Taft and Roosevelt: The Intimate Letters of Archie Butt Military Aide.* Garden City, N.Y.: Doubleday, Doran & Co., 1930.

Carpenter, William S. *Judicial Tenure in the United States.* New Haven, Conn.: Yale University Press, 1918.

Carrington, Paul D. "Hail! Langdell!" *Law & Social Inquiry* 20 (summer 1995): 691–760.

Carson, Hampton L. "Tribute to Chief Justice White." *Report of the Forty-Fourth Annual Meeting of the American Bar Association* (Baltimore: The Lord Baltimore Press, 1921) 6: 25–30.

Carter, Newman. "Edward D. White in Personal Retrospect." *Supreme Court Historical Society Yearbook* (1979): 5–7.

Cassidy, Lewis C. "An Evaluation of Chief Justice White." *Mississippi Law Journal* 10 (February 1938): 136–53.

Cavanaugh, Rev. John, C.S.C. "Recollections of Judge White." *Annals of Our Lady of Lourdes* 38 (1921): 88–91, 115–16, 144–46.

Chafee, Zechariah, Jr. *Free Speech in the United States.* New York: Atheneum, 1969.

Chambers, John Whiteclay, II. *The Tyranny of Change: America in the Progressive Era, 1900–1917.* New York: St. Martin's Press, 1980.

Clarke, John H. "Methods of Work of the United States Supreme Court Judges." *Ohio Law Reporter* 20 (1922): 398–408.

Clevenger, William M. *The Courts of New Jersey: Their Origin, Composition and Jurisdiction.* Plainfield: New Jersey Law Journal Publishing Co., 1903.

Closen, Michael L., and Robert J. Dzielak. "The History and Influence of the Law Review Institution." *Akron Law Review* 30 (1996): 15–53.
Cohen, Jeremy. "Schenck v. United States: A Clear and Present Danger to the First Amendment." Ph.D. diss., University of Washington, 1983.
Cohen, William. *At Freedom's Edge: Black Mobility and the Southern White Quest for Racial Control, 1861–1915*. Baton Rouge: Louisiana State University Press, 1991.
Coletta, Paolo E. *The Presidency of William Howard Taft*. Lawrence: The University Press of Kansas, 1973.
Conot, Robert. *A Streak of Luck*. New York: Seaview Books, 1979.
Cook, David A. *A History of Narrative Film*. New York: W. W. Norton, 1981.
Cook, Raymond Allen. *Fire from the Flint: The Amazing Careers of Thomas Dixon*. Winston-Salem, N.C.: John F. Blair, 1968.
Corwin, Edward S. *The Twilight of the Supreme Court: A History of Our Constitutional Theory*. New Haven, Conn.: Yale University Press, 1934.
Cray, William C. *Miles 1884–1984: A Centennial History*. Englewood Cliffs, N.J.: Prentice Hall, 1984.
Cripps, Thomas. *Slow Fade to Black: The Negro in American Film, 1900–1942*. New York: Oxford University Press, 1977.
Croly, Herbert. *The Promise of American Life*. New York: Macmillan, 1909.
Crosby, Alfred W. *America's Forgotten Pandemic: The Influenza of 1918*. Cambridge: Cambridge University Press, 1989.
Curtis, Michael Kent. *No State Shall Abridge: The Fourteenth Amendment and the Bill of Rights*. Durham, N.C.: Duke University Press, 1986.
Cushman, Barry. "Doctrinal Synergies and Liberal Dilemmas: The Case of the Yellow-Dog Contract." *The Supreme Court Review* (1992): 235–93.
Dale, Edward E., and Morris L. Wardell. *History of Oklahoma*. Englewood Cliffs, N.J.: Prentice-Hall, 1948.
Danelski, David J. "The Influence of the Chief Justice in the Decisional Process." In *Courts, Judges, and Politics: An Introduction to the Judicial Process,* 2d ed., edited by Walter F. Murphy and C. Herman Pritchett. New York: Random House, 1974.
Danelski, David J., and Joseph S. Tulchin, eds. *The Autobiographical Notes of Charles Evans Hughes*. Cambridge, Mass.: Harvard University Press, 1973.
Daniel, Pete. *The Shadow of Slavery: Peonage in the South, 1901–1969*. Urbana: University of Illinois Press, 1972.
Daniels, Josephus. *The Wilson Era: Years of Peace, 1910–1917.* Chapel Hill: University of North Carolina Press, 1944.
Dart, Henry P. *Louisiana Reports* 149 (1922): xii.
———. "Edward Douglas White." *Louisiana Historical Quarterly* 5 (April 1922): 145–51.
———. "Edward Douglas White." *Loyola Law Journal* 3 (November 1921): 1–13.
Dávila-Colón, Luis R. "Equal Citizenship, Self-Determination, and the U.S. Statehood Process: A Constitutional and Historical Analysis." *Case Western Reserve Journal of International Law* 13 (spring 1981): 315 74.
Davis, John W. "Edward Douglass White." *American Bar Association Journal* 7 (1921): 377–82.

DeSantis, Vincent P. *The Shaping of Modern America: 1877–1920.* 2d ed. Wheeling, Ill.: Forum Press, 1989.
Diner, Steven J. *A Very Different Age: Americans of the Progressive Era.* New York: Hill and Wang, 1998.
Dinnerstein, Leonard. *The Leo Frank Case.* New York: Columbia University Press, 1968.
Dishman, Robert B. "Mr. Justice White and the Rule of Reason." *Review of Politics* 13 (1951): 229–43.
Dubofsky, Melvyn. *We Shall Be All: A History of the Industrial Workers of the World.* 2d ed. Urbana: University of Illinois Press, 1988.
Dunn, Arthur Wallace. *From Harrison to Harding: A Personal Narrative, Covering a Third of a Century, 1888–1921.* New York: G. P. Putnam's Sons, 1922.
Early, Stephen Tyree. "James Clark McReynolds and the Judicial Process." Ph.D. diss., University of Virginia, 1954.
Epstein, Lee, Jeffrey A. Segal, Harold J. Spaeth, and Thomas G. Walker. *The Supreme Court Compendium: Data, Decisions, and Developments.* 2d ed. Washington, D.C.: Congressional Quarterly, 1996.
———. *The Supreme Court Compendium: Data, Decisions, and Developments.* Washington, D.C.: Congressional Quarterly, 1994.
Ernst, Daniel. "The Yellow-Dog Contract And Liberal Reform, 1917–1932." *Labor History* 30 (spring 1989): 251–74.
Farrelly, David G. "Harlan's Formative Period: The Years Before the War." *Kentucky Law Journal* 46 (1958): 367–406.
Fegan, Hugh J. "Edward Douglass White, Jurist and Statesman." Parts 1–3. *Georgetown Law Journal* 14 (November 1925): 1–21; (January 1926): 148–68; 15 (November 1926): 1–23.
Finkelman, Paul, ed. *Race, Law and American History, 1700–1990.* Vol. 4, *The Age of Jim Crow: Segregation from the End of Reconstruction to the Great Depression.* New York: Garland Publishing, 1992.
Fletcher, R. V. "Mr. Justice McReynolds—An Appreciation." *Vanderbilt Law Review* 2 (1948): 35–46.
Foraker, Joseph Benson. *Notes of a Busy Life.* 2d ed. 2 vols. Cincinnati: Stewart & Kidd Co., 1916.
Forman, William H., Jr. "Chief Justice Edward Douglass White." *American Bar Association Journal* 56 (1970): 260–62.
Fox, Eleanor M., and Lawrence A. Sullivan. "The Good and Bad Trust Dichotomy: A Short History of a Legal Idea." *Antitrust Bulletin* 35 (spring 1990): 57–82.
Frank, John P. *Marble Palace: The Supreme Court in American Life.* New York: Knopf, 1958.
———. "The Legal Ethics of Louis D. Brandeis." *Stanford Law Review* 17 (1965): 683–709.
———. "The Appointment of Supreme Court Justices: Prestige, Principles, and Politics." *Wisconsin Law Review* (1941): 172–210, 343–79, 461–512.
Frankfurter, Felix. "Chief Justices I Have Known." *Supreme Court Historical Society Yearbook* (1980): 3–9.

———. "The Supreme Court in the Mirror of Justices." *University of Pennsylvania Law Review* 105 (1957): 781–96.
———. "Chief Justices I Have Known." *Virginia Law Review* 39 (1953): 883–905.
———. *Mr. Justice Holmes and the Supreme Court*. Cambridge, Mass.: Harvard University Press, 1938.
Frankfurter, Frankfurter, and James M. Landis. *The Business of the Supreme Court: A Study in the Federal Judicial System*. New York: Macmillan, 1928.
Franklin, John Hope. "'Birth of a Nation'—Propaganda as History." *Massachusetts Review* 20 (autumn 1979): 417–34.
Garwood, Hiram M. "Chief Justice Edward Douglass White." *Report of the Louisiana Bar Association for 1923* 24 (1923): 151–66.
Gilbert, Stirling P. *James Clark McReynolds, 1862–1946, Justice of the Supreme Court of the United States of America* (1946), microform: Pamphlets in American History, Biography, B1517.
Goings, Kenneth W. *"The NAACP Comes of Age": The Defeat of Judge John J. Parker*. Bloomington: Indiana University Press, 1990.
Gompers, Samuel. *Seventy Years of Life and Labor: An Autobiography*. New York: E. P. Dutton & Co., 1925.
Gordon, Robert W., ed. *The Legacy of Oliver Wendell Holmes, Jr*. Palo Alto: Stanford University Press, 1992.
Gould, Lewis L. *Reform and Regulation: American Politics from Roosevelt to Wilson*. 2d ed. New York: Knopf, 1986.
———. "Willis Van Devanter in Wyoming Politics, 1884–1897." Ph.D. diss., Yale University, 1966.
Gramling, Oliver. *AP: The Story of News*. New York: Farrar and Rinehart, 1940.
Green, John W. "Judge Horace H. Lurton." In *Law and Lawyers: Sketches of the Federal Judges of Tennessee, Sketches of the Attorneys General of Tennessee, Legal Miscellany, Reminiscences by John W. Green*, 79–84. Jackson, Tenn.: McCowat-Mercer Press, 1950.
Grossman, Joel B. *Lawyers and Judges: The ABA and the Politics of Judicial Selection*. New York: John Wiley & Sons, 1965.
———. "The Role of the American Bar Association in the Selection of Federal Judges: Episodic Involvement to Institutionalized Power." *Vanderbilt Law Review* 17 (1964): 785–814.
Haig, J. F. "The Supreme Court of the United States." *Independent* 69 (November 1910): 1038-39.
Hall, Kermit L., ed. *The Oxford Companion to the Supreme Court of the United States*. New York: Oxford University Press, 1992.
———. *Civil Rights in American History: Major Historical Interpretations*. New York: Garland Publishing, 1987.
Hamilton, Virginia Van der Veer. "In Defense of Order and Stability: The Constitutional Philosophy of Chief Justice Edward Douglass White." *Reviews in American History* 10 (1982): 105–8.
Hamm, Richard F. "Southerners and the Shaping of the Eighteenth Amendment, 1914–1917." *Georgia Journal of Southern Legal History* 1 (1991): 81–107.

Harris, Joseph P. *The Advice and Consent of the Senate*. Berkeley: University of California Press, 1953.

Hart, W. O. "Edward Douglass White—A Tribute." *Loyola Law Journal* 7 (July 1926): 150–58.

Hendrick, Burton J. "Another Radical for the Supreme Court." *World's Work* 33 (November 1916): 95–98.

———. "James C. McReynolds: Attorney-General and Believer in the Sherman Law." *World's Work* 27 (November 1913): 26.

Highsaw, Robert B. *Edward Douglass White, Defender of the Conservative Faith*. Baton Rouge: Louisiana State University Press, 1981.

Hixson, William B., Jr. "Moorfield Storey and the Struggle for Equality." *Journal of American History* 55 (1968): 533–54.

Hoffheimer, Michael H. *Justice Holmes and Natural Law*. New York: Garland Publishing, 1992.

Hoffman, Frederick A. *Freudianism and the Literary Mind*. Baton Rouge: Louisiana State University Press, 1945.

Holsinger, M. Paul. "The Appointment of Supreme Court Justice Van Devanter: A Study of Political Preferment." *American Journal of Legal History* 12 (1968): 324–35.

———. "Willis Van Devanter, the Early Years: 1859–1911." Ph.D. diss., University of Denver, 1964.

Horwitz, Morton J. "The History of the Public/Private Distinction." *University of Pennsylvania Law Review* 130 (June 1982): 1423–28.

Hovenkamp, Herbert. "The Antitrust Movement and the Rise of Industrial Organization." *Texas Law Review* 68 (November 1989): 105–68.

———. "The Sherman Act and the Classical Theory of Competition." *Iowa Law Review* 74 (July 1989): 1019–65.

———. "The Marginalist Revolution in Legal Thought." *Vanderbilt Law Review* 46 (March 1993): 305–59.

Howe, Mark DeWolfe. *Justice Oliver Wendell Holmes: The Proving Years, 1870–1882*. Cambridge, Mass.: Belknap Press of Harvard University Press, 1963.

———. *Justice Oliver Wendell Holmes: The Shaping Years, 1841–1870*. Cambridge, Mass.: Belknap Press of Harvard University Press, 1957.

———, ed. *Holmes-Laski Letters*. Cambridge, Mass.: Harvard University Press, 1953.

———, ed. *Holmes-Pollock Letters: The Correspondence of Mr. Justice Holmes and Sir Frederick Pollock, 1874–1932*. Cambridge, Mass.: Harvard University Press, 1941.

Jehl, Francis. *Menlo Park: Reminiscences*. Dearborn, Mich.: Edison Institute, 1937.

Jesse, Richard Henry. "Chief Justice White." *American Law Review* 45 (May–June 1911): 321–26.

Johnson, John W. *American Legal Culture, 1908–1940*. Westport, Conn.: Greenwood Press, 1981.

Jones, Calvin P. "Kentucky's Irascible Conservative: Supreme Court Justice James Clark McReynolds." *Filson Club History Quarterly* 57 (January 1983): 20–30.

Jones, Eliot. *The Trust Problem in the United States*. New York: Macmillan, 1921.

Jowett, Garth S. "'A Capacity for Evil': The 1915 Supreme Court Mutual Decision." *Historical Journal of Film, Radio and Television* 9 (1989): 59–78.

Joyce, Walter E. "Edward Douglass White: The Louisiana Years, Early Life and on the Bench." *Tulane Law Review* 41 (June 1967): 751–68.
Keller, Morton. *Regulating a New Society: Public Policy and Social Change in America, 1900–1933.* Cambridge, Mass.: Harvard University Press, 1994.
Kellogg, Charles Flint. *NAACP: A History of the National Association for the Advancement of Colored People.* Baltimore: Johns Hopkins Press, 1967.
Kennedy, Randall. "Race Relations Law and the Tradition of Celebration." *Columbia Law Review* 86 (1986): 1622–61
Kerney, James. *The Political Education of Woodrow Wilson.* New York: Century Co., 1926.
Kerr, James E. *The Insular Cases: The Role of the Judiciary in American Expansionism.* Port Washington, N.Y.: Kennikat Press, 1982.
Klinkhamer, Sister Marie Carolyn, O.P. "The Legal Philosophy of Edward Douglas White." *University of Detroit Law Journal* 35 (December 1957): 174–99.
———. "Chief Justice White and Administrative Law." *Fordham Law Review* 13 (November 1944): 194–231.
———. *Edward Douglas White, Chief Justice of the United States.* Washington, D.C.: Catholic University of America Press, 1943.
Knight, Thomas J. "The Dissenting Opinions of Justice Harlan." *American Law Review* 51 (1917): 481–506.
Laidler, Harry W. *Boycotts and the Labor Struggle: Economic and Legal Aspects.* New York: John Lane Co., 1913.
Lamar, Clarinda Pendleton. *The Life of Joseph Rucker Lamar, 1857–1916.* New York: G. P. Putnam's Sons, 1926.
Landis, James McCauley. "Mr. Justice Brandeis: A Law Clerk's View." *Publications of the American Jewish Historical Society* 46 (1957): 467–73.
Landynski, Jacob W. "John Marshall Harlan and the Bill of Rights: A Centennial View." *Social Research* 49 (1982): 899–926.
Langum, David J. *Crossing over the Line: Legislating Morality and the Mann Act.* Chicago: University of Chicago Press, 1994.
Lash, Joseph, ed. *From the Diaries of Felix Frankfurter.* New York: W. W. Norton & Co., 1975.
"The Latest Addition to the Supreme Court." *Current Literature* 48 (March 1910): 271.
Leavitt, Donald Carl. "Attitudes and Ideology on the White Supreme Court, 1910 1920." Ph.D. diss., Michigan State University, 1970.
Levitan, David M. "Mahlon Pitney—Labor Judge." *Virginia Law Review* 40 (1954): 733–70.
———. "Jurisprudence of Mr. Justice Clarke." *Miami Law Quarterly* 7 (1952): 44–72.
Lillquist, Erik. "Constitutional Rights at the Junction: The Emergence of the Privilege Against Self-Incrimination and the Interstate Commerce Act." *Virginia Law Review* 81 (October 1995): 1989–2042.
Link, Arthur S., and Richard L. McCormick. *Progressivism.* Arlington Heights, Ill.: Harlan Davidson, 1983.
———. *Wilson and the New Freedom.* Princeton, N.J.: Princeton University Press, 1956.
———. *Woodrow Wilson and the Progressive Era, 1910–1917.* New York: Harper & Brothers, 1954.

Livesay, Harold C. *Samuel Gompers and Organized Labor in America.* Boston: Little, Brown, 1978.

Lofgren, Charles A. "*Missouri v. Holland* in Historical Perspective." *The Supreme Court Review* (1975): 77 122.

Lowry, Edward, G. "The Men of the Supreme Court." *World's Work* 27 (April 1914): 629–41.

———. "Justice at Zero: The Frigid Austerities Which Enrobe the Members of the United States Supreme Court." *Harper's Weekly Advertiser* (May 1910): 8, 34.

Marshall, Thomas R. *Recollections of Thomas R. Marshall.* Indianapolis: Bobbs-Merrill Co., 1925.

Mason, Alpheus T. *William Howard Taft: Chief Justice.* New York: Simon and Schuster, 1965.

———. *Brandeis: A Free Man's Life.* New York: Viking Press, 1946.

McAdoo, William Gibbs. *Crowded Years: The Reminiscences of William G. McAdoo.* Boston: Houghton Mifflin, 1931.

McDevitt, Brother Matthew. *Joseph McKenna: Associate Justice of the United States* (1946; New York: Da Capo Press, 1974 reprint).

McEvoy, Arthur F. "The Triangle Shirtwaist Factory Fire of 1911: Social Change, Industrial Accidents, and the Evolution of Common-Sense Causality." *Law & Social Inquiry* 20 (spring 1995): 621–51.

McHale, Francis. *President and Chief Justice, The Life and Public Services of William Howard Taft* (Philadelphia: Dorrance & Co., 1931).

McHargue, Daniel S. "President Taft's Appointments to the Supreme Court." *Journal of Politics* 12 (August 1950): 478–510.

———. "Appointments to the Supreme Court of the United States: The Factors That Have Affected Appointments, 1789–1932." Ph.D. diss., University of California, Los Angeles, 1949.

McLean, Joseph E. *William Rufus Day: Supreme Court Justice from Ohio.* The Johns Hopkins University Studies in Historical and Political Science. Vol. 64. Baltimore: Johns Hopkins Press, 1946.

McLellan, David C., and David C. Acheson, eds. *Among Friends: Personal Letters of Dean Acheson.* New York: Dodd, Mead & Co., 1980.

Mennel, Robert M., and Christine L. Compston, eds. *Holmes and Frankfurter: Their Correspondence, 1912–1934.* Hanover, N.H.: University Press of New England, 1996.

Minda, Gary. "The Law and Metaphor of Boycott." *Buffalo Law Review* 41 (1993): 807–931.

Morgan, H. Wayne, and Anne H. Morgan. *Oklahoma: A Bicentennial History.* New York: W. W. Norton & Co., 1977.

Morris, Jeffrey B. "Chief Justice Edward Douglass White and President Taft's Court." *Supreme Court Historical Society Yearbook* (1982): 27–45.

Mowry, George E. *Theodore Roosevelt and the Progressive Movement.* New York: Hill and Wang, American Century Series, 1960.

Murphy, Walter F. "In His Own Image: Mr. Chief Justice Taft and Supreme Court Appointments." *The Supreme Court Review* (1961): 159–93.

Murray, Robert K. *Red Scare: A Study in National Hysteria, 1919–1920* (1955; New York: McGraw-Hill, 1964 reprint).
Myers, Gustavus. *History of the Supreme Court of the United States.* Chicago: Charles H. Kerr & Co., 1925.
Nelson, Daniel A. "The Supreme Court Appointment of Willis Van Devanter." *Annals of Wyoming* 53 (fall 1981): 2–11.
Nelson, William. *The Fourteenth Amendment: From Political Principle to Judicial Doctrine.* Cambridge, Mass.: Harvard University Press, 1988.
Newland, Chester A. "Personal Assistants to Supreme Court Justices: The Law Clerks." *Oregon Law Review* 40 (1961): 299–317.
Novick, Sheldon M. *Honorable Justice: The Life of Oliver Wendell Holmes.* Boston: Little, Brown, 1989.
Nugent, Walter. *From Centennial to World War: American Society, 1876–1917.* New York: Macmillan, 1985.
———. *Structures of American Social History.* Bloomington: Indiana University Press, 1981.
Oliver, Gramling. *AP: The Story of News.* New York: Farrar and Rinehart, 1940.
Painter, Nell Irvin. *Standing at Armageddon: The United States 1877–1919.* New York: W. W. Norton & Co., 1987.
Peabody, James Bishop, ed. *The Holmes-Einstein Letters: Correspondence of Mr. Justice Holmes and Lewis Einstein, 1903–1935.* New York: St. Martin's Press, 1964.
Peritz, Rudolph J. "A Counter-History of Antitrust Law." *Duke Law Journal* 1990 (April): 263–320.
Polenberg, Richard. *Fighting Faiths: The Abrams Case, The Supreme Court, and Free Speech.* New York: Viking, 1987.
Pope, James G. "The Three-Systems Ladder of First Amendment Values: Two Rungs and a Black Hole." *Hastings Constitutional Law Quarterly* 11 (1984): 189–246.
Pound, Roscoe. "Liberty of Contract." *Yale Law Journal* 18 (May 1909): 454–87.
Pringle, Henry F. *The Life and Times of William Howard Taft.* New York: Farrar & Rinehart, 1939.
"The Progress of the World." *Review of Reviews* 43 (January 1911): 3.
Przybyszewski, Linda Carol Adams. "The Republic According to John Marshal Harlan: Race, Republicanism, and Citizenship." Ph.D. diss., Stanford University, 1989.
Purcell, Richard J. "Justice Joseph McKenna." *Records of the American Catholic Historical Society of Philadelphia* 56 (September 1945): 194–99.
Pusey, Merlo J. *Charles Evans Hughes.* New York: Macmillan, 1951.
Rabban, David M. "The Emergence of Modern First Amendment Doctrine." *University of Chicago Law Review* 50 (1983): 1205–355.
———. "The First Amendment in Its Forgotten Years." *Yale Law Journal* 90 (1981): 514–95.
Ragan, Fred. "Justice Oliver Wendell Holmes, Jr., Zechariah Chafee, Jr. and the Clear and Present Danger Test for Free Speech: The First Year, 1919." *Journal of History* 58 (June 1971): 24–45.
Rodes, Robert E., Jr. "Due Process and Social Legislation in the Supreme Court—A Post Mortem." *Notre Dame Lawyer* 33 (December 1957): 5–33.

Roelofs, Vernon W. "William R. Day: A Study in Constitutional History." Ph.D. diss., University of Michigan, 1942.
Rogin, Michael Paul. *Ronald Reagan, the Movie: and Other Episodes in Political Demonology.* Berkeley: University of California Press, 1987.
Romine, Ronald H. "The 'Politics' of Supreme Court Nominations from Theodore Roosevelt to Ronald Reagan: The Construction of a 'Politicization Index.'" Ph.D. diss., University of South Carolina, 1984.
Ross, William G. *A Muted Fury: Populists, Progressives, and Labor Unions Confront the Courts, 1890–1937.* Princeton, N.J.: Princeton University Press, 1994.
Schimmel, Barbara B. "The Judicial Policy of Mr. Justice McReynolds." Ph.D. diss., Yale University, 1964.
Semonche, John E. *Charting the Future: The Supreme Court Responds to a Changing Society, 1890–1920.* Westport, Conn.: Greenwood Press, 1978.
Shiras, George, III. *Justice George Shiras Jr. of Pittsburgh.* Pittsburgh: University of Pittsburgh Press, 1953.
Silva, Fred, ed. *Focus on "The Birth of a Nation."* Englewood Cliffs, N.J.: Prentice-Hall, 1971.
Sklar, Martin J. "Sherman Antitrust Act Jurisprudence and Federal Policy-Making in the Formative Period, 1890–1914." *New York Law School Law Review* 35 (1990): 791–826.
———. *The Corporate Reconstruction of American Capitalism, 1890–1916: The Market, the Law, and Politics.* New York: Cambridge University Press, 1988.
Spillenger, Clyde. "Elusive Advocate: Reconsidering Brandeis as People's Lawyer." *Yale Law Journal* 105 (1996): 1445–535.
Spring, Samuel. "Two Chief Justices: Edward Douglass White and William Howard Taft." *Review of Reviews* 64 (August 1921): 161–70.
Stagner, Stephen. "The Recall of Judicial Decisions and the Due Process Debate." *American Journal of Legal History* 24 (1980): 257–72.
Stansky, Peter. *On or About December 1910: Early Bloomsbury and Its Intimate World.* Cambridge, Mass.: Harvard University Press, 1996.
Stenzel, Robert D. "An Approach to Individuality, Liberty, and Equality: The Jurisprudence of Mr. Justice Pitney." Ph.D. diss., New School for Social Research, 1975.
Stevens, Robert. *Law School: Legal Education in America from the 1850s to the 1980s.* Chapel Hill: The University of North Carolina Press, 1983.
Stoddard, Henry L. *As I Knew Them: Presidents and Politics from Grant to Coolidge.* New York: Harper & Brothers, 1927.
Strum, Philippa. *Brandeis: Beyond Progressivism.* Lawrence: University Press of Kansas, 1993.
———. *Louis D. Brandeis: Justice for the People.* Cambridge, Mass.: Harvard University Press, 1984.
Sullivan, Mark. *Our Times: 1900–1925.* Vol. 3, *Pre-War America.* New York: Charles Scribner's Sons, 1946.
———. *Our Times: 1900–1925.* Vol. 4, *The War Begins, 1900–1914.* New York: Charles Scribner's Sons, 1946.

Swaine, Robert T. *The Cravath Firm and Its Predecessors: 1819–1948*. Vol. 2, *The Cravath Firm Since 1906*. New York: Ad Press, 1948.
Taft, Philip. "The Bisbee Deportation." *Labor History* 13 (winter 1972): 3–40.
Taft, William Howard, et al. "Appreciation of Edward Douglass White." *Loyola Law Journal* 7 (April 1926): 61–94.
Temin, Peter. *Taking Your Medicine: Drug Regulation in the United States*. Cambridge, Mass.: Harvard University Press, 1980.
Thompson, Charles W. "The New Chief Justice of the United States." *New York Times*, Dec. 18, 1910, magazine section, pt. 5, p. 2.
Timberlake, James H. *Prohibition and the Progressive Movement, 1900–1920*. Cambridge, Mass.: Harvard University Press, 1963.
Todd, Alden L. *Justice on Trial: The Case of Louis D. Brandeis*. New York: McGraw-Hill, 1964.
Trattner, Walter A. "The Federal Food and Drugs Act: A Complete but Familiar Story." *Reviews in American History* 18 (1990): 390–94.
Tucker, David M. "Justice Horace Harmon Lurton: The Shaping of a National Progressive." *American Journal of Legal History* 13 (July 1969): 223–32.
United States Senate. *"Judicial and Congressional Salaries"—Reports of the Task Forces of the Commission on Judicial and Congressional Salaries pursuant to Public Law 220, 83d Congress*. 83d Cong., 2d sess., 1954, S. Doc. 97.
Umbreit, Kenneth B. *Our Eleven Chief Justices: A History of the Supreme Court in Terms of Their Personalities*. New York: Harper & Brothers, 1938.
Urofsky, Melvin I. "The Brandeis-Frankfurter Conversations." *The Supreme Court Review* (1985): 299–339.
———. "Attorney for the People: The 'Outrageous' Brandeis Nomination." *Supreme Court Historical Society Yearbook* (1979): 8–19.
———. *A Mind of One Piece: Brandeis and American Reform*. New York: Charles Scribner's Sons, 1971.
Urofsky, Melvin I., and David W. Levy, eds. *Letters of Louis D. Brandeis*. Vol. 4 (1916–21), *Mr. Justice Brandeis*. Albany: State University of New York Press, 1975.
———, eds. *Letters of Louis D. Brandeis*. Vol. 3 (1913–15), *Progressive and Zionist*. Albany: State University of New York Press, 1973.
Usselman, Steven W. "Air Brakes for Freight Trains: Technological Innovation in the American Railroad Industry, 1869–1900." *Business History Review* 58 (1984): 30–50.
Vasicko, Sally Jo. "Justice Harlan and the Equal Protection Clause." *Supreme Court Historical Society Yearbook* (1982): 46–56.
Vose, Clement E. "State Against Nation: The Conservation Case of *Missouri* v. *Holland*." *Prologue* 16 (winter 1984): 233–47.
Walker, Thomas G., Lee Epstein, William J. Dixon. "On the Mysterious Demise of Consensual Norms in the United States Supreme Court." *Journal of Politics* 50 (1988): 361–89.
Waller, Spencer W. "The Antitrust Philosophy of Oliver Wendell Holmes." *Southern Illinois University Law Journal* 18 (1994): 283–327.
Warner, Hoyt Landon. *The Life of Mr. Justice Clarke: A Testament to the Power of Liberal Dissent in America*. Cleveland: Western Reserve University Press, 1959.

Warren, Charles. "The Progressiveness of the Supreme Court." *Columbia Law Review* 13 (1913): 294–313.
Warren, Samuel, and Louis Brandeis. "The Right to Privacy." *Harvard Law Review* 4 (1890): 193–220.
Watson, James E. *As I Knew Them.* Indianapolis: Bobbs-Merrill Co., 1936.
Weiss, Nancy J. "The Negro and the New Freedom: Fighting Wilsonian Segregation." *Political Science Quarterly* 84 (1969): 61–79.
Wetzel, Kurt. "Railroad Management's Response to Operating Employee Accidents, 1890–1913." *Labor History* 21 (1980): 351–68.
White, G. Edward. *Justice Oliver Wendell Holmes: Law and the Inner Self.* New York: Oxford University Press, 1993.
———. "The Canonization of Holmes and Brandeis: Epistemology and Judicial Reputations." *New York University Law Review* 70 (June 1995): 576–621.
White, Richard. *"It's Your Misfortune and None of My Own": A History of the American West.* Norman: University of Oklahoma Press, 1991.
———. "Judge Horace H. Lurton." *Tennessee Law Review* 18 (April 1944): 242–50.
Williams, Samuel C. *Phases of the History of the Supreme Court of Tennessee.* Johnson City, Tenn.: Watauga Press, 1944.
Witt, John Fabian. "The Transformation of Work and the Law of Workplace Accidents, 1842–1910." *Yale Law Journal* 107 (March 1998):1467–502.
Wittke, Carl. "Mr. Justice Clarke—A Supreme Court Justice in Retirement." *Mississippi Valley Historical Review* 36 (1949): 27–50.
Wood, Donna J. *Strategic Uses of Public Policy: Business and Government in the Progressive Era.* Marshfield, Mass.: Pitman, 1986.
———. "Strategic Use of Public Policy: Business Support for the 1906 Food and Drug Act." *Business History Review* 59 (1985): 403–32.
Wood, Stephen B. *Constitutional Politics in the Progressive Era: Child Labor and the Law.* Chicago: University of Chicago Press, 1968.
Woolf, Virginia. *Mr. Bennett and Mrs. Brown.* London: Hogarth Press, 1928.
Wright, George C. "The NAACP and Residential Segregation in Louisville, Kentucky, 1914–1917." *Kentucky Historical Society Register* 78 (1980): 39–54.
Wynn, Neil A. *From Progressivism to Prosperity: World War I and American Society.* New York: Holmes & Meier, 1986.
Yarbrough, Tinsley E. *Judicial Enigma: The First Justice Harlan.* New York: Oxford University Press, 1995.

INDEX

Adamson Act (1916), 169–74
administrative law, 45–46, 47–48, 62, 222, 230
advertising, 49, 84n. 30, 84–86 154–55
African Americans. *See* blacks
alcoholic beverages, 90–91. *See also* prohibition
amendments. *See* Sixteenth Amendment, Seventeenth Amendment, Eighteenth Amendment
American Bar Association, 140–41
American Federation of Labor, 50–51
American Tobacco Co., 27, 41–42, 74, 113
amicus briefs, 95, 190
Anti-peonage Act (1867), 132–33, 207
antitrust law, 27, 33–34, 37–44, 74, 80–81, 113. *See also* Clayton Antitrust Act; rule of reason; Sherman Antitrust Act
appointments to Supreme Court. *See* names of individual justices
automobiles, 49, 68, 195, 249, 253

Baldwin, Elbert: on justices 8–9, 20–21, 27, 30, 31; on Supreme Court, 44; on White's appointment as chief justice, 20
Bill of Rights, 240; application to states, 126, 130, 153–54, 238, 251, 253–54
Birth of a Nation, 127–28

blacks, 28, 132–35, 188, 190–93, 243–44
blue sky laws, 180
Bolshevik revolution, 4n. 18, 187, 217, 234
Borah, William E., 16
boycott, 51–52
Brandeis brief, 138, 196
Brandeis, Louis Dembitz, 8; appointment to Court, 114, 137–41; biographical information, 138–39; on contracts as coercive, 200–201; interpretation of language, 209; praise for McReynolds, 114; praise for Van Devanter, 156–57; reliance on experts, 168–69, 211–12, 239; style of opinions, 167–68, 182, 233, 238
Brewer, David, 4, 5, 11
Bryan, William Jennings, 143; reaction to antitrust decisions, 43
Butt, Archie, 22

Carmack Amendment (1906), 64, 151
censorship. *See* motion pictures
certiorari, writ of, 51, 157–59, 193, 228
Chafee, Zechariah, 235, 254
Child Labor Act (1916), 95n. 75, 202–4
Choate, Rufus, 19
circuit courts of appeal, 62, 157–58
citizenship, 147–48
Civil War, 31; commemorations, 96, 136; imagery in opinions, 70, 75,

107, 164, 201; military service of justices: Lurton, 10, 31; White, 17; Harlan, 25, 28, 31; Holmes, 29–30
Clarke, John: appointment to Court, 142–44; on dissents, 198–99
Clayton Antitrust Act (1914), 139
Cleveland, Grover: appointments to Supreme Court, 17, 57; relationship with Edward Douglass White in Senate, 17
commerce clause, 36, 41, 62–64, 68, 69, 92, 93–95, 106, 117, 118–19, 125, 202–4, 219; dormant aspect of, 96. *See also* police power
compulsory self-incrimination, 48, 130, 189
contempt of court, 50–52, 130, 205
contract, 43, 45, 64, 66, 75, 92, 98–99, 101, 104, 105, 121–23, 162–63, 188, 191–92, 198, 200–201, 226; excuse for nonperformance, 184, 195, 213–14
copyright, 83, 210
Corporation Tax Act (1909), 109
corporations, 48
Corwin, Edward, 16
Croly, Herbert, 123

Davis, John W., 40
Day, William Rufus: biographical information, 30–31; description, 30; on statutory construction, 82–83, 177–78, 208
Debs, Eugene V., 216–18; Socialist candidate for president, 2, 78
Democratic Party, 1
dissents, 46, 58, 60, 75, 102, 131, 137, 156, 170n. 69, 198–99, 206–7, 228
draft, 148–49, 187, 201–2, 215, 251. *See also* Thirteenth Amendment
due process, 8, 69, 73, 214; fifth amendment, 85, 121; fourteenth amendment, 121, 130, 191

Eighteenth Amendment, 228–32, 233, 250
elections, congressional: 1910, 1, 19, 58; 1914, 115, 137; 1918, 258
elections, presidential: 1912, 1–2, 4, 12, 55–56, 58, 71, 77, 78, 139, 143; 1920, 246
elections, primaries, 77, 257, 258–60; regulation of, 258–60
Eleventh Amendment, 145
employers' liability acts, 65–66, 116–17, 150, 154, 157, 159–60, 165–67, 222–26. *See also* workmen's compensation acts
employment agencies, state regulation of, 155, 181–82, 207, 253
equal protection, 8, 72–73, 89, 90, 134, 145, 191
Espionage Act (1917), 186, 215, 234–40, 253, 254
exclusionary rule, 255–57

fellow-servant rule, 65, 72–73, 143
Fifteenth Amendment, 134–35
Fifth Amendment. *See* compulsory self-incrimination; due process
First Amendment. *See* press, freedom of; speech, freedom of
Food & Drug Act (1906). *See* Pure Food and Drug Act
Fourteenth Amendment, 89, 91, 145, 192, 232. *See also* due process; equal protection
Fourth Amendment, 255–57
Frank, Leo, 130–32
Frankfurter, Felix, 174, 241; comment on White, 259; critical of McKenna, 262; praise for McKenna, 154

freedom of contract. *See* contract
freedom of press. *See* press, freedom of
freedom of speech. *See* speech, freedom of
Fuller, Melville Weston, 4, 5, 59, 60

Gompers, Samuel, 51
grandfather clause, 134–35, 191

habeas corpus, 131–32, 194
Hand, Learned, 235
Harding, Warren, 246
Harlan, John Marshall, 4; biographical information, 27–28; death, 54; dissent in *American Tobacco* case, 42; dissent in *Standard Oil* case, 39–41; swears in White as chief justice, 25
Hepburn Act (1906), 32, 36, 92, 103, 107–8
Holmes, Oliver Wendell, Jr.: antitrust views, 35, 81–82; biographical information, 29–30; comments on Brandeis's style, 168; friendship with Chief Justice White, 15, 18, 29, 264; statutory construction, 47, 71, 84; style of opinions, 59
Hours of Service Act (1907), 64
Hughes, Charles Evans: appears as counsel before Court, 258; appointment to Supreme Court, 12–13; biographical information, 13–14; comments on White as chief justice, 26, 60–61; considered as candidate for chief justice, 15; description, 31; presidential candidacy, 137; resignation, 141–42; service on postal rates commission, 84

immigration, 110n. 64, 144–47, 194
income tax

Industrial Workers of the World (IWW), 78, 123, 186, 217, 257–58
initiative, 70, 143, 145
injunction, 51
Insular Cases, 6n. 24, 18–19, 65n. 65, 87, 88
insurance, 13–14, 98–103, 105, 117–18, 162–63, 189, 253
Interstate Commerce Act (1887), 95, 96, 101, 107
Interstate Commerce Commission (ICC), 45, 101, 106–7, 170, 182–83, 188–89

judges, age 8, 11, 110–11
judicial recall, 3–4, 8, 55, 71
jury trials, 154. *See also* Seventh Amendment
justices: extra-judicial service, 84, 114–15; opinion writing, 58–59, 78–78, 110, 136–37; provisions for retirement, 5

Kentucky: residential segregation law, 188, 190–93; separate car law, 243–44
Ku Klux Klan Act (1870), 134

La Follette, Robert: 1912 election, 71, 139; reaction to antitrust decisions, 42–43; on recall of judges, 55
labor unions. *See* unions
Lamar, Joseph Rucker: appointment to Supreme Court, 20–22; childhood friendship with Woodrow Wilson, 21; death, 136; description, 31; dissenting opinions, 102; service on ABC Commission, 114–15
Langdell, Christopher Columbus, 100
Laski, Harold, 16, 235; on Brandeis's opinions, 168

law clerks to justices, 24, 60n. 34
law reviews, citation of, 182
liquor. *See* alcoholic beverages; prohibition
lottery, 94, 155, 176, 202
Lowell, A. Lawrence, 140
Lurton, Horace: appointment to Court, 9; biographical information 10–11; death, 112; style of questioning, 31
Lusitania, 147

mails. *See* post office
Mann Act (1910), 93–95, 177–80, 219. *See also* prostitution
maritime law, 165–67, 207, 225, 243
Marshall, Thomas, 186–87
McKenna, Joseph: biographical information, 29; description, 28–29; friendship with Chief Justice White, 18; on imprecision of language, 48–49, 69, 89–90, 99–101, 119, 126, 128, 175, 179–80, 181, 209; on national power, 94; on statutory construction, 46, 179
McKinley, William: friendship with Justice Day, 30; friendship with Justice McKenna, 29
McReynolds, James Clark: appointment, 112; biographical information, 113–14; delays trial in *Caminetti* case, 177; dislike of Justice Clarke, 219–20; proposal to replace elderly judges, 110–11
Mexico, relations with United States, 86–87, 114–15, 147, 169
Migratory Bird Treaty Act (1918), 222, 240–42
Moody, William T., 4–5, 9, 14
morality and law, 94, 178, 202–3
motion pictures, 125–29
Mowry, George, 1

Myers, Gustavus, 65; reaction to antitrust decisions, 43, 76

narcotics, regulation of, 220
National Association for the Advancement of Colored People (NAACP), 128, 141, 190–93
National Association of Manufacturers, 50–51
natural justice, 162, 224
New York: workmen's compensation act, 161, 165–68, 242–43

obscenity, 94n. 73, 126
Oklahoma: literacy test, 134–35, 191; separate coach law, 133; state capital, 49–50
Oregon: initiative and referendum, 70; maximum-hour law, 174–75

Palmer, A. Mitchell, 235
Parker, Alton B., 34
patents, 34, 73–75, 76–77, 80, 82–83, 185, 199, 247
Pinchot-Ballinger affair, 138–39
Pitney, Mahlon: appointment, 54; biographical information, 56–57
police power: of national government, 93, 228, 240–42; of states, 69, 72, 92, 93, 119–20, 122, 124–25, 145–46, 152, 155, 163, 180, 221, 222, 232, 248, 249, 251–52, 261. *See also* commerce clause
Pollock, Sir Frederick, 35
post office: delivery of mail, 97–98, 115–16, 195, 247, 248; regulations 85–86, 170n. 69; second-class mailing privileges, 84, 86, 254–55
Pound, Roscoe, 98, 141, 168
press, freedom of, 51, 85, 128–30, 205
price, regulation of, 101–3, 171–74

privacy, right to, 211, 252
privileges and immunities clause, 93n. 71, 191, 253, 258
Progressive Party: election of 1912, 77; formation, 4
prohibition: national regulation, 175–77, 219–20, 228–32, 249–50, 256; state regulation, 90–91
property rights, 103, 123, 173, 212, 253, 261; takings, 152–53, 188, 233, 234
prostitution, 93, 177, 218. *See also* Mann Act
public reaction to decisions: antitrust law, 42–43
public-private distinction, 101–3, 108, 121, 153, 171, 242, 255
Pure Food & Drug Act (1906), 32, 46, 72, 94, 109–10

railroads, 44, 62–64, 69, 73, 76–77, 95–96, 105, 169–74, 182–83, 194, 197
rate regulation: by states, 95–96, 105–6
recall. See judicial recall
referendum, 55, 70, 143, 145n. 40
rent control legislation, 260–62
republican form of government, 70
Republican party: insurgents, 1
resale price maintenance, 33, 199
restraint of trade, 34
Roosevelt, Theodore, 1–2, 17, 139; on antitrust law; on judicial recall, 3–4, 55, 71; election of 1912, 77, 78; death, 206
rule of reason, 6, 38–39, 42, 45, 68, 179, 200, 237, 238, 263. *See also* antitrust law

Safety Appliance Acts (1893 & 1903), 44, 63, 150, 162
salaries of justices, 12, 24

Seaman's Act (1915), 207–9
segregation, state-ordered, 133–34, 188, 190–93, 243–44
selective service. *See* draft; Thirteenth Amendment
Seventeenth Amendment, 258
Seventh Amendment, 239
Sherman Antitrust Act (1890), 38, 80–81, 113, 147
Sixth Amendment, 94n. 73
Socialist Party, 2, 78, 123, 215, 238
southerners: in executive branch, 2; in judicial branch, 58; in legislative branch, 2
speech, freedom of, 51, 125–26, 215–18, 234–40, 251–54
Standard Oil Co., 27, 37, 108
states: admission to union, 50; as constitutional category, 62–64, 67, 103–4, 230, 247
statutory construction, 36, 38, 62, 63, 66, 71, 80, 83–88, 109–10, 144, 148, 167, 177–80, 197, 208; deference to administrative agencies, 46, 47, 86
Storey, Moorfield, 141, 191
strikes, 78, 123, 169–70, 201, 227, 235
Sullivan, Mark, 2
Supreme Court of the United States: control over docket, 7, 58–60, 157–59; criticism of, 7–8, 204; facilities, 24; jurisdiction, 62, 81, 157–59; summary docket, 61. *See also* dissents; justices; law clerks to justices

Taft, William Howard, 139; appointments to the Supreme Court, 9, 58; correspondence with Lurton, 4; critical of Supreme Court, 4; interest in Supreme Court, 9; White, 9, 14–20; Lurton, 9–11; Hughes,

12–14; Lamar, 20–22; Van Devanter, 22–23; Pitney, 54–57; opposition to Brandeis's appointment to Court, 140
tariff, 61–62
taxing power: of national government, 117–18, 219–21; of states, 67–68, 89, 98, 103–4, 154–55, 189–90, 244–45, 248
telegraph, 210, 246–47
Thirteenth Amendment, 132–33, 148–49
Titanic, 97
tort, 65, 72, 76, 105, 160, 246–47. *See also* employers' liability acts; workmens' compensation acts
trading stamps, 154–55
treaty power, 62, 240
tying arrangements, 74, 82

unfair competition, 210–12
unions, 50–51, 121–24, 200, 253
United Shoe Machinery Co., 80–81, 140, 199–200
United States Supreme Court. *See* Supreme Court of the United States
urban planning, 152

Van Devanter, Willis: appointment to Court, 22–23; description, 31; leadership within justices' conference, 156–57, 229
Volstead Act (1919), 228–32, 250
voting rights, 134–35, 147–48

Waite, Morrison R., 59
war power, 201, 218–19, 232–34, 241, 251
War Revenue Act (1898), 117
Warren, Charles, 7–8
Washington: workmen's compensation act, 163–64

Watson, Thomas, 142
Webb-Kenyon Act (1913), 175, 243
Weyl, Walter, 2
Whipple, Sherman, 141
White, Edward Douglass: administrative law, 45; appointment to Supreme Court, 14–20; death, 263; description of, 27; friendship with Justice Holmes, 18; health problems, 156, 227–28, 245, 263; leadership style, 15–16, 26, 52–53, 59, 60–61, 157; nationalism, 50, 75, 169, 201, 259; number of opinions, 59; on dissent, 75, 156, 229–30; receipt of Laetare Medal from University of Notre Dame, 111; "rule of reason," 38–39, 42, 45; statutory construction, 85–88; style of opinions, 59–60, 85, 204
White Slave Traffic, 93, 178–79, 219
Wickersham, George W., 9, 139; advice on judicial appointments, 11, 15; opposition to appointment of Brandeis, 140
Wilson, Woodrow: appointments to the Court: McReynolds, 112; Brandeis, 137, Clarke, 142; childhood friendship with justice Lamar, 21; declaration of war, 147, 169; election of 1912, 2, 78; governor of New Jersey, 1
Winslow, Sidney, 140–41
work, right to, 146
workmen's compensation acts, 160–67, 242–43. *See also* employers' liability acts
World War I, 115, 147, 169, 183–84, 186, 201, 213–14

yellow dog contracts, 121–24